Pol

British Politics To

CW00938200

MACMILLAN COLLEGE INFORMATION CENTRE

This book is to be returned on or before the date stamped below

7/6/10

2 3 7 0 0

British Politics Today

Edited by

Colin Hay

Polity

Copyright © this collection Polity Press, chapter 6 © R. A. W. Rhodes, chapter 12 © Brendan O'Leary, 2002.

First published in 2002 by Polity Press in association with Blackwell Publishers Ltd.

Editorial office:
Polity Press
65 Bridge Street
Cambridge CB2 1UR, UK

Marketing and production:
Blackwell Publishers Ltd
108 Cowley Road
Oxford OX4 1JF, UK

Published in the USA by
Blackwell Publishers Inc.
350 Main Street
Malden, MA 02148, USA

MACMILLAN COLLEGE
CENTRO DE INFORMACIÓN

ACC			
CLASS	320 ONL Post 16		
LOC		DATE	4/11/02
DEPT		CAT	62

All rights reserved. Except for the quotation of short passages for the purposes of criticism and review, no part of this publication may be reproduced, stored in a retrieval system, or transmitted, in any form or by any means, electronic, mechanical, photocopying, recording or otherwise, without the prior permission of the publisher.

Except in the United States of America, this book is sold subject to the condition that it shall not, by way of trade or otherwise, be lent, re-sold, hired out, or otherwise circulated without the publisher's prior consent in any form of binding or cover other than that in which it is published and without a similar condition including this condition being imposed on the subsequent purchaser.

ISBN 0–7456–2318–2
ISBN 0–7456–2319–0 (pbk)

A catalogue record for this book is available from the British Library and has been applied for from the Library of Congress.

Typeset in 10 on 12 pt Sabon
by Kolam Information Services Pvt. Ltd, Pondicherry, India
Printed in Great Britain by MPG Books Ltd, Bodmin, Cornwall

This book is printed on acid-free paper.

MACMILLAN COLLEGE
INFORMATION CENTRE

Contents

Contributors

David Coates holds the Worrell Chair in Anglo-American Studies at Wake Forest University in North Carolina. He was previously Professor of Government at the University of Manchester. He has written extensively in the areas of labour studies and contemporary political economy, and has recently published *Models of Capitalism: Growth and Stagnation in the Modern Era* (2000) and jointly edited (with Peter Lawler), *New Labour in Power* (2000).

Stuart Croft is Professor of International Relations at the University of Birmingham. He has written, co-authored and edited eight books on security and diplomacy issues, and has published in a number of journals, including those of Chatham House and the Institut Français des Relations Internationales. His recent publications include *Security Studies Today*, with Terriff, James and Morgan (1999); *The Enlargement of Europe*, with Redmond, Rees and Webber (1999); *Strategies of Arms Control: A History and Typology* (1996); 'In Defence of Arms Control', *Political Studies*, vol. 44, no. 5 (Dec. 1996); 'European Integration, Nuclear Deterrence and Franco-British Nuclear Cooperation', *International Affairs*, vol. 72, no. 4 (Oct. 1996); and 'The Security Dangers of Double Enlargement: The Expansion of NATO and the WEU', *WeltTrends*, no. 10 (Mar. 1996).

Colin Hay is Professor of Political Analysis in the Department of Political Science and International Studies at the University of Birmingham. He is the author of a number of volumes, including *Political Analysis* (2002), *The Political Economy of New Labour* (1999) and *Re-stating Social and Political Change* (1996); he is also a co-author with David Marsh and others of *Postwar British Politics in Perspective* (1999) and co-editor with David Marsh of *Demystifying Globalisation* (2000).

Dennis Kavanagh is Professor of Politics and Communications at Liverpool University. Recent books include *The Powers behind the Prime Minister*, with Anthony Seldon (2001) and *The British General Election of 2001*, with David Butler (2001).

Ruth Lister is Professor of Social Policy at Loughborough University. She is a former Director of the Child Poverty Action Group and served on the Commission on Social Justice, the Opsahl Commission into the Future of Northern Ireland and the Commission on Poverty, Participation and Power. She is a founding Academician of the Academy for Learned Societies for the Social Sciences and a Trustee of the Community Development Foundation. She has published widely on the subjects of poverty, welfare and citizenship. Her latest book is *Citizenship: Feminist Perspectives* (1997).

David Marsh is Professor of Politics in the Department of Political Science and International Studies at the University of Birmingham. During the academic year 2000–1, he was a Visiting Fellow in the Politics Programme of the Research School of Social Sciences at the Australian National University, Canberra. He has published widely in British politics and is currently working on a book dealing with the British political tradition.

James Mitchell is Professor of Politics at the University of Strathclyde. His interests are in territorial politics: the politics of national and regional identity, multilevel government, and the territorial impact of public policy.

Pippa Norris is Associate Director (Research) of the Joan Shorenstein Center on the Press, Politics and Public Policy, Kennedy School of Government at Harvard University and she lectures in Public Policy at the Kennedy School of Government. A political scientist, she focuses on comparing elections, political communications, and gender politics. She has published over two dozen books including most recently *Britain Votes 2001*(2001); *Digital Divide: Civic Engagement, Information Poverty and the Internet Worldwide* (2001); *A Virtuous Circle? Political Communications in Post-industrial Democracies* (2000); *On Message: Communicating the Campaign* (1999); and *Critical Elections: Voters and Parties in Long-Term Perspective* (1999).

Brendan O'Leary is Professor of Political Science and the current convenor (head) of the Department of Government at the London School of Economics and Political Science. He is the author, co-author and co-editor of twelve books, including *Explaining Northern Ireland* (1995),

The Politics of Antagonism: Understanding Northern Ireland, 2nd edn (1996), *Right-Sizing the State* (2001) and *Theories of the State* (1987).

Rod Rhodes is Professor of Politics (Research) at the University of Newcastle-upon-Tyne; Professor of Politics and Public Policy in the School of Politics and Public Policy, Griffith University (Brisbane, Australia) and Adjungeret Professor, Institut for Statskundskab, Københavns Universitet (Denmark). Between 1994 and 1999 he was Director of the Economic and Social Research Council's Whitehall Research Programme. He is the author or editor of twenty books including recently *Understanding Governance* (1997); *Control and Power in Central–Local Government Relations*, 2nd edn (1999); and *Transforming British Government*, 2 vols (2000). He has been editor of the journal *Public Administration* since 1986. He is chair of the Political Studies Association of the United Kingdom.

Ben Rosamond is Senior Lecturer in Politics and International Studies at the University of Warwick. He is the author of *Theories of European Integration* (2000) and *Globalization and the European Union* (2002).

David Sanders is Professor of Government at the University of Essex. He has been an editor of the *British Journal of Political Science* since 1990. He has published numerous articles on various aspects of British politics. He is currently one of the Principal Investigators on the British Election Study.

1

British Politics Today: Towards a New Political Science of British Politics?

Colin Hay

For much of the postwar period, British politics was characterized, by mainstream and radical commentators alike, in terms of continuity, stability and the replication of long-enduring traditions. Concepts such as consensus, settlement, bipartisanship and, indeed, 'the British political tradition' featured prominently in the political science of British politics. As Peter Kerr has recently suggested, postwar British politics has conventionally been recounted in terms of an 'established narrative'. As he explains,

> the story which is told is one in which two principal protagonists, the Labour government of 1945 and the Conservative governments under Mrs Thatcher, succeeded in their respective attempts radically to reconstruct the nature of the British state. Between these two periods, British politics is said to have been dominated by a long period of consensus and relative stasis during which government policy exhibited an overall degree of continuity. (2001: 1)

In recent years, however, the internal grammar of that narrative has been challenged, as has the language in which that narrative was couched. That challenge has come from two quarters. The first is from revisionists, such as Kerr himself, critical of the account it offers of postwar British political development (see also Marsh et al. 1999). The second comes from those, somewhat greater in number, more favourably disposed towards such a narrative but nonetheless keen to emphasize the extent to which British politics today marks a departure from that which characterized the postwar period (see, for instance, Giddens 1994, 1998; Kavanagh 1997; Mulgan 1994; Seldon 2001; for a critical commentary see Fielding 2000). In recent years, then, attention has focused to a much greater extent on discontinuity, flux and change and the means by which to adjudicate between continuity and discontinuity, stability and flux, stasis and change (for a review see Hay 1999a). In the process the political science of British politics has become more reflexive theoretically as, arguably, its agenda has broadened. The contemporary political science of British politics is thus characterized by its references to discontinuity, transformation, novelty and crisis – in short, by its focus on the question of change.

Yet the greater awareness of and sensitivity to change is not all that sets the contemporary political science of British politics apart from its postwar counterpart. If anything, rather more significant has been the far greater extent to which British political dynamics have come to be contextualized (historically, comparatively and, above all, internationally) in the 'new' political science of British politics. Thus, while the established narrative described by Kerr tended to depict a hermetically sealed domestic politics whose evolutionary dynamic (such as it was) could be derived to a considerable extent from endogenous (or internal) factors such as the conduct of domestic political actors, recent analyses have tended by contrast to point to the significance of exogenous (or external) factors. The end of the Cold War (and the attendant need for a new international security architecture) and the contested processes of both European integration and globalization loom ever larger in accounts of contemporary British political dynamics.

While things were, arguably, ever thus, few self-respecting commentators on British politics today now fail to acknowledge the complex web of international interdependencies in which Britain is embedded. This has brought a welcome (and long overdue) recognition of the artificial and unhelpful polarization of international relations and domestic political analysis, with a growing recognition of 'the international conditions of existence of domestic political and economic dynamics' and 'the domestic conditions of existence of international/global political and economic dynamics' (Hay and Marsh 1999: 14).

This is the context in which the present volume should perhaps be situated. Its aim has been to bring together a distinguished array of internationally renowned scholars in the area of British politics (broadly conceived). Though given a substantial degree of latitude within the confines of the overall project, each author has been invited to present an assessment and critical commentary on key developments, both substantive and theoretical, in our understanding of British politics in recent years. They have been encouraged not only to summarize and reflect critically on recent work in their areas of expertise, but also to propose fruitful avenues for future empirical scrutiny and theoretical development.

Continuity, discontinuity, change and stability

As already indicated it is the question of change – its nature, extent, direction, reversibility and temporal characteristics – that emerges as the key and unifying theme of the present volume. In this sense the title *British Politics Today* is perhaps somewhat anomalous. For in so far as it implies a static snapshot of the condition of British politics at a particular, if nonetheless crucial, juncture, it does not capture well the contribution made by the following chapters. Indeed, not one chapter in this collection confines itself to a dehistoricized mapping of the present; each contextualizes contemporary dynamics historically and, in many cases, internationally (see, in particular, the chapters by Coates, Rosamond and Croft). Taken together, then, they make a significant contribution to the attempt to identify, describe and explain the processes and mechanisms linking British politics yesterday, today – and tomorrow. In so doing, they might be seen as contributing to a reconception of political analysis as an exercise in capturing the dynamism of an ongoing process of change rather than an attempt to map, detail or model an essentially static object of analysis.[1]

Given the centrality of questions of change to the analysis and, indeed, the discourse of contemporary British politics,[2] it is not surprising that assessments of change are highly contested – not least by the contributors to the present volume. It is thus important at the outset that we establish what we mean by terms such as change, continuity and discontinuity.[3]

Conceptualizing change

It is perhaps appropriate to begin by introducing two key conceptual distinctions frequently deployed within the analysis of institutional and/ or behavioural change yet all too often conflated: that between *change and stability* (or *dynamism and stasis*) on the one hand, and that between *continuity and discontinuity* on the other. It is certainly tempting to use these conceptual pairings interchangeably (and in so doing to confuse them); that temptation should be resisted.

Since the former is the more general it will be dealt with first. To do so requires that we consider what it is that we mean when we refer to change. Like many frequently used and taken-for-granted lay concepts, 'change' is difficult to define. We all know it when we see or experience it and, since we do, we do not spend very much time worrying about its definition. For current purposes, change implies a contrast between states or moments of a common system, institution, relationship or entity – a difference between the structuring of relations *then* and the structuring of relations *now*. Yet as Hermann Strasser and Susan Randall note, in order to identify change, 'the unit of analysis must preserve a minimum of identity' (1981: 16). This raises a crucial point. To speak of change is to imply some measure of continuity – it is, in short, to imply change *in* or *of something* and hence a common point or system of reference. The disintegration or termination of a system and its replacement by another is then not strictly an instance of *change* but one of *substitution*. Thus, if our system of reference is the feudal state, bourgeois revolutions represent not change but a substitution of the feudal state by the capitalist state; if our system of reference, on the other hand, is the state itself, then we can talk of institutional, ideational and behavioural change. To identify change over a given time frame is then, strangely perhaps, to make the simultaneous claim that the system exhibits some degree of continuity over this time frame; it is to suggest that it is indeed still the same system at the end of the time frame considered as it was at the start (even if its specific form may have altered).

Yet if change, despite being frequently conflated with *discontinuity*, does in fact imply a degree of *continuity*, it should not be regarded as synonymous with either. The distinction between continuity and discontinuity, though often mistaken for that between stability and change, in fact refers to types or modalities of change and, more specifically, to different *temporalities of change*. If we can then differentiate between issues relating to the extent of change on the one hand and those relating to the temporal characteristics of particular periods of change on the other, the distinction between continuity and discontinuity is concerned exclusively with the latter. While each chapter in this collection is concerned with identifying mechanisms and processes of change, opinions vary as to the temporal characteristics of that change – its continuous or discontinuous nature.

Continuity implies that whatever change occurs is incremental, iterative, cumulative and unidirectional.[4] Furthermore, it implies that all moments in this gradual or *evolutionary* process are of equal significance. It implies, in short, an even unfolding of events over time. By contrast, *discontinuity* implies rupture, transformation and an altering of trajectory (whether periodic, cyclical or random) – a process or processes of change punctuated by reversals, tipping points, turning points or other strategic moments of heightened significance. It implies an uneven conception of political time. Change is a necessary but not in itself sufficient condition of discontinuity.

Like the issue of change itself, whether we identify continuity or discontinuity will depend, essentially, on the system with respect to which we choose to assess such temporal characteristics of change. To return to our earlier example, if our system of reference is the feudal state, bourgeois revolutions will constitute a significant discontinuity (since arguably they destroy all that is distinctively feudal about such a regime). If, however, our system of reference is the state itself we may tend to emphasize significant elements of continuity – the national form of the state, its continued monopoly over the means of violence, its patriarchal character, its centralized nature and so forth.

The contested nature of change in contemporary British political discourse and analysis

Preliminaries aside, we are now in a position to examine in more detail some of the common conceptual and empirical issues raised in the chapters which follow. The first, and perhaps most striking, is the contested nature of change. For some commentators 1997 was a watershed election as significant as that of 1906, 1945 or 1979 (Seldon 2001). For others it marked little more than a return to consensus politics (Kavanagh, chapter 4 below) and a confirmation of the consolidation of much of the neoliberal economic legacy of Thatcherism (Heffernan 2000). Still others have argued that a growing process of either European integration or globalization – or both – has served to render domestic political interventions (and hence domestic electoral politics) essentially redundant as ever more potent external economic imperatives have flooded over Britain's increasingly porous borders (for instance, Giddens 1999; Gray 1997). This latter issue is especially contested, with yet others suggesting that globalization and European integration in fact pull in very different directions. For such authors, Britain's external trading relations have been Europeanized (more accurately EU-ized) not globalized, to reveal globalization as in fact little more than a convenient political excuse for a self-imposed path of political impotence in the face of rather more parochial constraints (Hay 2002a; see also Hirst and Thompson 1999, 2000). The evidence they present is stark indeed,

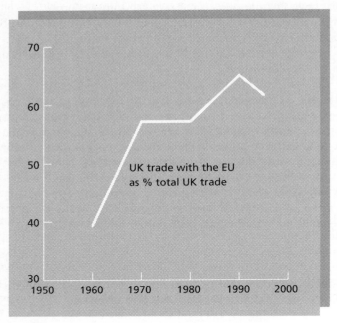

Figure 1.1 UK trade: a story of globalization or EU-ization?
Source: Based on Eurostat data.

and would seem to stand in marked contrast to the conventional orthodoxy (see for instance, figure 1.1).

What this serves to indicate is a staggering lack of consensus among
commentators and political scientists alike about the significance of
contemporary British political dynamics and the nature and severity of
the external constraints which may serve to condition or even circum-
scribe the realm of domestic political choice. Clearly not all of the above
interpretations can be accurate. Arguably they are mutually exclusive.
And the above list merely scratches the surface of ongoing dispute and
debate. In this context it is perhaps important to state that the purpose of
this volume is not to resolve such disputes but to bring together a range of
acknowledged experts who have written on such issues in the hope that
together they might clarify the nature of the issues at stake and the extent
to which they can be adjudicated empirically.

Were things not already complicated enough, they are only further
confused by the discourse in which much contemporary political debate
is conducted – a discourse which, again, places epochal change at centre-
stage. As I have elsewhere suggested,

No self-respecting critical analyst or commentator can possibly but shudder at the proliferation of entities, processes, institutions, theories, disciplines and now parties to which the prefix 'new' has been appended in recent years. We inhabit, variously, a 'new world order', a 'new world disorder' or 'new times'. Our politics exhibits all the characteristics of a new consensus fashioned around the ideas of the new right and reflected in the spirit of 'new realism' espoused, embodied and internalised most vigorously by New Labour. Should we require yet further evidence of the ubiquity of novelty, we need look no further than the world of political discourse. Here we discover, once again, New Labour leading us tirelessly and inexorably down the road to New Britain, armed with its post-neo-classical [or, simply, 'new'] endogenous growth theory, to find a new place within a new Europe aided and abetted by a renewed special relationship with Blair's fair-weather cousins across the pond, the New Democrats. (Hay 1999b: 1–2)

True, the New Democrats may now have departed the scene, taking with them the prospect of a renewed special relationship, but the point is surely made. In such a discursive environment it is perhaps difficult not to be taken in by talk of novelty. If we are to resist this natural tendency, it is perhaps useful to differentiate between a series of rather different subjects and objects of change. It is this that I attempt in the sections that follow.

Change: actual, claimed and projected

The key issue, and one addressed directly by each chapter in the present collection, is the extent of observed, empirical change in the light of that claimed, whether by commentators or politicians. Here three consistent themes emerge. The chapters by Croft, Mitchell, Rhodes and Rosamond, but also (if less directly) O'Leary and Sanders, point to the growing salience of political deliberations at spatial levels other than the national and hence to the emergence of multilevel governance as a significant determinant of contemporary political dynamics. A combination of constitutional reform and changing external relations, they suggest, presents a clear challenge to modes of political analysis, such as those that have tended to dominate the political science of British politics, which take as their starting point the notion of a bounded polity or 'unitary state'. As James Mitchell is surely right to point out, this was always something of a myth, but one that has become ever more cruelly exposed in a context of devolution and European integration. Similar arguments are made with respect to the changing exposure of the British economy in international, indeed global, markets by David Coates.

A second theme is changes in patterns of political representation, mobilization and participation and the relationship between such outcomes and existing patterns of structural inequality. Pippa Norris's important chapter examines in rich empirical detail the mechanisms underpinning the remarkable progress in the representation of women in British politics in recent years. It details the extent and nature of attitudinal and behavioural differences between women and men in the Commons, assessing the implications for legislative priorities and political debates. It is cautiously optimistic about the emergence – over time – of a process of political deliberation which gives voice to, and hence comes both to address and represent, the interests of women. The chapters by David Marsh and Ruth Lister also deal with these issues. In the midst of an impassioned critique of the legacy of pluralism for the practice and study of British politics, Marsh draws attention to the persistent structural inequalities which continue to characterize the British social and political system. He examines the uneven distribution of political resources and the implications for patterns of political mobilization and participation. Lister, too, focuses on issues of structural inequality, interrogating the distributional asymmetries associated with an emergent new welfare settlement in which welfare rights are rendered increasingly contingent on the (demonstrable) exercise of the claimant's responsibilities.

A third theme which emerges from a number of the chapters concerns the changing nature of political competition in Britain. This is addressed most directly in the chapters by Dennis Kavanagh and David Sanders, though it is a consistent theme of the volume as a whole. Kavanagh examines in detail the paradoxical nature of party competition in Britain which, in the space of a few years, has seen an almost unprecedented reversal of political fortunes. He assesses the extent to which contemporary British politics marks a return to bipartisan consensus, albeit on terms very different from those which characterized its postwar counterpart and examines the mechanisms which might have selected for such an outcome. Sanders, too, seeks to identify the key mechanisms driving party competition in contemporary Britain. He charts the growing electoral significance of emerging consumer and regional identities and the longer-term implications of such novel forms of identification in the context of ongoing constitutional reform.

Yet it is not only the extent of substantive change which concerns the contributors to this volume. Political rhetoric, as a growing number of commentators have suggested in recent years, may play an independent and causal role in the creation of social, political and economic outcomes (for useful reviews of this literature see Blyth 1997; Campbell 1998). This makes an assessment of changes in political discourse, such as that evidenced in the chapters by Stuart Croft and Ruth Lister, particularly significant. What both of these chapters draw attention to is the gulf between (invariably strategic) political rhetoric and the political reality to which the rhetoric purportedly refers. To be fair, there is nothing particularly unprecedented about a rhetoric–reality gulf in political discourse – indeed, for many, it is precisely to the duplicitous appeal to convenient myths that the adjective 'political' refers! Yet two points should perhaps be noted. First, historical examples of the gulf between political rhetoric and reality notwithstanding, political discourse has only recently come to feature prominently in the political analysis of British politics (see, for instance, Fairclough 2000; Hay 1999b). Second, what Croft and Lister also draw attention to is the way in which maintaining such a gulf presents both strategic opportunities but also potential legitimation problems to elected politicians. For Croft the substantive focus of attention is the 'ethical dimension' of Labour's foreign policy since 1997 and, specifically, the difficulties of reconciling such an unobjectionable discourse with the invariably habitual and institutionalized conduct of the Foreign and Commonwealth Office. If Croft points to the dangers of raising an undoubtedly laudable standard against which conduct might be judged in a context in which conduct may be difficult to reform, Lister's argument is rather different. For she demonstrates how a gulf between political rhetoric and political reality has opened up as a new welfare settlement has emerged and the role this has played in legitimating what might otherwise be seen as unpalatably inegalitarian and exclusionary welfare reforms. A similar observation is made by David Marsh, when he refers to the frequently strategic use made of ideas about globalization incompatible with the empirical evidence in justifying what might otherwise be seen as regressive social and economic reforms (see also Hay 2001).

As the above paragraphs suggest, it is not difficult to point to significant and ongoing shifts in political discourse and substantive political outcomes. Altogether more complex is the question of projected change. Few contemporary political analysts now hold out much hope for a science of the political capable of fashioning firm political predictions in the form of testable hypotheses. And, interestingly, those who do tend to confine themselves to post hoc rationalizations in the form of predictions of events that have already occurred! In the former respect, though thankfully not in the latter, this volume is no exception. Readers may well be disappointed not to find out whether New Labour is capable of becoming the natural party of government in the first half of the present century, or whether the Belfast Agreement of April 1998 will be successfully implemented. However, what they will gain is a series of detailed and measured assessments of the conditions of such outcomes (and a host of others) being realized. This is what a new and more modest and reflexive political science of British politics can offer – and, perhaps, all that it can *legitimately* offer (see also Rhodes, chapter 6 below).

That this is so is largely due to a growing recognition in contemporary political analysis (possibly to a rather greater extent in Europe than in North America and in international relations than in political science) of the inherent indeterminacy of political processes (on which see Hay 2002b). The future, for a growing number of political analysts, is necessarily unpredictable since, whether New Labour will become the natural party of government in the next forty years, for instance, is conditional on events which have yet to occur. Lest this be seen to qualify the extent to which political analysis might be regarded as a science, it is perhaps worth pointing to the implications of chaos theory for the natural sciences. For similar arguments are now made about the forecasting of meteorological outcomes – it now being widely accepted that the weather cannot be forecasted in the long term since the formation of weather systems is in fact contingent upon short-term events (famously, the flapping of a butterfly's wings). Of course, what sets political analysis apart from the natural sciences, rendering it all the more complex, is the indeterminacy injected into social and political dynamics by human agents. The recognition of this has led to a far greater emphasis on contingency and a far greater hesitation about the prediction of events yet to unfold (whose causal determinants have, arguably, yet to form).

Of course, some future outcomes are rather more contingent than others. At the time of writing, less than two weeks from polling day in the 2001 general election, that Labour will win seems a pretty safe bet. Yet the point is that such a prediction is not likely to discriminate well between contending accounts of contemporary British political dynamics. As such, it is not a very useful prediction. Altogether more helpful is to suggest the conditions of Labour's (presumed) success. It is this latter form of analysis which characterizes the contributions to the present collection.

A new political science of British politics?

It is perhaps premature to suggest, certainly on the basis of this volume alone, the emergence of a new political science of British politics. Indeed, the label is undoubtedly one which almost all of the present contributors would refuse. As the chapters which follow attest all too well, the contemporary political science of British politics is characterized by diversity and intellectual pluralism rather than conformity. Nonetheless, as I have been at pains to suggest in this brief introduction, a series of common themes do nonetheless emerge. Together they constitute a challenge to the modes of political analysis which have tended to dominate the political science of British politics in the postwar period. Among these, the following stand out.

1 A greater tendency to contextualize contemporary dynamics, both historically (temporally) and internationally (spatially).
2 A greater emphasis on institutional and ideational mediations and a concern to trace the process of political change from inputs to outcomes.
3 A greater recognition of the contingency and indeterminacy of political outcomes and an associated emphasis on the significance of unintended consequences.
4 An acknowledgement, linked to point 1 above, of the need to locate Britain comparatively.
5 An associated blurring of the once rigid demarcation of the domestic and the international and a growing recognition of the significance of processes of multilevel governance.
6 A broadening and respecification of the legitimate terrain of political analysis and a growing recognition of extrapolitical variables (such as cultural and/or economic factors) in the determination of political outcomes.
7 A greater recognition of the importance of ideational variables (values, paradigms, ideologies, rhetorics) in the causation of political outcomes and of the need to consider such ideational factors not in isolation but in their relationships to the material contexts in which they arise and on which they impact.

Some of these concerns are genuinely novel, others mark more of a return to older traditions of analysis. Yet together they map out the analytical terrain of British politics today. Their salience is amply illustrated in the chapters which follow.

NOTES

1 As this perhaps suggests given the theoretical diversity of the contributors to this volume, though frequently associated with the new institutionalism (par-

ticularly in its more historical variants), such developments are by no means confined to self-declared institutionalists. David Sanders's chapter is perhaps an important case in point. Though written by a prominent defender of behaviouralism (see, for instance, Sanders 1995), it provides an important assessment of the implications of constitutional-institutional change (current and potential) for party political dynamics (present and future).

2 Blair's first speech to the Labour Party Conference as leader, for instance, contained no fewer than thirty-seven references to the party's novelty (Butler and Kavanagh 1997: 64).

3 The following sections draw from a similar discussion of mine elsewhere (Hay 1999a: 25–7).

4 It should be noted that to identify continuity is not to imply that any change is taking place or to suggest that no change is occurring. The concept, unlike that of discontinuity, is neutral with respect to the identification of change.

REFERENCES

Blyth, M. M. (1997) '"Any More Bright Ideas?" The Ideational Turn of Comparative Political Economy', *Comparative Politics*, 29(1), 229–50.

Butler, D. and Kavanagh, D. (1997) *The British General Election of 1997*. Basingstoke: Macmillan.

Campbell, J. L. (1998) 'Institutional Analysis and the Role of Ideas in Political Economy', *Theory and Society*, 27, 377–409.

Fairclough, N. (2000) *New Labour, New Language?* London: Routledge.

Fielding, S. (2000) 'A New Politics?', in P. Dunleavy et al., *Developments in British Politics 6*. Basingstoke: Macmillan.

Giddens, A. (1994) *Beyond Left and Right: The Future of Radical Politics*. Cambridge: Polity.

——(1998) *The Third Way: The Renewal of Social Democracy*. Cambridge: Polity.

——(1999) *The Runaway World*. London: Profile Books.

Gray, J. (1997) *Endgames: Questions in Late Modern Political Thought*. Cambridge: Polity.

Hay, C. (1999a) 'Continuity and Discontinuity in British Political Development', in D. Marsh et al., *Postwar British Politics in Perspective*. Cambridge: Polity.

——(1999b) *The Political Economy of New Labour*. Manchester: Manchester University Press.

——(2001) 'The Invocation of External Economic Constraints: A Genealogy of the Concept of Globalisation in the Political Economy of the British Labour Party, 1973–2000', *European Legacy*, 6(2), 233–49.

——(2002a) 'Globalisation, EU-isation and the Space for Social Democratic Alternatives: Pessimism of the Intellect', *British Journal of Politics and International Relations*, 4.

—— (2002b) *Political Analysis*. Basingstoke: Macmillan.

Hay, C. and Marsh, D. (1999) 'Introduction: Towards a New (International) Political Economy?', *New Political Economy*, 4(1), 5–22.

Heffernan, R. (2000) *New Labour and Thatcherism*. Basingstoke: Macmillan.

Hirst, P. and Thompson, G. (1999) *Globalization in Question*, 2nd edn. Cambridge: Polity.

—— (2000) 'Globalisation in One Country? The Peculiarities of the British', *Economy and Society*, 29(3), 335–56.

Kavanagh, D. (1997) *The Reordering of British Politics*. Oxford: Oxford University Press.

Kerr, P. (2001) *Postwar British Politics: From Conflict to Consensus*. London: Routledge.

Marsh, D. et al. (1999) *Postwar British Politics in Perspective*. Cambridge: Polity.

Mulgan, G. (1994) *Politics in an Antipolitical Age*. Cambridge: Polity.

Sanders, D. (1995) 'Behaviouralism', in D. Marsh and G. Stoker (eds), *Theory and Methods in Political Science*. Basingstoke: Macmillan.

Seldon, A. (ed.) (2001) *The Blair Effect: The Blair Government, 1997–2001*. London: Little, Brown.

Strasser, H. and Randall, S. C. (1981) *An Introduction to Theories of Social Change*. London: Routledge and Kegan Paul.

2

Pluralism and the Study of British Politics: It is Always the Happy Hour for Men with Money, Knowledge and Power

David Marsh

In my view politics is about power and anyone who studies British politics is operating with an explicit, or more usually implicit, model of power. In this chapter I shall argue a number of related points: first, pluralism is the theory of power which underpins most studies of British politics; second, pluralism focuses almost exclusively on intentional, to the exclusion of structural, explanation; third, in doing so, it neglects perhaps the key feature of our social and political systems, that they are characterized by structured inequality; and, fourth, this structured inequality is reflected in the form and the outputs of government. In essence then, this chapter is a plea that students of British politics should look much more critically at their pluralist assumptions.

The dominance of pluralism

I shall first outline my understanding of the pluralist model of power before arguing that it underpins most political science and studies of British politics in particular.

The pluralist model

Pluralism is a slippery foe. Like other power theories it has changed significantly over time (see Marsh 1995). There are a number of ways of categorizing pluralism; here I shall merely distinguish between classical pluralism and elite or 'reformed' pluralism (Smith 1995). The rest of this chapter then focuses on the reformed pluralist model.

Classical pluralism   Classical pluralism, which is most associated with the views of Bentley (1967) and, later, Truman (1951), can be characterized in terms of the following features:

- Power is diffused, not concentrated; this distinguishes pluralism from both Marxism and elitism.
- Interest groups are the key feature of civil society; indeed they are the key actors in political life. This distinguishes pluralism from classical Marxism, which sees civil society under capitalism as divided predominantly on class lines, and elitism, which sees civil society as marked by an inevitable elite/mass dichotomy.
- To pluralists, politics involves conflict between a large number of interest groups which takes place within a consensus about the rules of the game.
- Pluralists usually use the term government because talk of the state suggests that rule involves both intervention in broad aspects of social and political life and coercion as well as consent. In classical pluralism, government is seen as having a relatively passive role; it acts like a weather-vane (Dunleavy and O'Leary 1984), buffeted by the wind of the representations of various interest groups and pointing in a direction which reflects a balance between those representations.
- Crucially however, the government is independent of any particular interest. As such, pluralism differs from classical Marxism, which argues that the state forwards the interest of the ruling class, and elitism, which sees the state as acting on behalf of the dominant elite.
- Pluralism has a normative as well as an empirical thrust. Pluralists believe that the outcome of pluralist interaction is beneficial. In particular, groups extend democracy by increasing and broadening participation. Of course, theorists from other positions are usually also normatively committed to pluralism, but argue that empirically it doesn't exist.

Elite or Reformed Pluralism   Pluralism has changed significantly in response to both theoretical and empirical critiques (see Marsh 1995). As such, modern elite or reformed pluralism is considerably more sophisticated. Moreover, as even this brief summary will suggest, there are a number of variants.[1]

- Interest groups are still the key feature of civil society, but elite pluralists recognize that a limited number of groups are particularly influential. In this, they have responded to critiques from within (see especially Dahl 1971; Lindblom 1977) and beyond pluralism (see especially Hunter 1953; Mills 1956). These authors argued that some groups – to Dahl, Hunter and Lindblom business, and to Mills the power elite – were particularly and consistently powerful in the United States.
- Consequently, although power is still viewed as diffuse, it is more concentrated than in the view of Truman and other earlier pluralists.
- There is an emphasis on the need to disaggregate. The government is seen as segmented. As such, there is considerable stress placed on the role of subgovernments or policy networks (for a review of this literature see Marsh 1998); that is, on the existence of close and sustained relationships between sections of the government and interest groups in many areas of policy-making. The argument is that these networks compete with one another for influence and therefore resources; this competition ensures that no one group dominates.
- There is a strong tendency in the more recent literature to equate pluralism with plurality (see Vogel 1987; McFarland 1987). So it is suggested that, while there are powerful groups in particular policy sectors, the identity of these groups varies over time and space. No one group dominates across a series of policy areas at any one time, so there is variation over space, and neither does any group dominate on one issue over time, so there is plurality over time.
- A number of authors acknowledge the crucial power of economic/ business interests; this view is most developed by Lindblom (1977).
- In contrast, some authors, especially McFarland (1987), place a great deal of emphasis on the importance of countervailing forces. To McFarland, powerful producer interests give rise to countervailing public interest groups, for example consumer groups, or, more broadly, to new social movements, for example in the environmental field. This leads McFarland to develop a triadic theory of power; so pluralist politics is essentially an exchange between government and

its agencies, producer interest groups and public interest groups/social movements.

- Reformed pluralism also acknowledges that the government or, perhaps more precisely, sections of it, have interests which they promote. Hence, the state is viewed as an active, rather than a passive, actor. In this view, the state has a large amount of autonomy; and indeed some strands of pluralism (especially Nordlinger 1981) or some of the new institutionalists (for a review see Peters 1999) regard the state as the dominant actor.
- The normative view is still that pluralism represents the best form of democracy. Indeed, this view has been reinforced by the contribution of what McLennan (1995) calls the 'radical pluralists'. The work of these authors is based on a very different epistemological approach; most are relativists, asserting and advocating a plurality based on the acknowledgement of difference, whereas the vast majority of the pluralists with whom we are concerned here are positivists.[2] Nevertheless, their advocacy of pluralism has contributed to its ascendancy as a normative position to the extent that McLennan claims: 'pluralism is nowadays part of a structure of feeling of Western intellectual culture to a degree which would have been unthinkable 10 to 15 years ago' (1995: 2).

Pluralism and the study of (British) politics

I have attempted to offer a fair characterization of modern pluralism. Indeed, I would argue that my appreciation of pluralism is considerably more sophisticated than the majority of pluralists who study British politics, most of whom work with an implicit pluralist theory which is probably some amalgam of the classical and the reform model. However, my argument doesn't fall on the detailed accuracy of this assessment. I am more interested here in the way in which pluralism underpins, and I shall suggest distorts, the study of British politics.

In this section I shall argue three related points, the first two of which concern the study of politics or political science[3] generally, while the third specifically concerns the study of British politics. First, it is important to acknowledge that the US dominates political science. Given that political science is a relatively young discipline, which has expanded very quickly in the last three decades, it is not surprising that something like 90 per cent of political scientists who have ever lived are still alive. It is more significant that over 80 per cent of them are from the United States. This has clear implications for what we study and how we study it. As such, and given that pluralism as a theory of power was developed in the

US, and is invariably used to characterize its power structure, it is not surprising that it has been the dominant perspective in political science.

Second, the very definitions of politics which most political scientists adopt are pluralist in inspiration. Obviously, this is crucially important because it sets the agenda for what is subsequently studied. There are two distinct, but linked, questions that anyone attempting to define politics has to address. What is involved in politics and where does it occur? Most definitions are pluralist in two ways: they are narrow, arena, rather than process definitions; and they see politics as involving limited conflict, resulting in incremental change. These points need brief elaboration.

In defining politics many people adopt an arena definition (see Left-wich 1984); that is to say they see politics as occurring within the sphere of government, but not in the broader social sphere. So what goes on in Whitehall, Westminster, Belfast, Edinburgh, Cardiff and town halls certainly involves politics, and possibly, although not inevitably, the educational system or the welfare state may have a political dimension, but the family would definitely lie outside the political arena. Here, a clear distinction is being drawn between the public and the private sphere, with the private sphere seen as outside politics. This position has been severely criticized, particularly by feminists who assert that 'the personal is political'. This is not the place to develop this argument (see Hay and Marsh 1999), but the crucial point is that the arena definition is a pluralist definition, or more precisely it is a definition which fits happily with pluralism as a theory of power.[4] Pluralists do focus on interest groups, but the emphasis is on their public role, their relations with government; pluralists recognize a distinction between the public and the private realm and regard politics as the preserve of the public realm.

At the same time, most definitions of politics see politics as involving the three Cs. Politics involves *conflict*, but limited conflict within a *consensus* about how that conflict should be resolved (by the legitimate authority; for instance, the democratically elected government), with the outcome being *compromise*. So change is incremental and both revolution and war are seen as marking the collapse or 'end' of politics. This, again, is clearly a pluralist, indeed a classical pluralist, definition. It stresses that the conflict between interests is resolved by an authoritative decision taken by government. In contrast, classical Marxists and classical elitists would have seen radical, indeed probably violent, change as the inevitable outcome of politics. Even modern Marxists are committed to the idea that political activity will lead to radical, although probably not revolutionary, change.

If pluralism dominates our conceptualizations of politics it is not surprising that most British politics textbooks, and more broadly most studies of British politics, are pluralist (for an excellent review of these textbooks see Smith, 1999). There are notable exceptions; so Kingdom (1999) presents an interesting, thorough, if a little strident, Marxist account, while the second edition of Dearlove and Saunders (1984) offers a sophisticated, if dated, radical-Weberian perspective. However, these are exceptions and perhaps, as such, they prove the rule. Elsewhere, much of the research on British politics is atheoretical, and indeed ahistorical and insular. So much so that the Political Studies Association, the professional body for British political scientists, has recently established a journal, the *British Journal of Politics and International Relations*, an aim of which has been to encourage alternative readings of British politics, while of course not neglecting mainstream approaches.

The consequences of the dominance of pluralism for the study of British politics

In my view, then, pluralism dominates the study of politics. Of course, not everyone would regard this as a bad thing. I would certainly argue that, as a normative theory, pluralism, with its emphasis on diversity and participation, should be encouraged. However, there are two other separate, though closely related, issues. Is the emphasis on pluralism as an empirical theory/model within political science limiting because it leads analysts to focus on some issues and ignore others? Does pluralism offer an adequate analysis of the power structure in Britain? The rest of this chapter addresses these questions and my conclusions are clear, although by no means uncontestable. The pluralist orientation of the study of British politics means that analysts neglect perhaps the crucial feature of British politics, the pattern of structural inequality that is reflected in political institutions and processes. In ignoring this pattern of structural inequality, analysts concentrate on a more surface level of politics at which pluralism may exist. In this section, I shall contend that pluralism neglects structural explanation. In the next section I argue that in studying British politics we need to take the patterns of structured inequality which exist within Britain more seriously.

Pluralism's neglect of structuralist explanation

My point here is a simple one: theory, definition, methodology and analysis/interpretation are inexorably linked. To study the distribution of power in Britain an analyst utilizes a particular theory of power, which underpins her or his definition of power. This definition leads the analyst to use a particular methodology that shapes the analysis of the distribution of power. So pluralism has a definition of influence, not power, that privileges a narrow methodology, which, in turn, confirms the pluralist position. It is important to develop this point at more length.

The pluralist model as here outlined underpins a definition of influence rather than power; power to a pluralist involves coercion as well as consent, but a pluralist system is one in which coercion is supposedly unnecessary. The definition pluralists normally adopt is Robert Dahl's (1957), although interestingly it has its origins in the work of Max Weber: A (an individual or an interest group) has influence over B (the government) in so far as she, he or they can make it do something it wouldn't otherwise have done.

There are three distinct, but linked, points about this definition. First, it is an open definition; that is, it leaves the question of whether, or not, an interest group has influence open to empirical investigation. This reflects two aspects of pluralism: its positivism and its emphasis on the plurality of outcomes over time and space. I have dealt with the second point above, but the first needs brief consideration. A positivist believes that we can establish an objective measure of the power distribution in any society by studying policy outcomes. In contrast, a relativist believes that power is a social construct and, as such, cannot be studied objectively, while a realist believes that not all aspects of a power structure can be directly observed. This is not the place to explore these epistemological positions,[5] but it is important to acknowledge that pluralism's positivist underpinnings have very important methodological implications; they point to a focus on directly observable and, to an extent, quantifiable indicators.

This inevitably brings into sharp focus the second characteristic of this definition; it sees influence/power as a zero-sum game. If an interest group gains concessions they are at the expense of government; the group 'wins' and government 'loses'. In contrast, many analysts would reject this conceptualization of power and argue that power is always relational, that it is not a commodity to be exchanged. As such, we must recognize that power is inscribed in all institutions and processes. So to study its distribution we must move beyond the study of the decisions governments take and analyse both the context within which they are taken and the meanings given to the exchange of resources by those involved.

This leads us inevitably to the key critique of pluralist methodology (see Bachrach and Baratz 1962; Lukes 1974; Hay 1997). Dahl's definition focuses on the outcome of government decision-making as the acid test of the influence of individuals or interest groups. Thus it is a very narrow definition advocating a very limited methodology. Bachrach and Baratz (1962) criticized this approach which they saw as focusing exclusively on what they called the first face of power (see figure 2.1). The researcher examines a particular policy decision and tries to establish why the government took that decision (X in the figure), rather than any of the other decisions it had considered (Y in the figure). In the view of Bachrach and Baratz, this approach ignored a crucial aspect of power: the capacity to prevent certain alternative policies being considered. They identified this as the second face of power, which they termed agenda-setting. They argued that a group also exercised power to the extent that it could prevent certain alternatives (Z in the figure) being considered; that is it kept them off the agenda (the divide between what is on and off the agenda is marked by // in figure 2.1). Lukes extended this critique. He argued that power doesn't necessarily involve behaviour; rather it can be inscribed in a dominant ideology that affects the perceptions, cognitions and preferences of the actors involved (politics takes place within a broader ideological climate which consistently favours certain interests, represented by the net in figure 2.1).

This discussion of faces of power is important here for at least three reasons. First, it makes it clear that pluralism focuses on the first and, particularly in its 'reformed' variant, the second face of power. In so far as we accept the notion that power has other faces, then the pluralist methodology is limited. Second, pluralism is behaviouralist and thus exclusively concerned with intentional, rather than structural, explanation; in so far as we accept that structures constrain or facilitate agents, then again the pluralist methodology is inadequate. As to the third reason, while Lukes is surely right to argue that power has other faces, his exposition of the third face is problematic. As Hay (1997) points out, Lukes's position rests on a distinction between the 'real' interests and the preferences of agents that is impossible to sustain. Rather, Hay argues that Lukes still adopts a behavioural approach; the exercise of power to

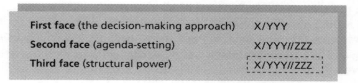

Figure 2.1 Three faces of power

Lukes still requires A to do something. In contrast, Hay argues that it is crucial to acknowledge that power can also be context-shaping and conduct-shaping; that is, that agents in changing structures affect both the context within which future agents act and those agents' conduct in that context.

In essence, Hay is suggesting that this is a structure/agency problem (see Hay 1995). The pluralists are essentially intentionalists, arguing that we can explain outcomes simply in terms of the actions of agents. Conversely, Lukes's third dimension of power focuses on structural explanation: the dominant ideology, conceptualized as a structure, shapes the preferences of the agents. However, both these positions are clearly inadequate. Structures don't determine the actions of agents, any more than agents act in an unstructured context. Instead, the actions of agents are constrained and facilitated by the structural and strategic context within which they operate, but they interpret those structures and their actions can and do change the structures. As such, this is an iterative and interactive, that is a dialectical, process.

This is a crucially important argument and it is where I fundamentally disagree with the pluralist conception of power. As indicated, many pluralists now acknowledge and study the process of agenda-setting. However, they fail to recognize the structural constraints within which the pluralist contestation of power takes place. To put it at its most simple, pluralism assumes that political contestation occurs on a fairly level playing field, whereas my argument is that it occurs in a context of structured inequality that favours some interests over others.

Structural inequality and British politics

Here I shall argue, against the pluralists, that decisions taken by government are structurally or, perhaps more accurately, strategically constrained; that they cannot be explained merely as the product of the interaction between interest groups and government or in terms of the intentions/actions of agents. However, I do not argue that these structural inequalities determine outcomes; while it may usually be the happy hour for men with money, knowledge and power, it is not necessarily always the case.

Of course, there are a number of bases of structured inequality and it is no part of my argument here to privilege one of these, or to suggest that they can all in some sense be reduced to one; although of course they do tend to be mutually reinforcing. I merely argue that these structured inequalities are a key feature of the context within which politics is conducted and decisions made. In other words, the structured inequality that characterizes British society must be taken seriously by those who analyse the British power structure. Yet pluralism fails to do this because of its emphasis on agency and the relationship between interest groups and the state.

More specifically, I shall argue that there are three reflections of these structural inequalities that have clear resonance for political outcomes. The structured inequalities are reflected in the broad balance between social forces in society; the resources which agents can utilize to influence the decision-making process; and the political institutions and processes within which agents act. These three reflections of structural inequality then affect, but again of course don't determine, the discursive construction of political problems and putative solutions; the strategic calculations of agents; and, hence, political outcomes (see figure 2.2).

An unequal balance between social forces: constraints on, and opportunities for, government autonomy

Structured inequality is reflected in the resources controlled by certain social forces; or, to put it another way, certain interests within society clearly control resources which constrain, without determining, government policy. In my view then, control over such resources privileges the representations by these interests and helps shape the deliberations of government.

In this section, for illustrative purposes, my focus is on control over economic resources; but obviously control over other resources is also crucial. I want to argue here that there are key features of the pattern of economic relations in society which constrain and facilitate political agents. It might seem easiest to sustain my argument if I accepted an extreme form of the globalization thesis, which emphasizes the dominance of economic over political forces. Indeed, Ohmae (1990) contends that the era of the national state is over and that national governments are ineffective in the face of globalized economic and social processes.[6] In Ohmae's view, two forces, global markets and transnational companies, are dominant in the world economy and no public authorities, either national or international, can control them. He views this development as beneficial because it has resulted in a strong economy and a weak state from which everyone will benefit.

However, as I have stressed, I am not a determinist and a critique of the work of Ohmae will allow me to clarify my position. Against Ohmae,

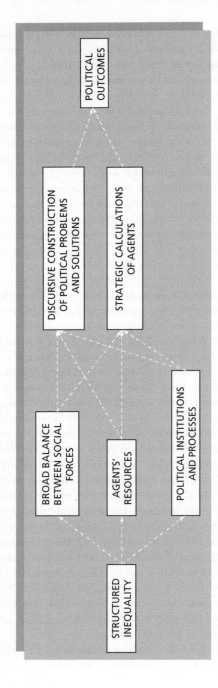

Figure 2.2 Structured inequality and political outcomes (the dotted lines indicate that the relationships are not determinant)

I argue here that the constraint exercised by economic forces cannot be seen solely in terms of a process of globalization, but, nevertheless, that control over economic resources constrains the autonomy of government. However, later I shall also emphasize that any simple economistic, that is determinist, reading of the relationship is untenable.

Domestic versus international capital   As Hirst and Thompson (1999) show, a process has been occurring which is perhaps more accurately called regionalization than globalization; as such, the British economy is still dominated by British domestic capital and British multinational corporations trade most in Britain and Europe and hold the majority of their assets in that region. However, it is interesting that British multinational companies are significantly more internationalized than those in the US, Japan or Germany (see Hirst and Thompson 1999: 82 table 3.10); a result not commented on by Hirst and Thompson.

However, Hirst and Thompson's discussion concentrates on one aspect of the character of British capital: its international nature. In my view, two other features are also crucial if our aim is to identify how it constrains the autonomy of government. First, British capital is highly concentrated, although this level has dropped slightly since the mid-1980s; so in 1994 on average 42.2 per cent of net output in each sector was concentrated in the largest five firms in that sector. To the extent that control over economic resources is important, this level of concentration means that a few firms have very significant resources. Second, the financial sector is particularly important. More specifically, there has been a particular growth in the size of financial markets. This of course is an international phenomenon; so daily turnover in the world currency markets jumped from $150 billion in 1985 to over $1,000 billion today. Of course, the vast majority of this activity is speculative rather than trade related; so these markets are an important constraint on economic policy-making. The City of London is one of the leading financial centres and plays a key role in the British economy, contributing a large surplus to the balance of payments. Certainly, the crucial role played by the financial sector in the British economy is well documented (Coakley and Harris 1983; Ingham 1984; Moran 1981). The links between the banking sector and industrial capital have historically been weak in Britain as compared with elsewhere (Hay and Watson 1998). In addition, the fact that it is the financial sector which holds much of government debt through the government bond market is a far from irrelevant consideration in economic policy-making.

Whether capital respects national boundaries or is genuinely transnational, its control over economic resources, and the discursive construction of that control, still constrains political outcomes. This point needs developing. Regardless of its international dimension, the crucial position which such institutions and firms occupy in the economy acts as a constraint on what governments can do.

This argument has been well made by heretic pluralists, as well as by more radical theorists. So, as an example, Lindblom (1977) emphasizes the structural power of business (he talks of business rather than capital and this reflects his pluralism). He argues that in policy areas of interest to business, for example economic policy, industrial policy, industrial relations policy, etc., government operates within an imprisoned zone of policy-making. His exposition focuses on the question of why and how this constraint operates. He suggests, in a manner which invokes Lukes, that government operates within a broad ideology (in his terms a set of volitions) which favours business; as such, the discursive construction of the issues and of the possible solutions to problems marginalizes alternatives which business would oppose (this argument is similar to that developed by Bachrach and Baratz). More positively, he argues that governments favour and forward the interests of business because the activities of business are crucial to economic success; an economic success which is, in turn, crucial to any government's chances of re-election (for a similar neo-Marxist argument, see Block 1977). Finally, Lindblom suggests that companies and interest groups representing the interests of business have significant resources for promoting pro-business policy preferences.

At the same time, government has resources which business wants (for example, government alone can make authoritative decisions and it also provides business with grants or tax breaks). As such, Lindblom conceptualizes modern pluralist politics as involving an exchange relationship between business and government; government has autonomy but this autonomy is significantly constrained by the structural position of business and the structural dependence of government on business confidence.

While there are major problems with Lindblom's position, particularly his failure to disaggregate the state, or capital, or the relations between the two (see Marsh 1983), this seems to me to be a powerful argument and a significant advance on most pluralist work. Business does constrain government and this constraint can operate independently of the interest group activity of business, because government, operating within a discursive framework which tends to promote business confidence and broadly favour business, anticipates the interests of business and the interests of business are inscribed in the institutions and processes of government.

Patterns of structured inequality and actors' political resources

Structured inequality is not only reflected in the unequal balance between structural forces which provides the broad framework within which political agents operate, it is also reflected in the resources on which individual political actors can draw.

Here, I briefly consider three key bases of structured inequality: class, gender and race. However, it is important to stress that the effect of these three structures on political outcomes is mediated through both education and knowledge and access to political power. While there is no simple relationship between social structural factors and political outcomes, these patterns of structured inequality are reflected in access to the three key resources used by actors in trying to shape political outcomes: money, knowledge and political power. Again my argument is not a determinist one. Rather, I contend that these factors interact to constrain and facilitate, that is to shape, political outcomes.

Structured inequality is reflected in each of these three resources' dimensions. There are significant inequalities of income and wealth in Britain (see tables 2.1 and 2.2). In addition, these inequalities have increased significantly in the last two decades; so Machin shows that 'from the late 1970s and through the 1980s, inequalities in earnings rose massively for both sexes' (1999: 187 and see 188–90, tables 11.1 a and b and 11.2). Indeed, he also emphasizes that wage inequality grew quicker during this period in the UK than in any developed country other than the United States (1999: 191, table 11.3). These inequalities are also clearly related to gender and race (see Reid 1998: ch. 2, esp. table 2.6); the richest section of the population in terms of both wealth and income are white males.

There has been considerable debate about the concept of an underclass, but there is no doubt that a significant section of the population is caught in a poverty trap (see Reid 1998: chs 3–6). During Mrs Thatcher's tenure in Downing Street average income rose by 36 per cent, but the

Table 2.1 Distribution of income in the UK in 1999 (pounds/week)

	All £	Male £	Female £	Female as prop. male	Manual as prop. non-manual
All workers	417.9	459.4	346.9	76%	
Non-manual	463.5	547.0	367.3	67%	
Manual	324.8	343.4	236.3	69%	70%

Source: Derived from government statistics on http://www.statsbase.gov.uk

Table 2.2 Distribution of wealth, 1996 (percentage of wealth owned by each group)

	Marketable wealth	Marketable wealth minus values of houses
Most wealthy 1%	19	27
Most wealthy 5%	39	50
Most wealthy 10%	52	63
Most wealthy 25%	74	82
Most wealthy 50%	93	94

Source: Derived from government statistics on http://www.statsbase.gov.uk

income of the bottom 10 per cent fell by 14 per cent, while that of the top 10 per cent rose by 65 per cent. The government's own figures show that 14 per cent of the population (8 million) is totally dependent on welfare. Other figures show 24 per cent of the population living in poverty, 17 per cent receiving income support, 19 per cent of households with no working adults, and so it goes on. Children from such backgrounds do much worse at school, are one and a half times more likely to have a long-standing illness and twice as likely to have a disability. They are much more likely to be black and women who are lone parents; so, for example, between 1979 and 1993 the proportion of lone parents in poverty increased from 19 per cent to 58 per cent (see Reid 1998: ch. 3; Burgess and Propper 1999; Stewart 1999; Nickell 1999).

Of course, there is social mobility, but while there is evidence to suggest that it is greater now than previously, it is still limited (compare Saunders 1996 with Marshall et al. 1997). However, upward social mobility is more common than downward social mobility. As just one example, the British Household Panel shows that 50 per cent of those in the bottom fifth of the population in income terms in 1991 remained in that position in 1997, while 57 per cent of those in the top 20 per cent remained in that category (British Household Panel Survey, Institute for Social and Economic Research). Origins still shape, although by no means determine, destinations.

Structured inequality is also reflected in education. The English public school system is a clear bastion of the white middle classes, as is Oxbridge (see Adonis and Pollard 1997: ch. 2). In a less extreme form the education system generally reflects similar patterns of privilege. Working-class children are less likely to stay on at school or to attend university. As far as race is concerned, Asian achievement is very similar to that of whites, but blacks are only a third as likely to obtain GCSE, AS and A levels or to go to university as other groups. In contrast, the educational achievement of men and women is similar, although there are clear differences in the subjects studied, with some researchers arguing that the fact that boys are much more likely to study maths and science benefits them on the labour market (on these relations see Reid 1998: ch. 7).

Moving to access to positions of political power, the under-representation of the working class, women and blacks in the political elite hardly needs demonstrating (see table 2.3 and 2.4). The dominant political elites in Britain are overwhelmingly white, male and middle class, if not by birth then by education.

In my view then there can be little doubt that there is a persistent structural inequality that is reflected in access to money, knowledge and power; and these are the key resources used in the struggle for political influence. This structural inequality provides actors with various structural possibilities, but any explanation of the outcomes must be in terms of both those structural possibilities and the strategic calculations of the actors.

Structural inequality and political institutions and processes

Structured inequality is also reflected in the institutions and processes within which, and through which, political decisions are made. The first point I would make here is one I have made before (Marsh 1980; Marsh and Tant, 1991; Marsh, Richards and Smith 2001). The British notion of representative democracy is a restrictive one; it is based on a limited liberal conception of representation and a conservative notion of responsibility. In fact, in the British political system the stress has consistently been on strong, centralized, efficient government, rather than responsive government. So, as Birch argues (1964), the British political tradition emphasizes 'first, consistency, prudence and leadership, second, accountability to Parliament and the electorate and third, responsiveness to public opinion and demands.'

In other words, the emphasis is on a normative commitment to elite or leadership democracy, rather than participatory democracy, and this is reflected in our institutions, processes and political discourse. Two examples should suffice here to illustrate this argument.

First, the core of the British political system, which I take to be the link between the electoral system, strong party discipline and executive dominance, is clearly a reflection of a leadership view of democracy. Supporters of these arrangements argue that a strong executive with a guaranteed majority is required in order to take necessary, decisive, even if unpopular,

Table 2.3 Access to political positions: social and educational composition of British cabinets, 1970–1997 (percentages)

	Class			Education			
	Aristocrat	Middle	Working	Public school	Eton	University	Oxbridge
Heath (1970–4)	22	78	0	83	22	83	83
Wilson/Callaghan (1974–9)	1	67	26	33	0	77	49
Thatcher (1979–90)	14	86	0	91	27	82	77
Major (1990–7)	14	77	9	64	9	91	77
Blair (1997–)	0	68	32	36	0	95	14

Source: D. Butler and G. Butler, *Twentieth Century British Political Facts, 1900–2000* (Basingstoke: Macmillan, 2000).

Table 2.4 Access to positions of political influence: social and educational backgrounds of Permanent Secretaries, 1979–1997 (percentages)

	1974–9	*1979–97*
All public schools	84	73.5
Eton/Harrow	11	3
Secondary school only	11	7.5
Oxford or Cambridge	75	63
All universities	88	93
Middle class	95	94
Working class	5	6
Women	2	3
Non-whites	0	0

Source: Calculated from Civil Service yearbooks.

action. It is also revealing that the unsuccessful challenges to this dominant view, from electoral reformers for example, have been underpinned by a normative commitment to participatory democracy. This tension between different views of democracy was evident in the deliberations of the Jenkins Commission on Electoral Reform established by the Labour government in 1997. However, what is most revealing is that the commission recommended a very limited form of electoral reform that would most probably ensure the continuance of majority government.[7] The British political tradition underpins not only the current institutions but also the terrain on which debates about reform take place.

Second, as I have argued elsewhere (Marsh and Tant, 1991), although Thatcherism is often seen as marking a crucial break with the past, it is in fact a perfect embodiment of the British political tradition rather than a challenge to it. As Gamble argues (1988), a key emphasis within Thatcherism was on the need for a strong state to provide decisive political leadership and establish the framework for a free economy. What is more, it is difficult to think of more appropriate political epithets for the British political tradition than the two epithets associated with the early years of the Thatcher Government: 'There is no alternative' and 'The Lady's not for turning'.

So, in my view, the institutions and processes are inscribed with a limited conception of democracy. I would also argue that this limited leadership view itself reflects and reinforces the broader socioeconomic inequalities in society. First, the nature of our leadership democracy reflects the outcome of the nineteenth-century struggle between social forces, a struggle that was effectively won by those defending the existing order; so the franchise was extended, but the elite still governed us.

Second, our democratic system discourages participation, the implicit view being that more participation leads to less efficiency, and, consequently, offers very limited sites for dissent. As such, there is a symbiotic relationship between this conception and practice of democracy and the existing social order that is elitist, patriarchal and racist.

If we return rather less heroically to a discussion of how our contemporary political structures reflect structured inequality, then much of the recent work on policy networks in British politics reflects my argument here. The main proposition of much of that literature is that policy networks are key political structures within which many decisions are made. These networks are characterized by clear patterns of inclusion and exclusion. So, as an example, the authors of the case studies in my edited book with Rhodes (Marsh and Rhodes 1992) identified networks which varied between tight policy communities and much looser issue networks (on this distinction see Marsh and Rhodes 1992: ch.1). However, all the networks were dominated by a combination of three sets of actors representing state, economic or professional interests. It will also surprise no one that few women or blacks were involved in the networks. Policy networks are thus political structures whose membership reflects, but again is not determined by, broader patterns of structured inequality in society (on this see Marsh and Smith 2000). In addition, it bears emphasizing that trade unions, consumer interests and non-economic interest groups were conspicuous by their absence from the networks studied; an observation which should make us look with some caution on McFarland's assertion of the importance of countervailing power.

Structured inequality and political outcomes

So far then I have argued that we need to acknowledge the importance of socioeconomic constraints which are reflected not merely in the balance of social forces but also in the resources available to political actors and the political structures and processes within which decisions are taken. However, I have repeatedly argued that my position is not determinist or economistic. My argument here is most easily made by a brief return to the work of Ohmae on globalization. The four points I wish to make will not surprise anyone who knows the globalization literature, but the argument is very important.

First, Ohmae and many others treat globalization as a process of structural determination; a process without a subject. Yet decisions about investments are taken by companies, or executives, and political decisions are taken by ministers, senior civil service or members of policy networks. These decisions are constrained or facilitated by structures, but those actors are strategically calculating subjects who attempt to realize their own interests within that constraint. In addition, the actors can negotiate and change the constraints because the actions of agents are what constitute and reconstitute the structure. So, for instance, at different stages, British governments have imposed or removed exchange controls, thus significantly altering the constraint. To put it another way, it is as misguided to argue that structures, in this case economic struc- tures, determine outcomes as it is to argue that outcomes can be ex- plained solely in terms of the actions of agents.

Second, while the process itself is important, it is often the discursive construction of that process which constrains political decisions. So, for example, there is a strong argument that in Britain the discourse of globalization has had more influence than the reality. As we saw earlier, there is considerable doubt about the extent of the process; however, the discourse of British politics in the 1980s and 1990s has taken the process for granted. The Conservative governments between 1979 and 1997 argued that the process meant that it was crucial to attract inward investment by offering incentives in the form of grants and creating an industrial relations system designed to reduce strikes and hold down wages. Even more revealing, the rhetoric of the Labour government in the last parliament argued that more radical policies, involving supply- side economics and increased public expenditure, would be unsustain- able in the modern global economy (Hay and Watson 1998).

Third, and following clearly from the prior discussion, it is misleading to treat economic forces as undifferentiated; domestic capital may have interests that differ from those of international capital and industrial and banking capital clearly have diverging interests.

Fourth, any form of economism ignores the importance of other social forces. It is not tenable to ignore the role that patriarchy, racism or control over knowledge plays in shaping both the structures of British government and the political decisions taken.

In conclusion

Most work on British politics deals in intentional explanations because it is based on an explicit or implicit pluralist theory of power. In contrast, my main argument has been that in studying British politics we need to acknowledge the importance of the structures that constrain or facilitate British governments. In my view, these structures are reflected in the overall balance between social forces, the resources available to political agents, and the institutions and process of governance. However, we also need to recognize that these are constraints – they are not determinants. There are a variety of structural constraints which cannot be reduced to one, and which, while they may reinforce one another, may also be contradictory. Agents operate within these constraints but

- their knowledge of these constraints is contingent;
- they have knowledge of a number of different constraints relevant to them, and these constraints may have contradictory effects;
- this knowledge is mediated by frames of meaning or discourses;
- actors are reflexive, so the relationship is not mechanical, but rather the actors strategically calculate their interests given their knowledge of the constraints;
- and, finally, agents affect structures.

However, while I'm not a determinist, I'm also not a pluralist. In my view it is misguided to equate plurality with pluralism. Pluralism is inadequate as a model of the power distribution in Britain because it fails to acknowledge the importance of the structural constraints such as those I have identified. In fact, in some ways, pluralism can itself be seen as a discursive construction of power, which protects the interests of the dominant forces in society, masquerading as an empirical analysis. What we need is a model of power which recognizes that power is not a zero-sum game; that power is a relational concept and the relationships involved are exchange relationships. Of course, modern pluralists would have little trouble with such a view. However, in my view, it is also crucial to recognize that most of these relationships are asymmetrical and that there are consistent and continuing patterns in that asymmetry. White men with money, knowledge and power do have a privileged position in the British polity (for a more detailed exposition of an asymmetric power model, see Marsh, Richards and Smith 2000).

NOTES

Table 2.3 is reproduced from D. Butler and G. Butler, *Twentieth Century British Political Facts, 1900–2000*, by kind permission of Macmillan Ltd.

1 For the most sophisticated statement of modern pluralism, see McFarland (1987).
2 In fact, I think McLennan makes a major mistake in conflating these two varieties of pluralism, see Marsh (1999).

3 I tend to use the term political science, but reject its positivistic overtones.
4 Of course, it is totally at odds with what McLennan calls 'radical pluralism', which has strong feminist origins and is based on an assertion of the need to recognize difference and a view that any distinction between the public and the private realms is a social construct that forwards the interests of the powerful.
5 For a brief exposition of these three positions, together with a statement of my own position, see Marsh et al. (1999).
6 It is important to emphasize that elite pluralists ignore globalization. More specifically, they stress the autonomy of the state and neglect both economic structural constraints particularly and the international dimension generally.
7 In addition, at the time of writing it seems unlikely that the Labour government will support even this limited reform.

REFERENCES

Adonis, A. and Pollard, S. (1997) *A Class Act*. London: Hamish Hamilton.

Bachrach, P. and Baratz, M. (1962) 'Two Faces of Power', *American Political Science Review*, 56, 947–952.

Bentley, A. (1967) *The Process of Government* (1908). Chicago: Chicago University Press.

Birch, A. H. (1964) *Representative and Responsible Government*. London: Allen and Unwin.

Block, F. (1977) 'The Ruling Class Does Not Rule', *Socialist Revolution*, 3, 6–28.

Burgess, S. and Propper, C. (1999) 'Poverty in Britain', in P. Gregg and J. Wadsworth (eds), *The State of Working Britain*. Manchester: Manchester University Press.

Chapman, J. (1995) 'The Feminist Perspective', in D. Marsh and G. Stoker (eds), *Theory and Methods in Political Science*. Basingstoke: Macmillan.

Coakley, J. and Harris, L. (1983) *City of Capital*. Oxford: Blackwell.

Dahl, R. (1957) 'The Concept of Power', *Behavioural Sciences*, 202–3.

—— (1971) *Polyarchy*. New Haven: Yale University Press.

Dearlove, J. and Sounders, P. (1984) *Introduction to British Politics*. Cambridge: Polity.

Dunleavy, P. and O'Leary, B (1984) *Theories of the State*. London: Macmillan.

Gamble, A. (1988) *The Free Economy and The Strong State*. London: Macmillan.

Gregg, P. and Wadsworth, J. (eds) (1999) *The State of Working Britain*. Manchester: Manchester University Press.

Hay, C. (1995) 'Structure and Agency', in D. Marsh and G. Stoker (eds), *Theory and Methods in Political Science*. Basingstoke: Macmillan.

—— (1997) 'Divided by a Common Language: Political Theory and the Concept of Power', *Politics*, 7(1), 45–52.

Hay, C. and Marsh, D. (1999) 'Introduction: Towards a New (International) Political Economy?', *New Political Economy*, 4(1), 5–22.

Hay, C. and Watson, M. (1998) 'Rendering the Contingent Necessary: New Labour's Conversion and the Discourse of Globalisation', Working Paper 8.4, Centre for European Studies, Harvard University.

Hirst, P. and Thompson, G. (1999) *Globalization in Question*, 2nd edn. Cambridge: Polity.

Hunter, F. (1953) *Community Power*. Chapel Hill: University of North Carolina Press.

Ingham, G. (1984) *Capitalism Divided?* Basingstoke: Macmillan.

Kingdom, J. (1999) *Government and Politics in Britain*, 2nd edn. Cambridge: Polity.

Leftwich, A. (1984) *What is Politics? The Activity and its Study*. Oxford: Blackwell.

Lindblom, C. (1977) *Politics and Markets*. New York: Basic Books.

Lukes, S. (1974) *Power: A Radical View*. London: Macmillan.

McFarland, A. (1987) 'Interest Groups and Theories of Power in America', *British Journal of Political Science*, 17, 129–47.

McLennan, G. (1995) *Pluralism*. Buckingham: Open University Press.

Machin, S. (1999) 'Wage Inequality in the 1970s, 1980s and 1990s', in P. Gregg and J. Wadsworth (eds), *The State of Working Britain*. Manchester: Manchester University Press.

Marsh, D. (1980) 'The British Political Tradition', mimeo, University of Essex.

—— (1983) 'Interest Group Activity and Structural Power: Lindblom's *Politics and Markets*', *West European Politics*, 6, 3–13.

—— (1995) 'The Convergence between Theories of the State', in D. Marsh and G. Stoker (eds), *Theory and Methods in Political Science*. Basingstoke: Macmillan.

—— (ed.) (1998) *Comparing Policy Networks*. Buckingham: Open Univeristy Press.

—— (1999) 'Pluralism versus the Politics of Plurality', mimeo, University of Birmingham.

Marsh, D. and Rhodes, R. A. W. (eds) (1992) *Policy Networks in British Politics*. Oxford: Oxford University Press.

Marsh, D. and Tant, T. (1991) 'Democracy Under Mrs Thatcher: Towards a Centralisation of Power', in M. Haralambos (ed.), *Developments in Politics*. Ormskirk: Causeway Press.

Marsh, D. and Smith, M. (2000) 'Understanding Policy Networks: Towards a Dialectical Approach', *Political Studies*, 48, 4–21.

Marsh, D., Richards, D. and Smith, M. J. (2000) 'Unequal Plurality: Towards an Asymmetrical Power Model of the British Political System', mimeo, University of Birmingham.

—— (2001) *Changing Patterns of Governance: British Central Government Departments 1974–1997*. London: Macmillan.

Marsh, D. et al. (1999) *Postwar British Politics in Perspective*. Cambridge: Polity.

Marshall, G. et al. (1997) *Against the Odds?* Oxford: Clarendon.

Mills, C. W. (1956) *The Power Elite.* New York: Oxford University Press.

Moran, M. (1981) 'Finance Capital and Pressure Group Politics', *British Journal of Political Science*, 11, 381–404.

Nickell, S. (1999) 'Unemployment in Britain', in P. Gregg and J. Wadsworth (eds). *The State of Working Britain.* Manchester: Manchester University Press.

Nordlinger, E. (1981) *On the Autonomy of the Democratic State.* Cambridge: Harvard University Press.

Ohmae, K. (1990) *The Borderless World.* London: Collins.

Peters, G. (1999) *Institutional Theory in Political Science: The New Institutionalism.* Washington: Pinter.

Reid, I. (1998) *Class in Britain.* Cambridge: Polity.

Saunders, P. (1996) *Unequal But Fair?* London: IEA.

Smith, M. (1995) 'Pluralism', in D. Marsh and G. Stoker (eds), *Theory and Methods in Political Science.* Basingstoke: Macmillan.

——(1999) 'Institutionalising the "Eternal Return": Textbooks and the Study of British Politics', *British Journal of Politics and International Relations*, 1(1), 106–18.

Stewart, M. (1999) 'Low Pay in Britain', in P. Gregg and J. Wadsworth (eds), *The State of Working Britain.* Manchester: Manchester University Press.

Truman, D. (1951) *The Governmental Process.* New York: Alfred A. Knopf.

Vogel, D. (1987) 'Political Science and the Study of Corporate Power', *British Journal of Political Science*, 17, 385–408.

3

Gender and Contemporary British Politics

Pippa Norris

Critical mass theory, derived from nuclear physics, suggests that nuclear reaction can be a contained process. Beyond a certain point, however, when enough uranium or other fissile material is assembled, there will be an irreversible meltdown, or unstoppable chain reaction of nuclear fission multiplying upon itself, producing an impact far beyond the quantity of the original material.

When applied to social science, the theory of critical mass suggests that the nature of group interactions depends upon size. When a group remains a distinct minority within a larger society, its members will seek to adapt to their surroundings, conforming to the predominant rules of the game. In many ways this is analogous to Elisabeth Noelle-Neuman's (1984) spiral of silence theory about the expression of dissonant views. But once the group reaches a certain size, critical mass theory suggests that there will be a qualitative change in the nature of group interactions, as the minority starts to assert itself and thereby transform the institutional culture, norms and values. Rosabeth Moss Kanter (1977) applied this account to gender relations in industrial corporations, identifying four categories. *Uniform* groups contain only men or women. *Skewed* groups contain a large imbalance of men or women, up to about 15 per cent of the minority group. *Tilted* groups contain about 15–40 per cent of the opposite sex. Lastly, *balanced* groups contain 40–50 per cent of each sex.

This theory can be applied to the position of women in public office. Drude Dahlerup (1988) and Jill M. Bystydzienski (1992) have argued that if women and men politicians differ in their underlying values, policy priorities and legislative styles, then when parliaments shift from skewed to tilted, or even balanced, groups there will be a transformation in the institutional culture, political discourse and policy agenda. The expectations are implicit in Clare Short's claims: 'As more women come into the Commons, the culture will change, the agenda of politics will broaden, and the institution itself will be transformed' (quoted in McDougal 1998). This theory suggests that in the past, we would expect few substantive differences between women and men MPs at Westminster, since, until recently, there have been so few female representatives. Previous research on parliamentary candidates and MPs in the 1992 election found that when compared with men within each party, women were slightly more supportive of feminist and left-wing values, expressed stronger concern about social policy issues, and gave higher priority to constituency casework. Yet in all cases the gender gap was modest, and overall party rather than gender proved the strongest predictor of values and attitudes (Norris and Lovenduski 1995; Norris 1996).

Has this situation changed by the entry of a new cohort of women politicians? The 1997 British general election, where the proportion of women MPs doubled overnight from 9.2 to 18.2 per cent of the Commons, provides a test case for critical mass theory. Much of the popular rhetoric supporting the introduction of gender quotas has stressed that, although there is a clear case to be made on the grounds of equity alone, in addition the entry of more women into Westminster would help to change the mainstream policy agenda, and the 'public school/boys club' atmosphere of Commons debate. A popular argument in favour of positive discrimination for women was that the new intake of female members would raise different types of concerns in the Commons, as well as in the Scottish Parliament, the Welsh Assembly and the European Parliament (see the discussion in Brooks, Eagle and Short 1990; Perrigo 1996; Short 1996; MacDougal 1998).

Yet although there has been much popular controversy about the impact of the new intake of women politicians, so far there has been little systematic research on this topic in Britain. The theory of a critical mass depends on the existence of underlying differences in the values, attitudes and behaviour of the groups concerned. If women and men MPs are similar in these regards, then even if women gradually became the majority at Westminster, British parliamentary politics will continue in familiar ways. The public face of politics will change more than the political culture. Critical mass theory can only operate if female politicians differ significantly from men, for example if they give greater priority to public spending on education rather than defence, or if they raise more parliamentary questions about childcare rather than foreign policy, or if they pay more attention to constituency service rather than parliamentary debate. While some studies demonstrate that women do make a distinct contribution to the policy agenda in legislatures else-where, such as in North America, Western Europe and Scandinavia, the evidence is equivocal, the debate ongoing (see for example, discussions in Thomas 1994; Karvonen and Selle 1996; Tremblay 1998).

This study analyses the entry of the new cohort of Labour women in the 1997 general election to see whether they have the potential to make a difference to the substantive policy agenda at Westminster. In particular this study draws on the 1997 British Representation Study (Norris et al. 1997) to examine whether women and men MPs differ within each party in two dimensions: their underlying values and their parliamentary activ-ities. The first part describes the dramatic growth in women's represent-ation in public office in the 1990s. The second part briefly summarizes the main causes of this development, focusing on changes in the gender gap in the electorate and the adoption of positive discrimination policies in Labour Party recruitment procedures. The third part examines the consequences of the entry of more women at Westminster, comparing their values and legislative activities. The conclusion considers whether the evidence supports critical mass theory, and the broader implications of the findings for understanding women's role in public life.

The growth in women's representation in public office in Britain

Recent years have seen remarkable progress in the representation of women in British politics. By the end of the twentieth century the British political elite had started to reflect the diversity of British society. From 1918 (when women were first allowed to stand for election to the House of Commons) to 1983, less than 5 per cent of MPs were women (see figure 3.1). The situation started to change in 1987, when the proportion of women grew to 6.3 per cent rising to 9.2 per cent in 1992. Following Labour's landslide victory on 1 May 1997, the line rocketed up the chart from 60 to 120 women MPs, or 18.2 per cent, including 101 in the Labour Party. To summarize developments in another way, half of all the women who had ever been elected to the British House of Commons were in Parliament as of 1 November 1999. Women were one-third of the Blair government, including five cabinet ministers, twenty-three minis-ters or under-secretaries outside the cabinet, and two whips in the House of Commons as well as one in the House of Lords. Moreover the appointments were not confined to the 'traditional' ministries like edu-cation or health: Margaret Beckett was President of the Council and Leader of the House of Commons, Ann Taylor was Chief Whip and

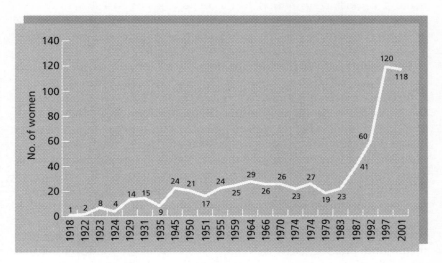

Figure 3.1   Women MPs in the UK Parliament

Parliamentary Secretary to the Treasury, Mo Mowlam, after a long spell in Northern Ireland, became Minister for the Cabinet Office, Clare Short was Secretary of State for International Development, and Baroness Jay was Leader of the Lords as well as Minister for Women.[1] Betty Boothroyd was Speaker of the House of Commons.

The breakthrough for women's representation in British politics was not confined to Westminster (see table 3.1 and figure 3.2). At the end of the twentieth century, women were 16 per cent of the House of Lords (doubling overnight with the abolition of most hereditary peers), one-quarter of British members of the European Parliament,[2] one-third of all government posts, 37 per cent of members of the Scottish Parliament, 40 per cent of the new Welsh Assembly, and 39 per cent of the 35,000 public appointments on boards of executive and advisory quangos, nationalized industries, public corporations and National Health Service bodies (Commissioner for Public Appointments 1999). The proportion of women in local government grew from about 15 per cent in the 1970s to just over one-quarter of all councillors (26 per cent) in 1999 (see figure 3.3), with slightly more in England.[3] Within each party women had made some gains as branch and constituency officers, the Labour Party was led by the first female General Secretary, Margaret McDonagh, and at the grassroots women were about 40 per cent of Labour Party members and 50 per cent of Conservative Party members (Lovenduski 1996). If not yet reflecting the proportion of women in the electorate,

Table 3.1 Women in public office, UK, 1999–2001

	Labour		Conservative		Liberal Democrat		Scottish National Party		Plaid Cymru		ALL	
	No.	%	No.	%	No.	%	No.	%	No.	%	No.	%
7 June 2001												
Cabinet/Shadow Cabinet	5/24	20.8	3/22	13.6								
House of Commons	95/412	23.0	14/166	8.4	5/52	9.6	1/5	20.0	0/4	0.0	118/659	17.9
Parliamentary candidates	146	22.8	92	14.4	135	21.1						16.8
11 June 1999												
European Parliament	10/29	34.4	3/36	8.3	5/10	50.0					21/87	24.1
6 May 1999												
Scottish Parliament	28/56	50.0	3/18	16.6	2/17	11.8	15/35	42.9			48/129	37.2
Welsh Assembly	15/28	53.5	0/9	0.0	3/6	50.0			6/17	35.3	25/60	41.7

Other parties and Independents not shown.

Sources: Pippa Norris, 'Apathetic Landslide: The 2001 British General Election', in Norris, *Britain Votes 2001* (Oxford: Oxford University Press, 2001); House of Commons Research Papers 98/104, 99/50 and 99/51, House of Commons Library; Tessa Keswick, Rosemary Pockley and Angela Guillame, *Conservative Women* (London: Centre for Policy Studies, 1999).

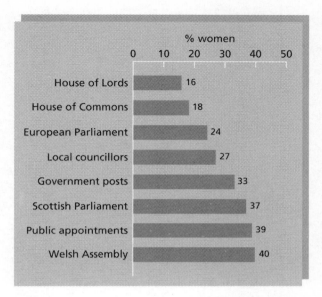

Figure 3.2   Women in public office, UK, 1 January 2000 (percentages)

after decades of either trendless fluctuations, or glacial improvements, the last few years of the century represented a major watershed for women's access to elected office. To compare this situation with the representation of women elsewhere, the Inter-Parliamentary Union (1999) estimated that by fall 1999 there were just under 5,000 women in parliament worldwide, constituting 13.4 per cent of the membership of lower houses and 10.9 per cent of upper houses. With the number of women in the Commons, Britain therefore ranks twenty-sixth globally, well above average, although not yet reaching Scandinavian levels.

The causes of gains in women's representation

Many factors have contributed towards this development in Britain. This includes long-term developments, like general cultural shifts associated with more egalitarian gender roles in the workforce and society, and socioeconomic trends such as a shrinking in size of the traditional manufacturing working class and an expansion of the service economy, with a growing role for women in the professional and managerial workforce, higher education and within the trade union movement. Nevertheless the sudden parliamentary breakthrough in the 1997 election, and its main

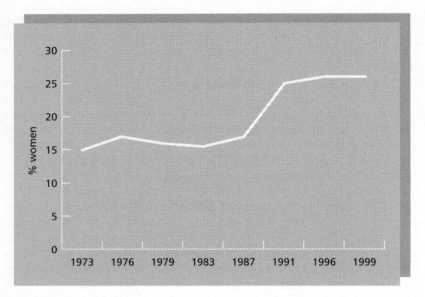

Figure 3.3 Women local councillors in English shire districts, 1973–1999 (percentages)
Source: C. Rallings and M. Thrasher, *Local Elections in Britain* (London: Routledge, 1997), updated from C. Rallings and M. Thrasher, *The Local Government Handbook 1999* (Plymouth: Local Government Centre, www.lgcnet.com).

impact within the Labour Party rather than across the British political landscape, means that secular or socioeconomic explanations are less plausible than political/institutional ones. This includes the growth of identity politics in a more multicultural British electorate, and in particular Labour's move towards the centre group of British politics in the attempt to maximize its appeal as a 'catch-all' party (Evans and Norris 1999). Pressure for reform of Labour's recruitment process were exerted by external associations like the Fawcett Society, the '300 Group', Socialist International Women, and Engender in Scotland, and by certain sectors of the trade union movement, as well as by an internal coalition of groups within the Labour Party like Tribune, and by women's organizations and Women's Officers. These pressures proved influential due to developments in the gender gap in the electorate, the modernization of the Labour Party organization leading to its adoption of gender quotas for parliamentary selection, and the Labour Party's legislative programme of constitutional reforms altering the structure of opportunities for women candidates.

One of the most important developments has been Labour's attempt to widen its electoral base by becoming a 'catch-all' party courting women voters. During the postwar decade the traditional gender gap meant that women leant strongly towards the Conservatives, while men gave greater support to Labour (Norris 1999). The size of the gender gap (the difference between the percentage Conservative–Labour lead among women minus the percentage Conservative–Labour lead among men) was substantial, peaking in the early 1950s, with women's votes giving the decisive edge to Conservative governments (see table 3.2). During the 1960s and 1970s the gender gap gradually shrank, becoming statistically insignificant in several elections after 1979. The process of gender dealignment weakened the traditional Conservative advantage among women. Moreover among younger voters the gender gap reversed so that by 1997 Labour had developed a ten-point lead among women in the youngest generation. The pattern of the 'gender-generation' gap fuelled the argument that Labour could maximize its electoral support by targeting women, either through policy initiatives like the proposal for a Minister for Women, or through changing its public face by selecting more women candidates. An influential study, presented to the leadership by Labour's Shadow Communication Agency, argued that if Labour was seen as a more women-friendly party this could help change voting behaviour in a way that could significantly affect the balance of power between the two major parties (Hewitt and Mattinson 1989; Short 1996).

During eighteen years on the Opposition benches, Labour had tried to modernize its electoral machine in the attempt to re-establish and widen its base of popular support. Parties out of power tend to be more receptive to organizational change, as shown by the Maxwell Fyfe overhaul of the Conservatives' party finances in 1948 after their crushing postwar defeat, or the equivalent Labour reforms following the Wilson Report in 1955. As Labour dragged itself back from the electoral abyss of 1983 under Neil Kinnock, John Smith and Tony Blair, and as the power of the trade unions waned within the party, the process of organizational modernization was given high priority. This meant that the general rules and procedures of the party were open to reform, and women, who had been mobilizing within the party for many years, including at all levels of the organization and as conference delegates, could use this process to push for their own demands.

In turning to positive discrimination strategies, Labour was following the path of many European parties of the left who had introduced gender quotas for party offices or for the selection of parliamentary candidates through legislative statute, internal party rules or informal agreements (see Dahlerup 1999). The use of positive discrimination policies for

Table 3.2 The gender gap in the British electorate, 1945–1997

	Conservative voters		Labour voters		Liberal voters		Gender gap
	% men	% women	% men	% women	% men	% women	
1945	35	43	51	45	11	12	−14
1950	41	45	46	43	13	12	−7
1951	46	54	51	42	3	4	−17
1955	47	55	51	42	2	3	−17
1959	45	51	48	43	7	6	−11
1964	40	43	47	47	12	10	−4
1966	36	41	54	51	9	8	−8
1970	43	48	48	42	7	8	−11
1974	37	39	42	40	18	21	−3
1974	35	37	45	40	16	20	−8
1979	45	49	38	38	15	13	−3
1983	46	45	30	28	23	26	−2
1987	44	44	31	31	24	23	−1
1992	46	48	37	34	17	18	−6
1997	29	31	53	51	18	19	−4
Difference 1992–1997	−17	−17	+16	+17	+1	+1	

Source: Pippa Norris, 'Gender: A Gender-Generation Gap?', in *Critical Elections: British Parties and Voters in Long-Term Perspective*, ed. Geoffrey Evans and Pippa Norris (London: Sage, 1999).

parliamentary candidates in the Labour Party recruitment process was accepted in 1993, carried by the general momentum of internal party modernization (for a discussion, see Norris and Lovenduski 1995; Perrigo 1996; Eagle and Lovenduski 1998). Labour Conference decided to introduce all-women shortlists in half their 'inheritor' seats (where a Labour MP had retired) and half their 'strong challenger' seats (defined in the conference motion as Labour's 'most winnable' seats). Conference, distracted by other debates, passed the motion by an overwhelming majority of votes (54 to 35 per cent) after relatively little debate. Nevertheless the policy attracted a backlash and the use of all-women shortlists was officially dropped after legal challenge in early 1996, but not before a record number of Labour women candidates had been selected. What produced the breakthrough at Westminster was less the number than the *type* of seats which Labour women fought. When Labour swept into office on a landslide of seats, women candidates were well placed in the key marginals. While women are not yet half of Labour Party candidates and office holders, the change within the space of a decade has been both dramatic and substantive.

The importance of the policy was made evident by the slower pace of change in other parties. So far, the Conservative Party has proved the most unresponsive to demands for gender equality. After the 1997 election women were only 14 out of 164 Conservative MPs, or 8 per cent of the parliamentary party. There were three women in William Hague's shadow cabinet compared to 19 men (14 per cent). Within the party, women were half of all grassroots members but only one-quarter of constituency chairs and one-fifth of senior staff at Conservative Central Office. A report by the right-wing Centre for Policy Studies recommended that to recover women's support in the younger age group, the Conservative Party should follow Labour's policy, setting minimum targets of 30 per cent for the proportion of women candidates for Westminster in the next election (rising to 40 per cent thereafter), as well as for senior party officials at Central Office (Keswick, Pockley and Guillaume 1999). In the event, women represented 21 per cent of the Conservative parliamentary candidates selected to fight the 2001 general election (16 out of 73), but most faced unwinnable seats. Although leadership speeches have continued to emphasize the importance of selecting more women candidates, to date the rhetoric has not been matched by serious internal reforms to recruitment procedures.

Liberal Democrats have also opposed positive discrimination measures such as compulsory quotas; in their candidate selection procedures their rules specify that at least one woman should be placed on any shortlists containing at least two contestants. A significant number of their shortlists, however, contain only one name and there are no special rules to place women in winnable seats. In the 1997 election, there were 122 women Liberal Democrat candidates, almost all in hopeless seats, and only three were elected. In the other British parties, the SNP returned two sitting women MPs, while Plaid Cymru's female candidates fought hopeless seats and none were returned.

The last major factor contributing to the transformation of women's presence in public office has been the process of constitutional reform under the Blair government. Developments in Scottish and Welsh politics have been important, particularly the opportunities for women in the new legislative bodies established by devolution (Brown, McCrone and Paterson 1996). Women mobilized early within the Scottish Constitutional Convention, under the Woman's Claim of Right Group, so that claims for gender balance and fair representation were written into the founding principles of the new Parliament.[4] In its first report, *Towards Scotland's Parliament*, in 1990 the Scottish Constitutional Convention committed itself to the principle of equal representation and it set up two working groups to establish the policies needed to achieve this objective in terms of the electoral system and procedures of the new body. This was implemented in the adoption of the proportional Additional Member system in the 6 May 1999 elections for the Scottish Parliament, and also for the Welsh Assembly. The constitutional reform initiative also led to the introduction of regional Party Lists for the 11 June 1999 elections to the European Parliament, scrapping first-past-the-post. Reform of the House of Lords has also contributed towards this process. The overwhelming majority of hereditary peers (98 per cent) were men and prior to reform there were 1,297 members who could sit in the House of Lords, of whom 103 (8 per cent) were women.[5] After most of the hereditary peers retired to their country estates, the proportion of women peers doubled to 16.1 per cent.

The Labour Party commitment to consider alternatives to the first-past-the-post electoral system at Westminster represents another opportunity for reform, since plurality single-member districts have long been a hindrance for women at Westminster (Norris 1985). Nevertheless the Jenkins Commission report on electoral reform for the Commons attached minimum priority (one paragraph) to this issue. The proposal from the commission is for a majoritarian Alternative Vote system based on 80 to 85 per cent of members elected in single-member districts, plus top-up list seats for the remainder in sixty-five small electoral districts. The small district magnitude (number of members per constituency) of the proposed system means that *if* this is eventually accepted and implemented, and at present it remains under debate, it is unlikely to have a substantial effect on women's representation.[6]

The consequences of women at Westminster

What have been the more general consequences of this development; in particular, has the new intake of women into public office 'made a difference' in terms of the substantive policy agenda? Previous research on women in the 1992 election found that there was a significant, although modest, difference between women and men politicians within each party. In particular, compared with men, within each party women tended to be more supportive of left-wing and feminist values, to give higher priority to social policy issues like education, pensions and the health service, and to devote more time to constituency service (Norris and Lovenduski 1995). Nevertheless the overall size of the gender gap was small, and in general party provided a stronger predictor of these factors. With the intake of far more women into the Commons, producing a shift from a 'skewed' to a 'tilted' minority, are the differences between male and female politicians becoming more marked, as critical mass theory suggests? For evidence we can use the 1997 British Representation Study,[7] a survey including almost 1,000 MPs and parliamentary candidates from all parties in Britain.

The gender gap in political attitudes

The attitudes and values of politicians were monitored in this survey using a series of ten-point scales monitoring their own position on six key issues dividing the parties. The scales measured left–right self-placement, the trade-off between inflation versus unemployment, taxation versus public spending, nationalization versus privatization, integration within the European Union, and gender equality. The questions were in the following form:

> Recently there has been discussion about women's rights. Some people feel that women should have an equal role with men in running business, industry and government. These people would put themselves in Box 1. Other people feel that a woman's role is in the home. These people would put themselves in Box 11. Other people have views somewhere in-between. Using the following scale . . . Where would you place your view?

Table 3.3 compares the breakdown of mean responses by gender and party for the pool of politicians, that is, parliamentary candidates and incumbent MPs. Three interesting and important patterns emerge.

First, the results confirm the pattern found in 1992, namely that across most policy issues it is party rather than gender which proves the strongest predictor of attitudes. Not surprisingly, given the strength of party discipline within Parliament, and the importance attached to collective adherence to manifesto programmes, Westminster politicians are primarily party standard-bearers first and foremost.

Second, across all the issue scales, women consistently tend to place themselves slightly to the left of men within their party with the exception of the left–right ideology scale, where women see themselves as slightly more right-wing than their male counterparts. In the Liberal Democrat Party, in particular, women politicians are significantly more left-wing than men across all policy scales. The gender differences within the Labour and Conservative parties are modest and rarely statistically significant.

Thirdly, on the issue of gender roles in the labour force and home, within each major party women are significantly more egalitarian than men. Despite expectations surrounding the new Labour cohort of women MPs, in fact the gap on this issue is strongest within the Conservative Party, where women and men present very different positions. Moreover within the other major parties, Liberal Democratic women proved more egalitarian on this scale not just than Liberal Democrat men, but also than Labour men.

This overall pattern replicates and thereby strengthens confidence in similar findings in the 1992 survey of parliamentary candidates (Norris 1996). The most logical conclusion is that although there are modest differences on the classic economic cleavages that have always divided Westminster parties, *the gender of politicians matters most substantively on gender-related issues*. If these findings can be extended further, it suggests that where Parliament debates issues where women and men have different interests – whether protective measures preventing domestic violence against women, equal opportunities in the paid labour force, or childcare provision in nursery schools – then potentially the attitudes and values which women bring into the parliamentary arena have the potential to make a difference to the outcome, especially within the Conservative Party where men proved the most traditional group of all politicians on the gender equality scale.

But can we extrapolate so far from a single issue scale? To explore this further, the British Representation survey monitored egalitarian attitudes towards women and men's roles using five further items, listed in table 3.4, designed to tap broader responses to matters like the appropriate

Table 3.3 Politicians' attitudes towards policy issues (mean score on scales coded from left (1) to right (10))

	Conservative				Labour				Liberal Democrat			
	Men (No. = 252)	Women (No. = 27)	Diff.	Sig.	Men (No. = 243)	Women (No. = 76)	Diff.	Sig.	Men (No. = 220)	Women (No. = 61)	Diff.	Sig.
Left v. right	7.35	7.41	+.06		3.32	3.58	+.26		4.01	4.12	+.11	
Jobs v. prices	7.44	6.88	−.56		2.45	2.09	−.36		3.62	2.68	−.94	**
Taxes v. spending	8.88	8.82	−.06		3.65	3.62	−.03		3.47	2.93	−.54	**
Nationalization v. privatization	9.93	9.54	−.39		4.75	4.65	−.10		5.68	4.50	−1.18	**
Unite fully with EU v. protect independence from EU	9.22	9.04	−.18		3.56	3.37	−.19		2.65	2.11	−.54	*
Women equal role v. women's role in the home	4.26	3.18	−1.08	*	1.39	1.02	−.37	**	1.63	1.18	−.45	**

Based on 999 MPs and parliamentary candidates all British parties. The difference is the % men in relation to % women. The significance of the difference in the mean score by men and women within each party is tested by ANOVA. * .01 ** .05. With the difference, a negative coefficient means that women are more left-wing than men in that party. A positive coefficient means that women are more right-wing than men in that party.
Source: 1997 British Representation Study.

Table 3.4 Politicians' attitudes towards gender equality (% pro-egalitarian response)

	Conservative				Labour				Liberal Democrat			
	Men	Women	Diff.	Sig.	Men	Women	Diff.	Sig.	Men	Women	Diff.	Sig.
All in all, family life suffers when the wife has a full-time job (Disagree)	32	68	+36	**	69	86	+17	**	62	67	+5	*
Being a housewife is just as fulfilling as working for pay (Disagree)	16	37	+21	*	43	51	+7		31	40	+9	
A husband's job is to earn the money; a wife's job is to look after the home and family (Disagree)	55	89	+35	**	96	99	+3	**	90	100	+10	**
Government should make sure that women have an equal chance to succeed (Agree)	63	78	+15		97	99	+2		92	97	+5	*
Most men are better suited emotionally for politics than most women (Disagree)	56	93	+37	**	91	94	+3	*	88	97	+9	**

Based on 999 MPs and parliamentary candidates all British parties. Q36: 'Recently there has been some discussion of women's rights. Can you tell me whether you agree or disagree with the following statements...' The figures represent the proportion who agree, or agree strongly, with the more egalitarian response (coded as indicated in parenthesis after the question). The difference is the % men in relation to % women. The significance of the difference in the mean score by men and women within each party is tested by ANOVA.
* .01 ** .05.

Source: 1997 British Representation Study.

division of responsibilities over domestic roles, the suitability of women for public life, and the government's role in implementing equal opportunities. The table presents the proportion that agreed with the most egalitarian response and the results confirm that on all these issues there was a large and significant gender gap. Although much attention has focused on the entry of a new cohort of Labour women, in fact again the gender gap in the elite proved greatest within the Conservative Party, particularly on whether women were suited to politics and work roles. For example, in the Conservative Party almost a fifth of the men agreed with the statement 'Most men are better suited emotionally for politics than most women', compared with none of the women.

Of course the gender differences that we have uncovered could be spurious if they were the result of other factors, such as systematic age differences or the incumbency status of women and men respondents. But when subject to multivariate OLS regression analysis (details not reported here), gender remained the strongest predictor of attitudes towards these issues within each party, even after controlling for age (the next strongest predictor), education, household income, whether the respondent was elected in 1997, and their general left–right ideology. In other words, we can treat the gender gap which has emerged from this study with some confidence for four reasons: the differences between women and men's attitudes towards egalitarian sex roles are consistent with previous studies of the 1992 election; they are not just a product of question design since they are evident when measured using different items; they cannot be explained as the product of Labour recruiting women sympathetic to feminist values, since the gender gap proved significant within all major parties; and lastly the multivariate analysis demonstrates that they are not simply the by-product of other factors that distinguish women and men politicians, like their age or education.

Legislative activities

Were there also differences in the legislative work that occupies MPs at Westminster and in their constituency? Previous work in the 1992 election found that women in every party gave higher priority to constituency work, especially the day-to-day casework dealing with individual grievances and problems (Norris and Lovenduski 1995: 223; Norris 1996, 1997). To examine this proposition we can compare the average amount of time that incumbent MPs estimated they usually devoted to a list of activities in the average week when the House is sitting. The study confirms the long hours and considerable demands of parliamentary life,

Table 3.5 Politicians' workloads: incumbent MPs (reported mean hours per week when the House is sitting)

	Conservative				Labour			
	Men (No. = 57)	Women (No. = 6)	Diff.	Sig.	Men (No. = 70)	Women (No. = 11)	Diff.	Sig.
At Westminster								
Informal meetings with other MPs	4.42	8.67	+4.25	**	5.41	6.09	+0.68	
Dealing with constituency casework at Westminster	15.93	19.50	+3.57	*	10.49	8.55	-1.94	
Attending debates on the floor of the House	6.36	7.60	+1.24		6.73	5.91	-.82	
Working in standing committees	3.17	1.80	-1.37		3.63	7.36	+3.73	**
Meeting group representatives	2.28	1.60	-.68		4.25	4.00	-.25	
Informal meetings with lobbyists	2.00	1.33	-.67		2.93	1.40	-1.53	*
Working in select committees	2.71	2.80	-.09		3.43	3.00	-.43	
Working in backbench party committees	2.32	1.00	-1.32		2.85	2.67	-.18	
Subtotal at Westminster	39.19	44.3	+5.11		39.72	38.98	-.74	
In constituency								
Dealing with constituency casework	5.91	13.50	+7.59	**	11.77	9.40	-2.37	
Attending other constituency functions	4.63	8.33	+3.70	**	4.75	5.45	-.70	
Travelling time from Westminster to constituency	5.58	10.50	+4.92	*	7.18	6.36	-.82	
Attending local party meetings	2.94	3.33	-.39		2.20	1.73	-.47	
Holding constituency surgeries	3.07	2.83	-.24		3.19	2.82	-.37	
Other activities	7.13	3.40	-3.73		6.07	8.91	+2.84	
Subtotal constituency	29.26	41.89	+12.63		35.16	34.67	-.49	
Total hours per week devoted to work as an MP	68.45	86.19	+17.74	**	74.88	73.65	-1.23	

The difference is the % men in relation to % women. The significance of the difference in the mean score by men and women within each party is tested by ANOVA. * .01 ** .05.
Source: 1997 British Representation Study.

with MPs estimating that they put in on average more than seventy hours per week (including travelling time between their constituency and Westminster).

If broken down by gender, the results are hampered by the relatively small number of cases, but nevertheless table 3.5 shows that in the Conservative Party, the estimates of women MPs (that is, incumbents elected prior to 1997) showed them to be spending far more time than men (up to twelve hours extra per week) on constituency service, especially on casework, attending other local functions, and travelling between Westminster and their constituency. In contrast to the 1992 study, this gender gap was not evident among Labour politicians. Similar patterns were found when Conservative MPs were asked to estimate how many letters they received from constituents or from others in the average week. Conservative women MPs estimated that they received about 325 letters from both sources, while their male counterparts said that they received far fewer, only 132 per week. The equivalent figures in the Labour Party were 146 for men to 101 for women MPs. In the same way, Conservative women members also said that they held about three constituency surgeries per month, compared with two for male Conservatives. Therefore the gender differences in the Conservative parliamentary party are consistent across different indicators, and with previous studies, although we would need more cases to see whether these results hold once they are controlled for ministerial status, which previous studies suggest may affect this pattern (Norris et al. 1997).

Conclusions and discussion

The last decade has witnessed substantial developments in the representation of women in Britain. Gender equality in public life is far from established but nevertheless, after decades where there were fewer than thirty women at Westminster, the 1997 general election and subsequent contests in Scotland, Wales and for the European Parliament have seen unprecedented progress in Britain. The main reasons for this development lie in strategies of positive discrimination within the Labour Party parliamentary recruitment process which led to the selection of many women in key target marginals, before the 1997 landslide swept Labour into power. This development has increased the pressures on the opposition parties to bring more women into office, although so far the doctrine and ethos of the Conservative Party means it has been reluctant to adopt gender quotas. The process of constitutional reform has altered the structure of opportunities for women in the new elected bodies in Scotland and Wales, without the barrier of established incumbents.

The growth of women in office has certainly altered the symbolic face of the British political elite. But has it had a significant impact on the policy agenda or ethos of parliamentary life? Prior to the last election, it was commonly claimed that more women at Westminster and in the devolved assemblies would transform the political agenda and the dominant political style. The more optimistic hopes have proved to be exaggerated, as British party politics has followed essentially familiar tracks. Nevertheless any fundamental change to the British political culture cannot be expected to occur overnight. The evidence within this study demonstrates that although British politicians differ far more by party than by gender, especially on the core cleavages over the economy and foreign policy, there are certain policy issues where there is a consistent gender gap within each of the major parties, and where the claim that women and men in politics speak 'in a different voice' seems most plausible. In short, the gender of politicians does not seem to matter on everything, but it does seem to matter most on gender-related values, which have significant implications for sex equality policy in the labour force and home. If these issues become more salient, as women move from a skewed to a tilted minority at Westminster, then critical mass theory suggests that this will gradually become evident in legislative priorities and political debates. The idea that gender matters most on gender-related issues may, perhaps, seem unsurprising, perhaps even commonsense. But it does provide a strong argument to counter exaggerated popular claims by both sceptical critics, who argue that nothing has changed, and more optimistic advocates, who hope that all will be transformed overnight.

NOTES

1 For details of initiatives taken by the Ministry for Women see http://www.womens-unit.gov.uk
2 The British elections to the European Parliament on 10 June 1999 returned 21 women and 66 men MEPs, or 24.1 per cent female, compared with 29.9 per cent of women MEPs across the whole European Parliament. The British Liberal Democrats and Greens elected 50 per cent women MEPs.
3 Rallings and Thrasher 1997, updated by Rallings and Thrasher 1999.
4 See http://www.engender.org.uk

5   Prior to reform, out of 1,326 members the House of Lords contained 118 women – 17 hereditary and 101 life peers. Out of 75 hereditary peers elected on 5 November 1999, four were women (all crossbenchers): Baroness Darcy de Knayth, Lady Saltoun of Abernethy, Baroness Strange and Baroness Wharton. After reform, out of 651 members, the total number of women in the Lords was therefore 105 or 16.1 per cent. Estimated from the House of Lords Briefing 1 Nov. 1999, http://www.publications.parliament.uk/pa/ld199798. See also HC Research Paper (1998: table Ib).

6   When discussing this issue the Jenkins Report mistakenly uses the Irish STV system as an example of a proportional electoral system, rather than a semi-proportional one, and seems unaware of the substantial body of evidence of a systematic relationship between PR and women's representation. See Jenkins Report (1998: para. 39).

7   The British Representation Study was conducted under the direction of Pippa Norris (Harvard University) in collaboration with Joni Lovenduski (Southampton University), Anthony Heath (Nuffield College/CREST), Roger Jowell (Social and Community Planning Research/CREST) and John Curtice (Strathclyde University/CREST). The research was distributed and administered from the School of Economic and Social Studies at the University of East Anglia and funded by the Nuffield Foundation. The 1997 BRS survey used a mail survey sent out to all candidates selected by the main British parties (Conservative, Labour, Liberal Democrat, SNP, Plaid Cymru, and Green) by 1 June 1996. Fieldwork was from 18 June to 3 July 1996. In total 1,628 questionnaires were distributed, producing 999 replies, representing a response rate of 61.4 per cent. The survey includes 179 MPs elected in 1992 and 277 MPs elected in 1997. The response rate produced a fairly even balance between parties, although the rate of return was higher among candidates than incumbent MPs. Full details can be found at www.pippanorris.com

REFERENCES

Brooks, Rachel, Eagle, Angela and Short, Clare (1990) *Quotas Now: Women in the Labour Party*, Fabian Tract 541. London: Fabian Society.

Brown, Alice, McCrone, David and Paterson, Lindsay (1996) *Politics and Society in Scotland*. London: Macmillan.

Bystydzienski, Jill M. (1992) *Women Transforming Politics: Worldwide Strategies for Empowerment*. Indianapolis: Indiana University Press.

Commissioner for Public Appointments (1999) *Fourth Report, 1998–9*. http://www.ocpa.gov.uk

Dahlerup, Drude (1988) 'From a Small to a Large Minority: Women in Scandinavian Politics', *Scandinavian Political Studies*, 11(4), 275–298.

—— (1999) 'Using Quotas to Increase Women's Political Representation', in IDEA discussion, Women in Politics: Beyond Numbers, International Institute

for Democracy and Electoral Assistance, Stockholm. http://www.idea.int/
women/

Eagle, Angela and Lovenduski, Joni (1998) *High Time or High Tide for Labour Women*. London: Fabian Society.

Equal Opportunities Commission (1999) *Facts about Women and Men in Great Britain 1999*. Manchester: EOC. http://www.eoc.org.uk

Evans, Geoffrey and Norris, Pippa (1999) *Critical Elections: British Parties and Voters in Long-term Perspective*. London: Sage.

HC Research Papers (1998) 'Lords Reform: Background Statistics', 15 Dec., House of Commons Research Paper 98/104, House of Commons Library.

——(1999a) 'Scottish Parliamentary Elections: 6 May 1999', House of Commons Research Paper 99/50, House of Commons Library.

——(1999b) 'Welsh Assembly Elections: 6 May 1999', House of Commons Research Paper 99/51, House of Commons Library.

——(1999c) 'Women in the House of Commons', revised Aug., House of Commons Information Office.

Hewitt, Patricia and Mattinson, Deborah (1989) *Women's Votes: The Key to Winning*. London: Fabian Society.

Inter-Parliamentary Union (1999) 'Women in World Parliaments', Nov., Inter-Parliamentary Union, Geneva. http://www.ipu.org

Jenkins Report (1998) *The Independent Commission on the Voting System*, Cm. 4090-I. London: Stationery Office.

Kanter, Rosabeth Moss (1977) 'Some Effects of Proportion of Group Life: Skewed Sex Ratios and Responses to Token Women', *American Journal of Sociology*, 82(2), 965–90.

Karvonen, Lauri and Selle, Per (1995) *Women in Nordic Politics*. Aldershot: Dartmouth.

Keswick, Tessa, Pockley, Rosemary and Guillame, Angela (1999) *Conservative Women*. London: Centre for Policy Studies. http://www.cps.org.uk/women.htm

Lovenduski, Joni (1996) 'Sex, Gender and British Politics', in Joni Lovenduski and Pippa Norris (eds), *Women in Politics*. Oxford: Oxford University Press.

Lovenduski, Joni and Norris, Pippa (1994) 'Labour and the Unions: After the Brighton Conference', *Government and Opposition*, 29(2), 201–17.

——(1996) *Women in Politics*. Oxford: Oxford University Press.

Lovenduski, Joni and Randall, Vicky (1993) *Contemporary Feminist Politics*. Oxford: Oxford University Press.

Lovenduski, Joni, Norris, Pippa and Burness Catriona (1994) 'The Party and Women', in Anthony Seldon and Stuart Ball (eds), *Conservative Century*. Oxford: Oxford University Press.

McDougal, Linda (1998) *Westminster Women*. London: Vintage.

Noelle-Neuman, Elisabeth (1984) *Spiral of Silence*. Chicago: University of Chicago Press.

Norris, Pippa (1985) 'Women in European Legislative Elites', *West European Politics*, 8(4), 90–101.

—— (1996) 'Women Politicians: Transforming Westminster?', *Parliamentary Affairs*, 49(1), 89–102.

—— (1997) 'The Puzzle of Constituency Service', *Journal of Legislative Studies*, 3(2), 29–49.

—— (1999) 'Gender: A Gender-Generation Gap?', in Geoffrey Evans and Pippa Norris (eds), *Critical Elections: British Parties and Voters in Long-Term Perspective*. London: Sage.

Norris, Pippa and Lovenduski, Joni (1995) *Political Recruitment: Gender, Race and Class in the British Parliament*. Cambridge: Cambridge University Press.

Norris, Pippa et al. (1997) 'The British Representation Study 1997'. http://www.pippanorris.com

Perrigo, Sarah (1996) 'Women and Change in the Labour Party 1979–1995', in Joni Lovenduski and Pippa Norris (eds), *Women in Politics*. Oxford: Oxford University Press.

Rallings, Colin and Thrasher, Michael (1997) *Local Elections in Britain*. London: Routledge.

—— (1999) *The Local Government Handbook 1999*. Plymouth: Local Government Centre.

Short, Clare (1996) 'Women and the Labour Party', in Joni Lovenduski and Pippa Norris (eds), *Women in Politics*. Oxford: Oxford University Press.

Stephenson, Mary-Ann (1989) *The Glass Trapdoor: Women, Politics and the Media during the 1997 Election*. London: Fawcett.

Thomas, Sue (1994) *How Women Legislate*. Oxford: Oxford University Press.

Tremblay, Manon (1998) 'Do Female MPs Substantively Represent Women?', *Canadian Journal of Political Science*, 31(3), 435–65.

4

The Paradoxes of British Political Parties

Dennis Kavanagh

Viewed from the perspective of the twentieth century the main British political parties in this new century are in a strange position. The traditional dominant party is at or near its weakest point; on virtually all the indicators of party strength – electoral support, membership, clarity, resources and support from the media and major interests – the Conservative Party is at or near an all-time low. Labour, traditionally the second party in the system, has perhaps never been so relatively well placed. Its electoral revival since the early 1990s has been accompanied by a transformation of its organization and its culture. Yet for some twenty years prior to 1997 many commentators warned that the forward march of Labour had been halted and that the party was in decline.

In the 1997 general election, the Liberal Democrats achieved the highest number (46) of seats of any third party since 1929. This success was only reinforced by the 2001 election result. The role of a third party has often been discussed in terms of how it would act if and when it held the balance of power in Parliament between Labour and Conservative. Ironically, the Liberal Democratic breakthrough was rendered irrelevant in the 1997 parliament because of the huge Labour majority which in turn ended Blair's mooted project of forming a progressive centre-left coalition with the Lib Dems.

In spite of the perception that Britain has until recently been the home of a model competitive two-party system, the historical record shows that this has been the case for only short periods. Since 1922 the two leading parties in votes and parliamentary seats have always been Labour and Conservative. Some of the dominance of the two parties in the Commons has been an artefact of the first-past-the-post electoral system which has penalized the 'other' parties, sometimes outrageously so. Dunleavy observes that if we regard an aggregate 85 per cent share of the popular vote as a major criterion for a two-party system, then only half of the general elections this century have produced such an outcome (1999:215). Fragmentation has increased since 1970 not least in Scotland and Wales and particularly so in the post-1997 elections for the Scottish Parliament and Welsh Assembly held under PR. The party system has also often been unbalanced in seats at Westminster, usually in favour of the Conservative Party, and Labour's huge parliamentary majority in 1997 (and in 2001) means that lack of balance still prevails.

This chapter explores the recent changes which have affected the three main UK political parties, explains why these changes have come about and, finally, speculates on future directions of change.

The electoral fortunes, internal organization, and positioning of parties are shaped by such forces as:

- *Socioeconomic and cultural trends*, including for example, the decline of manufacturing, the growth of the service sector, the embourgeoisement of society and the spread of more individualistic values. Since the 1960s these factors have, on balance, favoured the Conservative Party.
- *Constitutional features*, including informal 'rules' of the political game. In Britain, these have usually favoured a party in government and the first-past-the-post electoral system has supported the two main political parties. Again, the Conservative Party, as the normal party in office, has been the principal beneficiary.
- *Incumbency*, which tends to give the party leader in government more authority and patronage than he or she has in opposition. Until recently, the ethos and structure of the Conservative Party was shaped in part by the fact that it was normally in government and Labour's by the fact that it was normally in opposition.
- *Statecraft*, or the calculations of political leaders about the policies, party reforms and electoral appeals to adopt in order to win elections and govern effectively (Bulpitt 1986).

Labour Party

By the late 1970s there was ample evidence that Labour was in long-term decline. The party's share of the electorate had fallen at virtually each general election since 1951. Support was largely concentrated in declining social and economic groups, the party was closely associated organizationally and in the public mind with unpopular trade unions, and individual membership was steadily declining. The party's initial response to the 1979 general election defeat – and to the performance of the 1974–9 Labour government – was to move sharply to the left in policy and to reform the party institutions to give more power to the party activists as against the party leadership. The exit of a number of leading parliamentary figures to form the Social Democratic Party in 1981 was a substantive and a symbolic recognition of the party's change. The departures weakened the centre-right forces in the party and reinforced popular perceptions (aided by the right-wing press) that Labour was left-wing and extreme. Thatcher's radical policy initiatives weakened many Labour values and interests and cumulatively placed the party on the defensive during the 1980s.

It is important to dismiss any idea that the 'party' was a single actor making a conscious decision to lurch to the left and drive right-wingers out of the party. Internal recrimination, disillusion (and to some extent exit) among activists and supporters, a discredited parliamentary leadership and accidents all created a vacuum of authority (Shaw 1996). The 'capture' by activists of poorly attended constituency parties and trade union branches also facilitated the shift.

From the 1987 election defeat onwards, however, Labour abandoned a number of its left-wing policies and accepted a growing part of the Thatcherite agenda. Key party figures changed their perceptions of what was possible politically (in a more middle-class electorate) and economically (in a more globalized economy in which markets imposed constraints on governments regarding public spending, taxation and labour market policy). In a wide-ranging policy review (1987–9) the party abandoned its promises to repeal all the Conservatives' industrial relations legislation, accepted large parts of the Conservative privatization programme and ruled out any return to complete public ownership. The party leadership was gradually accepting the economic paradigm shift from Keynesian to neoliberal economic assumptions. It also accepted continued membership of the European Community, pressed for British membership of the European Exchange Rate Mechanism (ERM) and scrapped the policy of unilateral nuclear disarmament.

A precondition of the policy changes was a reform of the party structure, to overturn the effects of the constitutional victories won by the left in the early 1980s. Mandatory reselection of the MPs by local activists and election of the leader by an electoral college in which the trade unions and constituency parties held 70 per cent of the vote remained. But whereas these had initially reflected and reinforced the influence of the left, that effect was now undone. Neil Kinnock gradually won over the annual Labour Party Conference and the National Executive Committee (NEC), established a strong leader's office, created a policy forum which would take away the initiation of policy from Conference, and made the party more centralized (Kinnock 1994). The NEC assumed control over the choice of by-election candidates and exercised it against left-wing hopefuls. Much of the shift under Kinnock was inspired by crushing electoral defeats in 1983 and 1987 and evidence, both from surveys and candidates' personal experiences on the doorstep, that many Labour policies were unpopular.

It is worth restating just how lopsided the party system was between 1979 and 1992. In 1951, 1955 and 1959 the Conservatives had won three general elections in succession and there was much discussion about Britain having a 'dominant party' system (Abrams and Rose 1960). Yet over the three general elections in the 1950s, Labour trailed the Conservatives by an average of only 3 per cent of the vote. In the four general election defeats between 1979 and 1992 Labour trailed by an average 10 per cent of the vote. The decline of the British two-party system was almost entirely a Labour story.

Kinnock's organizational and policy changes, which can be described as the first stab at party modernization, were seen by voters as moving Labour to the centre ground. But they still failed to deliver election victory in 1992. Research showed that many of the negatives associated with 'old' Labour still remained. The party was widely seen as being wedded to high taxes and trade union power, and regarded as less trustworthy in managing the economy and tackling crime (Norris 1993). Although Kinnock's successor as party leader, John Smith, managed to achieve a move to one member one vote, so making Labour a mass party of individual members, much remained to be done. This task fell to Tony Blair when he became leader in June 1994.

Historically, Labour has rarely looked to the United States for political ideas (Pelling 1958). Yet Bill Clinton's victory in the 1992 contest for President provided lessons and encouragement for Labour strategists (Gould 1998). The Democrats had won only one of the previous six presidential elections. They were tied to the declining sectors of the economy, widely perceived as a party for minorities, and associated in the public mind with policies of excessive taxing and spending. Increasingly, the party was out of touch with the growing middle class and aspiring working class. Clinton was determined to reclaim these voters, many of whom had become Reagan Democrats. He promised a tax cut for the working middle class, tough social policies, including workfare, and distanced the Democrats from the trade unions.

The Clinton victory in 1992 (and again in 1996) showed Labour how a centre-left party could reverse electoral decline. The lessons were largely about campaign strategy rather than policy. Such campaign practices and tools as the war room, rapid rebuttal, continuous use of focus groups and opinion polling to reflect the views of mainstream voters, and disciplined adherence to a centrally devised message, were all subsequently to be accepted by Tony Blair's team. The assumed gains from central control of communications and the enhanced autonomy of the leader and his aides only reinforced what Blair planned for the party anyway (Gould 1998; Heffernan and Stanyer 1998). He was determined to transform the party from top to bottom, to make it 'new' Labour.

Modernization of the party meant that Labour had to become a professional electoral organization (Panebianco 1988), shifting from an activist-orientated to a voter-driven party. This transformation has had several elements. One was the use of a proactive media strategy, decided centrally. Blair's political office was heavily staffed with people who were skilled communicators and 'spin doctors'. Steps were taken to win over the Rupert Murdoch-owned newspapers, which had bitterly attacked Labour in the past and were regarded as crucial in setting the political agenda. A second was strong personal leadership; this inevitably meant a weakening of the party's traditional checks and balances, built on the ideas of inner party democracy and collective decision-making. Philip Gould advised Blair that the party should adopt a 'new unitary command structure' and 'There must be one ultimate source of campaigning authority, and it must be the leader' (Gould 1998:240). A third was the interest in and responsiveness to the concerns of target voters, defined as those who might defect from the Conservative Party to Labour or those who might vote Labour for the first time. Inevitably, responding to them involved a shift to the right, particularly on tax, trade union and law and order issues. Blair accepted that, in part because of Thatcher's policies, British society and values had changed in the 1980s. Many of the party's target voters resisted the idea of paying more taxes themselves but still wanted public services which were more responsive and provided more choice. Fourth, the party invested heavily in polling and focus groups to keep in touch with the concerns of these voters. Reliance on these techniques to assess the public mood involved a relegation of the role of the annual party conference, and the resolutions of trade unions and constituency parties. Finally, the party had to stay 'on message', a line defended and finessed by the leadership. Dissenting MPs were silenced down and marginalized.

The leadership (essentially Blair, Gordon Brown, the Shadow Chancellor, and their aides) took further steps to detach the party from the trade unions. The trade unions' share of the votes at the annual conference was further reduced to 50 per cent as a result of a conference vote in 1993, and their share of the electoral college vote for electing the leader was cut to a third (down from 40 per cent). In the ten years to 1996 trade union funding for the party fell from two-thirds of the total to less than half, with business contributions making up a large part of the difference. Increasingly, Labour was making successful overtures to business and the City, and was not prepared to allow its relationship with the unions to imperil its links with these two groups.

Blair also took advantage of Labour's revived individual membership to outflank activists. Amending Clause IV of the party constitution (and its commitment to public ownership) was an important symbolic statement of the extent to which the party had become 'new' Labour. The change was approved by a three to one majority at a special conference in April 1995, with support stronger among constituency parties and trade unions which balloted their members. Blair felt vindicated in his campaign to democratize the party. In autumn 1996 the draft election manifesto was also approved in a ballot of individual party members. Constitutional purists noted that the annual conference was bypassed on both occasions. This was a plebiscitary style of leadership, in which members participated in decisions, but the occasion and wording of the ballots were decided by the leader, and party members were confined to a yes or no vote.

By tradition, the party's commitment to inner party democracy has rested on a system of checks and balances in which the parliamentary leadership had to bargain over policy and appointments with the NEC, the trade unions and Conference (Minkin 1978). The voice of the individual member, however, was muffled as resolutions proceeded through different stages and various organs and a complex system of amendment, compositing, and block votes. Decision-making could also be extremely slow. The modernizers believed that an effective party, not least for electoral purposes, needed to be flexible so that it could respond quickly to events. In turn this required short lines of communication and greater autonomy for the leader and those the leader trusted (Heffernan and Stanyer 1998). For many modernizers the more leader-dominated Conservative party was actually a model they wished to emulate. They regarded Blair's high opinion poll ratings, Labour's improvements on a range of 'image' questions and the party's stunning election victory in 1997 as a vindication of the measures.

The modernizing project did not abate with Labour in government. The requisites for effective campaigning have been regarded as necessary tools for effective government. A proactive media operation was maintained as Blair strengthened his press office and also created a Strategic Communications Unit and an Intelligence and Research Unit in 10 Downing Street. Good communication(s) is regarded not merely as an add-on but an essential component for effective policy. Blair doubled the number of political and official staff working for him compared to

John Major and relegated the role of cabinet and cabinet committees in favour of working with project teams, groups of his own advisers and bilaterals with cabinet ministers and their officials. Some described this enhanced Number 10 operation as a Napoleonic style of government (Kavanagh and Seldon 1999; Hennessy 1999).

The emphasis on loyalty among MPs was strengthened by a code of conduct which laid down that Labour MPs could be disciplined for engaging in a sustained course of conduct judged to be prejudicial to the party. This could cover voting in defiance of the party whips or publicly criticizing the leadership. The party list system of proportional representation was used to reward loyalists and punish dissenters in selection for parliamentary and Assembly elections in Scotland and Wales and in the European elections. In Scotland, a number of allegedly 'unreliable' MPs and activists failed to be selected as Labour candidates or to be ranked high enough on the party list to be elected to the Scottish Parliament. Dennis Canavan, a left-wing MP, was so offended by his rejection that he stood and was elected as an independent. In Wales, Number 10 and Millbank intervened heavily to promote the election of Alun Michael over Rhodri Morgan as Leader of the Labour Party in Wales. In the Labour selection for London mayor, the leadership again intervened clumsily in favour of its candidate Frank Dobson against Ken Livingstone. It won that battle but lost the war, when Livingstone triumphed in the mayoral election in May 2000.

The party's traditionally bottom-up model structure which contained a mix of checks and balances and oligarchical practices, has been replaced by one that is more top-down and centralized. The party reforms in the early 1980s were designed to make the party safe for the left, strengthen the influence of the activists over MPs and elevate the extra-parliamentary organs over the Parliamentary Labour Party. In the short term they were successful. Over time, in an echo of Michel's iron law of oligarchy (Kavanagh 1998), the Blair leadership used the changes, and sometimes invoked the votes of members over those of activists to reverse the effects.

Conservative Party

The scale of the Conservative decline since 1992 has been remarkable, all the more so for one of the most successful parties in modern democratic politics. As the normal party of government throughout the twentieth century, Conservatives have celebrated their relatively strong sense of party unity, effective leadership, adaptability and good organization. It was not unreasonable for Ball and Seldon (1996) to entitle their book, *Conservative Century*. In the past, party strategists had expressed fears about the party's electoral future and ability to govern after successive extensions of the suffrage, the rise of Labour, and in the 1970s the growing power of the trade unions. Yet it withstood successive challenges and more often than not won general elections. It was also helped by its superiority in financial resources, media and business support, and by serious divisions within, first, the Liberal and then the Labour parties.

Under Mrs Thatcher's premiership (1979–90), the party reached a post-1945 peak of influence. More significant than gaining 42 per cent of the vote in general elections was that it gained over 60 per cent of the Labour-Conservative aggregate vote. As ever, it continued to attract voters across social classes, retained a reputation for economic competence (relative to Labour, at least) and was widely regarded as the party best able to defend the national interest. It also managed to reshape the political agenda. The reforms of industrial relations and creation of a more flexible labour market, privatization of many utilities, lower marginal rates of income tax, and abandonment of incomes policies all came to be accepted by the Labour Party. Conservative triumphalism was increased when John Major led the party to election victory in 1992, in the middle of a recession and against a strong public sentiment that it was time for a change. Major subsequently claimed that this election defeat for Labour was decisive in forcing Labour finally to abandon the socialist alternative. In fact Labour's accommodation to Thatcher's policy legacy was already considerable by 1992 and probably irreversible. Tony Blair's declaration in 1996 that the days of tax and spend were over was an acknowledgement that the Conservatives had won the argument.

Yet since 1992 the Conservative Party has encountered acute difficulties on four fronts. The first has been confusion over its identity and its message. Having won the battle of ideas – on many economic and social issues – what should it do next? John Major's consolidation of the Thatcherite settlement was less contentious because his rhetoric and style were more inclusive than his predecessor's; privatization, for example, was no longer seen as radical (it was being adopted elsewhere and widely advocated by international institutions such as the International Monetary Fund). The same could be said of direct taxation, industrial relations and reforms of Whitehall. Some Conservatives wanted to return to the 'pure' Thatcher policies, defined as going further in the direction of income tax cuts, privatization, cutting state spending and halting or even reversing the integration of Britain in the European Union. But only the last issue has commanded general support in the leadership as a means of putting 'clear blue water' between the party and

Labour. Under William Hague new issues divided the party. Some, like Michael Portillo, called for a more 'inclusive' and socially liberal party. Others, like Ann Widdecombe, took a more authoritarian stance on drugs, asylum seekers and gay rights.

Secondly, the Conservative Party lost its reputation for economic competence following the exit from the ERM in September 1992 (Black Wednesday). In the 1992 general election John Major had campaigned on continued membership of the ERM and held out the prospect of 'year on year' tax cuts. The party abandoned its election pledges by substantially increasing taxation in order to rebalance the public finances. In spite of a steady economic recovery from 1994, surveys showed that the party's reputation for managing the economy competently and delivering tax cuts had collapsed. It had forfeited the voters' trust, and Labour was now better placed. This still remained the case in 2001.

Thirdly, the party was hampered by its divisions on Europe. The party had been relatively united on income tax cuts, privatization, trade union reforms and encouraging cost effectiveness in the public sector. Until the late 1980s the European question had largely been pushed from centre-stage. Unfortunately, for Major, the Maastricht Treaty and the EU's moves to monetary union made it salient once more. The exit from the ERM only encouraged the Eurosceptics in the Conservative Party and in the press. Europe had been a growing source of instability under Mrs Thatcher, largely because the cabinet as a whole did not share her hostility to the European Community. It figured in Sir Geoffrey Howe's resignation from the cabinet in 1990 and the events which forced Mrs Thatcher from the leadership soon afterwards, as well as in the earlier explosive resignations from cabinet of Michael Heseltine and Nigel Lawson. The divisions spread under John Major. The government lost the vote on the paving motion for Maastricht in July 1993, when twenty-three Conservative MPs voted with the Opposition. In November 1994 eight MPs lost the whip, again defying a three line whip on a European issue. For the party to withdraw the whip from so many MPs was unprecedented.

Why did Europe prove so troublesome for the Conservative Party? After all, over the previous three decades the party had been decidedly more pro-European and more united than Labour. One reason was the change in the European project itself. In the 1990s the EU's extension of qualified majority voting for decisions, adoption of the social chapter, plans for the adoption of a single currency and the general shift, following Maastricht, towards greater integration all struck a sensitive nerve for many in the party. But Conservative MPs were also changing.

Successive cohorts of new MPs in each parliament were making the party more Eurosceptic; they believed that the more centralized EU was a threat to Britain's sovereignty and its market economy. Many regarded as too feeble John Major's line of 'negotiate and then decide' over whether Britain should enter the first stage of the European single currency. In the 1997 general election over two hundred Conservative candidates broke with this manifesto line and flatly declared their opposition to British membership of a single currency. The leading student of the party, Philip Norton, calculates that at the start of the 1997 parliament, 59 per cent of Conservative MPs were Eurosceptic-right and Eurosceptic-leaning, compared to 25 per cent who were Europhile and Europe-leaning (Norton 1998; Kavanagh 1998). Since then, the balance has probably swung further to the former.

But we still have to explain the particularly bitter form in which the divisions and disagreements were expressed. Traditionally, the party had managed to minimize the amount of publicity and recrimination accompanying its internal divisions. This is no longer the case. When he was Prime Minister, John Major, in an unguarded moment, spoke of the 'poison' coming from certain cabinet colleagues whom he described as 'bastards'. Conservative MPs have become more full-time, careerist and ideological as politicians, and dissenters are more willing to talk to journalists and to broadcast their views on radio and television (Berrington 1998; Riddell 1993). The party has also become more factionalized. One can point to the 'No Turning Back Group', the Bruges Group, the Tory Reform Group, Charter Movement and others. The upshot was that on Europe the Conservative Party was as internally divided as the Labour Party had been in the 1970s, and was seen to be so by the voters and media.

A final difficulty stemmed from Labour's transformation into what Blair always called New Labour. Historically, Conservative election successes and a reputation for competence have derived in part from Labour's failures. After the 1992 general election, and particularly after Blair's election as party leader in 1994, most of Labour's negatives were reduced, certainly amongst middle England voters. Many voters no longer regarded the party as untrustworthy on economic issues, agreed that it had changed for the better and had a strong leader, and claimed that New Labour now provided them with an effective electoral choice. This presented Conservative spokespeople with a problem. They were undecided whether to say that Labour had not really changed – it was still 'old' Labour in reality – that it had changed but was still dangerous because it was inexperienced, or that it was only copying the Conservatives (Butler and Kavanagh 1997).

The result of the above changes has been a striking reversal in the character of the Labour and Conservative parties (Berrington 1998). Hence the 'paradoxes' of the title of this chapter. The Conservative Party is now largely a Eurosceptical party, Labour a pro-European party. Reflecting the party's Eurosceptic outlook, William Hague ruled out membership of the European single currency for this and the next parliament at least. Conservative factionalism and disunity on the issue had undermined John Major's authority as party leader at a time when Blair was providing Labour with strong leadership. Hence, Hague's clear negative on the single currency. Here is another reversal in the two parties' positions. The weakening of the Conservative leader stemmed partly from the decline of solidarity and sense of hierarchy in the party, but also from the ease with which the leader could be challenged in annual elections. The leader was no longer granted a special eminence in the party's ethos. Since the Conservative Party adopted an annual system of electing the leader in 1975 four forced elections have been called (1975, 1989, 1990 and 1995), as a result of actual or potential challenges to the leader. In the same period the Labour leader has faced only one challenge (1988). The Conservative Party effectively ousted two of its last four party leaders, Heath (1975) and Thatcher (1990) through elections, and the possibility of a challenge each year undermined the authority of Margaret Thatcher and John Major.

In the aftermath of the 1997 election defeat the Conservative Party made radical changes to its structure. The party has often adopted wide-ranging reforms following election defeats – as after 1910 and 1945 – and it did in 1998. Long periods in government often produce some decay in a party's organization, as ministers rely more on civil servants than the party machine. Election defeat is then normally followed by a grassroots demand for reform, usually one which will give greater voice to the members *vis-à-vis* the parliamentary leadership, which is often discredited by the election defeat. William Hague's two most significant steps were to create a single mass membership party and to give party members a direct vote in the election of the party leader. Remarkably, until 1998 there was no single Conservative Party, but a separate Parliamentary Party and a National Union for the constituency associations, which organized the annual party conference, and the party bureaucracy at Central Office. The different units have been merged to form a unitary party. Until 1998 members joined autonomous constituency associations, and party headquarters had no list of individual members – making it effectively impossible to organize ballots of members. In 1998 the party at last adopted an individual membership scheme. This last step enabled Hague to follow Blair's plebiscitarian style in appealing directly to the party members in a ballot to approve the new constitution. In 1998 he also held a ballot on his stand over the single currency and was supported by 84 per cent of those voting.

In 1975 the party had adopted a system of annual election of a leader by MPs, so allowing a challenge to the incumbent. A rule change in 1990 required at least 10 per cent of MPs to petition for a contest to be held. As a result of reforms in 1998, 15 per cent of Conservative MPs now have to table a no-confidence motion in the leader for an election process to start. If the motion is carried by Conservative MPs, the leader resigns and a new election among the mass membership is held. If more than two candidates are nominated, a 'selection' ballot of MPs is held and the top two contest the election. If the no-confidence motion is defeated, no further motions are allowed for another twelve months. The new system of election by one member one vote means that MPs have lost their monopoly over the choice and the new rules have buttressed the leader's position.

Liberal Democrats

Since 1974 substantial popular support for a centre party has largely depended on dissatisfaction with the two main parties. The centre has worn different party 'labels', in 1974 and 1979 the Liberal Party, in 1983 and 1987 an alliance of the Liberals and Social Democrats, and since then Liberal Democrats. In general elections since 1970 in its various forms the centre has averaged 18 per cent of the vote. In an important strategic move, the party has abandoned its stance of being equidistant from both Labour and Conservative. As long as Liberal Democrat supporters distributed their second choice of party fairly evenly between Labour and Conservative, the even-handedness could be defended on the grounds that it enabled the party to gain from dissatisfied Conservative and Labour voters alike. Indeed, pollsters found that some part of the late swing to the Conservative Party in the 1992 general election was a result of the fear of some Liberal supporters that an anti-Conservative vote would allow Labour to form a government.

But after 1992 the Labour Party increasingly moved towards traditional Liberal Democrat ground. John Smith and, more openly, Tony Blair, sought cooperation with the party. Blair paid tribute to the work of Liberals like Keynes and Beveridge in inspiring the work of the 1945 Labour government, and to the Lib-Lab cooperation which existed before 1914. He calculated that if Labour was to become the dominant party in the future it would need the goodwill of the Liberal Democrats. Labour was also more sympathetic to two major Liberal themes, Europe

(by now the Conservatives were clearly the Eurosceptic party) and constitutional reform, including devolution, a Bill of Rights, reform of the
House of Lords and a willingness to consider proportional representation.
Indeed, the two parties worked together in a commission on constitutional
reform and unveiled an agreed package of measures before the 1997
elections. Throughout the 1992 parliament, and in the 1997 general
election there was evidence of tactical voting by some Liberal Democrats,
who supported a better-placed Labour candidate where this would help
oust the sitting Conservative MP. In government, leading Liberal Democrats sat alongside Labour cabinet ministers on a joint cabinet committee
(JCC), a step unprecedented in Britain outside of a coalition government.

The immediate future for the Liberal Democrats is unclear. Its electoral
support at Westminster has declined since the 1980s. As Labour has
moved to the political centre, and the Conservatives under Hague to the
right, so the party seems fated to play the role of a ginger group which is
to the left of Labour on many social and economic issues, and which
is more radical on constitutional and civil liberties issues. In Scotland
and Wales, it is already in coalition with Labour. In Westminster it is
likely that were Blair, at any point in the future, to find his majority
wiped out or substantially reduced, then coalition or something short of
it, may happen. What impact will such cooperation have on Lib Dem
electoral support if and when the public turns against a Labour government?

Future developments

As representative bodies, political parties respond to social changes. They
are also shaped by the political institutions under which they operate.
They are not, however, entirely passive in these relationships. Their
policies can influence social trends, for instance private home ownership,
public or private sector employment, trade union membership or equal
opportunities in employment. Moreover, they can change the political
institutions and electoral arrangements under which they operate. Parties
therefore are not entirely dependent variables in their relationship with
their environment.

A number of political changes have significantly affected the way
political parties operate. Because they are so recent the consequences
are still being worked out. They include:

1   *The evolving European Union*   If and when the EU becomes a more
    integrated entity it is likely that the European Parliament will become

a more influential body *vis-à-vis* national legislatures. If this happens it may also attract more weighty political figures away from national parliaments. The European elections in 1999 were the first United Kingdom nationwide elections to be held under proportional representation. As British MEPs are elected on a regional basis there is the opportunity for them to cooperate within the Parliament across party lines on issues of regional interest.

2 *Devolution, decentralization and elected mayors* To what extent will these reforms weaken the homogeneity and discipline of British political parties and be a force for decentralization and perhaps a less adversarial style of politics? To what extent will the non-nationalist parties in the EU, Wales and Scotland become more decentralized, insisting on a greater measure of autonomy in Brussels, Wales and Scotland? There were tensions among Welsh Labour members when the Westminster leadership intervened heavily in the choice in the election of the party's candidate for First Minister for Wales in 1999. Will a Labour Prime Minister's attempt to exercise central control over his party be undermined by a more pluralistic political system? (See the discussion by David Sanders in chapter 5.) Already there are distinctive patterns of politics in Scotland and Wales, with the main opposition to Labour coming not from the Conservatives but the nationalist parties.

3 *Electoral reform for Westminster* The adoption of proportional electoral systems for elections to the European Parliament, the Scottish Parliament, the Welsh and Northern Ireland assemblies, and for the London mayor, means that Westminster, with the first-past-the-post system, is now the odd one out. In 1998 the Independent Commission on Voting Systems, under Lord Jenkins, recommended the adoption of a more proportional system for Westminster. No action has yet been taken. Any reform increases the prospects of either minority rule (as in Wales initially) or coalition (as in Scotland and now Wales). Depending on the system adopted, PR might also encourage a breakaway by a disillusioned minority in a major party (see point 5 below).

4 *New financial regulations* The Registration of Political Parties Act (1998) and the Political Parties, Referendums and Elections Act (2000) have transformed the regulation of the party system. Parties are no longer private bodies but are open to scrutiny by the state. Following the recommendations of the Committee on Standards in Public Life under the chairmanship of Lord Neill, there is now a ceiling of £20 million per party to fight general elections over a twelve-month period. Some of the murkier aspects of party finance

will be cleaned up by tightening the rules on foreign donations and withdrawing the privilege of anonymity for those making contributions in excess of £50.

5 *Fragmentation of the party system* PR in elections for the Scottish Parliament, Welsh Assembly, London Assembly and European Parliament have seen 'other' parties gaining representation at the expense of Conservative and Labour, for instance Greens and the UK Independence Party in the European Parliament.

6 *Permanent campaigning* The large number of elections and referendums has imposed heavy demands on the parties' resources. Recent developments in the media allow the possibility of more *niche* campaigning, allowing parties to target groups via direct mail, telephone canvassing and placing advertisements in specialized magazines. Parties may go more directly to the public, bypassing the national media, by direct mail, telephone canvassing, phone-ins and public meetings. Communications technology also allows more co-ordination from the centre. In the run-up to and during the 1997 and 2001 general election campaigns Labour used faxes, mobiles, bleepers and computers to convey central 'messages' to all candidates and party spokespeople. Labour in government has continued with such centralized communications, and substantially strengthened the IT resources at Number 10. The Conservative Party has followed suit, with its own war room and rebuttal unit.

Party managers now plan campaigns in elaborate detail, organize prompt responses to daily events, record opinion trends through opinion polls and focus groups, counter the charges of political opponents and challenge the newsframes defined by journalists (Blumler and Kavanagh 1999). The parties have absorbed what may be termed the imperatives of the professionalization of political publicity. Presentation is not just an add-on to political decisions and policy-making but is an integral part of it. The objective is to get the media to report your agenda on your own terms and to put critics from your own party or opposition parties on the back foot. It is easy to see how this approach lends itself to what has been called a 'unitary command system' or a 'command premiership' (Gould 1998; Hennessy 1999). The requirements of effective party management and government appear to lead to the sacrifice of internal debate in the interest of presenting a clear and consistent message. The approach also enhances the power of the individual leader and the leader's entourage (Heffernan and Stanyer 1998). British political parties are increasingly becoming professional electoral organizations.

Discussion

Anthony Downs's (1957) thesis of rational parties as vote-seeking organizations is relevant in understanding the modernization and electoral revival of the Labour Party. Downs leads us to expect parties to behave in ways which gain sufficient votes to win elections. Habitual losing parties will try to attract key target voters, emulating the policy positions and other (non-policy) features of the dominant political party. In the 1980s the Conservative Party was dominant (Hay 1999; Kavanagh 1998).

Historically Labour, because of its complex organizational structure, the powerful position accorded to the trade unions, and an ideology represented by Clause IV, has not been well placed to respond easily to voters' preferences. Even when Labour shifted policies to move towards the centre ground, and was seen by voters to have done so in 1987 and 1992, it still failed to win general elections. Some voters agreed with Labour policies but did not vote for the party because in the real world voters also take account of the parties' past records, perceived competences, leaders' integrity and credibility, and the persuasiveness of their campaigns and policies. Policy change could achieve only so much. Election defeats, changes in demography and shifts in voters' values and policy preferences provided the incentives for Labour modernizers to try and transform the party's structure, ethos and policies. The leadership calculated that the party needed to change on all fronts if it was to move further to appeal credibly to 'middle England' voters. The reforms under Kinnock and Blair were designed to transform the party, weaken the influence of activists and enhance that of the leader, and make the party more of a single-minded unitary actor. In a word, it would have to become New Labour if it was to be able to respond to mainstream voters. Labour modernizers may never have read Downs, but they acted as if they accepted many of his main assumptions (Hay 1999).

If Downs is helpful in explaining the changes in Labour, how useful is he for explaining changes in the Conservative Party? A policy-based explanation for the collapse of the Conservative Party after 1992 is hardly persuasive, given that by 1997 Labour had steadily moved to accept so many Conservative positions, notably on the single European currency, industrial relations, markets and public spending and income tax. After 1992 the Conservatives lost out on precisely those features that had harmed Labour in the 1980s: leadership, party unity, economic competence and trust. Being out of office for so long sharpened Labour members' hunger for election victory and willingness to acquiesce in

what the leadership decreed was necessary for victory. The Conservatives, in office for so long, may have suffered a reverse effect. Moreover,
historically the Conservative Party has been most prone to internal
divisions on issues which affect questions of British economic relations
with other countries and of national sovereignty. Relations with the
European Union in the 1980s and 1990s, just like tariffs in 1906, have
provided just such an issue (Baker et al. 1993).

Here is a challenge for political actors and for Downsian thinking.
What does the party which has dominated the agenda do when its
policies are largely accepted (and seen as such by voters) by the Opposition? What does the preference-shaping party do when the Opposition
becomes preference-accommodating? One approach taken by the Conservatives has been to take advantage of electoral dissatisfaction with the
Labour government's perceived lack of competence on issues on which
public opinion is broadly unimodal in shape, for example asylum seekers,
law and order, and 'standing up for Britain' in the EU. Another is to
exploit a 'core' issue (such as 'save the pound' from joining the single
currency) on which public opinion is distributed in a more bimodal
direction, and seek to polarize voters and the press around the issue.
This made sense in terms of Conservative positioning for a general
election in which the single currency might be the major issue. There is,
however, no prospect that Labour will allow such policy difference on the
issue to emerge between it and the Conservatives, and there is no evidence that it is *the* most salient issue for many voters.

Has British politics moved to a new stage, one without sharp issue
divisions between the political parties? Since Mrs Thatcher's resignation
in 1990 the Conservative Party has shown no inclination to embark on
another Thatcherite crusade. In 1990, according to Norton (1990),
Thatcherites amounted to only 15 per cent of Conservative MPs, and
as yet it is not clear that the party wishes to move further in the direction
of implementing significant income tax cuts by means of cutting state
provision of public services. In the 1980s, Labour was on the defensive
over its plans for more public spending ('where's the money coming
from?'). In 2001 the Conservatives were on the defensive over proposed
tax cuts ('where will the spending cuts fall?'). The party has accepted
Labour's constitutional changes, the minimum wage, the social chapter
and the planned extra spending on health, education, transport and
police. Labour has given up socialism in the sense of defending state
ownership and using the income tax system to achieve a radical redistribution between the poor and the well-off. Under Blair it sought a middle
way, something between state ownership and the market, a pragmatic
acceptance of the best of both. Only the Conservatives' specific repudi-

ation of British entry to the single currency provides a significant divide between the two parties.

Political consensus has become a much contested term in recent years. In the post-Thatcher, post-socialist temper of British politics, convergence may be a more useful term. The evidence of convergence, though not of rhetoric, around many policy areas is clear-cut (Hay 1999). Two broad forces have been driving this convergence. One has been the Downsian logic of responding to the preference of 'target' voters. This heavily influenced Labour after 1987 and to a degree the Conservatives after 1997. The development of continuous opinion polling and focus groups has added to the pressure.

A second force has been globalization and its effect on politicians' perceptions of the policies needed to make the national economy competitive and to reassure holders of capital. Social democratic parties in many Western states have come to accept the need for market-friendly policies – low taxes, flexible labour regimes and a macroeconomic policy which promotes a stable framework.

REFERENCES

Abrams, M. and Rose, R. (1960) *Must Labour Lose?* Harmondsworth: Penguin.

Baker, D. et al. (1993) '1846 . . . 1906 . . . 1996? Conservative Splits and European Integration', *Political Quarterly*, 420–34.

Ball, S. and Seldon, A. (1996) *Conservative Century.* Oxford: Oxford University Press.

Berrington, H. (1998) 'Britain in the Nineties: The Politics of Paradox', *West European Politics*, 2, 10–27

Blumler, J. and Kavanagh, D. (1999) 'The Third Age of Political Communication: Influences and Features', *Political Communication*, 16(3), 209–30.

Bulpitt, J. (1986) 'The Discipline of the New Democracy: Mrs Thatcher's Domestic Statecraft', *Political Studies*, 34(1), 19–39.

Butler, D. and Kavanagh, D. (1997) *The British General Election of 1997.* London: Macmillan.

Cowley, P. and Norton, P. (1999) 'Rebels and Rebellions: Conservative MPs in the 1992 Parliament', *British Journal of Politics and International Relations*, 1, 84–105.

Downs, A. (1957) *An Economic Theory of Democracy.* New York: Harper Row.

Dunleavy, P. (1999) 'Electoral Representation and Accountability: The Legacy of Empire', in I. Holliday et al. (eds), *Fundamentals in British Politics.* London: Macmillan.

Gould, P. (1998) *The Unfinished Revolution*. London: Little Brown.

Hay, C. (1999) *The Political Economy of New Labour: Labouring under False Pretences*. Manchester: Manchester University Press.

Heffernan, R. and Stanyer, J. (1998) 'The Enhancement of Leadership Power: The Labour Party and the Impact of Political Communication', in C. Pattie et al. (eds), *British Elections and Parties Year Book*, vol 7. London: Cassell.

Hennessy, P. (1999) *The Blair Centre: A Question of Command and Control*. London: Public Management Foundation.

Kavanagh, D. (1998) 'Power in the Parties', *West European Politics*, 21, 28–43.

Kavanagh, D. and Seldon, A. (1999) *The Powers behind the Prime Minister*. London: HarperCollins.

Kelly, R. (1999) 'The Hague Effect', *Politics Review*, 8, 28–30.

Kinnock, N. (1994) 'Reforming the Labour Party', *Contemporary Record*, 8, 535–54.

MacIntyre, D. (1999) *Mandelson: The Biography*. London: HarperCollins.

Minkin, L. (1978) *The Labour Party Conference*. London: Allan Lane.

Norris, P. (1993) 'Labour Party Factionalism and Extremism', in A. Heath et al. (eds), *Labour's Last Chance?* Aldershort: Dartmouth.

Norton, P. (1990) 'The Lady's Not for Turning. But What about the Rest? Margaret Thatcher and the Conservative Party, 1979–89', *Parliamentary Affairs*, 43, 41–58.

——(1998) 'Electing the Leader', *Politics Review*, 7, 10–14.

Panebianco, A. (1988) *Political Parties: Organisation and Power*. Cambridge: Cambridge University Press.

Pelling, H. (1958) *America and the British Left*. London: Macmillan.

Riddell, P. (1993) *Honest Opportunism: The Rise of the Career Politician*. London: Hamish Hamilton.

Shaw, E. (1996) *The Labour Party since 1945*. Oxford: Blackwell.

Wickham-Jones, M. (1995) 'Recasting Social Democracy: A Comment on Hay and Smith', *Political Studies*, 43, 698–702.

5

Electoral Competition in Contemporary Britain

David Sanders

Electoral competition in Britain is currently experiencing a period of potentially radical transformation.[1] The 1997 election witnessed the highest level of electoral volatility since the 1930s, producing a massive 11 per cent swing from the Conservatives to Labour. Recent survey evidence (Brynin and Sanders 1997) suggests that less than half the electorate now exhibits a stable 'identification' with one or other of the major political parties (including the Liberal Democrats and the Scottish and Welsh Nationalists) – a situation that contrasts starkly with the high levels of party identification in the 1960s. The creation of the Scottish Parliament and the Welsh Assembly and the possibility of further moves towards proportional representation have opened up new arenas for party competition that promise both to supplement and contradict the traditional cleavage pattern of Westminster politics. The 'deepening' of the European Union and the potential strengthening of local (urban) government as a result of the introduction of elected mayors have added further layers of ambiguity to the electoral calculations that voters and parties will be obliged to make.

This chapter explores the origins of these changes in the electoral landscape and examines the ways in which parties and voters have reacted, and are likely to react, to them. This exercise is important in that the major parties have barely begun to comprehend the consequences that recent and projected institutional changes might have for the decision calculations of individual voters in different parts of the country and in different elections. Indeed, it is arguable that Labour's constitutional reform programme was introduced without an informed analysis either of its medium-term electoral consequences or its longer-term consequences for the functioning of British democracy. The first part of the chapter provides a brief overview of the 'traditional' two-and-a-half-party

Westminster model and considers the ways in which voters have reacted
to it and, more recently, begun to reject it with the rise of 'consumer' and
regional 'identity' voting. The second part examines the outcome of the
1997 general election and attempts to explain why Labour's subsequent
huge opinion poll leads did not translate into actual votes in the local,
regional and European elections that were held in 1999. The third part
considers the ways in which the juxtaposition of proportional representation and regional identity voting has already had a major impact on
electoral competition in Scotland and Wales. It also considers the potential 'knock on' consequences of these changes for English and UK party
politics, particularly in terms of ethnic identity voting. Finally, the fourth
part shows that, with the obvious exception of variations in national
identity, Scottish, Welsh and English voters are in general remarkably
similar to one another. This in turn implies that, once the devolution
process has stabilized (either through full Scottish and Welsh independence or through a broad acceptance in Scotland and Wales that sufficient
national autonomy has been acquired), the various parties will be making
appeals to similar sorts of voters across the country. As a result, the
future basis of party competition in the different parts of Britain may
not look so distinctive as current levels of nationalist support might
suggest.

The traditional UK party system and its recent variants

For much of the postwar period the UK had a 'two-and-a-half-party
system' at both national and local level. In general (that is, national)
elections, the Conservative and Labour parties between them consistently
won most of the votes and most of the seats in the House of Commons.
The 'half party' was represented by the Liberals (subsequently the Liberal
Democrats) who were usually some way behind the two major parties in
terms of their share of the popular vote. However, because of the geographical distribution of the Liberal vote and the impact of Britain's first-
past-the-post (FPTP) electoral rules, even when the Liberals achieved a
sizeable vote share (as in 1983, for example) they typically received only
a handful of Commons seats. This general position was complemented
by other spatial variations in party support. The Conservatives were
(until 1997) always the strongest party in England, particularly in the
suburbs, rural areas and small towns. Labour was generally strongest in
London and in other urban centres – particularly in the north of England,
in Scotland and in Wales. The Liberals, for their part, developed strong-
holds in the south-west of England and in rural parts of Scotland and

Wales. The outcome of this overall pattern, between 1945 and 1997, was an alternating sequence of majority Conservative and Labour governments, punctuated by brief interludes of minority government (Labour between February and October 1974) and coalition (the Lib-Lab pact of 1977–8).

This national pattern of Conservative and Labour dominance had its corollary in local government where, although turnout was almost always much lower than in general elections, the two major parties generally controlled most local councils. However, because of the geographical concentration of their vote, the Liberals were always better represented locally than they were nationally. Indeed, during the 1980s and 1990s the Liberal Democrats capitalized on the unpopularity of the Conservatives during the periods between general elections to build a very significant local presence. By the mid-1990s they controlled some thirty-one councils across the country and had overtaken the Conservatives nationally in terms of the number of local government seats held.

The changing calculus of voting in Britain, 1964–97

The two-and-a-half-party Westminster model described above was complicated from the 1970s onwards by the increasing presence of nationalist parties in Scotland and Wales. In part, this development reflected changes in the calculations made by large numbers of voters as to how they should cast their votes. At the time of the first British Election Study (BES) in 1964, the dominant influence on vote was a person's *social class* (Butler and Stokes 1971). Roughly two-thirds of working-class voters generally supported Labour and a similar proportion of the middle class usually voted Conservative. Underpinning these patterns, moreover, were high levels of 'party identification'. A high proportion of working-class voters had a long-term emotional attachment to Labour: they thought of it as 'their' party; the party that represented 'their' interests. Similarly, a high proportion of the middle class – together with a significant minority of the working class – felt an equivalent attachment to the Conservatives.

What is clear from subsequent BES surveys (conducted at the time of successive general elections) is that class has gradually become less and less important as a determinant of voters' partisan preferences. Table 5.1 provides illustrative evidence comparing the position in 1997 with that in 1964. The contrast is stark. In 1964, some 64 per cent of respondents voted with their 'natural' class party (the middle class for the Conservatives, the working class for Labour). By 1997, the equivalent figure had

Table 5.1 Voting and social class in 1964 and 1997

	Professional/ managerial	Intermediate/routine non-manual	Manual working class
1964			
Conservative	68	57	26
Labour	16	28	66
Liberal	15	14	8
Other	1	1	0
1997			
Conservative	39	29	21
Labour	37	43	58
Liberal Democrat	21	19	13
Other	3	9	8

Figures reported are all column percentages.
Sources: 1964 and 1997 British Election Studies.

fallen to 39 per cent.[2] It is possible to argue, of course, that this change in the class–vote relationship is less the consequence of 'class dealignment' and more the consequence of parties' ceasing to make appeals to the electorate on class grounds (Hay 1999). The standard counter-argument to this interpretation is that parties are so desperate for power that, if they seriously believed there were votes in making full-blooded class-based appeals, then they would certainly make them: they no longer do because such appeals have ceased to resonate sufficiently with voters.

Evidence from other surveys indicates that party identification levels are nothing like as high in the 1990s as they were in the 1960s. The early BES surveys found that in the region of 90 per cent of voters had a stable and enduring attachment to one or other of the three main parties. More recent panel data (which involve going back to the same respondents each year) suggest that no more than 50 per cent of voters have stable party identifica-tions (Brynin and Sanders 1997). These declines in class-based voting and in party identification have an obvious implication for the kinds of calculation that voters make when they decide which party to support. If class and identification are no longer so important as voting cues, then other factors must have replaced them as key determinants of voters' electoral choices.

Although it is not possible to go into detail here, recent years appear to have witnessed an increase in 'consumer voting'. Voters have been far less likely automatically to cast their votes on the basis of their perceptions of class interests and their party identifications. Instead, they have been far more likely to consider the competing merits and failings of the rival parties on offer, and to decide between them in the same way that they might decide to make one purchase rather than another. This 'consumer' approach has lead voters to accord more weight in their voting decisions to a range of factors. These include:

- voters' evaluations of the personal and leadership qualities of the party leaders (Clarke, Stewart and Whiteley 1997);
- the degree of similarity between the positions that the parties take on the major policy issues and the voter's own positions on these issues (Heath, Jowell and Curtice 1994);
- voters' sense that if the economy is prospering, it is better to support the party currently in power in order to sustain the political status quo that has produced prosperity (Sanders 1991, 1999);
- voters' evaluations of the main parties as to which is best able effectively to manage the economy in the future (Sanders 1996).

Of all of these factors, however, the last is probably the most important. Figure 5.1 shows the close correspondence between support for the governing Conservative Party and the perceived economic competence of the party in the 1991–7 period. The Conservatives' key failing during the 1992–7 parliament was the loss (at the time of the crisis over the Exchange Rate Mechanism (ERM) in September 1992) of their previous reputation for competent economic management. The crucial resource that the Labour opposition developed under Tony Blair was the confidence among voters that Labour in government – in comparison with the Conservatives – could be relied on to manage the economy responsibly and effectively.

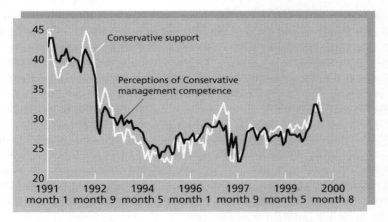

Figure 5.1 Conservative support and perceptions of Conservative management competence, 1991–2000

It is, of course, difficult to determine exactly *why* consumer voting appears to have increased in importance in the last twenty years. On the one hand, it seems plausible to argue that, in an age of class and partisan dealignment, voters have simply become discriminating – more rational, perhaps – in deciding how to cast their votes (Himmelwhite et al. 1984). The major parties have accordingly had to become much more sensitive to public preferences, on a range of different issues, in order to maximize their votes. On the other hand, it can also be argued that the parties' heightened consciousness of the need to make their policy appeals match the preferences and aspirations of voters has resulted from the more prominent role played by marketing and advertising executives in electoral campaigning over the last two decades (Hay 1999). Although cause and effect are difficult to disentangle in this sort of context, it seems unlikely that parties would have shifted their campaigning strategies from class-based to more consumer-oriented appeals unless there had first been changes in voters' thinking that made consumer-oriented appeals more fruitful electorally. In this sense, it seems likely that it was changes in the calculus of voting in the 1970s that generated changes in party electoral strategy in the 1980s and 1990s rather than vice versa. This is not to say, however, that those changes in calculus have not subsequently been reinforced by changes in party strategy.

But if the rise of consumer voting helps to explain recent developments in the fortunes of the Conservative and Labour parties, it is less helpful in explaining the rise of 'nationalist' voting in Scotland (for the SNP) and in Wales (for Plaid Cymru, hereafter PC). In these parts of Britain, although consumer voting has certainly increased, the decline of traditional *party identification* appears to have been accompanied by a concomitant rise in *regional* (that is, Scottish and Welsh) *identity*. (I refer to 'regional identity' in this context in order to avoid terminological confusion in the subsequent discussion. I reserve the use of 'national identity' to refer to the UK as a whole. This usage is not intended to deny that many people in Scotland and Wales regard their Scottish and Welsh identities as fundamentally 'national'). Crucially, this rise in regional identity has been associated with increased electoral support for regional parties. As table 5.2 indicates, in the 1997 general election voters in Scotland whose primary identity was Scottish were more than twice as likely to support the SNP than those whose primary identity was not Scottish. In Wales, the pattern (though based on a very small subsample of voters) was even more pronounced: voters whose primary identity was Welsh were four times more likely to support PC than those whose primary identity was not Welsh. The simple consequence of this association, given the relatively high levels of regional identity in Scotland and Wales, was that by

Table 5.2 Voting in Scotland and Wales and Scottish and Welsh identity, 1997

	Voters in Scotland		Voters in Wales	
	Respondent feels 'Scottish not British' or 'more Scottish than British'	Respondent feels 'equally Scottish and British' or 'more British' or 'British not Scottish'	Respondent feels 'Welsh not British' or 'more Welsh than British'	Respondent feels 'equally Welsh and British' or 'more British than Welsh' or 'British not Welsh'
Conservative	8	26	5	22
Labour	55	49	71	60
Liberal Democrat	12	14	11	15
SNP	25	11		
Plaid Cymru			13	3
No. of cases	417	235	63	68

Cell entries are column percentages.
Source: 1997 British Election Study.

the late 1990s both parties had achieved a firm foothold in Westminster politics and both had acquired a significant presence in their respective regional assemblies. Of course, this does not explain why regional identity developed so rapidly, over the previous thirty years or so, in the first place. However, one possible explanation lies in the fact that, during the 1979–7 period, the vast majority of voters in Scotland and Wales consistently voted against the Conservatives but equally consistently found themselves subject to an aggressively right-wing form of Conservative rule from Westminster. This situation proved fertile ground for the kinds of separatist arguments and definitions of political identity advocated by the SNP and by PC. It was perhaps not surprising in these circumstancı s that increasing numbers of Scottish and Welsh voters should come to sı e devolution (and, for some, independence) as a vehicle for limiting the damage inflicted on Scotland and Wales by a right-wing government in London. (The issues are explored in James Mitchell's discussion in chapter 11 below.)

In sum, then, over the last thirty-five years the basic decision calculus of voters in Britain appears to have shifted. Identification with class and party appears to have diminished in importance while 'consumer' calculation and regional identity appear to have become more significant. The next section explores how these changes affected the performance of the various parties in the 1997 general election and in subsequent local, regional and European elections that were held in 1999.

The 1997 general election and its aftermath

The most obvious feature of the May 1997 election was that it ended eighteen years of Conservative electoral hegemony. Indeed, such had been the Conservatives' dominance between 1979 and 1992 that one seasoned observer wondered if Britain's party system was beginning to look less like a two-and-a-half party model and more like the single-dominant party variant which had characterized Japan for so much of the postwar period (King 1992; Margetts and Smyth 1994). Yet the Conservatives' long-running series of election victories had been secured on a vote share of between 42 and 44 per cent – a classic consequence of a two-and-a-half party system in which support for the Opposition parties is relatively evenly divided. A key reason for Labour's success in 1997 was that it finally offered British voters what a significant proportion of them had always wanted: a competent, mildly left-of-centre government that was fiscally conservative, determined to preserve the welfare state and committed to law and order. Labour's cause had been ably assisted, moreover, by the disunity, incompetence and corruption that the Conservatives had managed to display during their final years in office.

But in the period after the 1997 election something remarkable seemed to happen in British party politics. For the first time in the postwar period, the government did not encounter the sort of 'mid-term blues' of low opinion poll ratings experienced by previous governments of all political hues. On the contrary, the popularity of the government and of the Prime Minister soared. Figure 5.2 graphically illustrates Labour's remarkable record. The figure shows how monthly opinion poll support for the governing party varied between 1947 and 1999. There can be no doubt that even if the question posed does not measure respondents' 'true' voting intentions, the way that the graph shoots up – and stays up – after May 1997 suggests that voters are reacting in a very distinctive, and new, way to questions about the governing party. In principle, of course, Labour's popularity could always have dissolved quite quickly – as it appeared to do, briefly, during the September 2000 fuel crisis. After all, the electorate demonstrated considerable volatility between 1992 and 1997. And as the long 'modernization' of Labour indicates, a reputation for economic competence is not easily gained and can be rapidly lost. This said, the prospects for Labour's re-election in 2001 always looked strong. The economy prospered and looked set to continue to do so for the medium term. The government, with its NATO allies, prosecuted a successful humanitarian campaign in Kosovo – even if this was not universally regarded as an unqualified success. It made some progress towards peace in Northern Ireland, even if a permanent solution seemed as intractable as ever. And the Conservatives continued to appear divided on Europe, dangerously right-wing for a party that needs to win back the electoral middle ground, tainted by scandal, and ineffectual in debates in all forums outside the House of Commons.

Yet in spite of its high opinion poll standing, Labour has had less success in garnering votes in actual elections. For almost all of 1999, over 50 per cent of voters said that they would vote Labour 'if there was a general election tomorrow'. As tables 5.3 and 5.4 show, however, in the 1999 local elections, regional elections (for the Scottish Parliament and Welsh Assembly) and European elections, Labour's vote share was consistently well below that implied by its opinion poll ratings. Indeed, such was its lack-lustre performance in the elections for the newly devolved assemblies that Labour was obliged to share power with the Liberal Democrats in Scotland and with Plaid Cymru in Wales.

How can this mismatch between poll performance and real votes recorded be explained? One obvious explanation is that the opinion polls are simply wrong; that respondents either deliberately conceal

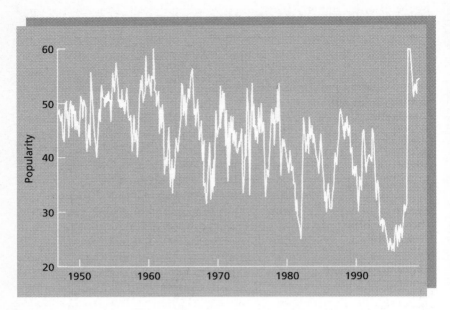

Figure 5.2 Governing party popularity in Britain, 1947–1999

their true voting intentions or else give responses they think the pollsters want to hear. The problem with this explanation is that there is no reason to suppose that these measurement difficulties are any more severe in the early twenty-first century than they were in the past. It is possible that voters are more familiar with opinion polls than they used to be – but polls have been conducted, widely reported and discussed in Britain for over half a century. There is certainly no evidence to suggest that voter cynicism about the polls (which might explain some polling inaccuracy) has increased significantly in recent years. Even bearing in mind the

Table 5.3 Vote shares of the major parties in local government elections in 1999

	Vote share (%)	Seats	Change in vote share since 1995 (last comparable elections)
Conservative	31.2	3,766	+7.4
Labour	33.7	4,802	−9.7
Liberal Democrat	23.7	2,609	+1.1

Source: *Local Election Chronicle*, University of Plymouth.

Table 5.4 Vote shares of the major parties in regional and European elections in 1999

	First-past-the-post vote share (%)	Proportional representation vote share (%)	Total seats
Scottish Parliament			
Conservative	15.6	15.1	18
Labour	38.8	33.1	56
Liberal Democrat	14.2	13.9	17
SNP	28.8	26.8	35
Other	2.7	11.1	3
Welsh Assembly			
Conservative	15.9	16.5	9
Labour	37.7	35.4	28
Liberal Democrat	13.5	12.5	6
Plaid Cymru	28.5	30.6	17
Other	4.5	5	0
European Parliament			
Conservative		35.8	36
Labour		28	29
Liberal Democrat		12.7	10
SNP		2.7	2
Plaid Cymru		1.8	2
Green		6.2	2
UK Independence		7	3
Other		5.8	0

Source: Centre for Research in Elections and Social Trends, Nuffield College, Oxford.

potential limitations of the polls, the evidence shown in figure 5.2 is compelling: between 1997 and 1999 the Labour government achieved unprecedented levels of popularity among voters – a pattern that continued through to the 2001 general election itself.

A second explanation of the mismatch focuses exclusively on the *local* and *European* election results. Local and European elections are widely regarded as 'second-order' elections – elections that most voters regard as relatively unimportant and in which they cast their votes largely on the basis of 'first order' – national – party considerations. On this account, Labour's relatively poor performance in the 1999 local and European elections resulted from a combination of mid-term apathy (which was reflected in very low *turnouts* in both sets of elections) and a tendency for some of Labour's traditional supporters to engage in third-party 'protest voting' in order to convey their concern that 'New Labour' in office was proving rather more centrist than they would have preferred.

This 'second order' argument, however, is less convincing in relation to the outcome of the *regional* elections – particularly those for the Scottish Parliament – where referendums had previously established the electorate's preference for devolved government. The most plausible explanation for Labour's relatively poor showing and for the nationalist parties' strong showing in the regional elections is that, just as regional identification exerted a powerful effect on SNP and PC voting in the 1997 general election, so regional identification also mattered in the elections for the Scottish Parliament and for the Welsh Assembly in 1999. Although the detailed empirical evidence necessary to support this conclusion is not available, it seems highly likely that voters in Scotland with a strong regional identity tended to vote SNP and that their counterparts in Wales tended to vote for Plaid Cymru. However – and this a crucial point – a novel feature of the 1999 regional elections (as with the subsequent European elections) is that they were fought under *proportional representation* rules – not under the UK's traditional first-past-the-post (FPTP) system. This significant constitutional rule change could have had important consequences for the way that voters approached the regional elections. It is these potential consequences that we now consider.

Devolution, proportional representation and the development of identity voting

Labour came into government in 1997 on a manifesto that committed the party to constitutional reform aimed at devolving power to Scotland and Wales, changing the character and status of the House of Lords and creating a fairer electoral system. Although there was no firm commitment to a reform of electoral rules, it was widely believed that pre-election negotiations with the Liberal Democrats had determined that some form of proportional representation (PR) would be introduced during New Labour's first term of office. Labour in fact moved very quickly. Referendums on devolution to Scotland and Wales were held within a year of Labour taking office. The new government also decided that the devolved assemblies would be elected by PR: like the poll tax, perhaps, another example of a Westminster government conducting a policy experiment on the Scots (and in this case on the Welsh as well) before trying it out on the English. Rather than showing gratitude to Labour for creating devolved assemblies, however, Scottish and Welsh voters turned disproportionately to the nationalists. As noted earlier, Labour obtained less support than it had received in the recent general election and failed to secure a majority of the seats in either of the new assemblies. It is also possible that voting Labour in the 1997 general election was, for many voters, simply a means to an end – devolution – and by the time of the regional elections in 1999 that end had, by definition, already been achieved.

There are two simple ways in which the simultaneous introduction of regional assemblies and PR could have weakened Labour's electoral position and strengthened that of the nationalists. First, regional assemblies almost inevitably increase the importance of regional parties because the latter are now by definition proportionately larger players in a smaller electoral pool. Given, as we saw earlier, that regional identity positively affects support for regional parties, it follows that the *impact* of regional identity is bound to be greater in regional elections because proportionately more voters are affected by it. Because the SNP and PC, respectively, have stronger regional identities (thus far) than Scottish Labour and Welsh Labour, Labour was always likely to perform less well in the regional elections than it had nationally.

The second way in which Labour's regional election performance was weakened, and that of the nationalists strengthened, relates to the impact of PR on the decision calculus of the individual voter. Under PR, votes are not 'wasted' in the same way that they are under FPTP. Under the particular form of PR introduced in the UK, a vote for Party X's 'hopeless' candidate in one constituency can help to elect someone from Party X's 'party list'. This simple logic encourages voters to support the party that most closely articulates their interests and concerns (and leads, other things being equal, to a fragmentation of the vote). This in turn means that, *in an era when party identification is in decline, PR increases the chances that other forms of identification will act as the basis of the vote.* In regional elections, regional identity is the obvious form of identification to exert itself. In *new* regional elections, when voters and activists alike are unsure of the ground rules of the new politics, regional identity is even more likely to offer a clear and attractive cue to voters. In these circumstances, it was hardly surprising that the SNP and PC should have enjoyed such success at Labour's expense. Astonishingly, this simple calculation seems to have been almost entirely discounted by Labour's strategists when they framed the electoral rules for the new assemblies.

What does all of this imply for the future of electoral competition in Scotland and Wales? In the first place, it seems likely that regional identity will continue to exert significant effects on voters' party preferences – at least until the devolution process itself 'stabilizes'. By 'stabilization', in this context, I mean either full independence for the region concerned or a general acceptance by the voters in that region that the

devolution process need go no further. This in turn implies that the
regional variants of the national parties – Scottish Labour, Welsh Liberal
Democrats and so on – will seek to redouble their efforts (which they
began in advance of the 1999 regional elections) to brand-differentiate
themselves from their parent national parties. These regional hybrid
parties were obviously less successful in 1999 than the SNP and PC
which had spent the previous thirty years and more creating strong
regional brand images. The future course of Scottish and Welsh politics
will depend heavily on the ability of the regional hybrid parties to
differentiate themselves from UK/English Labour in the years ahead. To
the extent that they are successful in this endeavour, they can reasonably
expect both to reduce the ability of the SNP and PC to recruit voters
primarily on the basis of regional identity and to garner the support of
regional identifiers for themselves. The key to the success of this strategy
will be the ability of the UK party leaderships to balance the need for
national policy consistency with the competing need to be seen to respond to specifically regional problems, concerns and priorities. How
well the various leaderships will perform this difficult balancing act
remains to be seen.

But if PR in regional elections means an increased role for regional
identity voting, what are the likely consequences of the introduction of
PR for Westminster elections? This question involves more than idle
speculation. The government has yet to make a definitive decision on the
future of PR in response to the Jenkins Report. If Jenkins's recommendations were to be accepted, then a future Labour government could in
principle introduce PR as the voting system for either the House of
Commons or a reformed House of Lords. Although, at the time of writing,
PR appears to be out of favour with the Prime Minister, a House of
Commons elected on the basis of PR remains more than a theoretical
possibility. The implications of such a reform could be far-reaching. As
noted above, at a time of declining national party identification, PR
increases the chances that *other* forms of identification will play a significant role in determining the vote. The obvious question that arises is:
'what sort of identity voting might be invoked by the introduction of PR
in the UK as a whole?' Two contrasting scenarios present themselves.

In the 'benign' scenario, PR stimulates the formation of a range of new
parties that represent the diversity of interests and identities (for
example, ethnic and religious identities or urban versus rural cleavages)
that now characterizes UK society. In this scenario, however, many
individuals retain multiple social identities and as a result British identity
also remains important for the vast majority of voters. This enables the
dominant national parties to retain their inclusive, national appeal

without prejudicing their support bases. The outcome is an enriched, more inclusive, political process that gives an enhanced voice to minority interests and concerns without adversely affecting majority interests.

In the 'malign' scenario, PR stimulates the formation of a range of new 'identity' parties that focus on 'exclusive' identities such as English 'white' nationalism, Islamic separatism or Afro-Caribbean solidarism. In this scenario, the attractions of these exclusionary movements undercut the support bases of the traditional, national, inclusionary parties. As a result, the main cleavages in the party system take on an increasingly ethnic character which leads, in the longer term, to that most dangerous of political mixtures – the politicization of ethnic cleavage. Extreme right-wing parties across Europe have frequently sought to elicit electoral support by appealing to the ethnic identity of the 'indigenous' population. The recent success of the Austrian Freedom party, which secured both 27 per cent of the vote and a place in government, illustrates how easy it can be for parties which make ethnic appeals to make electoral progress under PR rules.

It is, of course, entirely possible that both of these scenarios are hopelessly incorrect. Nonetheless, both scholars and politicians need to recognize that major constitutional changes – indeed policies in general – frequently have unintended and unforeseen consequences. The politicization of ethnic cleavage along party lines could have disastrous consequences for a multi-ethnic, multicultural state like Britain. The recent histories of Rwanda, Northern Ireland and the former Yugoslavia serve as extreme reminders of the damage that such politicization can inflict. If PR is to be introduced at a national level in Britain, its effects need to be monitored very carefully indeed and, if necessary, remedial action taken with all speed.

The future of electoral competition in Britain: how different are the English, Welsh and Scottish electorates?

As intimated in the previous discussion – and documented in detail elsewhere (McLean 1997; Norris 1997) – there are significant regional variations in UK party support patterns. Not only are the SNP and PC significant actors in Scotland and in Wales, but the fortunes of the Conservatives, Labour and the Liberal Democrats vary substantially across the different regions. Regional identities will continue disproportionately to benefit the SNP and PC unless and until the mainstream UK parties' regional hybrids develop sufficient regional brand differentiation to compete with the SNP and PC for regional identifiers' votes. On the assumption that such differentiation is forthcoming, the key question with regard to the future of electoral competition in Britain is whether voters in England, Wales and Scotland want noticeably different things from their prospective governments. In essence, do voters in England, Wales and Scotland view the political world differently or are the political perceptions and preferences of voters in the three countries broadly similar?

This question matters because, in order to get elected, parties need to develop policy stances that bear some resemblance to the views of the electorates that they seek to represent. How far do the values and opinions expressed by English, Welsh and Scottish voters suggest that there are distinct and separate electorates in the three regions? Clearly, if there is evidence of sharp differentiation, then we would expect parties (including hybrids) in the different regions to make rather different sorts of policy appeal in the future. Conversely, if there is no significant differentiation, then we would expect the bases of party competition – regional identification apart – to be substantially the same in the Scottish, Welsh and UK/English parliamentary contexts.

Tables 5.5–9 report the views of English, Scottish and Welsh voters on a range of key issues explored in the 1997 British Election Study. The overwhelming message from the data is how similar, rather than how different, voters are across the country.

Table 5.5 summarizes the views of the three groups of voters on three general aspects of *left–right ideology*: labour/capital relations, state involvement in the economy and the welfare state. The pattern of responses indicates that Scottish and Welsh voters are mildly to the left of their English counterparts in some of their responses, but not substantially so. For example, on labour/capital relations, fewer Scots and Welsh believe

Table 5.5 Attitudes of English, Welsh and Scottish voters on three aspects of left–right ideology, 1997

	English voters (%)	Welsh voters (%)	Scottish voters (%)
Labour/capital relations			
Business has too much power	72	74	74
Trades unions have too much power	22	21	23
Private enterprise is the best way to solve Britain's economic problems	29	25	21
There is a lot of conflict between social classes	17	17	16

There is little conflict between social classes	44	43	40
Workers get a fair share of national wealth	58	65	67
There is one law for the rich and one for the poor	70	74	79
The law should set a minimum wage	65	71	73
Low unemployment preferable to low inflation (score 1–3 on 11-point jobs vs prices scale)	57	57	61
State involvement in the economy			
Government has responsibility to find jobs for all	56	66	66
Favour more nationalization	24	32	32
Favour more privatization	10	4	7
Public services should be state owned	30	44	43
Favour nationalization as opposed to privatization (score 1–3 on 11-point scale)	27	32	33
Welfare state			
Taxes should be as low as possible even if people suffer: per cent disagreeing	74	69	75
More should be spent on social services even if it means increasing taxes	69	65	72
Would pay extra 1p in £ income tax for education spending	68	71	69
Selective schools should be available for clever children	48	33	27
Have used or would consider private education	11	7	6
Have not or would never use private education	89	93	93
It is good that schools should compete for pupils	30	23	23

The cell entries describe the percentage of the relevant group of voters who agree with the statement made. Full texts of the questions asked and response options available are provided in the BES questionnaire. Number of cases (with minor variations for different questions) for England is 2,551, for Wales 182 and for Scotland 882.
Source: British Election Study.

Table 5.6 Attitudes of English, Welsh and Scottish voters on democratic performance/governance, 1997

	English voters (%)	Welsh voters (%)	Scottish voters (%)
Satisfied/fairly satisfied with democracy in Britain	75	64	68
House of Lords needs reform	51	58	62
UK Elections are fair (score 1–2 on 5-point scale)	80	83	76
Trust British government all or most of the time	34	27	28
Trust MPs only some of the time	47	48	46
Almost never trust MPs	9	8	8
Moral standards in UK politics have declined	84	87	90
Political parties are only interested in votes	62	63	65

See note to table 5.5.
Source: British Election Study.

Table 5.7 Attitudes of English, Welsh and Scottish voters on social liberalism/illiberalism, 1997

	English voters (%)	Welsh voters (%)	Scottish voters (%)
Censorship is needed to uphold moral standards	67	68	68
The death penalty should be reintroduced	49	52	45
Equal opportunity policies in UK are about right	49	54	48
Race equal opportunities policies have gone too far	26	23	23
Black and Asian immigration has been bad for Britain	38	40	28
Disagree that 'A woman's place is in the home'	74	76	78
People should be allowed to organize public meetings against the government	66	63	70
People should tolerate unconventional behaviour	48	47	49

See note to table 5.5.
Source: British Election Study.

Table 5.8 Attitudes of English, Welsh and Scottish voters on political interest/efficacy, 1997

	English voters (%)	Welsh voters (%)	Scottish voters (%)
No interest in politics	30	40	38
Political knowledge quiz score, 4 out of 5 answers correct	38	38	36
People like me have no say in government actions	56	61	58
MPs know what ordinary people think	20	13	18
Political parties care what ordinary people think	34	36	30

See note to table 5.5.
Source: British Election Study.

Table 5.9 Attitudes of English, Welsh and Scottish voters towards the European Union, 1997

	English voters (%)	Welsh voters (%)	Scottish voters (%)
Britain should leave EU	19	18	14
EU's powers should be reduced	48	40	46
Should be single European government	7	7	8
UK should keep the £	62	71	61

See note to table 5.5.
Source: British Election Study.

workers get a fair share of the nation's wealth and more believe that there should be a statutory minimum wage; on state involvement, Scottish and Welsh voters are more in favour of state ownership; and on the welfare state, although they are similar to the English with regard to paying tax, the Scots and Welsh are slightly more supportive of state as opposed to private education. All of these differences, however, are relatively small. Table 5.6 describes the perceptions of the three groups of voters with regard to *democratic performance*. Again, although the Scots and Welsh are slightly less satisfied with government and trust it slightly less than the English, the differences are small. Table 5.7 summarizes the views of voters with regard to *social liberalism*. Although the Scots are slightly less

critical of immigration than voters in England and Wales, the remainder
of the responses suggest fundamentally similar attitudes across the three
regions. Table 5.8 reports the variations in voters' political interest and
sense of *political efficacy*. Again, the results suggest uniformity rather
than diversity, though the English appear marginally less interested in
politics than their Scots and Welsh compatriots. Finally, table 5.9 outlines
attitudes towards the EU, suggesting that there is virtually no regional
variation whatsoever in this regard.

In sum, the evidence reported in tables 5.5–9 suggests that there are
not distinct electorates in England, Wales and Scotland. The clear implication of this finding is that the future bases of party competition will not
be substantially different in the different parts of a devolved (or even
dismembered) UK. Of course, in the longer term, voters' attitudes and
preferences are not fixed, and parties will undoubtedly seek to influence
the way they develop in the future. It could be argued on this basis that
different regional parties will seek to shape opinion in different ways and
that therefore, in time, very different regional electorates will emerge. It
is debatable, however, whether parties are genuinely able to shape public
opinion in ways that suit their specific electoral interests. It is difficult
enough to explain changes in public opinion, let alone to manipulate
them in a particular desired direction. It is entirely possible that, over
time, Britain's regional electorates will develop distinctive attitudinal
profiles. The available evidence, however, suggests that this process of
attitudinal divergence is far from certain. And it would have a very long
way to go before the bases of electoral competition in Britain's regions
became highly differentiated from one another.

Conclusion

The creation of the Scottish Parliament and the Welsh Assembly has
inevitably complicated the electoral position of the established, national
political parties. It has raised the profile of the SNP and Plaid Cymru and
simultaneously allowed voters in Scotland and Wales to develop new
ways of exercising their democratic choices. Proportional representation
for the regional assemblies has complicated matters even further, by
enhancing the impact of regional identity on voters' electoral preferences.
The response of the Conservative, Labour and Liberal Democrat parties
has been to differentiate their respective regional hybrid variants from
the national 'parent' party itself in order to accommodate the concerns of
regional identifiers and to attract their votes. Thus far, the three national
parties have not been particularly successful in this endeavour. However,

it seems highly likely that they will continue to seek to devise new and more effective means of achieving a satisfactory degree of differentiation. By the same token, the regional parties will seek to carve out a support base for themselves that does not rely either primarily or exclusively on regional identifiers for electoral success.

Looking ahead, to a situation where regional identification has largely ceased to act as a recruiting sergeant for the SNP and PC, there is little support for the idea that there are distinctively different English, Scottish and Welsh electorates. On the contrary, the overwhelming impression that emerges from the available evidence is that voters in the three regions at present share similar views on most issues and problems. To be sure, the Scots, and to a lesser extent the Welsh, are slightly more left-wing than the English – but even this tendency is neither pronounced nor consistent. At most, it implies that the ideological centres of gravity of the Scottish and Welsh assemblies will be slightly to the left of the Westminster (and/or a devolved English) Parliament. But this is not a major difference. In most respects, English, Welsh and Scottish electors share remarkably similar views. This in turn implies that the competition among parties for their votes will not be radically different in the different parts of the UK.

NOTES

1 I am indebted to Colin Hay for his helpful comments on an earlier draft of this chapter.
2 The figure of 64 per cent voting for the 'natural' class party in 1964 is calculated as follows. Out of the 1,530 respondents to the BES who specified their vote choice, 147 'professionals/managers' voted Conservative; 259 'intermediate/routine non-manual workers' voted Conservative; and 565 'manual working class' voted Labour. This totals to 971 (64 per cent of 1,530) who voted for their 'natural' class party. In 1997, out of 2,028 respondents, 212 professionals/managers voted Conservative; 279 intermediates voted Conservative; and 310 manuals voted Labour. This totals to 801, or 39 per cent of 2,028.

REFERENCES

Brynin, M. and Sanders, D. (1997) 'Party Identification, Political Preferences and Material Conditions: Evidence from the British Household Panel Survey, 1991–92', *Party Politics*, 3, 53–77.

Butler, D. and Stokes, D. (1971) *Political Change in Britain*. Harmondsworth: Penguin.

Clarke, H., Stewart, M. and Whiteley, P. (1997) 'Tory Trends: Party Identification and the Dynamic of Conservative Support since 1992', *British Journal of Political Science*, 27, 299–319.

Hay, C. (1999) *The Political Economy of New Labour: Labouring under False Pretences*. Manchester: Manchester University Press.

Heath, A., Jowell, R. and Curtice, J. (eds) (1994) *Labour's Last Chance? The 1992 Election and Beyond*. Aldershot: Dartmouth.

Himmelwhite, H. et al. (1984) *How Voters Decide: A Model of Vote Choice Based on a Longitudinal Study extending over 15 years and the British Election Surveys, 1970–1983*. Milton Keynes: Open University Press.

King, A. (1992) 'The Implications of One-Party Government', in A. King et al., *Britain at the Polls, 1992*. Chatham, N.J.: Chatham House.

McLean, I. (1997) 'The Semi-Detached Election: Scotland', in Anthony King et al., *New Labour Triumphs: Britain at the Polls*. Chatham House, N.J.: Chatham House.

Margetts, H. and Smyth, G. (eds) (1994) *Turning Japanese? Britain with a Permanent Party of Government*. London: Lawrence and Wishart.

Norris, P. (1997) 'Anatomy of a Labour Landslide', in Pippa Norris and Neil Gavin (eds), *Britain Votes 1997*. Oxford: Oxford University Press.

Sanders, D. (1991) 'Government Popularity and the Next General Election', *Political Quarterly*, 62, 235–61.

—— (1996) 'Economic Performance, Management Competence and the Outcome of the Next General Election', *Political Studies*, 44, 203–31.

—— (1999) 'Conservative Incompetence, Labour Responsibility and the Feelgood Factor: Why the Economy Failed to Save the Conservatives in 1997', *Electoral Studies*, 18, 251–70.

6

The New Public Administration of the British State

R. A. W. Rhodes

Introduction

In this chapter I provide a brief intellectual history of that field of political science known as Public Administration.[1] First, I describe the traditional approach and show that it still lies at the heart of the subject by analysing trends in publications and research funding between 1979 and 1999. Second, I identify and describe the core ideas which inform debates in Public Administration in the 1990s. Third, I mount a critique of Public Administration from an interpretive perspective. Of necessity, I can provide only a brief introduction to this approach which I illustrate by decentring public sector reform in Britain. Finally, in the conclusions, I offer some reflections on the study of Public Administration, arguing that its students are too often attached to 'reformism', or designing solutions to practical (and therefore practitioner) problems, and are too rarely reflexive and critical.

Identifying the tradition

Writing in 1975, William Robson argued that the general approach in Public Administration was institutional. It focused on the history, structure, functions, powers and relationships of government, mainly central and local government (Robson 1975: 73). This description still accurately represents much work in the field (Rhodes 1997a: ch. 4).[2]

Research publications, 1979–1999

One way of assessing the state of any field of inquiry is to examine its changing pattern of publications and research funding. So I analyse the contents of *Public Administration*, the leading United Kingdom journal,[3] and funding by the Economic and Social Research Council (ESRC), easily the largest UK provider of research grants. I seek to show that the dominant institutional tradition persists today.

In my earlier commentaries on the state of the profession in the United Kingdom, I have described the dominant traditional approach and shown that the contents and methods of *Public Administration* since 1945 remained traditional.[4] Table 6.1 summarizes the subject-matter of the journal in the 1980s and 1990s.

Of course, there have been some significant changes. In the 1980s, public policy-making was flavour of the decade, replaced in the 1990s by public management. Most articles now employ empirical analysis and about a quarter use some form of statistical analysis (Rhodes 1995: 6). There was also a threefold growth in theory articles. Such long-standing, favourite topics as budgeting, personnel and planning have almost

Table 6.1 Subjects of articles in *Public Administration*, 1979–1999

	1980–1984		1985–1989		1990–1994		1994–1999	
	No.	%	No.	%	No.	%	No.	%
Administrative Theory	3	3	5	5	7	4	25	11
Public Management	12	13	7	5	50	32	33	15
Citizen Participation	1	1	1	1	1	1	3	1
Public Policy-Making	28	29	29	28	20	13	11	5
Planning	9	10	3	3	–	–	–	–
Accountability	4	4	7	7	1	1	6	3
Personnel	6	6	3	3	2	1	1	<1
Budgeting	6	6	2	2	3	2	6	3
Intergovernmental Relations	–	–	–	–	4	3	3	1
Local Government and other subcentral bodies	10	11	15	15	15	10	35	16
EU	1	1	4	4	3	2	15	7
Central Government	5	5	3	3	17	11	32	14
Comparative								
(a) Western Europe	4	4	6	6	11	7	30	13
(b) USA	4	4	1	1	1	1	4	2
(c) Others	1	1	6	6	20	13	9	4
Administrative Law	1	1	8	8	–	–	2	1
Other (mainly IT)	–	–	2	2	1	1	9	4

disappeared from the journal's pages. There was also a large increase in the number of comparative articles from an average of about 5 per cent in the 1970s and 1980s to 19 per cent in the 1990s. The main areas were the European Union (EU) and Western Europe. Also, at the risk of stating the obvious, British central and local government remained the primary research focus, not other institutions or processes. In short, the journal reflected both the long-standing institutional heart of the field and changes in public administration with the growth of the new public management and membership of the EU.

Research funding in the 1990s

The ESRC is the dominant source of funds for academic social science research in the UK. From 1979 to 1990, ESRC funding of Public Administration research declined continuously to reach an all-time low in 1990. Levels of funding did not pick up until 1996 and then peaked in the late 1990s (see Rhodes 1995: table 7; and table 6.2 here).

The reasons for the turnaround documented in table 6.2[5] were the ESRC's research programmes on 'Local Governance' and 'Whitehall' which accounted for 70 per cent of all grants in the 1990s. So, funding reinforced the traditional institutional foci of the field, although both programmes had several projects on public management (see below). Also, there was a noteworthy increase in funding for EU and comparative research, although even here most funds were for projects which were part of ESRC programmes. Such comparative work accounted for 22 per cent of research funding in the 1990s.

The Local Governance Programme ran from 1993 to 1998 and it sought to document the transformation of the structure of government beyond Westminister and Whitehall from a system of local government into a system of local governance involving complex sets of organizations drawn from the public and private sectors. It had several strands, including the history of the institutions of local governance from 1801 onwards; the changing context of local governance, particularly the Europeanization of local governance; the changing map of local power, examining, for example, the community power structures of London; changes in local politics – for example, the changing nature of political leadership; new forms of service delivery; and the changing role of management in local authorities.

The Whitehall Programme ran from 1994 to 1999 and aimed to describe, to explain and to create a better understanding of both recent and long-term changes in British government, comparing these changes

Table 6.2 ESRC research grants, Public Administration, 1990–1998 (£000s)

	1990	1991	1992	1993	1994	1995	1996	1997	1998	Total £/(%)
Administrative Theory										
Public Management										
Citizen Participation								9.6		9.6 (<1)
Public Policy-Making	43.8	63.5	21.5			69.5	59.6		43.5	301.4 (7)
Planning										
Accountability										
Personnel										
Budgeting										
Intergovernmental Relations										
Local Government and other subcentral bodies		29.3		24.5		54.6	501.4	845.1	375.1	1,830 (43)
EU			15.3	156.6	106.2	47.8	222.2		51.9	600 (14)
Central Government					15.9		98.8	523.2	504.6	1,142.5 (27)
Comparative	1.5	22.8	4.7				20.6	9.6	273.8	333 (8)
Administrative Law										
Other (mainly IT)										
Total	45.3	115.6	41.5	181.1	122.1	171.9	902.6	1387.5	1248.9	4216.5

with those in other EU member states and other states with a 'Westminister' system of government. It too had several strands: developing theories about the new governance; analysing the hollowing out of the state; providing an anthology of what was going on, especially up-to-date accounts of the impact of change on central departments and on the changing roles and relationships of ministers and civil servants; analysing changing patterns of accountability and of regulation; and analysing new forms of service delivery.

Although both programmes responded to the ESRC's call for policy-relevant research and involved users in their work, they were led by academic, not practitioner, concerns. For example the Whitehall Programme was explicitly set up as 'curiosity research' – that is, to reflect academic interests and concerns (see below). It was agreed with the ESRC and the Cabinet Office that its primary objective was not to provide policy-relevant advice, although in practice it combined basic research on the evolution of British government with policy-relevant research on present-day practice in Britain and Europe.[6]

Core ideas of the 1990s

So far I have identified the traditional topics of *Public Administration* and the changes of the 1980s and 1990s but I have said nothing about the substance of this work. What were the intellectual ideas which informed the field in the 1990s? There was a noteworthy broadening of focus which I seek to capture in the following four aphorisms: from bureaucracy to public management; from marketization to governance; from unitary state to differentiated polity; and from local to global and back again.[7]

From bureaucracy to the new public management

As a noviciate in Public Administration in the 1970s I read about its intellectual crisis. Subsequently I contributed to this continuing debate, describing both the pits of despond and such achievements as contingency theory and policy network analysis. Of the various crises, the challenge from the new public management (NPM) in the 1980s produced more gloom and doom than any crisis before or since.

NPM has two disparate, divergent sets of ideas: managerialism; and marketization. Managerialism refers to introducing private sector management in the public sector. It stresses hands-on, professional management; explicit standards and measures of performance; managing by results; value for money; and more recently closeness to the customer. It is often referred to as the '3Es' of economy, efficiency and effectiveness. Marketization refers to introducing incentive structures (such as market competition) into public service provision. It stresses the disaggregation of bureaucracies; greater competition through contracting out and quasi-markets; and consumer choice (for a more detailed discussion, see Hood 1991; Pollitt 1993).

The Conservative government elected in 1979 gradually evolved a reform strategy based on these ideas. Before 1988, managerialism was the dominant strand in Britain. After 1988, the ideas underpinning marketization became a major source of innovation. The causes of this managerial revolution have been oft rehearsed. It is commonly argued the changes are a response to:

- Economic depression and fiscal pressures leading to budget deficits.
- Ideological distrust from the 'New Right' of 'big government' and an accompanying determination to redraw the boundaries of the state.
- Europeanization, which further increased regulation and introduced new administrative pressures (for example, regionalization).
- Public disenchantment with government performance. Government is seen as doing too much, and whatever it does do, doesn't work.
- International management fashions, especially the new public management.
- Information technology, which made it easier to introduce NPM. (Wright 1994: 104–8).

The pace of change in Britain was greater than elsewhere in Western Europe for four reasons. First, a defining characteristic of British government is its strong executive and Margaret Thatcher used her position to push through reform of the civil service. Second, there are few constitutional constraints on that leadership. For public sector reform, the government used its prerogative powers and did not need to gain parliamentary approval. Third, the government evolved a clear ideological strategy to justify and 'sell' its various reform packages. It attacked big government and waste, used markets to create more individual choice and campaigned for the consumer. Finally, the government sought to cut public spending as part of an economic strategy designed to curb inflation. Administrative reform was part of a larger economic package which gave an urgency to the search for greater managerial efficiency which is not always found for such 'unexciting' topics. In sum, bureaucracies were no longer fashionable and marketizing public services, by for example contracting them out to the private sector, was the order of the day.

The coming of the New Right with its love of markets heralded lean times for Public Administration. Long concerned with the design of public institutions, especially with creating efficient and democratically controlled bureaucracies, it found its prescriptions roundly rejected for private sector management skills and marketization. Bureaucrats were recast as self-serving producers who sought to maximize the agency budget. The public interest was a myth. Students of Public Administration were sidelined, reduced to commenting on changes pioneered by others.[8]

From marketization to governance

NPM and its fashionable nostrums are already being challenged. Awareness of the unintended consequences of managerialism and marketization grows. Thus, marketing public services fragments service delivery, multiplying the organizations involved and creating pressures to build networks characterized by trust and management by negotiation rather than price and competition. After 1979, function-based policy networks based on central departments (or sections of them) changed in two ways. First, the membership of networks became broader, incorporating both the private and voluntary sectors. Second, the government swapped direct for indirect controls by, for example, contracting out services to the private sector. It also bypassed local authorities for special-purpose bodies and removed operational management from central departments and vested it in separate agencies. The policies of managerialism and marketization had the unintended consequence of speeding up fragmentation and multiplying networks.

These networks are difficult to steer and the term governance seeks to capture both the blurred boundary between state and civil society and the constraints on the capacity of the centre to steer. Inevitably there are many definitions of the term but perhaps the simplest for present purposes is 'network steering'. In sum, the last two decades have seen a shift from bureaucracy to markets to networks and the public sector is now characterized by a complex mix of service delivery systems (Rhodes 1997a: ch. 3 and 1999b).

Governance is part of Public Administration's fight back against the New Right. It is a description of the unintended consequences of corporate management and marketization. It is a response, therefore, to the perceived weaknesses of marketization and fragmented service delivery systems. The networks so central to the analysis of governance are a response to this pluralization of policy-making. Finally, the governance literature grapples with the changing role of the state after the varied public sector reforms of the 1980s and 1990s. In the UK context, where there is no state tradition comparable to the continental tradition of *Rechtsstaat*, governance explores how the informal authority of networks supplements and supplants the formal authority of government. The governance literature explores the limits to the state and seeks to develop a more diverse view of state authority and its exercise.

The literature on 'governance as steering networks' grows rapidly, although the labels vary, including holistic governance and joined-up government.[9] Governance as steering networks is used to describe public sector change; to interpret the changing British state and to prescribe the next round of reforms. It has become the defining narrative of British government at the turn of the century and the Public Administration community played a significant part in this discursive change. The Local Governance Programme and the Whitehall Programme provide a language for describing a world of networks and challenge the long dominant, managerial ideology. Both programmes describe a world in which networks rival markets and bureaucracy as an apt way of delivering services (see, for example, Rhodes 1999c).

From unitary state to differentiated polity

The British governmental tradition is unitary; political authority is centralized and undivided. The picture was always misleading because the British state has an equally long-standing tradition of divided functional authority. Britain always had extensive functional decentralization. It was always a union of territories. It is best characterized as a differentiated polity with a multiform maze of institutions (see Rhodes 1988; Rose 1982). Now, devolution to Northern Ireland, Scotland and Wales reunites divided functional authority with political authority and this union may well constitute a major challenge to the undivided political authority of the Crown in Parliament.[10] We may stand on the brink of the Dis-United Kingdom. The implications of this transition for the Union, for the civil services of the UK, for territorial local authorities, for English regional government, and for links with the EU will occupy the attention of students of Public Administration for years to come.

For example, Hazell and Morris (1999) argue that the civil service will have to deal with three devolved governments. Because devolution is a process not an event (see also Mitchell in chapter 11 below), and because each assembly has different powers, it will confront 'a rolling programme of asymmetrical devolution'. The civil service will also confront a patch-work quilt of regional assembles and directly elected mayors in England. There is also new machinery of government to manage intergovernmental relations both for domestic matters and the EU; most notably the Joint Ministerial Committee (Memorandum 1999) and the Council of the Isles. The consequences of these changes may include replacing the territorial secretaries of state with a single cabinet minister responsible for managing territorial (including fiscal) affairs. Despite UK government protestations to the contrary, devolution may also see the end of a unified civil service, with Scotland and Wales having their own civil service as is the case in Northern Ireland already. Diplomatic skill in intergovern-mental bargaining will become a prominent part of a civil servant's repertoire. Written understandings or 'concordats' will characterize rela-tions. They will not be legal documents and the topics may be less than exciting (for example, appointments to UK public bodies) but they will be public, transparent, and slowly but surely they will come to structure expectations. The Joint Ministerial Committee will become the main forum for negotiations between governments, giving Britain a taste of the federal-provincial diplomacy so characteristic of other Westminster systems such as Australia and Canada. Finally, individual Whitehall departments will set up devolution units to manage their links, and the devolved governments will not only have missions in London but also Brussels. Devolution will increase the workload on civil servants and place even greater strain on the centre's capacity to steer. In the words of the Head of the Home Civil Service, Sir Richard Wilson (1998) the civil service 'are going to have to learn skills that we haven't learned before'. In short, the networking skills increasingly required to manage service delivery are also at a premium in managing the intergovernmental rela-tions of devolved Britain.

From local to global and back again

Inflated claims surround 'globalization'; for example, that the global economy dominates national economies. The British debate is narrower, focusing on, for example, the hollowing out of the state or the loss of state capacity upwards to the EU and downwards to special-purpose bodies and sideways to agencies. This focus is too narrow and students of Public Administration must explore the constraints emanating from the inter-nationalization of production and financial transactions, international organizations, international law and power blocs (Held 1991). Globaliza-tion raises important questions about the impact of the international system on the administrative structuring and restructuring of the nation-state; the relationship between the nation-state, the rule of law and the international system; and the effect of the internationalization of policy-making on domestic steering capacities. But equally, national governmental traditions and state structures mediate the effects of globalization. The state remains a pivotal institution in the study of public administration. The challenge for Public Administration is to overcome its myopic concern with the details of public administration and explore not just the effects of the global on the local but also how the local produces both differentiated and shared responses to common international pressures.

For example, NPM is often treated as an example of globalization but, even allowing that the term refers to a discrete set of reforms (Hood 1995; Rhodes 1998), there are marked differences in the way individual countries respond to the 'same' international pressures. For example, the Danish government's response was a 'revolution in slow motion' (Olsen 1983: 188). The aim was to preserve a popular welfare state by selected reforms aimed at getting better value for money. Public sector reform is difficult to distinguish from any other policy area; it was characterized by a negotiated consensus and a pragmatism which avoided clear winners and losers. The choice of means was a technical matter, not dictated by party ideology. So, privatization and marketization were but two choices among many, to be used when there was agreement that they were the best way forward. Other means, such as regulation, were scarcely used at all. The government sought greater control through corporate management reforms and the use of 'flexible' contracts. It also distanced itself from problems by decentralizing to local government and citizens. Devolution was sought and won by the national associations of local authorities. User and citizen roles in public sector service delivery were strengthened. The description 'self-organizing' is apt and the consumer reforms in Britain are no parallel. Such reforms are distinctively Scandinavian and there is no reason to associate them with NPM, which never envisaged democratization as a means of delivering services let alone improving efficiency. If other reforms were 'interpreted' through the lens of Danish political traditions, the citizen reforms are a product of that tradition. The reform orthodoxy of the Ministry of Finance claims the reforms enhanced efficiency because, for example, agencies have clearer goals, but the outcomes are uncertain and ambiguous. Many changes continue 'the Danish tradition of foggy corporate governance in a different disguise' (Jensen 1998: 65). So, there are marked differences in the aims, measures and outcomes of the reforms (and for a more detailed account comparing reform in Britain and

Denmark see Rhodes 1999d). The example clearly shows that as well as looking at the effects of globalization on the public administration of nation-states, it is as important to look at local responses to those pressures.

Any attempt to identify trends will fail but the agenda for the next ten years will include some of my suggested topics. I am equally confident the 'scientific' pretensions of Public Administration will have to survive a major onslaught from the postmodern, anti-foundational, hermeneutic, constructivist – call it what you will – *Stimmung* (Bernstein 1991).

Anti-foundationalism and Public Administration

Anti-foundationalism provides an alternative epistemology to the luke-warm positivism which underpins much Public Administration. Anti-foundationalists explicitly reject the idea of given truths whether based on pure reason or pure experience. As a result, they typically look suspiciously on any claim to describe neutrally an external reality. They emphasize the constructed nature of our claims to knowledge (Rorty 1980).

'Constructivist' theories of the human sciences also suggest that an element of interpretation is inevitable. For example, Collingwood (1939 and 1993) argues that historians ask questions and answer them with stories to make sense out of 'facts' which in their raw form make no sense at all. He summarizes his position as follows:

> history should be (a)...an answering of questions; (b) concerned with human action in the past; (c) pursued by interpretation of evidence; and (d) for the sake of human self-knowledge. (1993: 10–11)

And Collingwood insists that knowledge is '*created*, not *discovered*, because evidence is not evidence until it makes something evident' (Collingwood 1965: 99, italics in original). This does not mean that there are no 'facts', only that historians construct them. The human sciences are constructed and shaped by the concepts and theories used. The resulting interpretation is always incomplete, always open to challenge. Such a view of the human sciences contrasts markedly with those commonly found in Public Administration where the influence of natural science models remains great.

Crucially, this anti-foundational epistemology in the human sciences still allows for the possibility of our judging competing theories or narratives by agreed standards of comparison. Objectivity arises from criticizing and comparing rival webs of interpretation about agreed facts using rules of intellectual honesty. The key rules are accuracy and openness. Accuracy means using established standards of evidence and reason; so, we will prefer one theory over another if it is more accurate, comprehensive and consistent. Openness means taking criticism seriously and preferring positive speculative theories which open new avenues of research and make new predictions supported by agreed facts. These rules provide the criteria for comparing webs of beliefs. The clear difference between this approach and conventional approaches to studying government is that all interpretations are provisional. We cannot appeal to a logic of vindication or refutation. Objectivity rests on criteria of comparison. The interpretation we select will not be one which reveals itself as a given truth. Rather, we will select the 'best' interpretation by a process of gradual comparison.[11]

Anti-foundationalism has implications beyond the epistemological domain. Neither scholars nor their subjects have pure perceptions or pure reason. Those we study do not have pure experiences or interests. So we cannot read off their beliefs, desires or actions from allegedly objective social facts about them. Rather, we must allow that they construct their beliefs against the background of a tradition (or episteme or paradigm) and often in response to dilemmas (or problems, or anomalies). Anti-foundationalism encourages us, therefore, to understand explanation in the human sciences through such notions as traditions, narratives, decentring and dilemmas (Bevir 1999a).[12]

Traditions

A tradition is a set of theories or narratives, and associated practices, that people inherit and that form the background against which they form beliefs and perform actions. Traditions are contingent, constantly evolving, and necessarily located in a historical context. Traditions emerge out of specific instances and the relations between them where the instances that make up a tradition are handed on from generation to generation, whether from parent to child in families or elder to apprentice in organizations and networks. Traditions must be composed of beliefs and practices relayed from teacher to pupil and so on. Moreover, because traditions are not fixed or static, it is not possible to identify or construct their particular instances by comparing them with the key features of the tradition. Rather, we can only identify the particular instances that compose any given tradition by tracing the appropriate historical connections back through time.

Narratives

Narratives are the form theories take in the human sciences; they are to the human sciences what theories are to the natural sciences. The point I want to make by evoking narratives is that the human sciences do not offer us causal explanations that evoke physically necessary relationships between phenomena. Rather, they offer us explanations of human affairs that work by relating beliefs, actions and institutions to one another through the appropriate conditional and volitional connections. Although narratives may follow a chronological order and contain such elements as setting, character, actions and happenings, their defining characteristic is that they explain actions by reference to beliefs and preferences. The human sciences rely, therefore, on narrative structures akin to those found in works of fiction. However, the stories told by the human sciences are not fiction. The difference between the two lies not in the use of narrative, but in the relationship of the narrative structures to the agreed facts about the world.

Decentring

A decentred study of an institution explores the way it is created, sustained or modified through the ideas and actions of subjects. Decentred studies are essential because we cannot read off the ideas and actions of individuals from knowledge of objective social facts about them. Although historians of ideas increasingly emphasize both how social discourses inform individual utterances and how social discourses are embedded in practices and institutions, it remains the case that individuals can exercise their particular reason in given social contexts. A decentred account will produce a radical emphasis on the capacity of the subject to imbue his or her actions with meaning and to redefine that meaning in, for example, organizational dialogue.

Dilemmas

In the *Oxford English Dictionary* a dilemma is a choice between equally unfavourable alternatives. Here I modify this definition to fit the specific context. So, a dilemma arises for an individual or institution when a new idea or ideas stands in opposition to an existing idea or ideas and forces a choice. We can understand how individuals change their beliefs and actions, and social practices, only by exploring the ways in which they conceive of, and respond to, dilemmas, not from their social or organizational position. Thus, an analysis of change and developments in British public administration must take place through a study of the relevant dilemmas. We need to explore the ways individuals have developed intellectual traditions to bring about change in the institutions of which they are a part.

Decentring public sector reform

The obvious way to illustrate this approach is to look at how individuals draw on traditions to understand changes. For example, to understand Thatcherism one needs to understand not only that Britain suffered from severe inflation in the 1970s but also the ways in which libertarians, conservatives, Whigs and socialists conceived the origins, nature and solution to such inflation (see Bevir and Rhodes 1998). Here, I look at the ways in which specific ideas about public sector reform changed through time by exploring how the beliefs of New Labour differ from Old Labour.[13]

New Labour has invoked a succession of visions, from the stakeholder society to 'the third way', all of which mark its distinctive response to dilemmas such as state overload.[14] Blair declared the Labour Party under his leadership as 'new in our means, but Labour in our aims' (*Observer*, 31 May 1998). The same theme was identified by Gordon Brown, Chancellor of the Exchequer, and Tony Wright, a Labour Member of Parliament, when they expressed their continuing faith in 'fundamental socialist values' that have 'an enduring quality' even though particular policies have to 'change in the light of new problems, knowledge and circumstances' (Brown and Wright 1995: 13, 29). The third way represents an attempt to keep many strands of the social democratic vision while accepting a need for new policies. Far from simply copying the neoliberal doctrines of the New Right, it draws on traditional social democratic ideas to condemn them. I illustrate this point by examining New Labour's construction of joined-up governance and the ways in which it differs from both traditional social democratic policies and those associated with the New Right.

The New Right argued that the minimal state required managerialism and marketization (see pp. 105–6 above). These changes and their causes are not given as brute facts. They are ideas that people construct as they experience the world and these experiences depend on their existing beliefs, or tradition, as well as on what is objectively out there. So, the

Table 6.3 New Labour and governance

	New Labour	Old Labour	New Right
Public philosophy	Stakeholding	Fellowship	Individualism
Service delivery:			
(a) Characteristic organization	Network	Bureaucracy	Market
(b) Characteristic relationship	Trust	Command	Competition

social democrats of New Labour see the dilemma of state overload significantly differently from the New Right. Social democrats traditionally believed in fellowship, enshrined in a bureaucratic state providing universal welfare. The New Right promoted individualism, with social relations based mainly on contracts and the market. New Labour favours a society of stakeholders enabled by a state that forms with them partnerships and networks based on trust (see table 6.3).

New Labour changed the Labour Party's attitude to delivering public services. It reinterpreted the concerns highlighted by the New Right from within the socialist tradition. The Old Labour model resembled a top-down, command-style bureaucracy based on centralized rules. The party became associated with hierarchic organization, with coordination secured by administrative orders. The New Right rejected this model, arguing that it was both inefficient and eroded individual freedom. The Thatcher governments tried to make public services more efficient through privatization, managerialism and marketization. Citizens became consumers able to choose between an array of public services. Although command bureaucracy remains a major way of delivering public services, privatization, the purchaser–provider split, and management techniques from the private sector have become an integral part of British governance.

New Labour's third way embodies a critique of the New Right's model of public service delivery. It suggests that the New Right has an exaggerated faith in markets. New Labour believes individuals are not just competitive and self-interested but also cooperative and concerned for the welfare of others. So, public services should encourage cooperation while continuing to use market mechanisms when suitable. For example, David Clark (1997), then the Minister for Public Services, explained that policies such as market testing 'will not be pursued blindly as an article of faith' but they 'will continue where they offer best value for money'. New Labour insists that markets are not always the best way to deliver public services. They can go against the public interest, reinforce inequalities and entrench privilege. Besides, much of the public sector simply is not amenable to market competition. Indeed trust and partnership are essential. With no market, one either has to rely on honest cooperation or specify standards in absurd detail. Far from promoting efficiency, therefore, marketization can undermine standards of service quality (Rhodes 1997b).

On the other hand, New Labour does not defend the command bureaucracy associated with Old Labour. Rather, we can identify a shift in the social democratic tradition inspired in part by the New Right's concerns with market efficiency and choice. For example, Mandelson and Liddle (1996: 27) explicitly rejected the 'municipal socialism' and 'centralised nationalisation' of the past. They insisted that New Labour 'does not seek to provide centralised "statist" solutions to every social and economic problem'. Instead New Labour promotes the idea of networks of institutions and individuals acting in partnership, held together by relations of trust. New Labour's concern with networks based on relations of trust does not exclude either command bureaucracy or quasi-market competition. Rather, New Labour proposes a mix of hierarchies, markets and networks, with choices depending on the service under consideration. So, government policy stated that 'services should be provided through the sector best placed to provide those services most effectively', where 'this can be the public, private or voluntary sector, or partnerships between these sectors' (HM Treasury 1998). Even a simple service is liable to display a mix of structures, strategies and relationships.

The Labour government uses networks to institutionalize its ideals of partnership and an enabling state. Blair (1998) stated the aims succinctly: 'joined-up problems need joined-up solutions' and this theme ran through the *Modernising Government* White Paper with its frequent references to 'joined-up' government and 'holistic governance' (White Paper 1999: 6, 7, 10–11, 15, 16, 20, 23, 24, 27, 32, 33, 40, 45, 46, 46, 53, 56; see also Cabinet Office 1999a). So services must be effective and coordinated and the principles of joined-up government apply also to voluntary and private sector organizations. The Cabinet Office took the idea further by setting standards for 'modernised' policy-making which included joining up (Cabinet Office 1999b: ch. 9 and Annexes A and B).

In these initiatives, joining up takes various forms. For example, there are area-based programmes or 'action zones' (twenty-six in health, twenty-five in education) linking central and local government, health authorities, the private sector and voluntary organizations; and group focused programmes such as the 'Better Government for Older People' pilot (White Paper 1999: 18, 26–7, 29). The state is an enabling partner that joins and steers flexible networks and public servants must adapt. Already the jargon breeds – diplomats, boundary-spanning roles, reticulists – but whatever the label, the task is to build bridges between the organizations involved in designing policies and delivering services. Networks are not just Third Way rhetoric because the notion has influenced and is changing substantive policy details about how organizations should work together. New Labour is implementing joined-up government and for all its flaws (Rhodes 2000c), it is a distinctive policy initiative.

New Labour's emphasis on individual choice and involvement may draw on themes developed by the New Right; for example promoting customer-focused services (Cabinet Office 1998). However, New Labour does not adhere strictly to the New Right's vision of the new public management. The third way stresses developing networks to promote cooperation and these networks are supposed to be based on trust. Blair described such trust as 'the recognition of a mutual purpose for which we work together and in which we all benefit' (Blair 1996: 292), and talked of building relationships of trust between all actors in society. Trust matters as we are interdependent social beings who achieve more by working together than by competing. Quality public services are best achieved through cooperative relations based on trust. Organizations from the public, private and voluntary sectors should exchange information about their practices to improve cooperation. Trust is promoted inside organizations by allowing individual responsibility and discretion to replace rigid hierarchical structures. Individuals should be trusted to decide and implement policies without following strict procedures.

The New Right portrays governance as made up of policies, such as marketization and the new public management, which are the fated outcomes of global economic pressures. But such pressures are not given as brute facts: they are constructed as different dilemmas from within various traditions. It suggests the policies a state adopts are not necessary responses to given pressures, but perceived solutions to one particular conception of these dilemmas. Also, adopting a set of solutions is a contingent outcome of a political contest.

In Britain, New Labour constructed the dilemma of state overload significantly differently from the New Right. These pressures do not have a given, inevitable content. They are identified, understood and explained differently by people from within various traditions. New Labour has a different conception of the dilemmas facing the British state; it has devised a set of administrative reforms different from those promoted by the Thatcher government. The New Right's concern to roll back the state has been replaced by a concern to transform the state into an enabling partner. And the New Right's belief in markets and competition within the public sector has been supplemented by a broader emphasis on networks based on trust.

To explore the ideas of the Socialist tradition, we have to explore their historical roots and see how they have mutated over the years; to explore ideas and their influence means we must analyse the contested processes by which ideas such as joined-up governance come to prominence. There is no ineluctable, inevitable process behind the new patterns; no abstract model of natural selection about capital mobility and competition between states. We need to highlight the political contests, including the use of coercion, that surround choosing and implementing policy. This shift of concern and emphasis would alter the research agenda, replacing the straightforward New Right assumption of convergence between states with a recognition of the possibility of continuing diversity. New Right writers typically understate variations in governance because they see them as less important than the shared characteristics imposed by global economic forces. This approach asks whether similar diversity does not appear in the aims, methods and outputs. Are the public sectors of different states becoming more and more similar, or are they becoming more similar in some respects but more diverse in others, or are they even becoming more diverse? However, there is danger in this stress on diversity. I do not wish to imply there is an open market in ideas. Obviously, some ideas and the traditions of which they are a part can be dominant. They can seem immutable and unchanging. So we must also ask if there are dominant traditions. Unpacking the notion of traditions and their associated practices in several countries should not blind us to the use of force at whatever level (local, national and international), whether overt or sedimented in institutional practices.

Conclusions

Public Administration is commonly seen as an applied social science with a reformist strand. The practice of public administration was criticized 'by reference to what may be crudely called "common sense"' (Mackenzie 1975: 9). The Fabians, with their belief in administrative engineering, epitomize this 'social critic' part of the British tradition (Rhodes 1979: 70). Dunleavy describes it as 'an area of study which is quite largely "applied" and closely linked with practical problems and practised solutions' (1982: 215). This orientation is too constraining and my final remarks aim to show that an anti-foundational or decentred approach can produce a different and challenging research agenda. I do so under two headings: chaos and ethnography.

Chaos

As White argues, 'the burden of the historian' is the 'moral charge to free men from the burden of history' (1978: 49). So: 'insofar as historical events and processes become understandable, as conservatives maintain, or explainable, as radicals believe them to be, they can never serve as the basis for a visionary politics...concerned to endow social life with meaning.' White emphasizes the nihilism of history, the endless search for meaning which continues to elude us as certainly as human aspiration drives us to construct shards of meaning from differentiation, discontinuity and disaster. So, the historian should abjure imposing order where there is none and focus on 'the notion of the historical sublime' because human dignity and freedom emerge out of our reaction against the meaninglessness of history; we are transmuted into something higher, nobler, or more excellent (see also Berman 1982).

Such grand sentiments may seem out of place in a chapter on British Public Administration but they point to a distinct advantage of a de-centred approach. It poses the question of how individuals make sense of, make and remake the institutions and processes which they inherit. A decentred account implies a microanalysis but does not imply necessarily a bottom-up approach. Equally, it does not privilege the 'myths' of elites about how government works, but treats the beliefs of practitioners as one narrative among many. Because the analysis is not restricted to any one category of actor, we need to include the street-level bureaucrats, who can make and remake policy; services users, whose experiences can differ markedly from the expectations of the service provider; as well as the beliefs and actions of the political and managerial elite who seek to steer other actors in the network.

As important, if we stop privileging elite accounts and definitions of 'problems', then the task will not be to create order, to explain continuity, to help governments show they are in control. Rather, the emphasis will fall on the complexities, ambiguities and confusions of institutional differentiation; the discontinuities induced by interrelated unintended consequences; and understanding policy disasters. The order of an anti-foundational *Stimmung* is an 'order' of differentiation, discontinuity and disasters. The summary term chaos does not overstate the point. Rather, it challenges students of Public Administration to understand institutions and their reform from the standpoint of those affected and excluded. For example, there are no accounts of how NPM affects individual middle-level managers or employees. Also, we have new 'tribes', vocal minorities with a predilection for direct action over representation in 'normal politics'. The new tribes include the environmentalists, the anti-roads lobby, the anti-smoking campaign, the campaign against blood sports, and the claims of religious and racial minorities. We have fetishized economy, efficiency and management over the past decade or so. Politics and Public Administration have been reduced to managerial and institutional fixes. We have marginalized the new tribes. They are outside 'normal' political and administrative processess, possibly from choice but definitely by exclusion; they are today's 'unauthorized identities'. Their challenge raises questions about sustaining the legitimacy of government.

Ethnography

An ethnographic approach: studies individual behaviour in everyday contexts; gathers data from many sources; adopts an 'unstructured' approach (that is, data is not collected to a preconceived plan); focuses on one group or locale; and, in analysing the data, stresses the 'interpretation of the meanings and functions of human action' (paraphrased from Hammersley 1991: 1–2. See also the 'grounded theory' of Glaser and Strauss 1967; and Geertz 1973 on 'thick descriptions'). The approach is directly relevant to the decentred study of public administration (see for example, Colville, Dalton and Tomkins 1993; Heclo and Wildavsky 1974; McPherson and Raab 1988: ch. 3).

Decentred ethnographic studies will build a multifaceted picture of how the several actors understand their world. There is no expectation that there will be the one 'true' account. The researcher constructs and compares stories about how other people understand what they are doing in their, for the sake of argument, public institutions. The task is to write 'constructions of other people's constructions of what they are up to' (Geertz 1973: 9), whether they be minister, permanent secretary, social worker or clerk. Ethnography provides the tools.

The focus on disasters and on the excluded is rare in British Public Administration. The nearest we get to adopting the standpoint of citizens is when we look at consultation and such managerial initiatives as the Citizen's Charter. Almost by reflex we approach the subject from the standpoint of the administrative elite. It is almost as if we seek to be *ersatz* permanent secretaries or chief executives. I have no wish to stop anyone dealing with practical problems or producing practised solutions. But this concern cannot define the subject. The subject needs more critical detachment; a scrutiny of core values and assumptions. The challenge is to create a reflexive Public Administration which takes heed of the anti-foundational, methodological critique and focuses on critical debates about the exercise of state power and its effects on all public employees and citizens (including the excluded).

Important changes have taken place and are taking place in British government. The shift from government to governance may not introduce the postmodern era but it is impossible to refuse the invitation to ponder the direction and pace of change at the start of the twenty-first century. Mainstream Public Administration may lack direction, and it was a by-stander to the new public management revolution. It does not need to adopt an anti-foundational epistemology to confront and interpret the changes. But there is a need for a reflexive Public Administration which confronts its own practices, traditions and narratives; eschews its fascination with administrative elites; and seeks to understand how citizens, users, employees and elites construct their administrative worlds.

NOTES

1   I employ the convention of capitals to refer to the subject – Public Administration – and lower case to refer to the activity – public adminis-tration. I cover the period 1979–99. I have chosen this period because the 'conventional wisdom' sees the advent of the Conservative government in 1979 as heralding a period of major change for public administration. The chapter explores the consequences for Public Administration of these changes in public administration. For an account of the changes see Rhodes 1997a: ch. 5; 2000c.

2   Perhaps the besetting sin of Public Administration the world over is its parochialism and British Public Administration is only a partial exception, although *Public Administration* carries far more international articles (de-fined either by author's country of origin or the country under study) than its American counterpart, *Public Administration Review* (see Rhodes 1995). On the distinctive characteristics of Public Administration in Britain and contin-ental Europe see Kickert et al. 1996.

3   *Public Administration* was ranked second in the list by the Political Studies Association of the United Kingdom of the top 100 journals, see *The BISA and PSA Directory 1999*, p. 181.

4   This section updates my earlier descriptions and analyses of trends in Public Administration. See Rhodes 1979, 1991, 1995, 1996 and Rhodes and Dargie 1996. See also Hood 1990, 1995, 1999; and Pollitt 1993, 1996. I also draw on my work with Mark Bevir and I must acknowledge his contribution to the anti-foundational analysis of British government.

5   Applicants nominate their main discipline on the grant application form and it is used to classify awards. This table is drawn from the applications

describing their main field as 'Political Science and Public Administration'. It excludes all political science topics and all awards to run seminars and workshops. It covers completed projects only. Several Whitehall grants did not finish until 1999. It does not cover all projects awarded under the Local Governance and Whitehall Programmes because several principal investigators named geography, history, law, management or sociology as their disciplinary field. All programmes are interdisciplinary.

6 On the Local Governance Programme see Stoker 1999b. On the Whitehall Programme, see Rhodes 2000a for further details, a list of publications and contact names and addresses; and Rhodes 2000b for summaries of the key findings.

7 On earlier periods see Rhodes 1997a: ch. 8 and citations; Hood 1990, 1999.

8 The extent to which NPM affected Public Administration is a matter of debate. For example, Greenwood and Robins (1999) argue that in undergraduate degrees there has been a shift in the curriculum from Public Administration to public management and the subject has been relocated away from social science departments to business schools. However, Boyne (1996: 692) suggests that 'the depth of the crisis appears to have been overestimated'. He disputes that there has been any significant relocation as opposed to endogenous growth in the business schools. Such territorial disputes matter less than the brute 'fact' that the world changed on Public Administration and so it too had to change.

9 For a review see Rhodes 1999b and the next section below. On its practical implications see Perri 6 et al. 1999; Stoker 1999a; Wilkinson and Appelbee 1999.

10 I focus on devolution because these changes are already in place but there are several other major constitutional changes on the way which could also have a significant impact on public administration and its study. The main examples are incorporation of the European Convention on Human Rights; and a freedom of information act. See Hazel 1999 for a broad survey of constitutional reform over the next few years.

11 This approach is not relativist but I do not have the space to develop the argument. See Bevir 1999a: ch. 3; Rhodes 1997a: ch. 9.

12 For a historical and philosophical defence of this choice of concepts compared to other anti-foundationalists see Bevir 1997 and 1999b.

13 This section draws on Bevir and Rhodes 2000; and Rhodes 2000c.

14 Of course I recognize that some of these ideas have been rhetorical flourishes with few if any substantive policy effects. Also in the space available I cannot trace the origins, development and uses of the several ideas associated with New Labour. I accept that 'stakeholding' has become less prominent and had few policy consequences. I would simply emphasize that my approach focuses on the formation and handing down of ideas, leaving the question of their effects for whom open to inquiry. Also, the idea of networks (and joined-up government) is not only an example of Third Way rhetoric but it also had substantive policy effects (see Rhodes 2000c).

REFERENCES

Berman, M. (1982) *All That Is Solid Melts Into Air*. London: Verso.

Bernstein, R. J. (1991) *The New Constellation*. Oxford: Blackwell.

Bevir, M. (1997) 'A Humanist Critique of the Archaeology of the Human Sciences', *Storia della Storiografia*, 32, 17–32.

——(1999a) *The Logic of the History of Ideas*. Cambridge: Cambridge University Press.

——(1999b) 'Foucault, Power and Institutions', *Political Studies*, 47, 345–59.

Bevir, M. and Rhodes, R. A. W. (1998) 'Narratives of "Thatcherism"', *West European Politics*, 21(1), 97–119.

——(1999) 'Studying British Government: Reconstructing the Research Agenda', *British Journal of Politics and International Relations*, 1(2), 215–39.

——(2000) 'Decentering Tradition: Interpreting British Government', *Administration and Society*, 33(2), 107–32.

Blair, T. (1996) *New Britain: My Vision of a Young Country*. London: Fourth Estate.

Boyne, G. A. (1996) 'The Intellectual Crisis in British Public Administration: is Public Management the Problem or the Solution', *Public Administration*, 74, 679–94.

Brown, G. and Wright, T. (1995) 'Introduction', in G. Brown and T. Wright (eds), *Values, Visions and Voices: An Anthology of Socialism*. Edinburgh: Mainstream.

Cabinet Office (1998) 'Service First: The New Charter Programme', Cabinet Office, June.

——(1999a) 'Modernising Government Action Plan', Cabinet Office, July.

——(1999b) 'Professional Policy Making for the Twentieth Century: Report by the Strategic Policy Making Team', Cabinet Office, September.

Clark, D. (1997) 'Delivering Better Government from the Bottom Up', speech by the Chancellor of the Duchy of Lancaster, 17 June, Queen Elizabeth Conference Centre, London.

Collingwood, R. G. (1939) *An Autobiography*. Oxford: Oxford University Press.

——(1965) *Essays in the Philosophy of History*. Austin: Texas University Press.

——(1993) *The Idea of History*, rev. edn. Oxford: Oxford University Press.

Colville, I., Dalton, K. and Tomkins, C. (1993) 'Developing and Understanding Cultural Change in HM Customs and Excise: There is More to Dancing than Knowing the Next Steps', *Public Administration*, 71, 549–66.

Dunleavy, P. (1982) 'Is There a Radical Approach to Public Administration?', *Public Administration*, 60, 215–33.

Geertz, C. (1973) *The Interpretation of Cultures*. New York: Basic Books.

Glaser, B. G. and Strauss, A. (1967) *The Discovery of Grounded Theory*. New York: Aldine.

Greenwood, J. and Robins, L. (1999) 'Public Administration Thematic Network: The United Kingdom', typescript, De Montford University, Leicester.

R. A. W. RHODES

Hammersley, M. (1991) *Reading Ethnographic Research: A Critical Guide.*
Harlow: Longman.
Hazell, R. (ed.) (1999) *Constitutional Futures: A History of the Next Ten Years.*
Oxford: Oxford University Press.
Hazel, R. and Morris, B. (1999) 'Machinery of Government: Whitehall', in
R. Hazell (ed.), *Constitutional Futures: A History of the Next Ten Years.*
Oxford: Oxford University Press.
Heclo, H. and Wildavsky, A. (1974) *The Private Government of Public Money.*
London: Macmillan.
Held, D. (1991) 'Democracy, the Nation State and the Global System', *Economy and Society,* 20, 138–72.
HM Treasury (1998) *Modern Public Services for Britain: Investing in Reform, Cm 4011.* London: Stationery Office.
Hood, C. (1990) 'Public Administration: Lost an Empire Not Yet Found a Role',
in A. Leftwich (ed.), *New Developments in Political Science.* Aldershot:
Edward Elgar.
—— (1991) 'A Public Management for All Seasons?', *Public Administration,* 69,
3–19.
—— (1995) 'Emerging Issues in Public Administration', *Public Administration,*
73, 165–83.
—— (1999) 'British Public Administration', in J. Hayward, B. Barry and
A. Brown (eds), *The British Study of Politics in the Twentieth Century.* Oxford:
Oxford University Press for the British Academy.
Jensen, L. (1998) 'Interpreting New Public Management: The Case of Denmark',
Australian Journal of Public Administration, 57(4), 55–66.
Kickert, W. J. M., et al. (1996) 'Changing European States; Changing Public
Administration', *Public Administration Review,* 56(1), 65–103.
Mackenzie, W. J. M. (1975) 'Public Administration in the Universities', in W. J.
M. Mackenzie, *Explorations in Government: Collected Papers 1951–1968.*
London: Macmillan.
McPherson, A. and Raab, C. (1988) *Governing Education.* Edinburgh: Edinburgh University Press.
Mandelson, P. and Liddle, R. (1996) *The Blair Revolution: Can New Labour Deliver?* London: Faber.
Memorandum (1999) *Memorandum of Understanding and supplementary agreements between the United Kingdom Government, Scottish Ministers and the Cabinet of the National Assembly for Wales, Cm 4444.* London:
Stationery Office
Olsen, J. P. (1983) *Organized Democracy: Political Institutions in a Welfare State – The Case of Norway.* Oslo: Universitetsforlaget.
Perri 6, Leat, D., Seltzer, K. and Stoker G. (1999) *Governing in the Round: Strategies for Holistic Governance.* London: DEMOS.
Pollitt, C. (1993) *Managerialism and the Public Services,* 2nd edn. Oxford:
Blackwell.

—— (1996) 'Administrative Reform and New Administrative Directions: Public Administration in the United Kingdom', *Public Administration Review*, 56(1), 81–7

Rhodes, R. A. W. (1979) *Public Administration and Policy Analysis*. Farnborough: Saxon House.

—— (1988) *Beyond Westminster and Whitehall*. London: Unwin-Hyman; repr. London: Routledge, 1992.

—— (1991) 'Theory and Methods in British Public Administration: The View from Political Science', *Political Studies*, 39, 533–54.

—— (1995) 'The State of Public Administration: A Professional History of the 1980s', *Public Administration*, 73, 1–15.

—— (1996), 'From Institutions to Dogma: Tradition, Eclecticism and Ideology in the Study of British Public Administration', *Public Administration Review*, 55, 1–11.

—— (1997a) *Understanding Governance: Policy Networks, Governance, Reflexivity and Accountability*. Buckingham: Open University Press.

—— (1997b) 'It's the Mix that Matters: From Marketisation to Diplomacy', *Australian Journal of Public Administration*, 56, 40–53.

—— (1998) 'Different Roads to Unfamiliar Places: UK Experience in Comparative Perspective', *Australian Journal of Public Administration*, 57(4), 19–31.

—— (1999a) 'Foreword: Governance and Networks', in G. Stoker (ed.), *The New Management of British Local Governance*. London: Macmillan.

—— (1999b) 'Public Administration and Governance', in J. Pierre (ed.), *Debating Governance*. Oxford: Oxford University Press.

—— (1999c) 'The ESRC Whitehall Programme: The Changing Nature of Central Government in Britain. Programme Director's End of Award Report, September 1999', Department of Politics, University of Newcastle.

—— (1999d) 'Traditions and Public Sector Reform: Comparing Britain and Denmark', *Scandinavian Political Studies*, 22, 341–70.

—— (2000a) 'A Guide to the ESRC's Whitehall Programme', *Public Administration*, 78(2), 251–82.

—— (2000b), *Transforming British Government*, 2 vols: vol. 1, *Changing Institutions*; vol. 2, *Changing Roles and Relationships*. London: Macmillan.

—— (2000c) 'New Labour's Civil Service: Summing-up Joining-up', *Political Quarterly*, 71(2), 151–66.

Rhodes, R. A. W. and C. Dargie (1996) 'Traditional Public Administration', *Public Administration*, 74, 325–32.

Robson, W. A. (1975) 'The Study of Public Administration Then and Now', *Political Studies*, 22, 193–201.

Rorty, R. (1980) *Philosophy and the Mirror of Nature*. Oxford: Blackwell.

Rose, R. (1982) *Understanding the United Kingdom*. London: Longman.

Stoker G. (1999a) 'Will Government Ever Get Joined Up?', paper to the ESRC Whitehall Programme Public Service Seminar, British Academy, London, 17 Sept.

Stoker G. (ed.) (1999b) *The New Management of British Local Governance*. London: Macmillan.

White, H. (1978) *Tropics of Discourse*. Baltimore: Johns Hopkins Press.

White Paper (1999) *Modernising Government, Cm 4310*. London: Stationery Office.

Wilkinson, D. and Appelbee E. (1999) *Implementing Holistic Government*. London: DEMOS.

Wilson, Sir Richard (1998) 'Modernising Government: The Role of the Senior Civil Service', speech, Senior Civil Service Conference, Oct.

Wright V. (1994) 'Reshaping the State: Implications for Public Administration', *West European Politics*, 17, 102–34.

7

Towards a New Welfare Settlement?

Ruth Lister

Summary and introduction

The last two decades of the twentieth century witnessed an ongoing process of renegotiation of the postwar welfare settlement (PWS) which is set to continue after the millennium. Under the Conservatives, a key aim was to diminish the role of the state in welfare provision and to increase individual responsibility. New Labour's response to the Conservative legacy has been described as 'an exercise in post-Thatcherite politics' (Driver and Martell 1998: 1), shaped by Thatcherism yet also representing a reaction against it. Neither 'old left' nor 'new right', New Labour is, it claims, forging a 'third way' in welfare.

While not as anti-state as the new right, the third way retains a scepticism about the state's role. Partnership is the watchword and, in a continuation of the new 'organizational settlement' forged by the Tories, 'the managerial state' rules OK over the welfare citizen as consumer (Clarke and Newman 1997; Hughes and Lewis 1998; Clarke 1997, 1998). Underpinning the third way is a paradigm shift in Labour Party thinking and rhetoric from the goal and discourse of equality to those of the trinity of responsibility, inclusion and opportunity (RIO).

Paid work, supported by education, is the primary mechanism for achieving all three. As the supreme citizenship responsibility, it stands at the heart of the 'new contract for welfare' which frames the welfare reform process. As all fit adults are to be encouraged to achieve independence through paid work, the new welfare settlement (NWS) marks a shift from a male breadwinner towards a 'universal breadwinner' model (Fraser 1997). In the social security field more traditional debates about benefit adequacy and the overall structure of social security, and in particular the balance between means-tested and non-means-tested benefits, are dismissed as irrelevant to an ideologically anaesthetized 'what works' approach couched in a discourse of modernization. Yet this approach could result in a significant shift in welfare regime mix and ideology further towards a more residual liberal model of welfare (which has already increased its hold on the UK welfare regime in recent years) and further away from institutional continental European models.

The first part of the chapter is contextual. It briefly discusses the notion and constitutive elements of the PWS and the challenge to it from the new right governments of 1979–87. The next section analyses the ways in which, in responding, New Labour has attempted to distance itself both from its own left ideological heritage and its new right inheritance. This leads into a discussion of the relationship between the state and the welfare subject in the emergent NWS and of the shift from an equality agenda to RIO in its underlying values.

The final sections focus more specifically on social security reform as pivotal to the emergent NWS. When Tony Blair declared that 'we will be the party of welfare reform' (1997c: 4), it was primarily social security which was his target.[1] The discussion of social security reform will be structured around the two interrelated themes of work and the new welfare contract. The conclusion will provide a cautious assessment of the emergent NWS, in the face of tensions between some of the rhetoric and the policy reality.

The challenge to the postwar welfare settlement

The postwar welfare settlement

The twentieth century has been marked by three 'waves' of preoccupation with citizenship during which the appropriate welfare settlement between individuals and the state has been contested and renegotiated: the decades prior to the First World War, the period after the Second World War, and the last two decades of the century (Rees 1996). Deliberately drawing historical parallels, in his 1945 Anniversary Lecture, Blair called for 'a new settlement on welfare for a new age' (1995a: 14).

The notion of a welfare settlement has been described as the establishment of 'a kind of framing consensus . . . which sets the limits within which compromises over what and how, and by whom and for whom, welfare services and benefits are delivered'. Negotiated by those with power, it represents 'a set of arrangements that create a temporary period of stability or equilibrium, even while they remain complex, contested and fragile' (Hughes and Lewis 1998: 4). Clarke and Newman (1997) distinguish three, overlapping types of settlement. The political-economic settlement hinges on the relationships between market and state and the relations of (in)equality which they promote. The social settlement, as embodied in the welfare state, shapes and is shaped by the intersecting institutions of family, nation and work (Williams 1989). The organizational settlement governs the ways in which welfare services and benefits are organized and delivered, thereby constructing welfare subjects as, for instance, supplicants, clients, customers or citizens (passive or active).

The PWS rested on a political-economic settlement in which the state played the leading role in the mixed economy of welfare, with walk-on parts for the private and voluntary sectors but a continued pivotal role played by the family as invisible understudy. The Beveridgean/Keynesian state was seen as responsible both for the provision and funding of welfare on a more or less universal basis and for the maintenance of full (male) employment. Public expenditure and taxation were regarded as key means to this end rather than as a problem. Social rights tempered the power of the market by decoupling the living standards of individual citizens from their market value so that they were not totally dependent on selling their labour power.

It was, to be more precise, male labour which was 'decommodified' in this way, for central to the social settlement was the male breadwinner heterosexist model in which families were peopled by family-wage-earning males and dependent female partners. This partnership was based on the latter's 'other duties': in the famous Beveridge phrase, 'housewives as mothers have vital work to do in ensuring the adequate continuance of the British race and of British ideals in the world' (Beveridge 1942: paras 114 and 117). It was, as this implies, a racialized model in which welfare citizens were implicitly assumed to be white, while black immigrants were subsequently, for a limited period, to be encouraged in order to staff the lower echelons of the health service in particular.

Organizationally, the model was a top-down one in which bureaucrats and professionals, working to a notion of public service, delivered services and benefits to passive and preferably deferential citizens (Clarke and Newman 1997; Hughes and Lewis 1998).

The late twentieth-century challenge

The challenge to the PWS and its component parts did not come simply from the new right government of Margaret Thatcher and its intellectual antecedents. The PWS was destabilized by a combination of economic, demographic and social trends, none of which was necessarily fatal in itself, but which together were interpreted and exploited as such by the new right. From the opposite corner, the PWS was the subject of attack from marginalized groups, most notably women and disabled people, no longer content to play the role of deferential welfare subject (Hughes and Lewis 1998). Nevertheless, the Thatcher government's deliberate ideological assault on the PWS, which skilfully manipulated these pressures, was critical, particularly in undermining its political-economic and organizational elements. At the heart of this assault was a determination (not totally successful in execution) to 'roll back the state' (or at least the welfare arms of it) and, in the latter stages of the Thatcher regime, to turn the provider state into a regulatory state operating in certain spheres through quasi-markets.[2] Strongly influenced by public choice theory, a new maxim ruled: 'private good, public bad'. The bureaucratic-professional state was, by the end of the Thatcher era, transmogrified into the target-setting, performance-centred, managerial state whose users were constructed as either consumers/customers or welfare dependants/scroungers (Clarke, Cochrane and McLaughlin 1994; Clarke and Newman 1997; Hughes and Lewis 1998; Clarke 1997; Hughes 1998).

It is the ideological assault on the PWS that represents the most significant legacy of eighteen years of Conservative government through its reshaping of the mainstream parameters of the politically possible. Particularly significant from the perspective of social security reform was its bequest of a powerful discourse of combating 'the dependency culture' in the name of promoting individual responsibility. In terms of specific social policy changes, the Conservative governments were more pragmatic than their rhetoric suggested, not always pursuing ideology to its logical policy conclusion. Nevertheless, some of the changes they did make created 'new institutional opportunities' for further more radical reform, by making possible options which previously would have been deemed politically impossible (Bonoli and Palier 1998: 329; Blackman and Palmer 1999).

Moreover, combined with regressive taxation and employment policies, in the context of an increasingly fissured labour market and globalizing economic forces, these changes helped to create a country scarred by levels of inequality and poverty exceptional by both postwar and international standards for an industrialized society. Between 1979 and 1996–7, the real incomes of the bottom tenth of the population fell by 9 per cent compared with an increase of 70 per cent for the top tenth and 44 per cent overall (DSS 1998b; see also HM Treasury 1999). This was no accident, for inequality was seen as an incentive to hard work and enterprise; as such, it was promoted as both inevitable and desirable (Johnson 1990).

New Labour's response: neither 'old left' nor 'new right'

New Labour responded to its Thatcherite inheritance by attempting to forge a third way which 'moves decisively beyond an Old Left preoccupied by state control, high taxation and producer interests; and a New Right treating public investment, and often the very notions of "society" and collective endeavour as evils to be undone' (Blair 1998a: 1).[3] The exact location of the third way, in terms of its political geography, remains unclear. Both Blair (1998a) and the third way's chief intellectual exponent Tony Giddens (1998) have claimed to be using the compass of a modernized social democracy committed to social justice to fix its bearings. This has not, however, satisfied those critics who believe that the third way veers to the right, under the continued magnetic pull of the Thatcherite legacy, and that talk of 'beyond left and right' implies 'a society which is no longer structured by social division' (Mouffe 1998: 13).

The defining characteristic of New Labour is that it is not 'old' Labour. In its attempt to distance itself from its own ideological past, New Labour has distorted existing thinking on the left, writing out of political and intellectual history a range of critical left positions. All pre-New Labour thinking is lumped together as 'old' and therefore, by implication, irrelevant to these new times. As we shall see, this kind of thinking encourages a false dichotomy at the heart of New Labour's welfare reform agenda.

The way was paved by a number of independent inquiries in the mid-1990s, which attempted to breath new life from the centre-left into the somewhat stagnant welfare debate. Of particular significance was the Commission on Social Justice whose report told a tale of 'three futures': a neoliberal 'deregulators' Britain', an egalitarian 'levellers' Britain' and an 'investors' Britain' combining 'the ethics of community with the dynamics of a market economy' where 'the extension of economic opportunity is not only the source of economic prosperity but also the basis of social justice' (Commission on Social Justice 1994: 95).[4] Although the commission firmly identified with an 'investors' Britain', some of its proposals bore something of the 'levellers'' hallmark, albeit cloaked in modernizers' language. Within a year of publication, the commission's report had effectively metamorphosed from a symbol of New Labour to one of old, as the juggernaut of accelerated modernization rolled over it.

Modernization is one of New Labour's favourite discourses. It is deployed not simply to distance New Labour from its own past, but also to present its policies as an inevitable response to change, in particular global change. It is a discourse which brooks no opposition and which creates a sense of inevitability, denying the choices involved in *how* politics responds to economic and social change and silencing alternative modernizing scripts (Finlayson 1998; Hay 1998; Andrews 1999; Rose 1999). Clarke and Newman suggest that this modernizing narrative represents 'the site of significant continuities between the New Right and New Labour' (1998: 10). Global and societal change have been invoked by both in order to justify the need for modernizing thinking and policy. Blair constantly reminds us that the third way 'is about traditional values in a changed world' (1998a: 1). Among those values that distance the party from the new right are social justice and community, as well as the 'middle way' Conservative vision of 'one nation' (see also Rose 1999). These underpin its determination to tackle social exclusion and Blair's pledge to end child poverty in twenty years.

At the same time, New Labour also invokes the 'changed world', together with perceived economic imperatives, in support of those positions that reflect its Thatcherite inheritance: the embrace of markets (albeit not untrammelled), low taxation, limited public spending (although with some relaxation post the 2000 Budget) and a macroeconomic policy that prioritizes the control of inflation, despite the centrality of employment to New Labour's welfare policy.

The foundations of the new welfare settlement

The managerial, partnership state

The thread that ties these new positions together is the acceptance of many of the key tenets of the new political-economic and organizational settlements forged under the Conservatives. A more limited state, in which enabling, brokerage and regulating is emphasized over providing, stands at the heart of the NWS (Miliband 1999a). As Blair underlined in his Beveridge Lecture, 'the welfare state need no longer be delivered only through the state or through traditional methods of Government. Public/ private partnership and the voluntary sector will have and should have a greater role to play' (1999b: 13). The growing importance attached to the voluntary sector was subsequently underlined by the Chancellor of the Exchequer, Gordon Brown: 'in the next five years the role of government will shift even more from the old "directing and controlling" to enabling and empowering voluntary action' (Brown 2001).

Partnership, a throwback to the 'middle way' in welfare thought as well as a legacy of the last Conservative government, is, in its multifarious guises and new suits of clothing designed for 'new times', the linchpin of the NWS's architectural foundations.[5] According to the welfare reform Green Paper, *New Ambitions for our Country: A New Contract for Welfare*, the third way in welfare is partly 'about combining public and private provision in a new partnership for a new age' (DSS 1998a: 19). Employers, private-sector financial institutions, trade unions, mutuals and voluntary organizations are all identified as important partners. Partnership is particularly emphasized in relation to pensions, the delivery of the New Deal (Theorore and Peck 1999; Finn 1999) and provision of welfare services. The second principle of welfare reform is that 'public and private sectors should work in partnership to ensure that, wherever possible, people are insured against foreseeable risks and make provision for their retirement' (DSS 1998a: 33). The aim of the proposals in the pensions Green Paper, *Partnership in Pensions*, is to shift the ratio of public–private pension provision from 60:40 to 40:60 by 2050 (for a critique, see *Benefits* 1999; Walker 1999).

In the service sector, partnerships are promoted between public and private or voluntary organizations, between different arms of the state and between providers and users (Cabinet Office 1999). In health, 'partnership, cooperation and collaboration are emphasised and mandated at every turn' (Paton 1999: 69), most notably in relation to trusts and health authorities, health action zones (Maddock 1999), and 'government, communities and individuals' in promoting good health (Labour Party 1999: vii). Health authorities face a 'new duty of partnership' with local authorities to promote the well-being of communities; *Partnership in Action* outlines 'a system of integrated care, based on partnership' in which social services 'have a key role' (DoH 1998: 5, 3). The White Paper, *Modernising Social Services*, devotes a chapter to a discussion of a wide range of partnerships (Johnson 1999). In terms of funding, of particular significance is the revitalization of the Tories' Private Finance Initiative in which hospitals and schools are privately built and leased to the state, probably at greater long-term cost than had they been built with public money. Education Action Zones are another site for public–private partnerships (Gewirtz 1999; Muschamp, Jamieson and Lauder 1999), while housing, community regeneration and neighbourhood renewal policy will also rely heavily on private and voluntary partners (Kemp 1999a, 1999b; Hulls 1999; Hall and Mawson 1999; Craig 1999; Social Exclusion Unit 2001).

If partnerships are the linchpin of the new organizational settlement, managerialism, another element in New Labour's inheritance, can be seen as the 'organizational glue' which holds it together (Clarke and Hoggett 1999: 15; Newman 1998). As Rouse and Smith observe, 'there will be no return to the public administration paradigm as the template for the organisation of the welfare state.... The performance management ethos has become even more pronounced under New Labour' (1999: 250 see also Dean and Woods 1999; Clarke, Gewirtz and McLaughlin 2000). In the context of a pragmatic discourse of 'what works', managerialism 'has become depoliticized' (Newman 1998: 369). It permeates the Comprehensive Spending Review, which plans to 'root out waste and inefficiency' and to 'provide efficient and modern public services' (HM Treasury 1998: 1). It is embodied in the government's enthusiasm for target-setting: in his introduction to the government's 1998–9 Annual Report, Blair pointed to 'over 600 testing performance and efficiency targets to transform the way the public services operate' (1999c: 7). The different, but related, notion of 'joined up solutions for joined up problems', particularly in tackling social exclusion (Mulgan 1998: 262; Miliband 1999a), provides a New Labour spin on the managerialist discourse, which also serves to further the goal of establishing New Labour's credibility as a party of government.

Under the Tories, managerialism cast welfare subjects as customers and consumers rather than citizens (Clarke 1997, 1998; Hughes and Lewis 1998). New Labour has attempted to marry the two in the person of 'the demanding, sceptical, citizen-consumer' who expects improved standards from public services in line with those in the private sector (DSS 1998a: 16). There is the same emphasis on individual customer service and user- rather than provider-led welfare as under the Conservatives (a model which was not necessarily realized in practice and which had more purchase in some arms of the welfare state than others[6]).

At the same time, though, there is something of a more collective approach: examples include the introduction of citizens' juries and various forums for 'listening to' particular groups such as women and older people, as well as resident participation in the Social Exclusion Unit's neighbourhood renewal action plan. According to Rouse and Smith, 'more accessible opportunities are being created for the public, through representative and participative means, to contribute to the shaping and control of the welfare state' (1999: 252). Yet, when Blair tells us that 'in all walks of life people act as consumers and not just citizens' (1998b) the suspicion is that it is the consumer rather than the citizen who represents the ideal New Labour welfare subject (see also Gamble and Kenny 1999).

In the social security field, the promise is of 'an active modern service' (DSS 1998c: 4). This will extend 'the exits from welfare dependency, moving from a mass-production service, which merely pays benefit, to one offering a professional, tailor-made service for each individual' (DSS 1998a: 19–20) through the deployment of personal advisers (an import from both the US (Deacon 2000) and Australia (Considine 1999)). However, the heavy emphasis on welfare 'dependency' and combating fraud tends to create a negative image of the welfare subject as dependant or fraudster, redolent of earlier 'scrounger' discourses.

The trinity of responsibility, inclusion and opportunity

Ending welfare 'dependency' is a, if not the, primary goal of welfare reform, as illustrated by the paradigm and discursive shift from an equality to a RIO agenda.

From equality to equality of opportunity   At the heart of this shift is the retreat from greater equality as an explicit goal and from redistribution of resources through the tax/benefit system as the primary mechanism for achieving it, despite continued vestiges of Labour's traditional vision of a more equal society. Back in January 1997, Gordon Brown promised that there would be no increase in income tax rates (including the top rate which is low by European standards) during the first term of a new Labour government. In 2000, he went further and cut the standard rate (at a cost of £2.8 billion) – to its lowest level for seventy years.[7] In an *Observer* interview (5 Sept. 1999), Blair spoke of achieving 'for ordinary families as low a tax burden as possible' and of 'people who need to keep more of their own money'. The Anglo-German document, 'Europe: The Third Way/Die Neue Mitte', lays similar emphasis on lower taxes while also declaring that 'public expenditure as a proportion of national income has more or less reached the limits of acceptability' (Blair and Schröder 1999: 29). Nevertheless, in 2000, public spending on services rose up the Government's agenda, reflecting growing public concern about the state of the welfare and transport infrastructure. The re-prioritization of spending on services over further tax cuts was reflected in the 2001 pre-election Budget.

Hugo Young warned after the 1997 tax pledge that 'we are on notice that it will be a government which has abandoned the fight against inequality by the standard method' (*Guardian*, 21 Jan. 1997). 'The standard method' of overt redistribution through the tax/benefit system has been rejected in favour of 'redistribution of opportunity' through education, training and paid employment, which are at the heart of 'a new supply-side agenda for the left' (Blair and Schröder 1999: 33). This agenda, which prioritizes investment in 'human capital' as the key to competitiveness, is driven by the perceived exigencies of the global marketplace.[8] Lifelong equality of opportunity is favoured over 'equality of outcome', which is repudiated in the classic anti-egalitarian caricature as associated with 'conformity and mediocrity rather than the celebration of creativity, diversity and excellence' (Blair and Schröder 1999: 28). The vision held out by Blair for the end of a 'ten year programme to tackle poverty and social exclusion' (1999a) is the American one of 'an expanded middle class, with ladders of opportunity for those from all backgrounds, no more ceilings that prevent people from achieving the success they merit'.

Higher income tax, perceived to be a vote-loser, has become a taboo subject (Commission on Taxation and Citizenship 2000). Even when Brown introduced mildly redistributive budgets, he could not bring himself to admit it. Redistribution has become the 'r' word, whose name the government dare not speak; instead Brown has pursued a strategy of 'quiet redistribution' or 'redistribution by stealth'. The retreat from noisy redistribution partly reflected a fear of frightening the voters of Middle Britain whom the party continued to woo in order to win a second term, but also a belief, typical of 'post-Fordism', that the constraints imposed by economic global forces mean that traditional 'tax and spend' policies are no longer sustainable.

While 'redistribution by stealth' may be a politically astute tactic in the short run, critics argue that there are limits to how much it can achieve in the face of the massive redistribution in the opposite direction under the Tories (see also Piachaud 1999). Moreover, in the longer run it fails to build the constituency of support for redistributive policies which is needed if they are really to take root among the tax-paying public. The case for such policies continues to be put by those who believe that equality of opportunity, even as defined by Brown as the chance for 'everyone to realise their potential to the full' (1996), will remain a mirage so long as massively unequal starting points affect the ability to grasp the opportunities opened up. David Marquand, for example, has observed that, in the context of a growing fault line 'between the winners and losers in the global marketplace . . . no project for social inclusion will work unless it captures some of the winners' gains and redirects them to the losers' (1998: 24).

From poverty to social exclusion   According to Giddens, 'the new politics defines equality as inclusion and inequality as exclusion' (1998: 102). The government has, in fact, rehabilitated the 'p' word 'poverty', expunged from the official lexicon under the Tories, and has used it increasingly following Blair's March 1999 pledge to eradicate child poverty in two decades. It does so alongside the language of social exclusion, which was its initial preference. It is a language spoken in a number of dialects, reflecting different values and models of society, encapsulated by Ruth Levitas (1998) in the three discourses of SID, MUD and RED.

RED refers to a redistributive, egalitarian discourse that embraces notions of citizenship and social rights, which Levitas associates with critical thinkers and activists, but not with the mainstream stance adopted by the UK government and the European Commission. The primary value here is social justice; the cartography is of a divided society in which the ability of the rich to exclude themselves from the bonds of common citizenship is also problematized. In contrast, the other two discourses are activated by the primary value of social cohesion rather than a concern about wider inequalities, reflecting a model of society in which the key relationship is a dichotomous, horizontal one of 'in' or 'out' rather than a hierarchical one of 'top' to 'bottom' (Duffy 1998; see also Driver and Martell 1997). It is also a model of social inclusion which stops at the borders of nation-states, as exemplified by the exclusionary stance adopted towards aslyum-seekers, thereby perpetuating the racialized construction of the nation in the postwar social settlement.

MUD (a 'moral underclass discourse') is a moralistic discourse, which deploys the divisive and stigmatizing language of the 'underclass' and 'dependency culture' to portray those excluded as culturally distinct from mainstream society. It emphasizes individual behaviour and values. SID, a 'social integrationist discourse', increasingly dominant in both the UK and the wider EU, is focused primarily, and sometimes exclusively, on exclusion from paid work. Levitas sums up the differences between the three discourses according to 'what the excluded are seen as lacking', namely money (and we might add power) in RED, morals in MUD and work in SID.

The government's approach to tackling social exclusion reflects an uneasy amalgam of SID, MUD and RED. Although it has, at times, deployed a definition of social exclusion in the RED tradition, its policies are firmly rooted in SID, most notably in their identification of paid work, supported by education and training, as the key route to social inclusion. There is also a good splattering of MUD as ministers speak the language of 'welfare dependency' and 'handouts', with negative implications for how those reliant on benefits are seen by the wider society.

The horizontal rather than hierarchical model of society, reflected in New Labour's conceptualization of social exclusion, shapes the remit of the Social Exclusion Unit, established 'at the heart of government' (Blair

1997b). The unit, heralded as the prototype of 'joined-up government', exemplifies a practical, problem-oriented approach which is paying dividends in the reports it has produced. Most notably, following widespread consultation, it has drawn up a National Action Plan for Neighbourhood Renewal, which emphasizes resident participation. Nevertheless, there have been concerns that the very speed with which the unit has had to work has meant that not enough has been done to include 'the excluded' in the process of policy development, especially at national level, thereby reinforcing the political exclusion bred by social exclusion (Metz 1999). Moreover, there is a danger that too great a focus on discrete problem groups and the areas they inhabit could encourage the belief that these groups are themselves the problem (Bennett 1998); while the problems they face are largely divorced from underlying structural processes of socioeconomic polarization in both the analysis and prescription (Kleinman 1998, 1999; Benington and Donnison 1999).

Although Blair's speech to launch the Social Exclusion Unit did speak of 'our national purpose to tackle social division and inequality', the discourse he used was otherwise more redolent of social cohesion (SID) than of social justice (RED). His argument was, in effect, that social division and inequality undermine social cohesion; the emphasis was more on behaviour and the threat to values and rules than on structures. Earlier Blair had argued that 'the only way to rebuild social order and stability is through strong values, socially shared, inculcated through individuals, family, government and the institutions of civil society' and that 'individuals prosper best within a strong and cohesive society' (Blair 1996: 8). A central value infusing such a society is that of community. This is the community of popular communitarianism, described by Nikolas Rose (1999: 476), in his critique of the third way, as 'an affective and ethical field' (see also Hughes and Little 1999). In an article to mark the launch of the unit, Blair explained that it 'will embody a core new Labour value: "community" or "one nation" . . . Our contract with the people was about opportunity and responsibility going together' (Blair 1997b).

From rights to responsibilities   The emphasis on responsibility underlines the social integrationist paradigm which frames Labour's analysis of and approach to tackling social exclusion. The statement of values, which replaced Clause IV of the party's constitution, sets as its ideal a community 'where the rights we enjoy reflect the duties we owe'. Giddens, in his exposition of the third way, goes so far as to propose '*no rights without responsibilities*' as 'a prime motto for the new politics' (1998: 65, emphasis in original).

Blair has set out to reorient the left towards 'a modern, responsible notion of citizenship' (*Observer*, 5 Sept. 1999). In his own third way statement for the Fabian Society, he argued that 'for too long, the demand for rights from the state was separated from the duties of citizenship and the imperative for mutual responsibility on the part of individuals and institutions' (Blair 1998a: 4). Back in 1995, he distanced himself from 'early Left thinking' in which the 'language of responsibility [was] spoken far less fluently' than that of rights. He argued for a two-way covenant of duties between society and citizens which 'allows us to be much tougher and hard-headed in the rules we apply; and how we apply them' (1995b). This 'hard-headedness' can be found in a range of social policy areas, most notably social security, but also anti-social behaviour and crime and disorder where the emphasis is on the responsibilities of families and parents to the wider community. Parental responsibilities are likewise emphasized in relation to family, education and child support policies (Home Office 1998; Blair 1998a; Gewirtz 1999; DSS 1999b) while, in tackling health inequalities, we are reminded that 'rights and responsibilities for health go hand in hand' (Labour Party 1999).[9]

Blair's emphasis on responsibilities reflects an ideological eclecticism which draws on a number of influences, including popular communitarianism, Christian Socialism and social liberalism as well as elements of a moral authoritarianism (Deacon 1997; Beer 1998; Freeden 1999; Heron and Dwyer 1999; Hughes and Little 1999). It draws on a view of human nature and motivation very different from that which animated the PWS. The welfare subject is now regarded as motivated more by self-interest than altruism (Deacon 1996, 2000; Le Grand 1997). Blair is, though, at pains to appeal to an 'enlightened view of self-interest' (1995b, 1999d) as the basis of the contract between individual and state, in contrast to the narrower, more selfish version promoted by Thatcherism (Deacon 2000). Where enlightened self-interest provides insufficient motivation, obligations have to be enforced and welfare becomes a (re)moralizing force for influencing behaviour (Davis 1999; Rose 1999; Deacon 2000).

Critics point to the dangers of an imbalance in the allocation of responsibilities and rights in an unequal society. Will Hutton, for example, while accepting a link between rights and obligations, has commented that 'most of the obligations that accompany rights in a New Labour order are shouldered by the bottom of society rather than those at the top, which is let off largely scot-free' (*Observer*, 5 July 1998; see also Fitzpatrick 1998; Dwyer 1998). Thus, for example, there is no talk of taxation of the better off as an expression of citizenship responsibility to balance the emphasis on work obligations for those at the bottom.[10]

'Reforming welfare around the work ethic'

The centrality of paid work

Work, or to be more precise paid work, lies at the heart of RIO. 'Reforming welfare around the work ethic' has become another New Labour mantra. The evils of 'welfare dependency' are a common refrain, as they were under the Tories, despite the lack of empirical evidence to support the notion of a 'dependency culture' (Lister 1996; Bennett and Walker 1998; Walker with Howard 2000).

The responsibility on benefit claimants to take up opportunities for paid work and training as the route to social inclusion and antidote to 'welfare dependency' is stressed continually by ministers, heavily influenced by thinking and policy in the US (Deacon 2000). The vehicle for exercising these responsibilities is the flagship New Deal 'welfare to work' scheme(s). The New Deal is to be administered by a new agency, Job Centre Plus, combining the Employment Service and Benefits Agency services for those of working age. Announcing the new agency, Blair described it as a cultural shift in which 'the aim is to accelerate the move from a welfare system that primarily provides passive support to one that provides active support to help people become independent' (2000: col. 257w).

The New Deal is buttressed by the introduction of a minimum wage (albeit at a level lower than campaigned for by trade unions and the 'poverty lobby') and social security reform, which combines 'sticks' and 'carrots'. On the 'carrot' side, there is a series of measures designed 'to make work pay' including tax credits, reform of national insurance contributions, the 'run-on' of certain benefits for the first few weeks in work and a new lump sum job grant to help the long-term unemployed with the transition into paid work.

Carrots, though, can quickly turn into sticks, as exemplified by Gordon Brown's message that 'work now pays; now go to work' (*Independent*, 6 Sept. 1999). Under the Conservatives, the 'stick' applied to unemployed benefit claimants had become progressively tougher. Labour has likewise made clear that for young people there will be 'no fifth option of an inactive life on benefit'. It has progressively tightened up the sanctions for non-compliance, as well as extending them to unemployed adults, in what a government insider told *The Times* (17 Sept. 1999) is 'the strongest ever attack on the workshy'. Spreading the regulatory net even wider, benefit sanctions for workless offenders who fail to comply with community sentences are being piloted. More generally, virtually all claimants of working age will be expected to attend a series of work-focused interviews with a personal adviser, as a condition of receiving benefit.[11]

This new obligation was announced in language that was both revealing and disturbing.[12] There were to be 'no apologies' for 'our tough benefits regime'. The Social Security Secretary, Alistair Darling, repeatedly underlined that fifty years on from the birth of the postwar welfare state, 'no one has an unqualified right to benefit' (*Independent*, 10 Feb. 1999). Blair explained to *Daily Mail* readers that the reforms epitomized 'the new ethic of rights and responsibilities at the heart of our welfare state', summed up as the 'end of a something-for-nothing welfare state' (10 Feb. 1999). In this way, Blair's 'vision for a popular welfare state' (1999b: 14) is built on the depreciation of the existing welfare state; 'the attempt to relegitimise "welfare"' (Bennett 1999a) is spun through the delegitimizing language of MUD.

The New Deal reflects a broad consensus that paid employment does represent the best route out of poverty for those able to take it, and, as such, it has been widely welcomed.[13] Nevertheless, there are critics. Some of these focus on particular aspects of the New Deal, but a more central object of criticism is the priority which the strategy gives to *employability* over *employment*. Demand-side policies to reduce unemployment have effectively been abandoned in the face of the constraints believed to be imposed by globalizing economic forces, again bearing out the 'post-Fordist' thesis (Jessop 1994; Deacon 1997). While, overall, unemployment has nevertheless been falling, others point to the inadequacy of reliance on 'supply-side' strategies alone in certain parts of the country where the jobs are simply not there for the various groups covered by the New Deal, who tend to be concentrated in the same low employment areas (Webster 1997; Peck 1998; Turok and Webster 1998). This criticism is only partially addressed by area-based policies such as the New Deal for Communities which will pursue intensive regeneration in a number of the most deprived areas (*New Economy* 1999). It will not, in particular, deal with what has been identified as a 'city-wide jobs gap' (Turok and Edge 1999).

More fundamentally, a few, largely unheard, voices have queried welfare to work's underlying philosophical premises that (a) paid work within a profoundly unequal labour market can necessarily be equated with social inclusion (an example of the subordination of social justice to social cohesion concerns), and that (b) it represents the primary obligation for all those of working age, discounting the value of community and voluntary activities and the unpaid work of reproduction and care carried out in the home, mainly still by women (Bauman 1998; Jordan 1998; Levitas 1998; Hirsch 1999)

From the perspective of the recasting of the work–family axis of the social settlement and of gender equity, the model pursued is increasingly that described by Nancy Fraser (1997) as 'the universal breadwinner model' (see also Fitzpatrick 1998; Lewis 2000). The breadwinner role is universalized so that women can be citizen-earners alongside men, as opposed to encouraging both men and women to combine paid work and family responsibilities through a 'citizen-earner/carer' model (Lister 1997). The launch of a childcare strategy, as an integral part of economic policy, comprising both childcare provision and family-friendly employment policies, can be seen as supporting the universal breadwinner model. No real attempt has been made to promote fathers' involvement in childcare, through, for instance, paid parental leave, as recommended by the European Commission and pursued in some Scandinavian countries. Nevertheless, for all the strategy's limitations, including those of resources, the symbolic importance of government recognition, in the UK, as in continental Europe, that childcare is, at least partially, a public responsibility is not to be underestimated.

Lone mothers taking up paid work are targeted as among the main beneficiaries of the childcare strategy, in the face of evidence suggesting that lack of affordable and suitable childcare acts as a major barrier to lone mothers' employment (Bradshaw et al. 1996).[14] It is in relation to lone mothers that the government's work-biased approach has come under greatest criticism, despite broad support for policies that make it easier for them to move into paid work, if they want to. The decision to implement the Tory plan to abolish additional benefits for lone parents (originally proposed as a means of supporting the institution of marriage) was justified in part with reference to the paid work opportunities opened up by the New Deal and the childcare strategy.[15] This was interpreted by many lone mothers and their supporters as a denial of the importance of the unpaid work they do caring for their children which, research suggests, some lone mothers prioritize over paid work as more consistent with good mothering, at least while their children are young (Ford 1996; Duncan and Edwards 1999; van Drenth Knijn and Lewis, 1999). Reports suggest that the 'Listening to Women' initiative met complaints that mothers who want to care for their children at home are not valued (*Observer*, 25 July 1999).

It is not true to say that those providing care at home have been ignored completely. The government can, for instance, point to its carers strategy, its enhancement of maternity benefits and its proposals for second pension credits for those caring for young children or adults (although, as observed by the Pension Provision Group (1999), these are more restricted than for the basic pension).[16] Moreover, the Office for National Statistics is now developing household accounts, which include an estimate of the value of unpaid care and voluntary work. Yet, welcome as such initiatives are, they do not fully address what Levitas identifies as a tension 'between treating paid work as the defining factor in social inclusion, and recognising the value of unpaid work' (1998: 145). Underlying that tension is a narrow, gendered, interpretation of the obligations of citizenship (Lister 1997, 1999a, 1999b).

A new contract for welfare

This is a central issue for the government's welfare reform strategy. It raises the wider question of what kind of support should be provided in order to guarantee the financial security of those unable to undertake paid work for whatever reason. In theory, support for these groups is covered by the central principle guiding the 1998 Green Paper on welfare reform: 'work for those who can; security for those who cannot'. In practice, ministers tend to erect a false dichotomy between the two halves of the principle and a number of question marks remain over the strategy to ensure 'security for those who cannot' undertake paid work.

The vision as presented in the Green Paper is of 'Welfare 2020', built on 'three core values of work, security and opportunity' (DSS 1998a: 79). 'At the heart of the modern welfare state', it declares, 'will be a new contract between the citizen and the Government based on responsibilities and rights' (1998a: 80). In line with the philosophy outlined earlier, the emphasis is more on the former than the latter, perhaps reflecting the nature of a contract that has been imposed by the more powerful party rather than negotiated between equal parties.[17] Having listed the duties of government and of the individual, the 'new welfare contract' sets out, as a 'duty of us all', 'to help all individuals and families to realize their full potential and live a dignified life, by *promoting economic independence through work*, by relieving poverty where it cannot be prevented and by *building a strong and cohesive society where rights are matched by responsibilities*' (DSS 1998a: 80, emphasis added).

In his foreword and introduction, Blair describes the essence of the strategy as a 'third way'. This is spelt out in the Green Paper as a choice between 'a privatised future' with a residual safety net for the poorest, which is rejected as divisive, and a status quo supported by those who 'believe that poverty is relieved exclusively by cash hand outs'. This too is rejected in favour of the third way: 'a modern form of welfare that believes in empowerment not dependency' (DSS 1998a: 19).

Paid work is the route to empowerment, through an *active* welfare state (pursued more widely in the European Union also), while improving benefit levels is equated with a *passive* welfare state which encourages dependency, a dichotomy frequently emphasized by Blair (for instance, 1999b; for a critique, see Hirsch 1999). The research evidence which suggests that inadequate benefits for those out of work could undermine the government's educational and welfare-to-work policies (summarized in Lister 1998) is discounted. In fact, a few carefully targeted benefit increases have been announced for groups who are not expected to seek work (poorer pensioners, severely disabled people and carers). This reflects a distinction borrowed from the influential American analyst, David Ellwood, between 'those who should look to the labour market and those who should not', designed to ensure that work disincentives do not undermine the credibility and effectiveness of the benefits system (Deacon 2000; Glennerster 1999).

Perhaps surprisingly, the targeted improvements included an 80 per cent phased real increase in the income support rates for those with children under eleven by October 2001. The first phase in the 1998 Budget can be understood as an attempt to take the sting out of the unpopular cuts in lone parents' benefits announced earlier. The later phases were, though, announced rather quietly (perhaps so that *Daily Mail* readers would not notice). By focusing on children, partly in the name of 'strengthening family life' (Miliband 1999b), the government is able to do what it said it would not do. In a new twist in the politics of quiet redistribution, Brown has defended this as redistribution based on 'people exercising responsibilities' to bring up their children, in contrast to old forms of 'something for nothing' redistribution (*Today Programme*, 29 Mar. 1999). What we are perhaps seeing is an implicit acknowledgement of the criticisms of New Labour's work-biased construction of citizenship responsibilities, and that genuine equality of opportunity does require some redistribution of resources as well as of endowments. What it adds up to is 'redistribution with a purpose', that is, not redistribution for its own sake in the name of greater equality, but redistribution to promote RIO.

More consistent with the New Labour philosophy was another announcement in the 1999 Budget: a doubling of the maternity grant to £200 (increased by a further £100 in 2000, with a promise of £500 in 2002). This was, though, 'in return for parents meeting their responsibilities', that is, the grant will be conditional on attendance at child health check-ups, which is a completely new departure in British social security policy but a long-established practice in France.

For all the improvements that have been made, the more general case for a comprehensive review of the adequacy of benefit levels for those not in work has not been conceded, despite the fact that there has been no such public, official review since the levels proposed by Beveridge. Indeed, Darling continues to promote a false dichotomy between promoting paid work and improving benefits (*Guardian*, 16 June 1999). For those in work, means-tested tax credits are preferred over cash benefits, typical of a trend towards 'fiscalized social policy' in the Anglo-American world (Bashevkin 2000: 2).[18] This both reflects and reinforces an increasingly central role for the Treasury in the forging of the NWS, which could have significant, and potentially damaging, long-term implications (Piachaud 1999).

What the third way in welfare reform means for the *structure* of social security is still ambiguous. The Green Paper's rejection of a residual safety net model and espousal of a welfare state 'from which we all benefit' points to a more institutional model of social security. Yet the lack of any commitment to reduce the scope of means-testing and the heavy emphasis on private forms of provision, especially of pensions (as part of the more general emphasis on 'partnership'), do indicate a more limited two-tier model rather than one that gives the state a central role in ensuring the financial security of all its citizens.

The future of national insurance, widely viewed as the hallmark of the Beveridge model of social citizenship, has not been addressed explicitly either in the Green Paper or subsequently (apart from a couple of opaque mentions). Yet social insurance can be seen as promoting many of the government's own principles and objectives, including the notion of a welfare contract, the centrality of paid work and the provision of security in the face of risk (Bennett 1999b). One of the main criticisms of the current national insurance scheme is that it no longer adequately provides security to help people cope with the changing nature of economic and social risk. This was addressed by the Commission on Social Justice, which put forward proposals for a modernized, more inclusive social insurance system, better attuned to the position and needs of women. These proposals, which offered an alternative modernizing path, have been, more or less, ignored by the government. While there have been some policy initiatives consistent with them, overall the drift towards greater reliance on means-testing implicit in reforms to a number of contributory benefits disadvantages women (Lister 1992).

According to Nicholas Timmins, public policy editor of the *Financial Times*, 'national insurance is dead . . . ministers know they are accelerating its destruction, but do not want to talk about it much' (*Financial Times*, 22 Nov. 1999). Indeed, ministers are disinclined to debate the shape of the social security system's underlying architecture more generally. Such debates are dismissed as 'arid' and as about 'dogmatic preferences' (DSS

1999; *House of Commons Hansard* 1999). Blair used his Beveridge lecture to stress that in the mix of 'universal and targeted help', 'the one is not "superior" or "more principled" than the other' (1999b). The government's view is that 'the contributory principle, means-tested benefits or universal benefits are not an end in themselves but merely a means of delivering the Government's policy objectives – it is the outcomes which are important' (DSS 2000: para. 2). The result is, that as Darling pursues his 'benefit by benefit' review (a tactic adopted also by his Conservative predecessor, Peter Lilley, to minimize opposition), there is a danger that the shift in the fulcrum of the social security system under the Conservatives towards means-testing is being continued by default. This is without public debate about the appropriate balance between the different kinds of benefits – contributory, means-tested and categorical (Social Security Committee 2000).[19]

The Economist has declared approvingly that 'Tony Blair's Government has crossed the Rubicon from . . . the left bank of welfare-for-all to the right bank of means testing' (6 Mar. 1999). Likewise, in Timmins's view, 'the country is witnessing the last death throes of universalism, although its ghost will live on' (*Financial Times*, 19 Nov. 1998). Even if possibly something of an overstatement (given, for example, counter-indications such as an increase in the real value of child benefit and some limited improvements to national insurance benefits), his observation acts as a hazard warning. Instead of a 'third way' in social security reform, we may be moving further down the highway towards the very model rejected in the Green Paper, that of a more residual social security system typical of liberal regimes such as the US, even if, as argued by Howard Glennerster (1999), the specific policy lane is different from that adopted in the US.[20] This takes us even further away than previously from more institutionalized continental and nordic European models. Although these models are themselves also under pressure (Cox 1998), there is considerable resistance among other centre-left governments in the European Union to following Blair down the third way (Taylor 1999).

Conclusion

It is still too soon for any definitive assessment as to the destination of the route being mapped out towards a NWS.[21] Cutting through the thickets of rhetoric to discern the actual path is not always easy, particularly when the two appear to be pointing in different directions. Nevertheless, as this chapter has demonstrated, there are a number of clear signposts.

Welfare increasingly will be delivered through partnerships between state, private, voluntary and informal sectors. The state sector itself will promote 'joined-up government' as part of the managerial mode that defines the new organizational settlement. Typical of this managerial mode is a 'what matters is what works' (Blair 1998a: 4) approach, which stands in contrast to, and sometimes in tension with, the rhetoric of 'radical welfare reform', although the two are bound together by a discourse of modernization.

This tension is most apparent in the field of social security, which stands at the heart of the welfare reform project. On the one hand, there is a clear determination to forge a 'third way' of responsibility, inclusion and opportunity through paid work. The central aim of social security reform is to reduce 'welfare dependence' as part of a moral crusade (Darling 1999). This is primarily what the 'new contract for welfare' is about. The principle of 'work for those who can' takes priority over that of 'security for those who cannot' so as not to jeopardize work incentives. Although the concern with work incentives is hardly new, what is novel is the way in which paid work is elevated to the primary motor of welfare reform, as part of a concerted attempt to change the culture of the social security system from that of 'passive' provider of benefits to 'active' routemaster towards independence.

On the other hand, incremental reforms to the structure of social security are presented as simply cost-effective, modernizing changes. This serves to divert attention from important issues of principle that they raise (Powell and Hewitt 1998). Darling, in particular, is impatient of suggestions that the broad direction of reform is to shift the welfare regime mix further towards a liberal, residual two-tier model and away from more institutionalized continental European models. Yet, even if this is not the *intention*, the sum effect of a series of pragmatic steps could be a significant shift in the overall model of social security. As Esping-Andersen's welfare regime analysis (1990) underlines, this has implications for the overall fabric of social relations, which are more likely to be exclusionary than inclusive. It is likely to spell greater financial insecurity for many than under a more institutionalized model, as means-tested and private forms of provision play a more dominant role.

How far down this particular road the government is prepared to go is not yet clear. It is not primarily what the NWS is about, even though the destination will be crucial to it. What the NWS *is* primarily about is a modern citizenship contract in which the social rights of citizens are contingent upon the exercise of responsibilities. The essence of these clauses of the contract are likely to survive any future change of government, thus suggesting we *are* moving towards a new welfare settlement.

It is also a contract that promises social inclusion and opportunity rather than greater equality. Whether it will be able to deliver genuine social inclusion, together with the pledge to end child poverty in twenty years (and halve it in ten), through the policies outlined here and in the face of entrenched inequalities of income, wealth and power remains to be seen.[22]

NOTES

This is an expanded version of a paper given at the 1999 Social Policy Association conference, published in abbreviated form in Edwards. R. and Glover, J., *Risk and Citizenship: Key Issues in Welfare*, (London: Routledge, 2001). Other versions have been published in E. Broadbent (ed.), *Equality and the Democratic State*, (Toronto: University of Toronto Press, 2001) and *Renewal*, 8(4) (2000). I am grateful to Fran Bennett, John Clarke and Colin Hay for their very helpful comments on the first draft.

1 The language of 'welfare' is itself instructive. In New Labour parlance it can refer both to the welfare state as a whole and more specifically to social security. This second usage bears the mark of US discourses in which welfare refers to means-tested assistance and as such has pejorative overtones which taint its deployment as a synonym for social security in the UK.
2 In fact, as Clarke and Newman (1997) argue, the process of 'rolling back' the state involved a '"rolling out" of state power but in new, dispersed, forms', as its regulatory powers were extended through, for instance, contracts with the voluntary sector.
3 The negative construction of 'producer interests' is a key discursive legacy from the new right critique of public services.
4 The Commission on Social Justice was established as an independent commission by the leader of the Labour Party, the late John Smith, 'to develop a practical vision of economic and social reform for the 21st century'.
5 George and Wilding (1994) describe public–private partnerships as a key 'plank' in the 'middle way' which was embraced both by traditional Conservatives and key figures such as Beveridge and Keynes. I am grateful to Jane Lewis for the insight into the significance of 'partnership' to the NWS.
6 The greatest purchase of the user-led model has been in the area of community care. There has been little attempt to apply it to the social security system.
7 According to estimates supplied by the Institute for Fiscal Studies, the potential gain for those in the top decile was about thirty times that for those in the bottom three deciles (see Lister 1999c).
8 This exemplifies Jessop's formulation of the post-Fordist, 'Schumpetarian workfare state' in which 'redistributive welfare rights take second place to a productivist re-ordering of social policy' (Jessop 1994: 24). See also Holden

(1999) who argues that the emphasis on education is primarily about promoting international competitiveness.

9   The potential and actual tension created for lone parents between parental responsibilities for the good behaviour and education of their children and paid work responsibilities is glossed over (Standing 1999).

10 See the Report of the Fabian Society's Commission on Taxation and Citizenship (2000), which calls for a debate about the role of taxation in citizenship.

11 The Explanatory Notes on the Welfare Reform and Pensions Bill outlined the rules. 'People who are terminally ill, over pension age, or getting housing benefit/council tax benefit while in full-time work, will be exempt from interviews'. Interviews will be deferred where a person is 'recovering from a major operation'; where 'a lone parent has recently had a baby'; or where 'someone's mental illness is such that it would not be appropriate for him or her to have the interview'. There will be 'no group exemptions for severely disabled people, full-time carers, or people with children under 5' on the basis that people should be treated as individuals, not categories (*Welfare Rights Bulletin*, 150 (June 1999)).

12 For an insightful analysis of New Labour's welfare discourses see Fairclough (2000).

13 For a useful overall assessment, see Bennett and Walker (1998) and Oppenheim (1999).

14 In-depth research, however, suggests that childcare is only one factor in the complex decisions involved for lone parents considering whether to take paid work (Ford 1996).

15 The government's more general stance on lone parenthood is one of ambivalence, in the face of the decomposition of the postwar social settlement. It acknowledges that family policy cannot 'turn the clock back' but also wants 'to strengthen the institution of marriage' (Home Office 1998: 4).

16 There has also been some easing of the rules governing the undertaking of voluntary work while on benefit.

17 Nancy A. Naples has analysed the discursive power of the notion of the 'social contract' in the US context. She argues that it has 'privileged individualist and coercive behavioural strategies such as workfare and inhibited the incorporation of structural analyses into the resultant welfare policy' (1997: 908). For a more general critique of social contract theory see Pateman (1988).

18 This is likely to have an adverse impact on the gendered distribution of income in one-earner couples, where payment of working families tax credit is made through the wage packet (Goode, Callender and Lister 1998). However, from 2003 it is proposed that a new 'integrated child credit' will be paid direct to the caring parent. This will be complemented by an 'employment tax credit' paid through the wage packet to low paid adults.

19 Between 1979 and 1997–8, the proportion of social security spending devoted to means-testing increased from 16 to 34 per cent.

20 In some ways the route points more towards the Australian model under which means-tested benefits and tax credits are not confined to the very poorest.
21 For a more comprehensive interim assessment, see Powell (1999).
22 On the basis of a careful analysis of the prospects for delivering the pledge to end child poverty, Piachaud (1999: 160) concludes that its achievement will depend, in part, on 'much more redistribution'.

REFERENCES

Andrews, G. (1999) 'New Left and New Labour: Modernisation or a New Modernity?', *Soundings*, 13, 14–24.

Bashevkin, S. (2000) *Road-testing the Third Way: Welfare Reform in Canada, Britain and the United States*. Jerusalem: Hebrew University of Jerusalem.

Bauman, Z. (1998) *Work, Consumerism and the New Poor*. Buckingham: Open University Press.

Beer, S. (1998) 'The Roots of New Labour: Liberalism Rediscovered', *The Economist*, 7 Feb. pp. 23–5.

Benefits (1999) 'The Future of Pensions', 26.

Benington, J. and Donnison, D. (1999) 'New Labour and Social Exclusion: The Search for a Third Way, or Just Gilding the Ghetto Again?', in H. Dean and R. Woods (eds), *Social Policy Review 11*. Luton: Social Policy Association.

Bennett F. (1998) 'Comment: Unravelling Poverty', in C. Oppenheim (ed.), *An Inclusive Society: Strategies for Tackling Poverty*. London: Institute for Public Policy Research.

—— (1999a) 'Commentary on A. Darling, "Rebuilding the Welfare State: The Moral Case for Reform"', in G. Kelly (ed.), *Is New Labour Working?* London: Fabian Society.

—— (1999b) Evidence to the Social Security Committee Inquiry on the Contributory Principle.

Bennett F. and Walker, R. (1998) *Working with Work: An Initial Assessment of Welfare to Work*. York: Joseph Rowntree Foundation.

Beveridge, W. (1942) *Social Insurance and Allied Services*. London: HMSO.

Blackman, T. and Palmer, A. (1999) 'Continuity or Modernisation? The Emergence of New Labour's Welfare State', in H. Dean and R. Woods (eds), *Social Policy Review 11*. Luton: Social Policy Association.

Blair, T. (1995a) 'Let us Face the Future – the 1945 Anniversary Lecture', Fabian Society, London.

—— (1995b) 'The Rights We Enjoy Reflect the Duties We Owe', Spectator Lecture, London, 22 Mar.

—— (1996) 'My Vision for Britain', in G. Radice (ed.), *What Needs to Change: New Visions for Britain*. London: HarperCollins.

——(1997a) Speech given regarding the launch of the government's new Social Exclusion Unit, Stockwell Park School, 8 Dec.

——(1997b) 'Why We Must Help Those Excluded from Society', *Independent*, 8 Dec.

——(1997c) 'Introduction', in *New Labour Because Britain Deserves Better*, election manifesto. London: Labour Party

——(1998a) *The Third Way: New Politics for the New Century*. London: Fabian Society.

——(1998b) 'The Government's Strategy', in *The Government's Annual Report 97/98*. London: Stationery Office.

——(1999a) Speech to the Institute for Public Policy Research, London, 14 Jan.

——(1999b) Beveridge Lecture, Toynbee Hall, London, 18 Mar., reproduced in R. Walker (ed.), *Ending Child Poverty*. Bristol: Policy Press.

——(1999c) 'Introduction', in *The Government's Annual Report 98/99*. London: Stationery Office.

——(1999d) 'The Fight against Poverty – "The One Nation Coalition of Haves and Have-nots"', speech to Centrepoint, London.

——(2000) Written answers to questions, *House of Commons Hansard*, 16 Mar.

Blair, T. and Schröder, G. (1999) 'Europe: The Third Way/Die Neue Mitte', reproduced in *The Spokesman*, 66, 27–37.

Bonoli, G. and Palier, B. (1998) 'Changing the Politics of Social Programmes: Innovative Change in British and French Welfare Reform', *Journal of European Social Policy*, 8(4), 317–30.

Bradshaw, J. et al. (1996) *The Employment of Lone Parents: A Comparison of Policy in 20 Countries*. London: Family Policy Studies Centre.

Brown G. (1996) 'New Labour and Equality', Second John Smith Lecture, Edinburgh, 19 Apr.

——(2001) 'Let the People Look after Themselves', *The Times*, 11 Jan.

Cabinet Office (1999) *Modernising Government*, Cm 4310. London: Stationery Office.

Chen, S. (1999) *Citizens and Taxes*. London: Fabian Society.

Clarke, J. (1997) 'Capturing the Customer', *Self, Agency and Society*, 1(1), 55–73.

——(1998) 'Consumerism', in G. Hughes (ed.), *Imaging Welfare Futures*. London: Routledge.

Clarke, J. and Hoggett, P. (1999) 'Regressive Modernisation? The Changing Patterns of Social Services Delivery in the United Kingdom', in H. Wollmann and E. Schröter (eds), *Comparing Public Sector Reform in Britain and Germany*. Aldershot: Ashgate.

Clarke, J. and Newman, J. (1997) *The Managerial State*. London: Sage.

——(1998) 'A Modern British People? New Labour and the Reconstruction of Welfare', paper presented to the Discourse Analysis and Social Research Conference, Copenhagen, Sept.

Clarke, J., Cochrane, A. and McLaughlin, E. (eds) (1994) *Managing Social Policy*. London: Sage.

Clarke, J., Gewirtz, S. and McLaughlin, E. (eds) (2000) *New Managerialism, New Welfare?* London: Sage.

Commission on Social Justice (1994) *Social Justice: Strategies for National Renewal.* London: Vintage.

Commission on Taxation and Citizenship (2000) *Paying for Progress. A New Politics of Tax and Spending.* London: Fabian Society.

Considine, M. (1999) 'Markets, Networks and the New Welfare State: Employment Assistance Reforms in Australia', *Journal of Social Policy*, 28(2), 183–203.

Coote, A. (1999) 'Labour's Love's Lost on Worcester Woman', *Fabian Review*, 111(2), 2–3.

Cox, R. H. (1998) 'The Consequences of Welfare Reform: How Conceptions of Social Rights are Changing', *Journal of Social Policy*, 27(1), 1–16.

Craig, G. (1999) 'Take your Partners?' *Benefits*, 26, 34–6.

Darling, A. (1999) 'Our Children's Future', speech at St Bart's Centre, East Ham, London, 18 July.

Davis, E. (1999) 'The Way through the Welfare Wood', in A. Kilmarnock (ed.), *The Social Market and the State.* London: Social Market Foundation.

Deacon, A. (ed.) (1996) *Stakeholder Welfare.* London: Institute of Economic Affairs.

——(1997) ' "Welfare to Work": Options and Issues', in M. May, E. Brunsdon and G. Craig (eds), *Social Policy Review 9.* London: Social Policy Association.

——(1998) 'The Green Paper on Welfare Reform: A Case for Enlightened Self Interest?', *Political Quarterly*, 69(3).

——(2000) 'Learning from the US? The Influence of American Ideas upon "New Labour" Thinking on Welfare Reform', *Policy and Politics*, 28(1), 5–18.

Dean, H. and Woods, R. (eds) (1999) *Social Policy Review 11.* Luton: Social Policy Association.

DoH (1998) *Partnership in Action.* London: Department of Health.

Driver S. and Martell L. (1997) 'New Labour's Communitarianisms', *Critical Social Policy*, 17(3), 27–46.

——(1998) *New Labour: Politics after Thatcherism.* Cambridge: Polity.

DSS (1998a) *New Ambitions for our Country: A New Contract for Welfare.* London: Stationery Office.

——(1998b) *Households below Average Income 1979–1996/7.* Leeds: Corporate Document Services.

——(1998c) *A New Contract for Welfare: The Gateway to Work.* London: Stationery Office.

——(1999a) 'Means Testing: The History', note for meeting with Social Security Consortium.

——(1999b) *A New Contract for Welfare: Children's Rights and Parents' Responsibilities.* London: Stationery Office.

——(2000) *Report on the Contributory Principle*, Cm 4867. London: Stationery Office.

Duffy K. (1998) 'Combating Social Exclusion and Promoting Social Integration in the European Union', in C. Oppenheim (ed.), *An Inclusive Society: Strategies for Tackling Poverty.* London: Institute for Public Policy Research.

Duncan S. and Edwards R. (1999) *Lone Mothers, Paid Work and Gendered Moral Rationalities.* Basingstoke: Macmillan.

Dwyer, P. (1998) 'Conditional Citizens? Welfare Rights and Responsibilities in the Late 1990s', *Critical Social Policy,* 18(4), 493–517.

Esping-Andersen, G. (1990) *The Three Worlds of Welfare Capitalism.* Cambridge: Polity.

Fairclough, N. (2000) *New Labour, New Language?* London and New York: Routledge.

Finalyson, A. (1998) 'Tony Blair and the Jargon of Modernisation', *Soundings,* 10, 11–27.

Finn, D. (1999) 'From Full Employment to Employability: New Labour and the Unemployed', Social Policy Association Annual Conference, Roehampton Institute.

Fitzpatrick T. (1998) 'The Rise of Market Collectivism', in E. Brunsdon, H. Dean and R. Woods (eds), *Social Policy Review 10.* London: Social Policy Association.

Ford R. (1996) *Childcare in the Balance.* London: Policy Studies Institute.

Fraser N. (1997) *Justice Interruptus.* New York and London: Routledge.

Freeden, M. (1999) 'The Ideology of New Labour', *Political Quarterly* 70(1), 42–51.

Gamble, A. and Kenny, M. (1999) 'Now We Are Two', *Fabian Review,* 111(2), 10–11.

George, V. and Wilding, P. (1994) *Welfare and Ideology.* Hemel Hempstead: Harvester Wheatsheaf.

Gewirtz, S. (1999) 'Education Action Zones: Emblems of the Third Way?', in H. Dean and R. Woods (eds), *Social Policy Review 11.* Luton: Social Policy Association.

Giddens, A. (1998) *The Third Way: The Renewal of Social Democracy.* Cambridge: Polity.

Glennerster, H. (1999) 'A Third Way?', in H. Dean and R. Woods, (eds), *Social Policy Review II.* Luton: Social Policy Association.

Goode J., Callender C. and Lister R. (1998) *Purse or Wallet? Gender Inequalities and Income Distribution within Families on Benefits.* London: Policy Studies Institute.

Hall, S. and Mawson, J. (1999) 'Joined Up Regeneration', *New Economy* 6(4), 209–14.

Hay, C. (1998) 'Globalisation, Welfare Retrenchment and the "Logic of no Alternative"; Why Second-Best Won't Do', *Journal of Social Policy,* 27(4), 525–32.

Heron, E. and Dwyer, P. (1999) 'Doing the Right Thing: Labour's Attempt to Forge a New Welfare Deal between the Individual and the State', *Social Policy and Administration,* 33(1), 91–104.

Hirsch, D. (1999) *Welfare Beyond Work: Active Participation in a New Welfare State*. York: Joseph Rowntree Foundation.
HM Treasury (1998) *Modern Public Services for Britain: Investing in Reform*, pocket guide. London: HM Treasury.
——(1999) *Tackling Poverty and Extending Opportunity*. London: HM Treasury.
Holden, C. (1999) 'Globalization, Social Exclusion and Labour's New Work Ethic', *Critical Social Policy*, 19(4), 529–38.
Home Office (1998) *Supporting Families*, London: Stationery Office.
Hughes, G. (ed.) (1998) *Imagining Welfare Futures*. London: Routledge.
Hughes, G. and Lewis, G. (1998) *Unsettling Welfare*. London: Routledge.
Hughes, G. and Little, A. (1999) 'The Contradictions of New Labour's Communitarianism', *Imprints* 4(1), 37–62.
Hulls, D. (1999) 'Tackling Social Exclusion', *New Economy*, 6(4), 183–7.
Jessop, B. (1994) 'The Transition to Post-Fordism and the Schumpeterian Workfare State' in R. Burrows and B. Loader (eds), *Towards a Post-Fordist Welfare State?* London and New York: Routledge.
Johnson, N. (1990) *Reconstructing the Welfare State*. Hemel Hempstead: Harvester Wheatsheaf.
——(1999) 'The Personal Social Services and Community Care', in M. Powell (ed.), *New Labour, New Welfare State?* Bristol: Policy Press.
Jordan, B. (1998) *The New Politics of Welfare*. London: Sage.
Kemp, P. (1999a) 'Housing Policy under New Labour', in M. Powell (ed.), *New Labour, New Welfare State?* Bristol: Policy Press.
——(1999b) 'Making the Market Work? New Labour and the Housing Question', in H. Dean and R. Woods (eds), *Social Policy Review II*. Luton: Social Policy Association.
Kleinman, M. (1998) *Include Me Out? The New Politics of Place and Poverty*. London: Centre for the Analysis of Social Exclusion.
——(1999) 'There Goes the Neighbourhood: Area Policies and Social Exclusion', *New Economy*, 6(4), 188–92.
Labour Party (1999) *Modernising the NHS*. London: Labour Party.
Le Grand, J. (1997) 'Knights, Knaves or Pawns? Human Behaviour and Social Policy', *Journal of Social Policy*, 26(2), 149–69.
Levitas R. (1998) *The Inclusive Society? Social Exclusion and New Labour*. Basingstoke: Macmillan.
Lewis, J. (2000) 'Work and Care', in H. Dean, R. Sykes and R. Woods (eds), *Social Policy Review 12*. Newcastle: Social Policy Association.
Lister, R. (1992) *Women's Economic Dependency and Social Security*. Manchester: Equal Opportunities Commission.
——(1996) 'In Search of the "Underclass"', in R. Lister (ed.), *Charles Murray and the Underclass: The Developing Debate*. London: Institute of Economic Affairs in association with the *Sunday Times*.
——(1997) *Citizenship: Feminist Perspectives*. Basingstoke: Macmillan.
——(1998) 'Fighting Social Exclusion ... with One Hand Tied behind our Back', *New Economy*, 5(1), 14–18.

—— (1999a) 'What Welfare Provisions do Women Need to become Full Citizens?', in S. Walby (ed.), *New Agendas for Women*. Basingstoke: Macmillan.

—— (1999b) '"Reforming Welfare around the Work Ethic": New Gendered and Ethical Perspectives on Work and Care', *Policy and Politics*, 27(2), 233–46.

—— (1999c) 'Fabian Debate: Should Labour be Seeking a Lower Basic Rate of Income Tax?', *Fabian Review*, 111(2), 18.

Maddock, S. (1999) 'Health Action Zones', *Renewal* 7(2), 62–7.

Marquand D. (1998) 'The Blair Paradox', *Prospect*, May.

Metz, E. (1999) 'Towards a National Anti-poverty Strategy?', *Poverty Matters*, 20, 3–5.

Miliband, D. (1999a) 'This is the modern world' *Fabian Review*, 111(4), 11–13.

—— (1999b) 'The Third Way is Not Just Hot Air and Spin', *Daily Telegraph*, 15 June.

Mouffe, C. (1998) 'The Radical Centre: A Politics without Adversary', *Soundings*, 9, 11–23.

Mulgan G. (1998) 'Social Exclusion: Joined Up Solutions to Joined Up Problems', in C. Oppenheim (ed.), *An Inclusive Society: Strategies for Tackling Poverty*. London: Institute for Public Policy Research.

Muschamp, Y., Jamieson, I. and Lauder, H. (1999) 'Education, Education, Education', in M. Powell (ed.), *New Labour, New Welfare State?* Bristol: Policy Press.

Naples, N. A. (1997) 'The "New Consensus" on the Gendered "Social Contract": The 1987–1988 US Congressional Hearings', *Signs*, 22(4), 907–45.

New Economy (1999) 'Neighbourhoods and Exclusion', 6(4), 183–214.

Newman, J. (1998) 'Managerialism and social welfare' in G. Hughes and G. Lewis, *op cit*.

Oppenheim, C. (1999) 'Welfare Reform and the Labour Market: A "Third Way"?', *Benefits*, 25, 1–5.

Pateman, C. (1988) *The Sexual Contract*. Cambridge: Polity.

Paton, C. (1999) 'New Labour's Health Policy: The New Healthcare State', in M. Powell (ed.), *New Labour, New Welfare State?* Bristol: Policy Press.

Peck J. (1998) 'New Labourers? Making a New Deal for the Workless Class', paper, Manchester University.

Pension Provision Group (1999) *Response to the Pensions Green Paper*. London: Department of Social Security.

Piachaud, D. (1999) 'Progress on Poverty', *New Economy*, 6(3), 154–60.

Powell, M. (ed.) (1999) *New Labour, New Welfare State?* Bristol: Policy Press.

Powell, M. and Hewitt, M. (1998) 'The End of the Welfare State?', *Social Policy and Administration*, 32(1), 1–13.

Rees, A. M. (1996) 'T. H. Marshall and the Progress of Citizenship', in M. Bulmer and A. M. Rees (eds), *Citizenship Today*. London: UCL Press.

Rose, N. (1999) 'Inventiveness in Politics', *Economy and Society*, 28(3), 467–93.

Rouse, J. and Smith, G. (1999) 'Accountability', in M. Powell (ed.), *New Labour, New Welfare State?* Bristol: Policy Press.

Social Exclusion Unit (2001) *A New Commitment to Neighbourhood Renewal: National Strategy Action Plan*. London: Cabinet Office.

Social Security Committee (2000) *The Contributory Principle*, HC56. London: Stationery Office.

Standing, K. (1999) 'Lone Mothers and "Parental" Involvement: A Contradiction in Policy?', *Journal of Social Policy* 28(3), 479–95.

Taylor, R. (1999) 'The Social Democrats Come Roaring Back', *New Statesman*, 20 Dec., pp. 25–7.

Theodore, N. and Peck, J. (1999) 'Welfare-to-Work: National Problems, Local Solutions?', *Critical Social Policy*, 19(4), 485–510.

Turok, I. and Edge, N. (1999) *The Jobs Gap in Britain's Cities: Employment Loss and Labour Market Consequences*. Bristol: Policy Press.

Turok, I. and Webster, D. (1998) 'The New Deal: Jeopardised by the Geography of Unemployment?', *Local Economy*, 13, 309–28.

van Drenth, A., Knijn, T. and Lewis, J. (1999) 'Sources of Income for Lone Mother Families: Policy Changes in Britain and the Netherlands and the Experiences of Divorced Women', *Journal of Social Policy*, 28(4), 619–41.

Walker, A. (1999) 'The Third Way for Pensions (by Way of Thatcherism and Avoiding Today's Pensioners)', *Critical Social Policy*, 19(4), 511–27.

Walker, R. with Howard, M. (2000) *The Making of a Welfare Class?* Bristol: Policy Press.

Webster D. (1997) 'Welfare to Work: Why the Theories behind the Policies Don't Work', *Working Brief*, June, 10–11.

White S. (1998) 'Interpreting the Third Way: Not One Road, but Many' *Renewal*, 6(2), 17–30.

Williams, F. (1989) *Social Policy: A Critical Introduction*. Cambridge: Polity.

8

The New Political Economy of Postwar Britain

David Coates

Throughout the entire postwar period, the state of the British economy has preoccupied and constrained the British political class with a consistency and a potency unmatched by any other issue. The Attlee government was confronted, from its earliest days in office, with the awesome consequences of the US's abrupt cancellation of lend-lease; and it spent the remainder of its term struggling with inadequacies in economic supply, problems of overseas payments, and difficulties created by the exchange rate of sterling. So too did many of the governments that followed. From the Macmillan government's balance of payments crisis of 1961, the devaluation battles of the 1960s and the IMF loan of 1976, through to John Major's 'Black Wednesday' and New Labour's difficulties with the economy's entrenched deficit on its balance of payments, the British economy has been a persistent source of *difficulties* for its politicians. But it has also been an immense source of *strength* to them as well, generating as it has a rising level of general prosperity that was literally beyond the conception of both politicians and their electorate as the postwar period opened. Since 1945 the more favoured section of each successive generation has known a new plateau of prosperity: a plateau in the 1960s for perhaps two-thirds of the baby boomers in their young adulthood; and an even more bountiful plateau of prosperity in the 1990s, for the same segment of that same generation in their middle age, and for their children. The postwar British economy has thus generated prosperity and poverty among the electorate, and problems and possibilities for the politicians; and it has imposed its Janus-faced presence on all aspects of postwar British social and political life. Because it has, if we are adequately to grasp the complex interplay of politics and society in Britain since 1945, it is with issues of political economy that we ought properly to begin: by looking in sequence at the changing shape of the British economy (the first section of this chapter), at its changing performance over time (the second section), and at the political projects which have competed to enhance that performance over time (the third section).

The changing state of the British economy

The British economy that emerged from the Second World War possessed a manufacturing sector stretched to full capacity, the legatee in its troubles of a powerful mixture of interwar underinvestment and wartime erosion. It was an economy in which employment was still heavily concentrated in the primary sector and in heavy industry. The civilian labour force in 1946 was just over 18 million in total. More than a million of those workers were still in agriculture, and just under three-quarters of a million worked in the mines (Cairncross 1985: 394). Ship-building, railways and textiles remained major employers of labour; and they remained so well into the 1950s. Employment in the textile industry, for example, peaked as late as 1951, at 1.1 million: twice as many as were then employed in the key motor vehicle and component industries that were later to fuel postwar British manufacturing growth. The new industries (and the new geographical centres) of major postwar employment and output growth were there in embryonic form during the Attlee years, but the bulk of the immediate postwar economy remained where the interwar one had been. It remained centred in the northern river valleys and it remained locked in industries and companies that could trace their heritage (and their periods of greatest success) back to Britain's brief Victorian period of world manufacturing supremacy.

Wartime levels of demand, and the immediate postwar conditions of pent-up domestic consumption and disrupted overseas competitors, gave this older British economy one last breathing space; but that respite proved both short-lived and (as we will see later) in the long term extremely costly. Thus one important element in the postwar British economic story line is the sequential rundown of many of those industries as sources of employment and output growth. Cotton was the first of the old industries to contract dramatically, railways were the second, mining the third: all against a background of steady labour expulsion from an increasingly mechanized and chemical-based agricultural sector. The employment numbers for cotton fell from 200,000 to 54,000 between 1961 and 1980. Those for the rail industry fell from 649,000 to 192,000 between 1948 and 1992. By then agricultural employment was down to 134,000, and the numbers employed in mining were in free-fall. There were 697,000 people working for the National Coal Board in 1956. That number was down to 287,000 by 1971. It had fallen to 184,000 by the start of the 1984–5 miners' strike; and by 2000 (in the tiny privatized remnants of a once proud industry) was down to 13,000. In the last forty years of the twentieth century, most of the old industries on which Britain's Victorian supremacy had been built shrank away to a shadow of their former selves. The British mining industry just went that one stage further, and quite literally disappeared.

For a generation however, this contraction of the older industrial base was more than matched by the employment and output growth produced by Britain's new industries. These were, in the main, located further south than their older predecessors. The centre of gravity of the new industries lay in the British Midlands rather than the British North. The new industries were also more consumer focused than the old ones – directed at mass markets both at home and abroad in a way that only textiles had been in the Victorian period. The British car industry was the flagship industry of this industrial renaissance, driving an expansion of employment and output in a series of component industries, and integrating with linked processes of expansion in the production of other consumer durables, in new science-based petrochemical and pharmaceutical industries, and in the new energy industries (electricity, oil and even to a limited degree, nuclear power). In fact, 'nearly one-third of industrial growth in the economy in the 1950s and 1960s has been attributed to the motor industry and its suppliers' (Church 1994: 54). Whole new communities sprang up around its new production sites, communities which in their turn stimulated employment in the construction of houses, factories and roads. Employment in the car industry (and its linked suppliers) reached 800,000 by 1973 as manufacturing employment in total (which had stood at 4.3 million in 1946) peaked in 1966 at 9.2 million. More than one worker in three in Britain in 1966 worked directly in the UK's expanding manufacturing sector.

The other two-thirds then worked either in that shrinking older base to which we have already referred, or in the other two great growth points in employment and output in the postwar UK economy in its pre-1973 prime. They either worked in the expanding private service sector – in retailing and in banking (though the great expansion in banking employment was still yet to come) – or they were numbered among the expanding ranks of public sector welfare employment. By 1975 public sector employment had reached 7.2 million in the UK, with 2 million people working in the nationalized industries and 3 million in education, welfare and local government (Coates 1984: 220). Then, as employment in publicly provided services stagnated after 1975, private sector service employment soared. Employment in distribution, hotels and catering rose between 1980 and 1997 from 4.3 million to 5.1 million. Employment in banking and finance rose even more quickly over the same period: from 2.4 million to 3.9 million (*Financial Times*, 2 Mar. 1998, p. 8). As the domestic strength of British retailing and the international standing of British-based financial institutions emerged as powerful new points of strength in the British economy in the 1980s, employment in those sectors began dramatically to outstrip that in a manufacturing sector that was by then rapidly shrinking. In fact by the year 2000 twice as many people worked in retailing and banking as in the entirety of British-based manufacturing, so giving credence to the claim that Britain had genuinely become, by then, a nation of shopkeepers.

For by the 1980s the earlier expansion of employment in manufacturing in the mass production consumer industries of the British Midlands had given way to substantial deindustrialization. In the wake of the first oil crisis, and lower levels of output and productivity growth in the global economy as a whole, the depth and range of international competition in manufactured goods intensified, and British-based producers found themselves increasingly threatened in first export and then domestic markets. Occasionally, whole British-based industries succumbed to that competition: for a period, that was true of the British motor-bike industry, and of British-based white goods and television production. Foreign-owned transplants would, in the 1990s, restore some of that British-based output; but for two decades at least, British-based manufacturing industries that were geared to mass consumer markets shrank (in both output and – more dramatically – in employment) under a gale of foreign competition. The British car industry was the major casualty of that gale. It reset its centres of ownership from British companies (and for a time, the British state) to foreign ones (not just American, as in the past, but also French, Japanese and briefly – with BMW's disastrous purchase and later sale of Rover in the 1990s – German companies too). It also dropped its employment levels from 505,000 in car assembly in 1971 to 280,000 in 1993 and to 218,000 by 1999. Not all sectors of British-based manufacturing lost out in this way. Pharmaceuticals did not; aircraft production did not; and in both those sectors, Britain remained the home base of leading edge companies in the global economy. But overall, domestically based manufacturing suffered a significant shrinkage in world strength and in local employment. Overall indeed British manufacturing shed employment – particularly full-time employment – at an unprecedented rate. In the 1980–2 recession, in particular, 'manufacturing employment fell from 7.4 million to 5.4 million – a reduction of 2.0

Table 8.1 Structure of employment (percentages)

	Agriculture	Industry	Services
1951	8.9	43.6	47.4
1961	6.6	44.3	48.7
1971	4.3	42.9	52.8
1981	3.2	35.3	61.5
1991	1.9	26.9	71.2
1998 (Nov.)	2.0	22.0	76.0

Sources: S. Glyn and A. Booth, *Modern Britain* (London: Routledge, 1996); *Employment Audit*, 10 (1999), p. 4.

million or 27 per cent of the 1979 manufacturing labour force' (Wells 1989: 25). A further 1.8 million jobs were lost in the 1989–92 recession, though this time that job loss spread south as well, taking in not just northern and Midlands manufacturing jobs, but also service jobs in the hitherto prosperous and recession-immune South East: to leave British manufacturing employment by 1993 at 4 million. By then, only 18 per cent of British workers were employed in manufacturing, against 51 per cent in the non-governmental service sector, and 15 per cent in public service; and the manufacturing sector, which as late as 1979 had contributed 30 per cent to total GDP, contributed only a modest 21 per cent (Beavis 1997: 1)

This changing pattern of performance between economic sectors over the postwar period as a whole had three main consequences. It changed the economy's spatial and industrial centres of gravity; it triggered fundamental shifts in ownership and control; and it created whole new sets of economically based social and political actors.

Shifting centres of gravity

The spatial rearrangement of the economy's centre of gravity in the postwar period was particularly stark, leaving as it did once prosperous areas in decay and decline. Over the last fifty years the broad movement of prosperity in postwar Britain has been south and east. Immediately after the war, industrial activity remained largely the business of northern England, Scotland, Northern Ireland and southern Wales. Britain in the 1940s was still an economy based primarily on coalfields, located in river valleys, and positioned alongside major ports. By the 1960s, however, all that had changed. The new industries of the long postwar boom were largely Midlands based and electricity powered. As Newcastle and

Glasgow slipped in prosperity, Birmingham and Wolverhampton rose. But by the year 2000 much of that prosperity too had gone. Now the new industries strung themselves out along the M4 corridor (and in Scotland's 'silicon glen'), or huddled together around the financial institutions and large corporate headquarters firmly fixed in London and the South East. For by then both the earlier industrial leaders (textiles and coal) and the later ones (cars and steel) had been replaced in dominance by new knowledge-based industries and by financial institutions: industries and institutions that no longer required either northern coal or Midlands semi-skilled labour. By the end of the century the successful parts of Britain's manufacturing base were primarily those within/alongside the military industrial complex (particularly aerospace and defence electronics), or those reimplanted into greenfield sites by foreign investment (Japanese car plants being the major example). The economy by then had world-quality companies only there, and in petroleum, in pharmaceuticals and chemicals, in food, drink and tobacco and in international financial services (Porter 1990: 484–94; Walker 1993: 168–9; Coates 1996a: 14–17). This new distribution of leading sectors left Britain as a whole regionally unbalanced – with pockets of high prosperity outside the South East (particularly in those parts of Scotland possessing the new oil and computer industries), but with the bulk of the nation's prosperity heavily concentrated well south of a line from the Severn to the Wash.

Shifting structures of ownership

These changing patterns of performance and employment both triggered (and were then accentuated by) changing patterns of ownership within the postwar British economy. Underperformance by particular industries (and in the 1970s even individual companies) triggered a changing pattern of public ownership. The boundary of the public and the private ebbed and flowed persistently in the postwar period. Public ownership expanded in two great waves. It expanded first in the 1940s, with the nationalization of a series of industries hitherto starved of extensive investment (mining, rail and road transport, and eventually the steel industry). It expanded again in the 1960s and 1970s, as both new industries came into public ownership (steel once more, ports and shipyards, even sections of the car industry) and as individual large but struggling firms were bought by the state (most notably Rolls-Royce and Ferranti). Then, of course, the whole expansion process was sent into reverse by the Thatcherite privatizations of the 1980s: privatizations which (as in coal and in steel) were then followed by significant reductions in employment

Table 8.2   The changing boundaries of the public sector

	To public ownership	To private ownership
1946–9	Railways, road haulage, major airlines, coal, gas, electricity, steel, plus the Bank of England	
1953		Road haulage, steel
1967	Steel	
1971–3		Thomas Cook, Carlisle Breweries
1973	Rolls-Royce	
1975–8	British Leyland, British National Oil Corp., British Shipbuilders, British Aerospace, ICL and INMOS, plus holdings in Ferranti, Amersham International, Cable and Wireless...	
1980–9		British Petroleum, ICL, Ferranti, British Aerospace, British Sugar, Cable and Wireless, Amersham International, Britoil, British Ports, BR hotels, INMOS, Sealink, British Telecom, British Shipbuilders, British Gas, Rolls-Royce, water authorities
1990–5		Electricity generation and distribution, British Rail, British Coal, National Power and Power Gen

and production outlets. The resulting boundary lines of public and private ownership are captured in table 8.2.

Alongside this ebb and flow of public ownership, the British private sector went through its own process of ownership restructuring. The 1960s and 1970s in particular witnessed a merger boom of unprecedented proportions. By 1980 the British economy still retained a significant small and medium-size business sector in which even its microbusinesses (those employing ten workers or fewer) still provided 28 per cent of all employment (Storey 1994: 20). But by then the entire economy was nonetheless dominated by a series of large companies – six or fewer in each of the twenty-two industrial sectors listed by the Department of Employment – which were collectively responsible for probably two-thirds of the economy's output as a whole. In fact, as early as 1976 'a mere 87 giant enterprises were responsible for over half of British exports' (Harris 1985: 12); and by 1986 over one and a quarter million

British workers – some 5 per cent of the total – had jobs with the forty largest manufacturing firms in the UK (Coates 1995: 83). By the 1990s a significant element of those large companies had themselves become foreign owned. Japanese, German, Swiss and American companies were all big players in the British economy by 2000: to the point that probably 'one in seven workers in manufacturing is [now] employed by a foreign-owned firm' (Auerbach 1989: 263). Behind the surface of company names, large degrees of cross-ownership were by then evident; and leading British banks had by now begun to link blocs of companies together in complex networks of ownership and control. By as early as 1980, London's four major banks, seven insurance companies and nine merchant banks between them had a controlling interest in ten of Britain's top fifty manufacturing companies (Coates 1989: 26); and many of the familiar industrial names in the postwar British economy (ICI, Unilever, GEC and the like) were already transforming themselves from local concerns into genuinely global companies – and ones with a developed propensity to relocate employment and production *out* of Britain into Europe, the United States and East Asia. Karel Williams and his colleagues calculated that their sample of twenty-five of Britain's largest companies created some 200,000 jobs abroad between 1979 and 1989 while shedding more than 300,000 jobs at home – in a veritable 'hollowing out' of British manufacturing that continued apace through the 1990s (Williams, Williams and Haslam 1990: 472).

Shifting patterns of class

These changes in location and control had profound effects too on those who worked in the postwar British economy, and on how those working there defined their own position and their relationship to others. In the broadest sense the rise of large private companies, the development of extensive service provision and the expansion of public sector welfare bureaucracies expanded dramatically both the number and proportion of workers who occupied managerial positions or worked as administrators and clerks. Britain in the postwar period, that is, like other major industrial economies, experienced a rapid growth in white collar employment. It also experienced the destruction of skilled and semi-skilled manual work in declining industries, and the creation of new skill categories and new semi- and unskilled positions in the new industries and in the expanding service sector. Most of the jobs lost in that process (certainly those lost in the 1980s) were full-time jobs, traditionally filled by men. Many of the new jobs created were part-time or even temporary ones –

many now filled by women. 7.3 per cent of all jobs by century's end were of a temporary nature (fixed contract, temping, casual and seasonal), where two decades before the figure had been only 5 per cent (Philpott 1999: 1, 3). In 1971 the British economy employed 21.6 million workers, 18.3 million of whom worked full-time. A generation later, in 1993, the total was down to 20.7 million, of whom only 15 million worked full-time; and by 1997, after half a decade of recovery, the numbers were still only 22.8 million and 17.1 million respectively. In 1997 83 per cent of the by then 5.7 million part-time jobs were filled by women workers, and 44 per cent of all women working for wages in Britain were doing so on a part-time basis (*Employment Audit*, 7 (1998), p. 8).

The cumulative result of all these changes in employment was the creation of a more complex and socially divided labour force than that which had initially emerged from the Second World War. The end-of-century British labour force was divided between two or even three working classes: an old one predominantly northern, unionized, and in traditional industries; a Midlands working class heavily unionized and largely dependent on the car industry; and a new southern working class that in general was less unionized and more based in new industries and service employment than its northern equivalents. The end-of-century British labour force also included a much expanded white collar and new middle-class sector: a white collar sector of routine office workers, and a middle class that was itself divided between the managerial strata of the large private firms and public sector semi-professionals in education and healthcare. And it was a labour force that was still heavily divided by gender and ethnicity: with a core of white male employment and a periphery of less well-paid and less secure jobs disproportionately filled by white women and by Afro-Caribbean and Asian workers. By century's end the glass ceiling holding women in subordinate employment positions was easing slightly (Walby 1999: 197–8; Desai et al. 1999: 175–6) but that holding ethnic minority populations in insecure employment and disproportionate unemployment had shifted hardly at all. In fact Britain ended the old century more spatially divided in social terms than it had been in 1945. By the year 2000 it had become a country of middle-class suburbs and urban ghettos: one divided – in Will Hutton's telling phrase – into a 40/30/30 mould (40 per cent of its population affluent and secure, 30 per cent in employment without job security, and 30 per cent in marginalized unemployment and poverty) (Hutton 1995: 105). Theirs was a poverty tied directly to that other key feature of postwar Britain's political economy – not so much the shape of its economy as its performance – to which we now need to turn.

The changing performance of the British economy

Measured solely against its own past the postwar British economy has been a huge success story, generating a level and range of output, and a scale and quality of employment, never achieved in Britain before. The resetting of the centres of gravity of the economy from heavy industry to light, the shift in its basic energy sources from coal to electricity and oil, and its full participation in first the semi-automated production systems pioneered by the US car industry and later in computer-based technologies, all had one major effect. They transformed qualitatively the *productivity* of both labour and capital across the British economy as a whole. Between 1950 and 1980 GDP in Britain more than doubled, and consumption per head rose 80 per cent, and in the next twenty years GDP grew by more than one-third again. Year on year from 1950 to 1973 the economy grew on average at 3.7 per cent, from 1974 to 1979 at 2.4 per cent, in the 1980s at 2.6 per cent and from 1992 at variously 2.0 per cent, 2.5 per cent and even (in 1977) 3.8 per cent per year. The economy did not expand every year – 1974–5 were particularly bad years, as were 1980–1 and 1989–92 – but overall the economy remained on a consistently upward growth trajectory; and in the process completely transformed the material and social experience of the entire population.

In relation to living standards, economic growth of that scale and length did two things. It completely transformed the *level* of personal consumption, raising it to heights unimaginable at the start of the postwar period; and it completely transformed the *range* of goods and services consumed, introducing into conventional consumption an ever expanding stream of new products and services. Over the postwar period as a whole in Britain, some of that consumption took the form of a rising social wage – a steady improvement in the quality and availability of publicly provided education and health services, unemployment benefits, pensions and social assistance. But that social wage was always a contested one: never enough to equalize consumption, always too burdensome to be easily sustained by generalized taxation, and always prone to be understood by the bulk of the population (Hutton's top 40 per cent or 70 per cent) as an unwelcome drain on their ability to expand their private consumption. In fact, that private purchase and consumption of an ever expanding supply of goods and services was the single most striking consequence of the prolonged productivity growth of the postwar British economy. People coming into young adulthood in Britain in 1945 still faced a decade of acute shortages – the rationing of basic foodstuffs, the absence of manufactured consumer goods, housing shortages and the paucity of resources in the newly created public welfare networks. But decade on decade all that changed. By the 1950s the long postwar housing boom was well underway: first a boom in publicly provided housing, and from the 1960s increasingly a boom in private housing. By the 1960s the first wave of consumer durables was beginning to transform daily life in significant numbers of both middle-class and upper working-class homes: televisions, washing machines and fridges, telephones and cars. A decade later more and more people began to add foreign holidays to their regular consumption pattern, and from the 1980s participated enthusiastically in the contemporary explosion of electronic equipment, leisure goods and domestic services.

As we will see next, access to this perpetually expanding stock of wealth was never equal. It was always structured by class, by ethnicity, by gender and by age. Relative poverty remained a huge feature of British life throughout the period – poverty known disproportionately by the very old and the very young, by women bringing up children alone, by ethnic minorities cut off from employment options, and by manual workers subject to industrial downsizing. But for Hutton's more fortunate 70 per cent consumption became – over the postwar period as a whole – the leisure activity they participated in most: a consumption bonanza made progressively easier down the years by the parallel revolution in modes of payment. Shopping in the 1950s was, except for the very rich few, an exercise performed with cash, out of a weekly pay packet. Shopping in the 1970s, for significant parts of the expanding middle class, was an exercise performed by cheque and bank account; and by 2000 it was an exercise largely lubricated by 'plastic'. As Janet Ford put it, 'in the mid 1960s bank credit cards were unknown' but a generation later there were thought to be some 6 million retail cards in circulation. Certainly by as early as 1986 the average family in Britain 'owed £1,500 and spent 6 per cent of its income servicing the agreements' (Ford 1988:3).

But to stop the story here would be seriously to distort the record. For the postwar expansion of the British economy, though striking by its own previous standards, was problematic – in comparative terms – in at least two key ways. Its bounty did not extend to everyone within its own territory, and its performance did not match that of economies territorially located elsewhere. Rising prosperity in postwar Britain came hand-in-hand with persistent poverty, and with entrenched economic under-performance; and must be understood in relation to both.

Certainly Britain remained scarred by serious inequalities of income and wealth throughout its postwar years of generalized economic growth, and those inequalities actually intensified as the half-century progressed. The initial postwar welfare settlement established a more systematic safety net beneath the vast numbers of working-class poor than had hitherto been provided by the prewar mixture of limited state assistance and variable private charity. But that settlement could not by itself dent the inherited inequalities of housing, income, education and social contacts characteristic of the social order of mid-century British capitalism; and indeed those inequalities persisted, generation on generation, in spite of the generalized prosperity of the postwar period as a whole. Free schooling to age fifteen, then sixteen, produced a social revolution of sorts; but still the children of the middle class monopolized the selective grammar schools and the universities as these expanded. Healthcare spread systematically through the UK as a whole, but still the actual consumption of publicly provided healthcare was skewed by class, and private healthcare remained the preserve of those with income and authority. The post-1973 downturn and subsequent restructuring of the UK economy then accentuated these inequalities, adding large-scale unemployment to the sources of renewed poverty in the 1980s and creating new sectors of low-paid service employment that trapped their occupants in paid labour and relative poverty at one and the same time. By the mid-1980s, official reports were recording anywhere between 17 and 29 per cent of the population living at or just above Supplementary Benefit level, with as many as 12 million people close to poverty and at least 2.6 million living in acute poverty. During the Thatcher years income inequality in Britain actually *widened*, so that by 1991 as many as 4 million children in Britain were living in households whose total income was less than half the national average. By the end of the century the latest official figures were showing about one in five Britons living in poverty, as against one in ten in 1979 (Burgess and Propper 1999: 259); and the British economy stood alongside those of the US and Canada in its propensity to generate poverty through low-wage employment. In Belgium, Finland and Sweden, less than one worker in ten was in poverty because of low wages, and in Germany one worker in seven. But the OECD found that in 1996 'low-wage employment [was] most prevalent in the United Kingdom where about one in five full-time workers is low-paid, and in Canada and the United States, where this fraction is about one in four' (*Employment Audit*, 10 (1999), p. 18).

If the persistence of poverty constitutes the postwar British economy's most acute internal failure, the economy demonstrated an external failure as well. Over the postwar period as a whole, its rate of economic growth failed to match that of other leading industrial economies, and in consequence British standards of living began to slide in international terms. The postwar British economy grew, but it did not grow as quickly as others. In 1950 the UK stood sixth in real GDP per head, marginally behind Canada, Australia and New Zealand, and with a living standard roughly 20 per cent less than that of Switzerland and two-thirds that of the United States. By 1970 it had slipped to tenth, by 1975 to fifteenth, and by 1985 to nineteenth in that same league table; and by 1995 had clawed its way back merely to sixteenth, still two-thirds short of the USA, but now behind a whole string of European economies too (Scandinavian economies, Germany, the Low Countries, France and Italy) and behind Japan (Bain 1997: 17; Coates 2000: 3). The productivity levels achieved in the British economy over the postwar period as a whole continued to fall short of those achieved in the US, Japan and Germany (the McKinsey Institute still had British labour productivity 40 per cent lower than in the US, and 20 per cent lower than in Germany, as late as 1998); and the capacity of British-based firms to hold on to world market share of manufactured exports persistently fell. British-based firms held a 25.4 per cent share of all manufactured exports from the world's eleven leading industrial nations in 1950; but that figure was down to 9.1 per cent by as early as 1971 and was only 7.9 per cent by 1992 (Crafts 1997: 30). The percentage of trade in manufactured goods captured by British firms fell particularly rapidly between 1950 and 1973; and yet it was only after 1973 that the weakness of the manufacturing sector began particularly to show. As the Select Committee on Trade and Industry reported in 1994:

> Taking [those] last two decades as a whole, the UK is the only major industrial country whose manufacturing output...remained virtually static, although there [was] some catching up in respect of France and Germany [from] the early 1980s. Not until 1988 did UK manufacturing output recover its peak level of 1973, and in 1992 it was [still] less than 1% higher than in 1973, whereas output increased by 27% in France, 25% in Germany, 85% in Italy and 119% in Japan during the same period. (Select Committee on Trade and Industry 1994: 16)

The retreat of British manufacturing

By the late 1980s, that is, the British economy had lost its capacity to produce what Wells called 'a sufficient volume of manufacturing capacity capable of producing the sort of products which people require in both overseas and domestic markets' (Wells 1989: 58). Since British consumers continued to desire such manufactured goods, the result of this diminished international competitiveness and stagnant overall output was a sizeable and persistent deficit on the UK balance of payments.

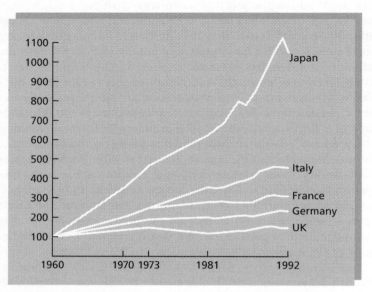

Figure 8.1   Manufacturing output 1960–1992 (1960 = 100) (UK manufacturing is 'manufacturing and mining less energy-related products')
Source: US Bureau of Labor, *Monthly Labor Review* (Jan. 1994), from Select Committee on Trade and Industry, *Competitiveness of Manufacturing Industry* (London: HMSO, 1994), p. 16.

Though the output of the British economy may have fundamentally shifted from manufacturing to services through the 1980s, the structure of British demand did not. British consumers at the end of the 1980s were still spending the same percentage of their income on manufactured goods and the same percentage on services as they had in 1979 (before the deep cuts in manufacturing employment of the 1980s). They actually increased their total demand for manufactured products by 30 per cent in that key decade while manufacturing output remained broadly unchanged (Wells 1989: 36, 46). The British economy became in consequence a net importer of manufactured goods for the first occasion in peacetime in 1983, and throughout the second half of the 1980s and the 1990s the economy's overseas trade account remained in deficit. Throughout the 1980s and 1990s the British economy balanced its books – and protected internal living standards – only by holding interest rates higher in London than elsewhere in the world system. The persistence of poverty at home was matched by improvidence abroad – and the price of that was expensive money in London, and hence yet another barrier to easy investment in the economy's weakening manufacturing base. The UK's current balance of payments – which was in deficit consistently from 1988 to 1995 but which had been pulled back into surplus by 1998 – ended the decade once more in deficit, forecast, on the government's own figures, to move from £15.5 billion in 1999 to £28 billion by 2002 (*Observer*, 26 Mar. 2000).

The origins and causes of this pattern of economic performance are immensely controversial. Indeed, as we will see, different understandings of why the British economy slipped from its 1961 position (as still the second most productive large-scale economy in the capitalist bloc) to its present position in the second division of world economic players are still the key issue dividing dominant political projects on offer to the British electorate. The Thatcherite explanation that took hold in the 1980s placed responsibility for prolonged underachievement firmly at the door of trade union power, excessive state spending and the absence of a proper enterprise culture. More centre-left explanations both before

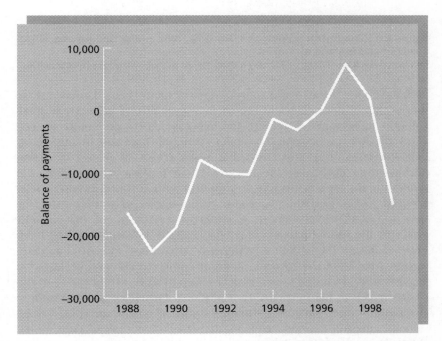

Figure 8.2 The British economy's balance of payments, current balance, 1988–1999 (£m)
Sources: *NIER* (Oct. 1997), p. 117; *NIER* (July 1999), p. 116; *Observer*, 26 Mar. 2000.

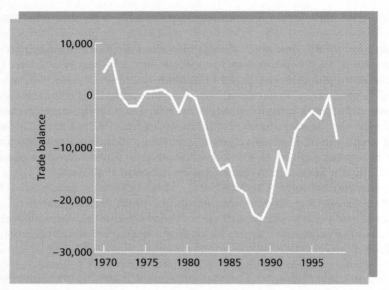

Figure 8.3 The British economy's trade balance in goods and services, 1970–1998 (£m at 1991 prices)
Sources: NIER (Oct. 1997), p. 117; *NIER* (July 1999), p. 116; *Observer*, 26 Mar. 2000.

and since have located the sources of underperformance elsewhere: in long-standing deficiencies in the financing of British industry, in inadequacies in managerial training and expertise, in the preference of state elites for imperial adventures and global policing, and in underlying deficiencies in state education. For some critics of British economic performance, decline set in as early as 1890 (Hobsbawn 1968). For others the lost opportunity to restore economic fortunes occurred later (Pollard 1982). For some it lay in the privileging of welfare provision over industrial investment supposedly characteristic of British state policy in the second half of the 1940s (Barnett 1986). For others it lay in the failure of the Labour governments' attempts at industrial modernization after 1964 (Marquand 1988); and for yet others in the Thatcher governments' failure to seize one last opportunity at industrial reconstruction before the intensification of global economic interconnections squeezed out the space for nationally triggered economic repositioning. (On this literature, see Coates 1994; Cox, Lee and Sanderson 1997.) What Angus Maddison referred to as 'the ultimate causes' of economic performance are therefore, in the British case at least, in fierce dispute (Maddison 1995: 86).

The investment record

Less contentious, however, are what Maddison would term the 'proximate causes' of weakening international competitiveness. For it is quite clear that, whatever else was wrong with British economic institutions and organization throughout the postwar period, at the very least those institutions were short of investment. UK manufacturing industry suffered throughout the period from an incapacity to attract to itself the share of GNP for investment purposes characteristically attained by its key competitors. Gross non-residential investment as a percentage of GDP ran at 26.5 per cent in Japan between 1960 and 1973 and at 24 per cent between 1980 and 1993. The German figures were 19.6 per cent and 16.2 per cent, the British only 14.6 per cent and 13.7 per cent (Crafts 1997: 35). The result was that by 1989 the capital/worker hour in British manufacturing was only three-quarters that of American, German or French manufacturing, a gap likely to widen 'as, through cumulative causation processes, the expectation that the manufacturing sector is not investing becomes self-fulfilling' (Kitson and Michie 1996: 201).

The British economy suffered in consequence from what some have termed 'flawed Fordism' (Jessop 1992: 20), the inability fully to exploit the productivity potential released by the generalized application of semi-automated production processes to key sections of manufacturing industry in the first half of the postwar period. It suffered too from the resulting cumulative loss of international competitiveness, finding itself excluded from the 'virtuous circles of growth' enjoyed by economies with high levels of investment, productivity and profits: trapped instead in a mutually reinforcing trajectory of low investment, low productivity, low competitiveness and low profits. That trajectory deepened decade on decade, as British-based manufacturing firms relocated overseas, as the distribution of investment funds in Britain shifted from manufacturing to services (especially financial services, but also retailing), and as the volume of foreign direct investment attracted into the British economy by its key position within the affluent markets of the European Union was offset by the greater outflows of British-generated capital to industrial investment opportunities in Western Europe, Asia and North America. Manufacturing firms and financial institutions had never established the close working relationships characteristic of more successful capitalisms elsewhere (particularly those in Germany and Japan). Indeed the gap between industry and finance in Britain had long been a key feature of economic underperformance (Hutton 1995); and certainly by the

1980s a weakened manufacturing base proved incapable of attracting sufficient investment funds from what was by then becoming a truly global set of financial lenders.

Instead, in the key decade of the 1980s, manufacturing investment within Britain (for the purchase of new factories and machinery) rose by just 12.8 per cent 'whereas investment by the financial and business services sector (new offices, computers, etc.) grew by 320.3 per cent. In 1979 investment by the latter sector was around one-third of investment in manufacturing: in 1979 it was around one-third more than manufacturing investment (with financial investment alone over one-half that of manufacturing)' (Glyn 1992: 84–5). That, in spite of the by then general recognition (underscored by the report of the Select Committee on Trade and Industry) that manufacturing still mattered: that 'manufacturing, though only around 20% of GDP, provides over 60% of UK exports, compared to less than 25% in the case of services', that 'the UK's share of world export of services' was currently declining 'faster than its share in manufactured exports', and that 'given the composition of the UK's exports, every 1% decline in exports of manufactures requires more than a 2.5% rise in exports of services to compensate' (Select Committee on Trade and Industry 1994: 21–2). The shortfall in the trade balance that resulted from this pattern of investment was, by the century's end, financed by an inflow of short-term capital, attracted to London by the strength of sterling and London's internationally high rates of interest; but it was not financed by any long-term net inflow of funds. On the contrary, the British economy closed out the century as a net exporter of capital on a considerable scale. Certainly between 1991 and 1995 the outflows of direct investment from the UK averaged out at $25.4 billion a year, the inflows at only $17.2 billion (Barrell and Pain 1997: 65); and as table 8.3 demonstrates. This was nothing new. Outflows of

Table 8.3 Long-term capital transactions, 1979–1992 (£ billion)

	Direct investment			Portfolio investment			Total
	Outward	Inward	Balance	Outward	Inward	Balance	Balance
1979–80	−5.4	3.7	−1.7	−2.1	1.5	−0.6	−2.3
1981–3	−5.2	3.1	−2.1	−6.5	0.6	−5.9	−8.0
1984–6	−8.7	3.4	−5.3	−16.3	7.7	−8.6	−13.9
1987–92	−15.1	13.0	−2.1	−20.2	17.1	−3.1	−5.2

Source: H. Radice, 'Britain in the World Economy', in D. Coates and J. Hillard (eds), *UK Economic Decline: Key Texts* (Hemel Hempstead: Prentice Hall/Harvester Wheatsheaf, 1995), p. 238.

capital from the UK exceeded inflows into the UK through the 1980s as well.

Work and wages in a weakening economy

A pattern of capital investment of that kind had consequences for both political projects and the British labour movement. As far as labour was concerned, the years of persistent underinvestment produced wage levels that were, by European and North American standards, increasingly inadequate. The British economy began the postwar period as a relatively high wage economy. It ended it as a low wage one. Indeed by as early as 1970 it had become 'the industrialised country in Western Europe with the lowest labour costs, with the sole exception of Ireland' (Ray 1987: 71: Nolan 1992: 112). It also ended the century as the main economy in northern Europe in which the working of long hours, and intensifications of the work process, most compensated for the absence of internationally adequate levels of investment in new plant and equipment. That work intensification was a key consequence of the Thatcherite assault on trade union power and full employment in the 1980s. The 1980s did see a 'productivity miracle' of a sort, and a narrowing of the productivity gap between the British economy and its leading Western European rivals (Lansbury and Mayes 1996: 21). But it was a gap in unit labour costs that was narrowed less by investment than by downsizing and work intensification (Nolan 1992: 101–21). At century's end British workers still worked the longest hours in northern Europe for the lowest wages, and experienced unprecedented levels of job insecurity (Toynbee 2000: 13). By then, 3 million of the 7 million workers in the European Union who regularly worked in excess of a fifty-hour week did so in Britain; and significantly, those working the longest hours earned less than those who did not (*Employment Audit*, 10 (1999), p. 13). The British economy in the 1990s produced more jobs (and hence lower unemployment) than its main European rivals. In that the 1990s marked a distinct change, and an improvement, on the high unemployment of the decade before. Late in 1999 the level of employment in the British economy 'for all people aged 16 and over was 27.6 million, higher than at any time since 1973' (*Employment Audit*, 10 (1999), p. 4). But the bulk of those new jobs remained predominantly low paid, and low skilled, and in the service sector (British manufacturing actually shed 20,000 more jobs in the three months to September 1998); and in all those ways the last decade of the century saw the persistence of a pattern which, thus far, none of the political projects canvassed for economic reconstruction has managed to rupture.

Political projects and economic performance

Politics in Britain since the late 1950s has been dominated by a developing awareness – in both policy circles and the wider electorate – of this
diminishing international competitiveness of key sectors of the British
economy. Parties in government and parties in opposition addressed
themselves consistently to the adverse internal consequences of the economy's international slippage, and have regularly generated programmes
designed to redress it. The Macmillan government was the first postwar
government systematically to do so, opening a phase of economic intervention by successive governments (both Labour and Conservative) that
persisted (with only a brief hiatus in the first half of the Heath administration) right through until 1979. The Thatcher government, persuaded
of the inappropriateness of state intervention of the kind pioneered by
the Macmillan government and extended by the Labour administrations
of first Wilson and then Callaghan, then reset economic and industrial
policy on entirely different lines, bringing into British politics what we
can now see was a 'second way' to economic recovery. Currently the
Labour government led by Tony Blair is pursuing its own 'third way'.

   At the heart of the Macmillan–Wilson 'first way' was the deployment
of the state as an active (though in comparative terms still a 'cautious')
agent of industrial modernization. In the 1960s much of this was necessarily tentative, as governments moved into policy territory that was new
to them, and as the severity and depth of the task they faced only
incrementally became clear. For much of the 1960s, policy was directed
at effects rather than causes: concentrating on exchange rates and levels
of demand, and struggling to balance an overvalued currency with a
labour movement reluctant to engage in income restraint. In the early
phases of that 'first way', politicians and civil servants were themselves
touched by inherited attitudes – deep in the British state system – that
argued against any detailed intervention by public institutions into the
peacetime workings of private industry. The 'first way' was slow to build
momentum in part because of an ingrained 'liberal militarism' in the
British state system, a tradition allowing governments to establish a
hands-on relationship only with industries producing military (and mili-
tary-related) commodities and allowing governments to regulate industries producing for the civilian market only in times of war (Edgerton
1991; Coates 1996b). But by the late 1960s, with the creation of the
Ministry of Technology, and after the 1972 and 1975 Industry Acts,
successive administrations did make a sustained if belated attempt to
facilitate the reconstruction of an internationally competitive manufac-

turing base. They took industries and firms into private ownership. They funded industrial investment. They provided regional aid. They restrained the export of capital. They opened new markets by entry into the European Economic Community. They 'picked national winners', and through complex structures of consultation with both sides of industry sought to strengthen their competitive position in particular. They funded industrial retraining, provided help with the redeployment of labour, and endured considerable political damage holding down welfare provision and sustaining wage-cutting incomes policies. And, of course, they failed.

The Thatcherite reaction to that failure, and to the problem of Britain's 'decline' out of which it arose, was distinctly different. The post-1979 Thatcher government dismantled the complex structures of consultation and abandoned the state-led pursuit of national champions. It looked to market forces to resuscitate the UK's international economic position, and was not overconcerned initially about whether that position needed to be built around a strong manufacturing sector. The Major governments of the 1990s came to believe so again, whereas the Thatcher governments of the mid-1980s were more content to see the service sector flourish alone. But in both decades, Conservative administrations looked to international competition to trigger economic modernization. They allowed the export of capital and courted foreign direct investment; and they sought to create a favourable environment for capital accumulation by cutting what they identified as high rates of income and corporate taxation, privatizing large sections of the publicly owned manufacturing base, restraining the growth of the welfare sector, and curbing trade union rights to negotiate and strike. Between 1982 and 1989 such a dramatic shift in policy seemed to open a renewed period of economic recovery, but the depth and length of the 1989–92 recession dented that optimism. In the event, the British economy in the 1990s remained significantly short of investment, not simply in plant and equipment, but also in a skilled labour force able fully to exploit the new information-based production systems then developing in the US and Asia; and eventually popular support for the neoliberal 'second way' eroded as that for Old Labour's 'first way' had eventually done.

The New Labour 'third way' sees itself as a synthesis of what was best in each of those preceding packages, and as a strategy capable of succeeding where they had failed precisely because of its awareness of the pitfalls associated with each of its predecessors. The policy distance is greatest between Old Labour and New. That between Thatcherism and New Labour is more subtle and nuanced. New Labour has set its face against the picking of winners, the extensive subsidization of industrial investment, or any return to direct public ownership. It has also kept its trade union allies firmly at a distance, with their rights as organizations and as workers largely unchanged from the Thatcherite settlement imposed on them in the 1980s. New Labour's enthusiasm for market solutions to economic underperformance, its belief in the opportunities provided by global trade and the flow of foreign direct investment, and its determination to leave British business free of government regulation and taxation, are at least as great as those of the Conservative governments which preceded it; but New Labour has a passion for education and training, as the key long-term solution to the lack of economic competitiveness, that was largely absent from the Thatcherite (if not from the Major) policy litany (Hay 1999: Coates and Lawler 2000).

For understandable political reasons, many of the advocates of these three models as 'ways' tend to emphasize the *discontinuities* in British economic policy over time: treating 1979 and 1997 in particular as key moments of policy realignment. And in one sense it is right to do so, since each date marks that point at which a new cohort of politicians took office, determined to change dominant understandings of how best to revive the economy's flagging fortunes. But in another sense it is not wise to draw lines in time so sharply as that; for across those dates powerful strands of policy *continuity* remained. Certainly much of Margaret Thatcher's initial monetarism was foreshadowed in the post-1976 policy stance adopted by Labour's then Chancellor of the Exchequer, Dennis Healey; and many of the dominant themes of New Labour's current industrial and employment policies were embryonically present in the policy mix developed by Michael Heseltine's Department of Trade and Industry during John Major's long tenure as Conservative Prime Minister (Coates 1999). Table 8.4 demonstrates one important aspect of that later policy continuity: the shared determination of both the Major and Blair governments to combine limited regulation of private industry with systematic support for investment (in both research and development, and in human capital) as their route to economic growth. Indeed table 8.4 makes clear that the New Labour targets for educational achievement, for all the 'hype' surrounding their launch after 1997, were actually slightly more modest than those adopted more quietly by the Heseltine-led DTI prior to 1997. And perhaps this should not surprise us, given how powerful are the imperatives imposing policy continuity on British governments trapped between a still weak economy and the strictures of an increasingly globally dominant neoliberal discourse.

For here is the rub. Successive generations of British politicians have now spent more than half a century presiding over an economy in decline in terms of international competitiveness. It was a decline that the first

Table 8.4 White Papers compared, from John Major's Conservative government and Tony Blair's Labour government

	Competitiveness: Forging Ahead (1995)	Our Competitive Future: Building the Knowledge-Driven Economy (1998)
Problem	'In a market economy, the primary responsibility for improving competitiveness must lie with firms; this is recognised by business itself . . . when market imperfections limit the scope for firms to improve competitiveness, the Government may need to intervene. The Government creates the climate within which business can improve its performance by':	'Britain's goal must be to reverse a century of relative economic decline by raising the sustainable rate of growth. To achieve this, more British businesses have to match the best in the world. . . . Business must lead this process of modernisation by responding to the spur of competition and by exploiting market opportunities. In addition to establishing macroeconomic stability and improving education standards, the Government has a key role to play as a catalyst, investor and regulator to strengthen the supply-side of the economy. . . . To strengthen the UK's capability to compete in the modern economy, the Government will':
Policy towards capital	• providing the stable macroeconomic environment based on low inflation, sound public finances and competitive tax rates, which is essential to give business confidence to invest • maintaining and developing open and competitive world markets and fighting to bring down barriers to trade • removing unnecessary burdens on business through deregulation, aimed particularly at SMEs • making markets work better through liberalisation,	• invest . . . in partnership with the Wellcome Trust to modernise the British science and engineering base • vigorously promote the commercialisation of university research • help . . . small businesses to harness information and communication technologies to compete more effectively in the digital marketplace • launch a new round of the Foresight programme • create a new Enterprise Fund • Improve the help given to start-ups

(continued)

Table 8.4 (*continued*)

	Competitiveness: Forging Ahead (1995)	Our Competitive Future: Building the Knowledge-Driven Economy (1998)
	sharpening incentives by the reform of personal and business taxation, and extending markets through privatisation • helping business help itself through better informed decision-making and the spread of best practice • ensuring a favourable environment for inward investment; and • improving value for money and standards in services, such as education, which are best provided by the public sector • with the private finance initiative in the forefront	• change the insolvency laws to give businesses in difficulties a better chance of turning around • back proposals to...drive up performance among suppliers • back the CBI's campaign...to encourage a massive increase in the number of companies adopting best practice • provide funds for the Regional Development Agencies • set up a public–private action team to promote clusters in biotechnology • examine the planning system to ensure it encourages enterprise and promotes the needs of industrial clusters
Problem	'To improve the UK's international competitiveness by raising standards and attainment levels in education and training to world class levels by ensuring that' by the year 2000:	'Successful modern economies are built on the abilities of their people. People are at the heart of the knowledge-driven economy. Their knowledge and skills are critical to the success of British business. People are the ultimate source of new ideas. In a fast moving world economy, skills must be continually upgraded or our competitiveness will decline.' So by 2002:
Policy towards labour	• By age 19, 85% of young people to achieve five GCSEs at grade C or above, an intermediate GNVQ or an NVQ level 2	• 50% of 16 year olds should have five GCSEs (grades A–C) 60% of 21 year olds should have a level three qualification (2 A levels or equivalents)

- 75% of young people to achieve level 2 competence in communication, numeracy and IT by age 19; and 35% to achieve level 3 competence in these core skills by age 21
- By age 21, 60% of young people to achieve 2 GCE A levels, an Advanced GNVQ or NVQ level 3
- Life-long learning: 60% of the workforce to be qualified to NVQ level 3, Advanced GNVQ or two GCE A level standard...
- 50% of economically active adults should have a level 3 qualification
- 28% of economically active adults should have a level 4 qualification

postwar generations of politicians failed to stem even during capitalism's so-called 'golden age' when the battery of policy instruments available to them was, at least by later standards, both wide and effective. Certainly the Japanese state had its successful 'development' moment in those years, as the British state did not (Abe and Gourvish 1997; Brown 1998). Contemporary British politicians now live in the shadow of that past failure; while simultaneously facing an international economic order whose governing ordinances and understandings militate against the deployment of the very range of policy instruments once used to fundamentally reset growth paths. Against the scale of the problems they have inherited, the policy instruments currently being canvassed by today's generation of economic ministers seem puny indeed; making it hard to avoid the conclusion that New Labour's 'train and reskill' panacea will be no more capable of lifting the British economy on to a new and higher growth trajectory than were the Thatcherite 'deregulation' or the Wilsonite 'planning and subsidy' ones. After all, the British economy has been locked into its particular global position now for over half a century, and the institutional forces and practices keeping it there have throughout that period proved totally immune both to ambitious political rhetoric and to modest state reform. It is not clear why suddenly they should change now. Of course, there is no iron law dictating that past failures must always repeat themselves, and a chapter like this cannot arbitrarily foreclose on what is an on-going process. So perhaps it is safer (certainly it is more neutral) merely to conclude with the observation that *whether* New Labour's 'skills revolution' can reverse this half-century pattern of economic underperformance is still *the* central unanswered question of contemporary British political economy. On the success or failure of that 'skills revolution' turns not simply the electoral fate of the New Labour government, but also the living standards, social rights and possibly civil peace of those that New Labour currently governs. There is therefore much at stake, as ever, in this interplay of economic performance and political projects; and it would be good to think that perhaps at last the political project being canvassed is up to the task. The jury is still out, and time alone will tell; but the portents are not good.

REFERENCES

Abe, E. and Gourvish, T. (eds) (1997) *Japanese Success? British Failure? Comparisons in business performance since 1945*. Oxford: Oxford University Press.

Auerbach, P. (1989) 'Multinationals and the British Economy', in F. Green (ed.), *The Restructuring of the UK Economy*. Hemel Hempstead: Harvester Wheatsheaf.

Bain, G. (1997) *Promoting Prosperity: A Business Agenda for Britain*, Report of the Commission on Public Policy and British Business. London: Vintage Books for the Institute for Public Policy Research.

Barnett, C. (1986) *The Audit of War*. Basingstoke: Macmillan.

Barrell, R. and Pain, P. (1997) 'The Growth of Foreign Direct Investment in Europe', *National Institute Economic Review*, Apr. 63–75.

Beavis, S. (1997) 'CBI Calls for Drive to Catch International Rivals', *Guardian*, 23 Sept. p. 1.

Brown, K. D. (1998) *Britain and Japan: A Comparative Economic and Social History since 1900*. Manchester: Manchester University Press.

Burgess, S. and Propper, C. (1999) 'Poverty in Britain', in P. Gregg and J. Wadsworth (eds), *The State of Working Britain*. Manchester: Manchester University Press.

Cairncross, A. (1985) *Years of Recovery: British Economic Policy 1945–51*. London: Methuen.

Church, R. (1994) *The Rise and Decline of the British Motor Industry*. Cambridge: Cambridge University Press.

Coates, D. (1984) *The Context of British Politics*. London: Hutchinson.

—— (1989) 'Britain', in T. Bottomore and R. Brym (eds), *The Capitalist Class: An International Study*. Brighton: Harvester Wheatsheaf.

—— (1994) *The Question of UK Decline*. Hemel Hempstead: Harvester-Wheatsheaf.

—— (1995) *Running the Country*. London: Hodder and Stoughton.

—— (1996a) 'UK Underperformance: Claim and Reality', in D. Coates and J. Hillard (eds), *UK Economic Decline: Key Texts*. Hemel Hempstead: Prentice Hall/Harvester Wheatsheaf.

—— (ed.) (1996b) *Industrial Policy in Britain*. Basingstoke: Macmillan.

——(1999) 'The Novelty of New Labour: A View at Half-time', paper to the APSA conference, Atlanta, Sept.

——(2000) *Models of Capitalism*. Cambridge: Polity.

Coates, D. and Lawler, P. (eds) (2000) *New Labour in Power*. Manchester: Manchester University Press.

Cox, A., Lee, S. and Sanderson, J. (1997) *The Political Economy of Modern Britain*. Cheltenham: Edward Elgar.

Crafts, N. (1997) *The Conservative Government's Economic Record: An End of Term Report*. London: IEA.

Desai, T., Gregg, P., Steer, J. and Wadsworth, J. (1999) 'Gender and the Labour Market', in P. Gregg and J. Wadsworth (eds), *The State of Working Britain*. Manchester: Manchester University Press.

Edgerton, D. (1991) 'Liberal Militarism and the British State', *New Left Review*, no. 185, 18–69.

Ford, J. (1988) *The Indebted Society: Credit and Default in the 1980s*. London: Routledge.

Glyn, A. (1992) 'The Productivity Miracle: Profits and Investment', in J. Michie (ed.), *The Economic Legacy 1979–1992*. London: Academic Press.

Glynn, S. and Booth, A. (1996) *Modern Britain*. London: Routledge.

Harris, L. (1985) 'British Capital: Manufacturing, Finance and Multinational Corporations', in D. Coates, G. Johnston and R. Bush (eds), *A Socialist Anatomy of Britain*. Cambridge: Polity.

Hay, C. (1999) *The Political Economy of New Labour*. Manchester: Manchester University Press.

Hobsbawm, E. (1968) *Industry and Empire*. New York: Pantheon.

Hutton, W. (1995) *The State We're In*. London: J Cape.

Jessop, B. (1992) 'From Social Democracy to Thatcherism: Twenty Five Years of British Politics', in N. Abercrombie and A Warde (eds), *Social Change in Contemporary Britain*. Cambridge: Polity.

Kitson, M. and Michie, J. (1996) 'Britain's Industrial Performance since 1960: Underinvestment and Relative Decline', *Economic Journal*, 106 (434), 196–212.

Lansbury, M. and Mayes, D. (1996) 'Productivity Growth in the 1980s', in D. Mayes (ed.), *Sources of Productivity Growth*. Cambridge: Cambridge University Press.

Maddison, A. (1995) *Explaining the Economic Performance of Nations*. Cheltenham: Edward Elgar.

Marquand, D. (1988) *The Unprincipled Society*. London: Cape.

Nolan, P. (1992) 'The Productivity Miracle', in F. Green (ed.), *The Restructuring of the UK Economy*. Hemel Hempstead: Harvester Wheatsheaf.

Philpott, J. (1999) 'Temporary Jobs, Constant Opportunity?', *Employment Report*, special edition, 14 (3).

Pollard, S. (1982) *The Wasting of the British Economy*. London: Croom Helm.

Porter, M. (1990) *The Competitive Advantage of Nations*. Basingstoke: Macmillan.

Radice, H. (1995) 'Britain in the World Economy: National Decline, Capitalist Success?', in D. Coates and J. Hillard (eds), *UK Economic Decline: Key Texts*. Hemel Hempstead: Prentice Hall/Harvester Wheatsheaf.

Ray, G. F. (1987) 'Labour Costs in Manufacturing', *National Institute Economic Review*, May, 71–4.

Rhys, G. (1995) 'The Transformation of the Motor Industry in the UK', in R. Turner (ed.), *The British Economy in Transition: From the Old to the New*. London: Routledge.

Select Committee on Trade and Industry (1994) *Competitiveness of Manufacturing Industry*. London: House of Commons.

Storey, D. (1994) *Understanding the Small Business Sector*. London: Routledge.

Toynbee, P. (2000) 'Caught in the Whirl of Work', *Guardian Weekly*, 20–26 Jan. p. 13.

Walby, S. (1999) 'Transformations of the Gendered Political Economy: Changes in Women's Employment in the United Kingdom', *New Political Economy*, 4(2) 195–214.

Walker, W. (1993) 'National Innovation Systems: Britain', in R. Nelson (ed.), *National Innovation Systems: A Comparative Analysis*. Oxford: Oxford University Press.

Wells, J. (1989) 'Uneven Development and De-industrialisation in the UK since 1979', in F. Green (ed.), *The Restructuring of the UK Economy*. Hemel Hempstead: Harvester Wheatsheaf.

Williams, K., Williams, J. and Haslam, C. (1990) 'The Hollowing Out of British Manufacturing', *Economy and Society*, 19, 456–90.

9

Britain's European Future?

Ben Rosamond

> The stake we would acquire in the success of the Community as a whole might change our concept of what were vital UK interests, whether in domestic or external relations. Progress towards integration is bound to be gradual . . . The possibility of further erosion of the power of independent decision and perhaps ultimately of some loss of national identity must nonetheless be faced.
>
> Report of the Economic Steering (Europe) Committee (the Lee Committee), 1961, on Britain's relations with the EEC

Introduction

The European issue has long been the fly in the ointment of British politics. The question of Britain's relationship with and its role within what is now called the European Union (EU) has consistently failed to fit the established patterns of political cleavage in the country. As a consequence political parties have been exposed as bitterly divided and successive governments have been engaged less in conventional statecraft and more and more with the business of balancing contending intraparty factions. Britain has been a member state since 1973 and this continues to raise a series of profound questions. To what extent has formal engagement with European integration transformed patterns of governance and influenced the degree to which national governments are able to remain authoritative and decisive? In what respect has integration and the Europeanization of policy-making spurred change in the British political economy? Is Britain locked into a European future, and to what extent do the British have choices about what this future might be?

In terms of the political sciences, the topic of Britain and Europe has tended to bring to the fore two venerable issues. The first is the relationship between 'politics' and 'economics'. The second is the linkage between domestic and external policy-making or, put another way, the link between national and international politics.

The first of these – what we might call the political economy problem – reminds us that the study of Britain and Europe must not be confined to a discussion of the changing positions of governments or the shifts in the European policy of parties. Aside from widening our parameters of enquiry, the problem charges us to think about two things. Firstly, it alerts us to the relationship between the logic of markets and the actions of private economic actors on the one hand and the formal processes of authority and control on the other. Put a little more crudely, it directs research to the relationship between (informal) economic integration and (formal) supranational institution building. Do economic processes and the logic of market imperatives force governments into particular sorts of collective decision-making? Do governments 'sign up' to or instigate schemes of integration or regimes of supranational rule-making at the behest of particularly powerful domestic economic constituencies? Secondly, the proper interrogation of political economy problems requires a wide historical lens. Conventionally, Britain's relations with processes of European integration are discussed in terms of the post-1945 period. It will be argued here that exploring the relationship between European economic integration and the Europeanization of governance functions may require a rather longer-term view.

The second of these dilemmas is a particularly pertinent question in the context of European integration. Traditionally national governments have been viewed as 'gatekeepers' between domestic political processes and international affairs. There is still a lively debate about the degree to which this is the case in contemporary Europe. Also at stake is the matter of how domestic political economies are transformed by European integration – whether, in the case explored here, 'British politics' has been altered as a consequence of British membership of the EU. Indeed many now argue that the distinction between politics within the member states and EU politics has become hopelessly blurred. Rather than being an arena in which *international* politics takes place separately from national politics, many now see the EU as a multilevel polity where the erstwhile boundaries between European and domestic policy-making have been deeply eroded. Following this logic means not only that the discussion of British politics is not complete without reference to the European dimension, but also that the processes associated with the EU herald the demise of 'British politics' as a meaningfully autonomous sphere of action.

The extent to which Britain's political future will be European is, to a large degree, mapped out by these issues. If British actors are enveloped by European structures or Europeanizing processes, then the capacity to think otherwise about alternative political and economic pathways is likely to be constrained. If governments operate a step behind the actions of crucial sections of society and if those key constituencies are 'Europeanizing' their mental horizons and behavioural patterns, then the capacity for authoritative strategic choice is severely circumscribed. If the boundaries between the British and the European political economies have ceased to be meaningful, then it becomes meaningless to speak of disengagement.

This chapter arrives at a consideration of these issues via a relatively brief discussion of the place of the 'European issue' in British politics and the relations over time between British governments and the European Communities (EC) and the EU. It moves on to think about the extent to which Britain is genuinely out of step with or awkward in relation to other member states. In pursuit of explanations it moves on by thinking about the historical trajectories of the British political economy in relation to 'Europe' and offers a short survey of how different theoretical approaches have told the 'Britain and Europe' story. The final section thinks about the question of Britain's European future through a discussion of some of the dynamics at work within the contemporary European Union.

The European question in postwar British politics

Most studies of Britain and Europe – understandably perhaps – have tended to concentrate on the period since the end of the Second World War. This has led to a focus on the relationship between British politics broadly defined and the formalization of European integration through the institutions of the European Communities commencing with the creation of the European Coal and Steel Community (ECSC) in 1951. The United Kingdom was not formally admitted to the European Communities until 1973, but the previous twenty years were characterized by an increasing engagement between British politicians and interest groups and the solidifying institutions of West European integration founded by the 'Six'.[1] The period since 1973 has involved sticky diplomacy and domestic political turmoil over European integration, but arguably has seen the British political economy fully immersed in the new multilevel polity represented by what is now called the European Union (EU). This is an important and fascinating story that has been told well many times (Camps 1963; Dennan 1996; Gamble 1998; Geddes 1999; George, 1991, 1998; H. Young 1998; J. W. Young 1993) and from which we should not divert our gaze.

Despite the presence of creative thinking about the nature of West European political order in the immediate aftermath of 1945 and despite an evident interest in the outcomes of attempts to develop a system of peace on the continent, successive governments in the 1940s and 1950s were largely hostile to British participation in such ventures. For the most part, the economic unification of core West European states was consistent with the British foreign policy goal of developing a coherent non-communist continental block. Yet, the desire to coordinate such a scheme ran up against resistance to the idea of supranational organization that seemed to involve loss of sovereignty in crucial areas. In addition, the abdication of Britain from European unification was thought in some quarters to run the risk of allowing the development of a non-Atlanticist grouping among West European countries. These dilemmas were played out within the British state in interdepartmental exchanges leading up to and following the Schuman Declaration of 1951 (George 1991: 37–9; J. W. Young 1993: 28–35). The Schuman Plan – named after the French foreign minister of the time – proposed the integration of the French and German coal and steel sectors as a first step towards broader integration and ultimately a peaceful settlement among these two erstwhile combatants. The insertion of supranational coordination of these strategically important sectors would create significant interdependencies between member states, thereby reducing the likelihood of conflict. But the integration of certain aspects of economic governance was also thought likely to generate pressures for the integration of cognate economic sectors. Thus the Schuman Plan, inspired as it was by the thinking of Jean Monnet, was rather more than a 'quick fix' to a local European security dilemma.

The failure of the 1954 Pleven Plan, proposing a European Defence Community, had much to do with domestic opposition in France. Yet the lack of interest of the Conservative government and the large-scale hostility of Whitehall to the scheme did little to advance the idea of an integrated West European military structure. It has been suggested that this period saw European statesmen losing faith in the idea of British leadership of a new West European order (George 1991: 40). But it is also clear that two important ideas were central to the calculus of British foreign policy elites: national sovereignty and Atlanticism. The embeddedness of the former doctrine meant that any apparent challenge to policy-making autonomy was likely to be met with suspicion. Commitment to the Atlantic Alliance prohibited involvement in the construction of exclusively *European* security schemes, but also sat at the heart of a more general ambivalence towards involvement in European integration.

That said, the enthusiasm of the American administration for the Messina negotiations which opened in 1955 did little to dissuade the British government from its reluctant and eventually detached posture in relation to the proposed European Economic Community (EEC). The Conservative government first sought to shift the emphasis away from the putative supranational (and apparently narrow) grouping by refusing to send high level negotiators to the Messina talks and preferring the alternative negotiating forum of the Organisation for European Economic Cooperation (OEEC) for diplomatic encounters regarding European reconstruction and integration (Camps 1963). In the longer term, the British withdrawal from Messina was accompanied by a leading role in the creation of the European Free Trade Association (EFTA), a looser more avowedly intergovernmental organization.

EFTA came into being in 1960, yet within twelve months Britain had lodged an application to join the EEC. The rationale for the shift in policy is much discussed and is usually attributed to a mixture of factors: a sense of diminishing world power significance following the Suez crisis, encouragement from the new Kennedy administration in the US and the first realization within the political classes that urgent solutions were needed to the problem of British relative economic decline. While this first application for membership of the Communities was rejected, largely at the behest of the French administration under de Gaulle, the issue of membership quickly made inroads into domestic political debate in Britain. European integration quickly ceased being an issue of pure diplomacy and elite calculus (Ludlow 1997; Wilks 1996).

Labour Party leader Hugh Gaitskell's speech to the 1962 Labour Party Conference characterized the prospect of British membership as imperilling 'a thousand years of history' (Gaitskell 1996). The politics of membership (that is whether or not the UK should join or remain within the European Communities) became the main and most overt way in which British politics interacted with European integration from the early 1960s until the early 1980s. For the most part the issue flared at particular junctures. These included the period of the membership applications during the 1960s, the period leading up to and following British accession in the early 1970s, the referendum campaign of 1975 and the 1983 general election when the Labour Party presented an explicit manifesto commitment to curtail British membership. The pattern of this politics of membership – to an extent – followed the dictates of Britain's oppositional political culture. But from the early exchanges of the 1960s it was also apparent that the European issue was capable of dividing political parties and producer groups like no other. The established fault line of twentieth-century British politics, 'state versus market' which translated into the left–right cleavage between the Labour and Conservative parties, proved insufficient to capture the many questions raised under the rubric of the 'European problem'. True, it became common within the left to package opposition to British membership of the EC with hostility to Conservative governments (this is true of both the early 1960s and the early 1970s), but the presence of strong voices in the Labour movement favouring British involvement was indicative of the profound difficulties European unity would eventually cause for British politicians.

Debate exists within political parties on all issues and by their very nature parties are broad churches. Yet the intrusion of the membership questions into the everyday cut and thrust of party politics created tensions unlike any others witnessed in the postwar period. These became especially salient within the Labour Party during the 1970s. In the run-up to the referendum on continued British membership in 1975, the Prime Minister Harold Wilson took the remarkable step of removing the constraints of collective cabinet responsibility as a measure to keep his government united. The hardening of official party policy towards membership in the late 1970s and early 1980s was instrumental in persuading several leading figures to create the rival Social Democratic Party (SDP).

The Conservatives had seemed relatively united on the membership question throughout the 1960s and 1970s. Yet as the 'politics of European integration' shifted away from purely membership concerns, divisions became quickly apparent as 'Euroscepticism' became not only a significant tendency within the party, but also a feature of the political discourse of Conservative leaders, notably Margaret Thatcher. As the stark issue of membership receded from debate after the 1983 election, the overt 'politics of European integration' came to revolve around the place of Britain within the Communities and the nature of the 'Europe' that further integration looked set to produce (Rosamond 1998). Following the Conservative victory in the 1979 election, the Thatcher government adopted an aggressive negotiating posture within the EC's intergovernmental institutions over the issue of British contributions to the Community budget. The eventual settlement of this problem at the Fontainebleau European Council of 1984 paved the way – at the diplomatic level at least – for the moves towards the completion of the Community's internal market.[2] At first sight the creation of an EC-wide liberalized market space chimed well with the domestic neoliberal project of Thatcherism in the UK, but the freeing of the Community market also logically entailed a degree of transfer of regulatory and authoritative capacity to supranational institutions. This potential for 'spillover' was not lost on the relatively cohesive and strategically minded Commission that took office under Jacques Delors in 1985. EC-level social standards (especially in the area of workers' rights), the 'deepening' of market integration to monetary union, fiscal harmonization and macroeconomic convergence all became serious agenda items in EC circles from the late 1980s.

The ferocious rhetorical exchanges between Thatcher and Delors helped to define political fault lines in Britain from the late 1980s. Not only did Euroscepticism become normalized as a feature of Conservative Party (and thus government) policy, but the Labour Party under the leadership of Neil Kinnock moved quite decisively away from hostility to British membership of the EC (Baker and Seawright 1998a; George and Rosamond 1992; Rosamond 1990). The party's policy review process, the dictates of oppositional political culture and the appearance of quasi-social democratic sentiments at the peak of the European Commission all helped to 'convert' the British left. But the centrality and ubiquity of 'Europe' in British political debate from the late 1980s reflected the growing intimacy between the British political economy and the processes of European integration. The advent of the single market from the mid-1980s had alerted British firms and trade unions to the growing importance of the EC legislative framework, and the volume of directives to be incorporated into UK law had increased steadily. The extensive involvement of Whitehall and local government in the monitoring and implementation of EC legislation meant that the entire British polity became suffused in a wider European polity. Interest organization and local authorities were among those establishing a presence in Brussels in order to seek resources and gain an input into the Community's policy-making processes (Mazey and Richardson 1996).

The relatively settled nature of the membership question combined with the purposeful activism of the Commission, the European Parliament and the European Court of Justice to produce a politics focused around the question of the future shape and extent of European integration and Britain's place therein. This did not mean that the long-standing ideological bases of pro- and anti-Europeanism disappeared, but that they were deployed differently in alternative contexts.

The Conservative government's reputation for 'awkwardness' and tough negotiating was reinforced by its posture at the Maastricht European Council in 1991. This was the culmination of the negotiations that produced the Treaty on European Union (TEU). By common consent, the shape of the TEU was shaped crucially by the influence of the British delegation in the negotiations (Forster 1998). The TEU was significant for its extension of policy competencies and the significant overhaul of the architecture of the Communities. The Major government was instrumental in creating the EU's so-called 'three pillar' design that ensured that extensive supranational competence would not intrude into the proposed Common Foreign and Security Policy (CFSP).[3] Additionally, the provisions on social policy (the 'Social Chapter') were removed from the main text of the treaty and annexed as a protocol enabling the other eleven member states to borrow the Community's institutions to make progress in this area. Britain would not be subject to any legislation made through this route. For most, though, the TEU's key provisions related to the setting of criteria and a timetable for the achievement of monetary union by the member states. It was here that the British successfully negotiated a right to choose whether to proceed to the irrevocable aspects of monetary union – fixing of exchange rate parities and movement to a common currency (Council of the European Communities/Commission of the European Communities 1992: 191–3). Prime Minister John Major claimed to have secured a 'best of both worlds' deal for Britain in that membership would only occur at Britain's behest if it could be established that joining European Monetary Union (EMU) was in the country's best interest. It also meant that confrontation with the troublesome issue of monetary sovereignty could be postponed.

On the other hand, it would be misleading to suggest that Maastricht had given the British government total freedom of manoeuvre in relation to monetary union. Quickly, the thrust of UK economic policy came to focus on the achievement of the convergence criteria necessary for economies to be judged ready for admission to EMU. Indeed, close attention had been paid to the Europeanization of macroeconomic policy well before the TEU was negotiated. The Conservatives had taken Britain into the Exchange Rate Mechanism (ERM) of the European Monetary System (EMS) in October 1990, but under the Chancellorship of Nigel Lawson had already engaged in a de facto exchange rate alignment by shadowing the Deutschmark. Indeed, it now seems clear that influential ministers within the Conservative government (supported eventually by officials within both the Treasury and the Foreign Office) had been engaged in the long-term endeavour of persuading Margaret Thatcher of the merits of British membership of the ERM (H. Young 1998: 341–53).

The arguments about ERM membership and EMU revealed at least two interesting facets of British politics at the time. Firstly, Thatcher's hostility to joining the ERM (the first prerequisite stage of EMU according to the Delors Report of 1988) was based on an argument about the sanctity of British monetary sovereignty. The countercase, presented by Lawson and Geoffrey Howe, was based on the claim that Britain would be best placed to influence, and therefore subvert, the path to full EMU within the Communities (Buller 1999). But there was also a distinct sense in these exchanges of the inadequacies of existing British monetary policy frameworks, and methods of exchange rate management in particular (Thompson 1996). Exchange rate stability and currency strength were vital in a world of increasingly mobile capital and EMU had always been built on the premise that these virtues could best be achieved through collective action among the member states of the Communities. In short, the ideological preference for policy autonomy was rubbing against the real fears that this very autonomy was under serious threat. Secondly, as Helen Thompson has shown, policy-making in relation to European monetary arrangements was chaotically muddled: 'the British government missed out on the possible benefits of ERM membership offered during the 1980s in terms of interest rates and exchange rate stability, whilst incurring the costs that the system imposed in the early 1990s' (1996: 218). Her analysis suggests both a long-term and a short-term policy failure. In the long term a mixture of ideological fog and the failure to understand the inadequacies of domestic monetary policy kept the UK out of the ERM. In the short term, a rational approach to policy-making would have foreseen the immediate dangers of joining the ERM in the circumstances of 1990.

Britain left the ERM in spectacular fashion in September 1992 following a colossal speculative attack on vulnerable European currencies including sterling (Barrell, Britton and Pain 1994; Michie 1998). The circumstances of 'Black Wednesday' revealed enormous amounts about the power of international financial markets, the vulnerability of national governments and the prospects for attempts to pool monetary sovereignty. It also showed how an event of this sort might have significant political repercussions. If opinion polls are right, the ERM episode left the Conservative government mortally wounded (King et al, 1998). The image of economic competence was shattered and the fault lines within the Conservative Party became open sores. Internal party management became a priority for Major in the context of a dwindling parliamentary majority. The challenge to Major's leadership of the party by John Redwood, the removal of the party whip from a troublesome group of Eurosceptic Conservative backbenchers and further crisis occasioned by the issue of BSE[4] were all manifestations of the chaos wrought by European integration in British politics (Baker et al. 1996).

The Labour government of Tony Blair assumed office in 1997 with an explicit commitment to engage more constructively with its European partners. Nevertheless, the EMU issue remained deeply troublesome. The continued suspension of British membership of the ERM provided a technical obstacle to joining the first group of countries to enter EMU in January 1999. Although the British economy met the other criteria for inclusion, it was made clear in 1997 that the UK would not join the currency union without firm judgements being made on the suitability for Britain of such an enterprise. The language of public ministerial statements presented EMU as a largely technical matter, not to be handled with ideological zeal on either side. As the then Foreign Secretary Robin Cook put it:

> It is a rational approach that puts a cool calculation on the national interest first. It does not make the mistake of a commitment out of a romantic affection for Europe to join the euro, even if the economic conditions were not right. And it avoids the mistake on the other extreme which is to rule out joining the euro out of a distaste for all things European. (Cook 1999: 5; see also T. Blair 1999)

But few doubt that this technocratic language masked potentially damaging divisions within the Labour Party (Baker and Seawright 1998a). At the same time, the Conservative Party under the leadership of William Hague moved in a more decisively and explicitly Eurosceptic direction. A party slogan 'In Europe, not run by Europe' (Conservative Party 2000a) was accompanied by a commitment to fight the next election on the platform of opposing British membership of the single currency (Conservative Party 2000b).

The emergence of a pro-European Conservative Party in the 1999 elections for the European Parliament was indicative of continuing tensions on the centre right of the political spectrum. This was reinforced by the launch of the cross-party 'Britain in Europe' campaign in October 1999 which claimed the support of senior Conservatives such as Michael Heseltine and Kenneth Clarke (see http://www.britainineurope.org). But Euroscepticism also organized itself beyond the Conservative Party. Sir James Goldsmith's Referendum Party fought the 1997 election conspicuously if not particularly successfully, while the longer-standing UK Independence Party benefited from changes in the electoral system to win seats in the 1999 elections for the European Parliament.

The impact of membership

Britain's formal involvement with the processes of European integration and the construction of an EU governance regime has had a number of discernible effects within the British political economy. Most obvious has been the growth of European calculus in foreign policy decision-making (Reynolds 1991). British external relations – especially in forums such as the World Trade Organization – take place most obviously under EU auspices. This is not to say that British foreign policy has ceased to exist, but that a good deal of the business of the Foreign and Commonwealth Office, as well as that of other departments of state, is taken up with European affairs (Henderson 1998). It might be that certain agencies of the British state have become 'internationalized' or linked more intimately to authoritative structures of governance elsewhere than to the agencies and clients of the British state.

A second obvious effect has been the considerable upsurge in inter- and intraparty debate about European integration combined with the 'European issue' (however defined) becoming a staple item of popular and journalistic discourse. Prior to the mid-1980s, questions of European integration intruded only periodically (albeit significantly) into British political consciousness. By the late 1990s, internecine party warfare over European integration had become the norm. It has been argued that the battle lines defined by the European issue have been difficult to accommodate within the conventional party political cleavages of British politics (Baker, Gamble and Ludlam 1993). The conventions of opposition as cemented by the evolution of Britain's bipolar party system have tended to align opposing forces on a classic left–right distinction: roughly 'state versus market'. But the European issue brings another axis of conflict into play: roughly 'sovereignty versus interdependence'. Historically, divisions along this axis have tended to divide parties within rather than intensify the conflict between them.

Beyond these obvious manifestations of the European issue, policy-making in Britain has become 'Europeanized'. This may be defined in various ways. For Jim Buller (1999), Europeanization represents the growth of European legislation as a core element of the business of Whitehall. By definition, membership of the EU requires the incorporation of the body of EC law – the *acquis communautaire* – into UK law. Simon Bulmer and Martin Burch (1998) cast the net a little wider by offering a two-pronged definition. They argue that Europeanization occurs when the EU has an impact on the main policy agendas and goals of member state governments. The second dimension of Europeanization is the shift in the norms, practices and values of policy-making as a consequence of EU membership. Bulmer and Burch explore the second of these dimensions and conclude that the *modus operandi* of Whitehall has remained largely intact despite British membership of the European Communities. However, distinct new procedures have developed in response to the pervasiveness of EC law. Moreover, it seems that the central arms of the civil service now find themselves faced with relatively new international policy imperatives. The need for ministers to bargain, coalition-build and do deals within the EU's intergovernmental institutions provides an additional focal point for Whitehall's activities.

Other aspects of British life can be thought of as Europeanized. The jurisprudence of the European Court of Justice is frequently sought by British courts in need, in accordance with Article 177 of the Treaties, of preliminary rulings on domestic cases where issues of EC law are at stake. This is rather more than a technical procedure. It opens up new battle lines in the politics of law by arming lower courts with significant leverage in relation to higher national judicial bodies (Alter 1996). Europeanization also extends to the wider organization of politics. Patterns of negotiation, lobbying and interest intermediation have all been recalibrated in light of the emergence of new loci of authority. The growth of interest organizations and local authorities with offices in Brussels has been explosive since the mid-1980s. Interested actors had to adapt both to a new level of policy-making and to distinct patterns of liaison and consultation between the Commission and its clients (Mazey and Richardson 1996). The evidence is that the levels of engagement vary from sector to sector and that different groups within the same policy sector often use the opportunity of EU-level lobbying in quite distinct ways (Egdell and Thomson 1999).

At a deeper level it is often argued that the stimulus for recent debates about constitutional change in the UK has come predominantly from the repercussions of British membership. Wolfram Kaiser (1998) maintains that the visibility of European integration has been an important catalyst for elite reflection on issues of modernization and constitutional reform in the UK since the early 1960s. Similarly, P. W. Preston (1994) has suggested that the participation of Britain in the European project brings the UK's traditionalist political-institutional culture directly into conflict with more modern, rationalist, decentralized and democratic continental variants. The moves to devolution for Scotland and Wales, attention to the iniquities of the electoral system, moves to reform some of the more obviously archaic elements of the British state and the growing concern in political discourse for the theme of 'modernization' can all be seen as flowing from a form of constitutional Europeanization. At the same time, of course, there is a powerful argument to suggest that the form of economic integration practised by the EU via the single market and EMU represents a triumph for essentially Anglo-Saxon capitalist values.

The precise economic consequences of British membership are hard to discern. It is probably true to say that the UK economy is tightly locked into the wider European economy and that the single market has become the defining feature of the 'business environment' of UK firms. The fourteen other member states collectively constitute the UK's most important trading partner (Lintner 1998). More difficult to estimate are the economic consequences of membership and thus the implications of the UK withdrawing from the EU. The short term 'impact costs' of joining the Communities (notably a competitive shock to UK manufacturing industry) may have been offset by longer term dynamic gains (such as access to continental markets and the availability of cheap imports). Precise measurement of these phenomena is almost impossible, since broader changes in the global economy have also impacted on the performances and practices of the British economy since 1973, especially following the elimination of capital controls in 1979.

Perhaps the most telling consequence of membership is the removal of certain policy instruments. The status of the Communities as a customs union means that external trade policy can no longer be based on the unilateral application of tariffs or the creation of non-tariff barriers (Lintner 1998). Agricultural support policies – a feature of all advanced industrialized countries – are conducted at the European level, as are polices and regulatory frameworks in an increasing range of economic, social and environmental areas. The big issue here is the extent to which this 'drift' of policy-making to Europe compromises the autonomy of the British state. A lot of the British debate about European integration revolves around the issue of sovereignty. However, it has been argued that the concept of autonomy, defined as 'the ability of a state to transform its policy preferences into authoritative actions' (Kassim and Menon 1996), is a more useful entry point to thinking about these questions. For example, it might be that British pretences are more effectively realized through the transfer of governance capacity to the European level.

Awkwardness?

One favoured interpretation of Britain's dealings with the Communities is the so-called 'awkward partner' thesis. The argument – found not just in academic analysis, but also journalistic treatments – tends to proceed in two steps. The first step claims that successive British governments have taken a negative and zero-sum attitude to the Communities since 1973 and that this displays continuities with the diplomatic dealings of governments prior to the attainment of membership. The second step is to seek explanations for these periodic outbreaks of awkwardness.

Examples of awkwardness are easy to chronicle: the initial reluctance of Britain to engage with the integration project in the 1950s, the need to hold a referendum on continued membership in 1975, the Labour Party's commitment to terminate British membership at the 1983 election, periodic disputes about the size of the British contribution to the Community budget, the persistent refusal to join the ERM, the Thatcher government's running battle with the Delors Commission, the Major government's tough negotiating posture at Maastricht and its policy on non-cooperation within EU institutions at the height of the BSE crisis, and the Blair government's refusal to enter EMU (to name but a few). Depictions of the EU in the British press often relied on caricature and 'us versus them' language (Wilkes and Wring 1998)

It would be difficult to treat these instances of negativity in British dealings with the EU as the outcome of a systematic and deliberate negotiating strategy. But there is an evident tendency (Wilks 1996). Whether this places Britain at odds with the other member states is another matter though (Buller 1995). For example, since 1973 Britain's record of incorporating Community directives into British law compares remarkably well with most of the other member states (George 1995, 1998). Indeed Britain has one of the lowest rates of Commission censure or Court action for non-compliance or mis-implementation of Community legislation (Nugent 1999: 376, 378–9).

It is probably safer to say that successive British governments have encountered difficulties when operating in the EC/EU context. To an extent this can be explained by the lack of British influence over the shape of the Communities that it eventually joined sixteen years after their initiation. For instance, the Common Agricultural Policy (CAP) was a system of agricultural support devised by the Six to take account of the structures of their domestic farming sectors. The fact that a very high proportion of the Community budget was devoted to the CAP meant that the British would be heavy net contributors. Others look to the peculiar processes of British domestic politics that give rise to particular governmental positions in intergovernmental negotiations (George 1995, 1998). Thus it is difficult to understand the orientations of the British government in the late 1980s and early 1990s without attending to the delicacies of internal Conservative Party politics.

Delving deeper, the character of British institutions and political culture might help to explain tendencies to awkwardness. Instead of awkwardness being the diplomatic expression of fundamental differences of national interest between the UK and the rest, British reluctance could be attributed to the existence of (from the British viewpoint) 'unusual' decision-making cultures and procedural norms in the European institutions. Thus Stephen George (1994) suggests that the British fall foul of the continental tendency to set goals and then work on how to achieve them, which contrasts with a British tradition of 'muddle-through' incrementalism in policy-making. He also reports the initial bafflement expressed by some British MEPs – hitherto socialized into the cut and thrust of Westminster – at the non-adversarial culture of the European Parliament. Stuart Wilks (1996) argues that two well-established features of the British state intervene in the relationship between Britain and the EU. These are the tendency to centralize power and the dominant doctrine of parliamentary sovereignty. Together, they promote opposition to integration because the British political class finds it difficult to contemplate ceding authority either upwards (to the supranational level) or downwards to local authorities, both of which feature heavily in the recalibration of governance functions associated with the growth of a multilevel European polity. Centralizing tendencies also allow the executive to maintain relatively tight control over the conduct of EU business. So an additional counter-democratic effect is the potential emasculation of parliamentary control of the executive.

The debate about awkwardness or semi-detachment is useful because it alerts the student of Britain and the EU to deep sources of explanation. The next section tries to provide a little historical depth, while the following section offers a series of alternative readings of the UK–EU relationship.

History

This chapter has concentrated largely on the period since 1945 and has begun to assemble some of the explanations for the way in which European integration has been a significant factor in British politics. The previous section suggested that we may have to dig a little deeper to gain a proper understanding of the longer-term dynamics of British policy and the impact of 'Europe' on Britain. This section offers a brief historical detour with a view to fleshing out the story yet further.

Andrew Gamble (1998) argues that a number of strategic choices made by British elites have influenced subsequent attitudes and that these strategic choices have been determined largely by the type of capitalism and the form of state that emerged from the industrial revolution in Britain. Britain's leadership of the international economic order in the nineteenth century was underwritten by its advocacy of policies of free trade and *laissez-faire*. The repeal of the Corn Laws in 1846 took protectionism and agricultural self-sufficiency off the domestic political agenda and locked Britain decisively into the rhythms of the international economy. Interestingly enough, the growth of free trade advocacy and commercial liberal practices across Europe in place of mercantilism (economic nationalism) had much to do with Britain forcing the pace of change and acting as an exemplar to other countries. A cluster of bilateral tariff reduction treaties throughout the 1860s can be traced to an initial compact between Britain and France in 1860 (Pollard 1981). In some ways, therefore, Britain can be seen as a material and ideational driving force of European economic integration after the Napoleonic Wars. It is also salutary to remember that European economic integration did not begin with the ECSC in 1951 (Klausen and Tilly 1998). Thinking about the longer-term trajectory of the processes of cross-border economic activity helps us to remember that certain core principles of the European economic order were laid down in the nineteenth century and that the role of Britain was significant in displacing various versions of national political economy (Gamble 1994a).

That said, the British engagement with the emerging European economy was only part of the story. The strength of France as a continental economic force had contributed to the search by British commercial and industrial capital for markets beyond Europe (Overbeek 1990: 39–40). British dominance of world trade was such that by 1870 the UK was 'directly involved in nearly one quarter of all world trade' (Williams 1971: 10). The associated growth of the British empire saw a gradual reorientation of British capital exports to non-European areas, certainly by the turn of the twentieth century. The need to police the empire had augmented Britain's world power status, and while it was not an insignificant player in the European power balance, the economic and military dimensions of hegemony meant that the British state's gaze extended well beyond its immediate European locality.

This, of course, meant that the residues of this world power status influenced dealings with Europe after the Second World War and made alignment with the 'European circle' a less obvious option. However, the residue of the move to empire is not the only historical factor used to explain the lack of European impetus in the British state in the second half of the twentieth century. The failure of successive British governments to deal with the manifest problems of relative economic decline has been the subject of much historiographical scrutiny (Gamble 1994a: Coates 1994). One significant theme has been the retention by the British state of pre-democratic legacies and affinities to circulating or financial capital rather than indigenous productive capital. In combination these legacies failed to generate the type of developmental or strategic ethos to execute the necessary modernization of the British economy. Engagement with 'Europe' might have been a central component of such a strategy, but recognition of the deep nature of Britain's economic malaise did not emerge until the early 1960s. Only at this point did the necessity of a European future for the British economy begin to become apparent (Fay and Meehan 1999). This was compromised in any case by the lack of commitment to the competitive needs of British industrial capital and the continued favouring of the City and circulating capital.

A further legacy of Britain's imperfect industrial modernization was the abiding commitment across the political spectrum to the doctrine of 'parliamentary sovereignty' – a translation of absolutist monarchical precepts into quasi-democratic langauge. Most obviously, this meant that ceding authority to another level of governance or pooling sovereignty have always been difficult concepts for the British political class. The doctrine also found expression on the left, through the Fabian belief in the capacity of (an unreformed) Westminster to deliver progressive social democratic outcomes. Nation-state socialism was perhaps the dominant tendency on the British left until the late 1980s (Rosamond 1990, 1993). But the legacies of this doctrine have been expressed most forcefully on the right of the political spectrum through the Conservative Party (Lynch 1998). In a broader sense, this historical detour shows not only how the legacies of the past influence the present, but also how much is at stake in the politics of Britain's European future. In a sense Europeanization may represent an opportunity for the modernization of the British political economy.

Interpreting Britain and Europe

The Britain/Europe question has commanded voluminous literature, but perhaps not enough of this work has posed theoretical questions. Quite clearly, the way in which we read the story is likely to be influenced by the theoretical framework we choose. The purpose of this section is to identify a number of theoretical lenses and to explore briefly how each would treat the relationship between Britain and European integration. It is argued here that each of these theoretical clusters can be used as a springboard not only for thinking about the way in which the relationship between Britain and Europe has developed to date, but also to examine ways of thinking about the future. Four broad theoretical clusters are identified here. All are mainstream to the study of the EU (Rosamond 2000).

Realism/neorealism

Conventional theories of international relations tend to make a separation between domestic politics and international relations. The claim is that politics *among* nations is quite distinct from politics *within* nations. In realist international relations, foreign policy is a matter of strategic choice where state elites evaluate appropriate diplomatic postures to deal with their perceived position in relation to other states. In most realist and neorealist analysis[5] international alliances and intergovernmental organizations are fragile creations rooted in the short-term self-help logic created by the pursuit of states' self-interest in conditions where there in no overarching global authority. At the forefront of states' calculus is the question of security in this anarchic environment. Moreover, the continued capacity of states to monopolize the means of destruction and violence gives them significant primacy over non-state actors in world politics. From this type of perspective there is a definite distinction between processes of domestic politics and foreign policy. The former is, by and large, separate from the latter and international politics operates largely on the basis of foreign policy elites' strategic calculus. Domestic political considerations and pressures do not feed into this process. Alliance structures and international organizations are bodies that serve coincident strategic interests of groups of states, but they are likely to dissolve when interests shift (Mearsheimer 1991).

From this perspective it is best to read Britain's involvement with European integration as a matter of elite strategic choice. The decision to join the Communities could be read as a decision based on the exigencies of Britain's place in the international system in the 1950s. Rather than representing a decision to abdicate sovereignty and thereby dissolve the integrity of the British nation-state into a supranational Europolity, joining the EC can be read as a deliberate decision to insert the UK more definitely in its European foreign policy 'circle' (Sanders 1990). The decision may have reflected Britain's declining status as a world power, a fact evident to the British political class in the wake of the Suez fiasco of 1956. It may also have indicated an understanding of the growing importance of European markets and the relative retreat of the significance of the Commonwealth. Either way, the depiction of involvement in the European game as a matter of strategic self-interest suggests that the decision could and should be reversed if British interests altered.

An alternative way of thinking about British relations with Europe from an elite-strategic perspective is through the concept of statecraft (Bulpitt 1986; Buller 1999; Thompson 1996). 'Statecraft' refers to the ways in which governments seek to maintain themselves in office and secure domestic political support. Jim Buller (1999) argues that successive twentieth-century British governments have sought international economic solutions to domestic policy dilemmas. Membership of the Communities represented a preference for a European external support mechanism over the failing empire/Commonwealth method of the first half of the century. Jim Bulpitt's classic analysis (Bulpitt 1986) suggested that Conservative governments in particular have tried to secure a space for independent action by the executive by insulating government from domestic and external pressures. This would be consistent with the tendency of 'awkwardness' described above, but could also be used to explain why governments move towards the potential haven of European-level intergovernmentalism.

Liberal intergovernmentalism and domestic politics

Realists are often criticized for their failure to see the importance of domestic pressures on foreign policy-making, their rigid separation of economic from security concerns and the dismissal of international institutions as insignificant in explaining behaviour. Liberal intergovernmentalism (LI) is a perspective native to EU studies, but has its roots in the critiques of realism and neorealism by scholars of international relations. The key claim of LI is that the integration process takes place as a two-level game. 'Demands' for integration outcomes emerge in the domestic policy-making processes of the member states, whereas integration outputs are supplied through processes of intergovernmental bargaining at the EU level. At the interface of these two levels sit member state governments. Governmental preferences emerge out of processes of domestic politics. These preferences in turn are the basis of bargaining strategies in the EU's intergovernmental institutions, notably the Council of Ministers and the European Council. The principal exponent of LI, Andrew Moravcsik (1993, 1998), argues that the key junctures of European integration are moments of treaty creation and revision. It is at these points that the gatekeeping role of governments is most salient. Thus to understand either the Single European Act or the Treaty on European Union, we need to attend to the bargaining strategies deployed by national executives, the relative power of those governmental actors, the preferences from which those strategies emerge and the processes of domestic political bargaining within individual member countries.

The two-level game analogy can be seen to have two contradictory effects on our conception of the autonomy of national governments.

Firstly, involvement with international cooperation is a recipe for their progressive emasculation. Governments seek to retain office. To do so they need to secure the support of powerful domestic coalitions (for example 'finance capital' or firms in particular sectors). If the balance of domestic forces favours a particular integration outcome (say European-level liberalization and regulation or progress to monetary union), then it makes sense for rational power-seeking office holders to adopt those preferences. However, the enactment of those outcomes is likely to enhance the relative power of those powerful domestic constituencies in relation to government – and so the process continues (Milner 1998).

Secondly, on the other hand, European integration can be read as a way of strengthening the state in relation to the domestic polity. The transfer of decision-making capacity to the European level has the dual effect of keeping governments involved in the management of accumulation and the regulation of their respective societies while releasing national executives from 'troublesome' democratic controls on the decision-making process (Moravcsik 1994). In a similar vein, it has been argued that 'integration' was the only choice for modern European welfare states seeking to secure long-term durability through the delivery of policy programmes. In Alan Milward's famous and counter-intuitive phrase, postwar integration constituted the 'rescue of the nation-state' (Milward 1993). More recently it has been suggested that the European Union has evolved out of two sets of pressures on the modern European nation-state: the demands of national publics socialized into the norms of the modern welfare state and the challenges to effective macroeconomic control posed by 'globalization' (Wallace 1996).

The British case can be slotted into these scenarios with some ease and plausibility (though see Forster 1998). As one of the larger member states, it carries significant voting weight and tacit power within the EU's intergovernmental fora. Moravcsik (1991) attributes the successful negotiation of the Single European Act to preference convergence among the West German, French and British governments around a neoliberal economic agenda in the mid-1980s. Moreover, the UK's tendency to be attitudinally 'out of synch' with the rest of the member states could be attributed to the highly distinctive pressures that emerge in the context of British politics. Thinking in this way also raises some significant paradoxes. The Thatcher government (1979–90) could be read as fostering accumulation strategies consistent with the preferences of internationally oriented productive and finance capital – hence the support for European-level market liberalization in the form of the Single European Act. Yet its simultaneous revulsion for the loss of particular aspects of its autonomy shows up beautifully the 'push-me-pull-you' aspect of the two-level game as well as the intriguing free economy/strong state dialectic that lay at the heart of Thatcherism (Gamble 1994b).

Institutionalism

A third cluster of theoretical accounts lies under the umbrella term 'institutionalism'. Both realism and LI offer largely state-centric versions of the dynamics of European integration and EU governance. While emphasis on the significant actions of governmental actors is not ruled out, institutionalists choose rather to focus on the impact on behaviour and policy outcomes of institutions. Institutions can be defined as formal, procedural, rule-bound entities, but the term also embraces established patterns of interaction and routinized practices among actors. Most institutionalists begin with the premise that institutions constitute an intervening variable between preferences and behaviour and/or policy output. For some, institutions make agreement easier to achieve by increasing trust among participants and reducing transaction costs. Others occupy a more radically 'sociological' position to argue that institutions are venues for socialization and induction into norms that actually create preferences. Actors' notions of their identity, their interest and their environment can all arise and develop within institutions. They are social constructs that are not straightforwardly located in an external material reality.

A further variant of institutionalist analysis asks an alternative set of questions. Historical institutionalists are interested in two things: the long-run impact of institutions and the actual processes of institutional choice and design. In terms of the first of these, institutions often 'lock in', producing patterns of interaction and policy styles that are not easily displaced, even if the overall context of policy-making changes (Pierson 1998). The ECSC was created in quite distinct circumstances and in the context of quite different imperatives from those confronting Europeans in the early twenty-first century. Yet the basic institutional pattern de-vised by the Six – involving a relatively heavy load of supranationalism – remains more or less intact. New external challenges such as competitive threat in the 1980s or perceptions of globalization in the 1990s had to be filtered through an institutional architecture that arose in very different circumstances. This leads to the second question about the mechanisms of institutional choice: how and why particular configurations are chosen by actors at particular times. This begs in turn a third set of queries about the consequences of new members participating in institutional forums designed by others.

This last observation could be applied to Britain which, as we saw above, was 'absent at the creation' of the Communities. It might be argued that the British eventually came to participate in a set of path-dependent institutions that were playing out a series of logics inspired by the circumstances of their design. But institutional perspectives also remind us that British actors are in many ways enmeshed into the day-to-day workings of the Brussels policy process. Institutions can also possess socializing qualities. The Council of Ministers is difficult to describe as a purely intergovernmental forum (Hayes-Renshaw and Wallace 1997) since individual councils have developed distinctive ways of doing business and in some cases, such as the Council of Agricultural Ministers, have moved away from being bargaining forums to becoming venues of advocacy for the needs of the sector in question (Grant 1997). This means that it is potentially difficult to discern 'British interests' or 'British preferences' that either arise externally to the EU's institutional environment or are not heavily mediated by the influence of institutional practices. Research also suggests that exposure to the practices and habits of the European Parliament has contributed to greater sympathy for the deepening of European integration among British MEPs (Westlake 1994)

Multilevel governance

Critique of the state-centric explanation favoured by LI is perhaps best encapsulated by the literature on multilevel governance (Marks, Hooghe and Blank 1996; Rosamond 2001). Here the twin depictions of national governments as gatekeepers and intergovernmental institutions as the most important venues in the EU come under sustained attack. The EU is portrayed instead as a fluid, variegated multilevel and multi-actor policy. The multilevel governance (MLG) metaphor is used to show that the EU policy process is not simply confined to bargaining forums and institutions in Brussels. Rather it embraces and envelops the full range of political institutions within the member states. This also means that actors often operate at more than one level of action, that states are not the exclusive sites of authority in the system and that levels of integration vary from policy area to policy area. The MLG picture is consistent with the claim that the growth of policy competence and the deepening of integration can happen through informal means (the inter-action of non-state actors, the development of the technicalities of EC law and the incremental growth of regulatory frameworks) as much as through the formalities of intergovernmental bargaining. As one analyst puts it, the EU is 'a system of complex, multitiered, geographically overlapping structures of governmental and non-governmental elites' (Wessels 1997: 291).

Such depictions have radical implications for the way we 'read' the Britain and Europe issue. Conventional academic, journalistic and political discourse treats British politics and the EU as separate spheres of action. Acceptance of the MLG perspective carries with it the claim that this classical separation may be a falsehood. The British government remains, of course, a key player in EU affairs, but it lacks the capacity to gatekeep and the institutions within which it bargains are not necessarily the key determinants of the EU's pattern of evolution. An MLG approach also cautions against taking a cross-the-board view of British relations with Europe. Sectoral variations in policy-making may be more important than national variations.

Conclusion: Britain's European future?

Andrew Gamble argues that 'what is at stake in the European controversy in British politics is a major choice about Britain's role in the global political economy' (1998: 12). It is, as suggested above, a choice conditioned by the playing out of the logic of previous choices, some of which stretch back into the mists of history. The consequences of making that choice are significant in all kinds of ways. Gamble goes on to suggest that the point at which key choices are made is likely to be a moment of realignment that alters the texture of the political system. Governments fall, parties split and political coalitions fragment and others form. The period since the Second World War can be viewed as a prolonged deferment of that inevitable decision. The statecraft of successive governments has (just about) kept the main political parties from splitting, but it has not stopped governments receiving reverses at the polls and experiencing deeply troublesome displays of disloyalty in the House of Commons.

However, the dawn of EMU presents a point at which the choice will have to be made. Joining monetary union will commit Britain to the irrevocable fixing of exchange rates and the phasing out of sterling as a distinct unit of account. The UK government will cease to have monetary policy autonomy and pressures for the pooling of fiscal policy competencies might not be far behind. To join EMU would align Britain decisively within the deeply integrated European economy and lock the governance of the British economy into a system of supranational rule-making and macroeconomic control. The debates about the pros and cons of such a move continue to fascinate. Conservative Eurosceptics raise the spectre of catastrophic losses of policy-making autonomy and, therefore, the effective dissolution of Britain as a nation-state. A range of technical arguments form the superficial case for entry. These include the virtues of exchange rate and interest rate stability, low inflation and increased transparency (Johnson 1996). The deeper questions arise out of a more profound issue of political economy: how to secure these policy goals in a turbulent, globalized economy? The debates on the intellectual left in Britain give some clue to the complexity of these matters. For some, the stability offered by EMU gives the space for the pursuit of core social democratic values without the underlying fear of speculative attack and capital flight (Corry 1999). Others see EMU as nothing less than the imposition of deflationary market discipline on the economies of the EU (Michie 1999).

Another argument is that – aside from any deeper objections to the EMU project – the British economy continues to be structured in peculiar ways that mean that the ways in which EMU is calibrated will not render Britain more prosperous. The distinctiveness of Britain in relation to its continental counterparts is not simply a matter of the outward orientation of the economy or the oddities of geography (Chisholm 1995), but also about its peculiar business cycle and the internal structures of – for example – the housing market. For some these peculiar economic structures make EMU membership nothing short of folly (Baimbridge, Burkitt and Whyman 1997).

However, the EMU issue will not be resolved through technocratic debate. It must be filtered through the prism of interparty debate and intraparty management. Given the preferred use of the referendum option, it will also be a matter of public opinion – or more precisely the management of public opinion and exercise of statecraft. Opinion poll data suggests a comfortable majority of the British public continues to be hostile to the prospect of a single currency. During late 1999 and early 2000, the pollsters ICM found that when people were posed with the question 'If there were to be a referendum would you vote to join the single European currency or vote not to join?', around 60 per cent replied negatively (*Guardian*, 19 Jan. 2000). Against that is the fear of the withdrawal of foreign direct investment from the UK and/or the dissatisfaction of powerful domestic economic constituencies should Britain not join the 'euro zone' (*Financial Times*, 18 Jan. 2000).

Aside from these intriguing matters of statecraft yet to come, all of this raises the question of the extent to which Britain is bound into the European project. An immediate point to make is the fact that the European issue is not a constant. The key question (roughly sovereignty or loss of autonomy) is often portrayed in a particular way in the British press and in political rhetoric. But scholars of the EU increasingly take the view that the EU contains multiple logics, is unevenly developed and, therefore, should be conceived as a sort of complex political system. So rather than thinking about integration as a progressive adventure *en route* to a particular destination, it is rather a fluid polity characterized by several levels of authority where actors move between levels and where politics revolves around matters of mundane regulatory policy as much as it does about the contest about 'integration'. Crucially, in this image of multilevel governance, authority has dispersed, but is not drifting unequivocally from national governments to 'Brussels/Strasbourg'.

Therefore, there is no straight choice about whether Britain's political future is to be 'European' or otherwise. This reflects not just the domestic complexity and combustibility of the debate about European integration, but also a profound sense of ambiguity about what the European Union is now and what it might yet become. The idea that it is a putative federal superstate is a sentiment capable of igniting rhetorical bonfires, but one that is extremely difficult to sustain empirically. Of course, European integration and the observable growth of EU-level economic governance do represent challenges *to* and possible transformations *of* established patterns of authority associated with the nation-state. At the same time it is imperative to heed John Ruggie's warning that we should not imagine challenges to the state only in terms of entities that are 'institutionally substitutable' for the state (Ruggie 1998). Intellectually, this means that the evidence of transformation in European politics might not only reside in the growth of formal authoritative capacity at the EU level. Politically, it means that politicians and opinion formers could usefully look for ways of 'thinking otherwise' that might help debate to shift beyond a set of rather jaundiced categories.

NOTES

1   The six founding member states of the ECSC were Belgium, the Federal Republic of Germany, France, Italy, Luxembourg and the Netherlands. The same six – as signatories of the Treaties of Rome – formed the EEC and Euratom (the European Atomic Energy Community) in 1957. The three Communities were effectively 'merged' in 1965, after which time it became commonplace to use the shorthand EC (for European Communities).

2   It should be remembered that debate rages among scholars of European
    integration about the dynamics that might explain the reactivation of Euro-
    pean integration with the internal market programme of the mid to late
    1980s. One view is that the preferences of the key member states converged
    in ways consistent with the pursuit of market liberalization. The emphasis
    here is on processes of elite interaction and diplomacy (Moravcsik 1998).
    Ranged against this position are a series of views that emphasize the key role
    played by non-state actors such as the Commission in alliance with the
    European Court of Justice (Wincott 1995). Yet others stress the development
    of 'informal' economic integration that led to the emergence of genuinely
    transnational economic actors who soon came to look beyond national
    governments for the supply of market regulations (Sandholtz and Stone
    Sweet 1998).

3   The TEU formally created the European Union in a three pillar structure.
    Pillar I consolidated and developed the existing commitments of the European
    Communities. Pillar II created the CFSP, while a framework for cooperation
    in matters of Justice and Home Affairs (JHA) was the basis of pillar III. Pillars
    II and III were to use rather more robustly intergovernmental modes of
    decision-making than the more supranational style of pillar I, reinforcing
    the impression that advocates – such as the British – of keeping issues of
    'high politics' as matters of interstate bargaining won a significant victory.
    That said, it has been argued that the outcome of the CFSP negotiations went
    well beyond the original negotiating position laid out by the British govern-
    ment (A. Blair 1998) and that the claims of British success at Maastricht
    might be rather overblown (Forster 1999).

4   The BSE (bovine spongiform encephalopathy) crisis dented consumer confi-
    dence in the safety of British beef and became one of the most explosive
    political issues in Britain during the 1990s. The issue spilled over into the
    European arena, not just because beef exports suffered (and were ultimately
    banned), but also because of the EU's administration of agricultural markets
    through the Common Agricultural Policy (for an informed commentary see
    Grant 1997: 123–9).

5   The realist tradition is the most influential in the study of international
    relations. Realists such as Hans Morgenthau (1985) emphasized the centrality
    of states and the consistent lack of overarching authority in the international
    system. In this anarchic environment, states pursue self-interest and survival.
    Security is thereby elevated to the primary issue in world affairs. International
    institutions lack the capacity to shape these basic premises and realists depict
    international and domestic politics as very distinct spheres of action. Neore-
    alism, usually associated most readily with the work of Kenneth Waltz (1979)
    takes a more 'scientific' view by placing emphasis on the importance of the
    structural properties of anarchy rather than the inherent characteristics of
    states.

REFERENCES

Alter, K. (1996) 'The European Court's Political Power', *West European Politics*, 19(3).
Baimbridge, M., Burkitt, B. and Whyman, P. (1997) 'Economic and Monetary Union in Europe: A Critical British Perspective', *New Political Economy*, 2(3).
Baker, D. and Seawright, D. (1998a) 'A "Rosy" Map of Europe? Labour Parliamentarians and European Integration', in D. Baker and D. Seawright (eds), *Britain For and Against Europe: British Politics and the Question of European Integration*. Oxford: Clarendon Press.
—— (eds) (1998b) *Britain For and Against Europe: British Politics and the Question of European Integration*. Oxford: Clarendon Press.
Baker, D., Gamble, A. and Ludlam, S. (1993) '1846.... 1906.... 1996: Conservative Splits and European Integration', *Political Quarterly*, 64(4).
Baker, D. et al. (1996) 'The Blue Map of Europe: Conservative Parliamentarians and European Integration', in C. Rallings, D. Farrell, D. Denver and D. Broughton (eds), *British Elections and Parties Yearbook 1995*. London: Frank Cass.
Barrell, R., Britton, A. and Pain, N. (1994) 'When the Time was Right? The UK Experience of the ERM', in D. Cobham (ed.), *European Monetary Upheavals*. Manchester: Manchester University Press.
Blair, A. (1998) 'Swimming with the Tide? Britain and the Maastricht Treaty Negotiations on Common Foreign and Security Policy', *Contemporary British History*, 12(3).
Blair, T. (1999) 'The Case for Britain in Europe', speech by the Prime Minister, Tony Blair, at the launch of the Britain in Europe Campaign, BFI IMAX Cinema, London, 19 Oct. http://www.fco.gov.uk/news/speechtext.asp?2886
Buller, J. (1995) 'Britain as an Awkward Partner: Reassessing Britain's Relationship with the EU', *Politics*, 15(1).
—— (1999) 'Britain's Relations with the European Union in Historical Perspective', in D. Marsh et al. *Postwar British Politics in Perspective*. Cambridge: Polity.
Bulmer, S. and Burch, M. (1998) 'Organizing for Europe: Whitehall, the British State and the European Union', *Public Administration*, 76(4).
Bulpitt, J. (1986) 'The Discipline of the New Democracy: Mrs Thatcher's Domestic Statecraft', *Political Studies*, 34(1).
Camps, M. (1963) *Britain and the European Community 1955–1963*. Princeton: Princeton University Press.
Chisholm, M. (1995) *Britain on the Edge of Europe*. London: Routledge.
Coates, D. (1994) *The Question of UK Decline*. Hemel Hempstead: Harvester Wheatsheaf.
Conservative Party (2000a) 'In Europe, Not Run by Europe', http://195.224.205.213/ccoinformation/ campaigns/europe/europe1.htm
—— (2000b) 'Keep the Pound' (http://www.keepthepound.org.uk)

Cook, R. (1999) 'Britain's Future in Europe', speech by the Foreign Secretary, Robin Cook, Britain in Europe Campaign Event, Victoria Plaza, London, 23 Nov. http://www.fco.gov.uk/news/speechtext.asp?3031

Corry, D. (1999) 'Why the Left Should Be For EMU', in EMU: the Left Debate, PERC Policy Papers 4. Sheffield: Political Economy Research Centre, University of Sheffield.

Council of the European Communities/Commission of the European Communities (1992) Treaty on European Union. Luxembourg: Office for Official Publications of the European Communities.

Daniels, P. (1998) 'The Europeanisation of the Labour Party', West European Politics, 21(1).

Dennan, R. (1996) Missed Chances: Britain and Europe in the Twentieth Century. London: Cassell.

Egdell, J. M. and Thomson, K. J. (1999) 'The Influence of UK NGOs on the Common Agricultural Policy', Journal of Common Market Studies, 37(1).

Fay, M.-T. and Meehan, E. (1999) 'British Decline and European Integration', in R. English and M. Kenny (eds), Rethinking British Decline. Basingstoke: Macmillan.

Forster, A. (1998) 'Britain and the Negotiation of the Maastricht Treaty: A Critique of Liberal Intergovernmentalism', Journal of Common Market Studies, 36(3), 347–68.

——(1999) Britain and the Maastricht Treaty Negotiations. Basingstoke: Macmillan.

Gaitskell, H. (1996) 'The Common Market' (1962), speech introducing the National Executive Committee's Statement on the Common Market to the 1962 Labour Party Conference, in M. Holmes (ed.), The Eurosceptical Reader. Basingstoke: Macmillan.

Gamble, A. (1994a) Britain in Decline: Economic Policy, Political Strategy and the British State. Basingstoke: Macmillan.

——(1994b) The Free Economy and the Strong State: The Politics of Thatcherism, 2nd edn. Basingstoke: Macmillan.

——(1998) 'The European Issue in British Politics', in D. Baker and D. Seawright (eds), Britain For and Against Europe. Oxford: Clarendon Press.

Geddes, A. (1999) Britain and the European Union, 2nd edn. Manchester: Baseline Books.

George, S. (1991) Britain and European Integration since 1945. Oxford: Blackwell.

——(1994) 'Cultural Diversity and European Integration: The British Political Parties', in S. Zetterholm (ed.), National Cultures and European Integration. Oxford: Berg.

——(1995) 'A Reply to Buller', Politics, 15(1).

——(1998) An Awkward Partner: Britain in the European Community, 3rd ed. Oxford: Oxford University Press.

George, S. and Rosamond, B. (1992) 'The European Community', in M. J. Smith and J. Spear (eds), The Changing Labour Party. London: Routledge.

Grant, W. (1997) *The Common Agricultural Policy*. Basingstoke: Macmillan.
Hayes-Renshaw, F. and Wallace, H. (1997) *The Council of Ministers*. Basingstoke: Macmillan.
Henderson, D. (1998) 'The UK Presidency: An Insider's View', *Journal of Common Market Studies*, 36(4).
Johnson, C. (1996) *In with the Euro, Out with the Pound: The Single Currency for Britain*. Harmondsworth: Penguin.
Kaiser, W. (1998) 'The Political Reform Debate in Britain since 1945: The European Dimension', *Contemporary British History*, 12(1).
Kassim, H. and Menon, A. (1996) 'The European Union and State Autonomy', in H. Kassim and A. Menon (eds), *The European Union and National Industrial Policy*. London: Routledge.
King, A. et al. (1998) *New Labour Triumphs: Britain at the Polls*. Chatham, N. J.: Chatham House Publishers.
Klausen, J. and Tilly, L. A. (eds) (1998) *European Integration in Social and Historical Perspective*. Lanham: Rowman and Littlefield.
Lintner, V. (1998) 'The Impact of Membership on the UK Economy and UK Economic Policy', in T. Buxton, P. Chapman and P. Temple (eds), *Britain's Economic Performance*, 2nd edn. London: Routledge.
Ludlow, N. P. (1997) *Dealing with Britain: The Six and the First UK Application to the EEC*. Cambridge: Cambridge University Press.
Lynch, P. (1998) *The Politics of Nationhood*. Basingstoke: Macmillan.
Marks, G., Hooghe, L. and Blank, K. (1996) 'European Integration from the 1980s: State Centric v. Multi-level Governance', *Journal of Common Market Studies*, 34(3).
Mazey, S. and Richardson, J. (1996) 'The Logic of Organisation: Interest Groups', in J. Richardson (ed.), *European Union: Power and Policy-Making*. London: Routledge.
Mearsheimer, J. J. (1991) 'Back to the Future: Instability in Europe after the Cold War', *International Security*, 15(1).
Michie, J. (1998) 'Economic Consequences of EMU for Britain', in B. H. Moss and J. Michie (eds), *The Single Currency in National Perspective*. Basingstoke: Macmillan.
—— (1999) 'Why the Left Should Be Against EMU', in *EMU: the Left Debate*, PERC Policy Papers 4. Sheffield: Political Economy Research Centre, University of Sheffield.
Milner, H. V. (1998) 'Regional Economic Co-operation, Global Markets and Domestic Politics: A Comparison of NAFTA and the Maastricht Treaty', in W. D. Coleman and G. R. D. Underhill (eds), *Regionalism and Global Economic Integration: Europe, Asia and the Americas*. London: Routledge.
Milward, A. S. (1993) *The European Rescue of the Nation-State*. London: Routledge.
Moravcsik, A. (1991) 'Negotiating the Single European Act', in R. O. Keohane and S. Hoffmann (eds), *The New European Community: Decision making and Institutional Change*. Boulder, Col.: Westview.

—— (1993) 'Preferences and Power in the European Community: A Liberal Intergovernmentalist Approach', *Journal of Common Market Studies*, 31(4).

—— (1994) 'Why the European Community Strengthens the State: International Cooperation and Domestic Politics', Center for European Studies Working Paper 52, Harvard University.

—— (1998) *The Choice for Europe: Social Purpose and State Power from Messina to Maastricht*. London: UCL Press.

Morgenthau, H. J. (1985) *Politics Among Nations: The Struggle for Power and Peace*, 6th edn. New York: Knopf.

Nugent, N. (1999) *The Government and Politics of the European Union*, 4th edn. Basingstoke: Macmillan.

Overbeek, H. (1990) *Global Capitalism and National Decline: The Thatcher Decade in Perspective*. London: Unwin Hyman.

Pierson, P. (1998) 'The Path to European Integration: A Historical Institutionalist Analysis', in W. Sandholtz and A. Stone Sweet (eds), *European Integration and Supranational Governance*. Oxford: Oxford University Press.

Pollard, S. (1981) *The Integration of the European since 1815*. London: Allen and Unwin.

Preston, P. W. (1994) *Europe, Democracy and the Dissolution of Britain: An Essay on the Issue of Europe in UK Public Discourse*. Aldershot: Dartmouth.

Reynolds, D. (1991) *Britannia Overruled: British Policy and World Power in the Twentieth Century*. London: Longman.

Rosamond, B. (1990) 'Labour and the European Community: Learning to be European?', *Politics*, 10(2).

—— (1993) 'National Labour Organizations and European Integration: British Trade Unions and "1992"', *Political Studies*, 41(3).

—— (1998) 'The Integration of Labour? British Trade Union Attitudes to European Integration', in D. Baker and D. Seawright (eds), *Britain For and Against Europe: British Politics and the Question of European Integration*. Oxford: Clarendon Press.

—— (2000) *Theories of European Integration*. Basingstoke: Macmillan.

—— (2001) 'Functions, Levels and European Governance', in H. Wallace (ed.), *Interlocking Dimensions of European Integration*. Basingstoke: Palgrave.

Ruggie, J. G. (1998) *Constructing the World Polity: Essays on International Institutionalization*. London: Routledge.

Sanders, D. (1990) *Losing an Empire, Finding a Role: British Foreign Policy since 1945*. Basingstoke: Macmillan.

Sandholtz, W. and Stone Sweet, A. (eds) (1998) *European Integration and Supranational Governance*. Oxford: Oxford University Press.

Thompson, H. (1996) *The British Conservative Government and the European Exchange Rate Mechanism, 1979–1994*. London: Pinter.

Wallace, H. (1996) 'Politics and Policy in the European Union: The Challenge of Governance', in H. Wallace and W. Wallace (eds), *Policy-Making in the European Union*. Oxford: Oxford University Press.

Waltz, K. (1979) *Theory of International Politics*. New York: McGraw Hill.

Wessels, W. (1997) 'Ever Closer Fusion? A Dynamic Macropolitical View of the Integration Process', *Journal of Common Market Studies*, 35(2).

Westlake, M. (1994) *Britain's Emerging Euro-Elite? The British in the Directly Elected European Parliament, 1979–1992*. Aldershot: Dartmouth.

Wilkes, G. (ed.) (1997) *Britain's Failure to Enter the European Community, 1961–3*. London: Frank Cass.

Wilkes, G. and Wring, D. (1998) 'The British Press and European Integration, 1948–1996', in D. Baker and D. Seawright (eds), *Britain For and Against Europe: British Politics and the Question of European Integration*. Oxford: Clarendon Press.

Wilks, S. (1996) 'Britain and Europe: An Awkward Partner or an Awkward State?', *Politics*, 16(3).

Williams, L. J. (1971) *Britain and the World Economy 1919–70*. London: Fontana/Collins.

Wincott, D. (1995) 'Institutional Interaction and European Integration: Towards an Everyday Critique of Liberal Intergovernmentalism', *Journal of Common Market Studies*, 33(4).

Young, H. (1998) *This Blessed Plot: Britain and Europe from Churchill to Blair*. London: Macmillan.

Young, J. W. (1993) *Britain and European Unity, 1945–1992*. Basingstoke: Macmillan.

10

Ethics, Labour and Foreign Policy

Stuart Croft

Introduction

The advent of Labour governments after years of Conservative rule often brings an expectation that, in Britain's relations with the world, 'things will be different.' It has been a feature of such times that a view of a more moral Britain is often put forward, whether that be in 1945, 1964, 1974 or 1997. However, only in the latter case has the Labour government embraced the idea of morality formally in its foreign policy orientation.

Such expectations for change are often disappointed, and it has been the case that the left of the party, relatively quickly after the post-election honeymoon, begins to express disillusionment. In the 1940s, the government was accused of being too anti-Soviet; in the late 1960s, too pro-American; in the late 1970s, too pro-nuclear weapons. Change in foreign policy has appeared to be much more difficult to bring about in government than it had looked in opposition. To those who remained outside government, whether on the back benches of Parliament, or in non-governmental organizations, such difficulties have smacked of compromise, and of the assimilation of ministers into establishment culture.

Perhaps, then, the negative reaction to the notion of an ethical dimension to foreign policy, as espoused by Foreign Secretary Robin Cook in the immediate aftermath of the 1997 landslide election victory, and subsequently endorsed publicly by Prime Minister Blair, was rather predictable. Traditional constructions of interests have seemed to overpower ideas based on morality. When the ethical dimension to foreign policy seemed to be running into trouble, it was bolstered by the moral crusade launched by the Prime Minister to 'save' the population of Kosovo. Critics such as John Pilger, however, would have us believe that 'Like the famous hoax of an "ethical" foreign policy, the "new moral crusade" is designed for compliant headlines. Translated, it means the Orwellian opposite...Hypocrisy continues to rain on [Blair's] victory parade...' (Pilger 1999).

For critics such as Pilger, Labour fails to deliver on its promises in foreign policy, and will continue to do so, because it is either naive or disingenuous, and hence unable to understand the relationship between ideas and interests. There is nothing new in this. In 1945, Labour's radical domestic agenda, and traditional support for internationalism, raised expectations about its future foreign policy (Shlaim 1978: 86–96). But in policy, continuity reigned. Virtually all of the long-term objectives outlined under Eden and the National government were continued by Ernest Bevin. Not only were the policies the same, but so were the personnel. In the Commons Bevin was pointedly asked whether 'the present diplomats with their present outlook [were] to carry on the policy in Europe, or are we to have diplomats with a Labour and Socialist outlook?' (Dr Morgan MP cited in Bullock 1985: 73, see also 65–6). Both the Permanent Under-Secretary, Sir Alexander Cadogan, and the Senior Deputy Under-Secretary, Sir Orme Sargent, had feared dismissal in the aftermath of Labour's victory; but instead Cadogan was sent to represent Britain at the United Nations, and Sargent was promoted to Permanent Under-Secretary (Dalton 1962: 104). Even more astonishingly, Lord Halifax, the former Conservative Foreign Secretary, was allowed to continue as Ambassador to the United States, while Duff Cooper, another former Conservative minister, was allowed to continue as Ambassador in Paris.[1]

But care must be taken with arguments over continuity. Bevin and Attlee did seem to be following conservative precepts in their foreign policy. They, after all, did authorize the development of Britain's atomic bomb, despite arguments in cabinet to the contrary.[2] They also contributed further to the development of Cold War structures with the creation of NATO. However, this is not to argue that had the Conservatives won the 1945 general election, the history of Britain's foreign policy would not have been different. Churchill had by the middle of 1945 already decided that a break with Moscow was inevitable, and was resolutely determined that India (and hence Pakistan) would not become independent. A Churchill-inspired Conservative foreign policy would have been different in important aspects.

Although one must be careful with continuity, surely the relationship between interests and ideas is straightforward in British foreign policy? Perhaps British diplomacy is successful when it focuses on national interests, and leaves moral ideas to one side, because of the anarchical nature of international relations. One can find reflections of this view throughout at least the last two centuries of British foreign policy. George Canning, for example, expressed satisfaction with such a situation in the 1820s: 'So things are getting back to a wholesome state again. Every nation for itself, and God for us all' (quoted in Bourne 1970: 13). Lord Palmerston, as Prime Minister, noted that England had no permanent friends or enemies, only permanent interests. Sir Eyre Crowe, the then permanent under-secretary in the Foreign Office, noted in 1907 that 'it has become almost an historical truism to identify England's secular policy with the maintenance of [the] balance of power...' (Gooch and Temperley 1928: 403). Churchill explained in the 1930s that British – he noted English – planning 'takes no account of which nation it is that seeks the overlordship of Europe.... it has nothing to do with rulers or nations...' (Churchill 1961: 186–7).[3] The Maud Committee was set up in 1940 to consider the possibility of building an atomic bomb, and concluded that 'no nation would care to be caught without a weapon of such decisive possibilities' (Gowing 1964: 394). And nuclear weapons thus became a central part of this view. Margaret Thatcher asserted that 'Conventional weapons alone do not deter, and two world wars in Europe have already proved that. We want a war-free Europe, and we need to keep nuclear weapons to achieve that' (Thatcher 1988).

But this view of unchanging interests over long periods of time is flawed, however superficially attractive it may be. Of course it would be ridiculous to argue that interests are not at the heart of foreign policy. But interests are not exogenously provided. Interests and ideas are mutually constituted: one does not make sense without the other. And this must lie at the heart of an examination of 'New' Labour's foreign policy. Does the integration of an idea of the ethical change the way in which British interests are perceived?

The origins of an ethical dimension to foreign policy

Britain's new emphasis on the ethical dimension of foreign policy was to many an unexpected development. In the Labour Party's manifesto for the 1997 general election, foreign policy did not appear as one of Tony Blair's core ten areas, except with regard to the specific issue of providing leadership in Europe (Labour Party 1997). In the section on foreign policy, the components of an ethical dimension to policy were outlined: support for human rights and democracy, and an ethical curb on the arms trade. However, these were not presented explicitly in the broad framework of an ethical dimension to policy (1997: 37–9). Largely, this was due to Labour's interpretation of its recent traumatic past.

The Labour Party had spent much of the late 1980s and early 1990s trying to convince the electorate that on issues concerning overseas matters they were responsible, not radical, and hence would be interest rather than idea based in government. Primarily this had been focused on defence policy, and specifically nuclear weapons policy. It had become an accepted truism among the leadership in the latter half of Neil Kinnock's tenure as party leader that a commitment to unilateral nuclear disarmament had been the symbol of the unelectable character of Labour to a majority of the electorate, and so, under Kinnock, Labour began the return to nuclear 'acceptability'. This began before the 1987 general election; marking a deliberate difference with the Campaign for Nuclear Disarmament, the party had made a commitment to nuclear strategy with its statement that 'Labour's defence policy is based squarely and firmly on Britain's membership of NATO' (Labour Party 1987: 15).[4] George Robertson, Labour's Defence Secretary a decade later, argued that '... at a deeper level, Labour's changed attitude to defence was an important component in our [election] victory... events in the 1980s showed that, without a clear and unambiguous commitment to strong defences as an essential part of Britain's foreign policy, the British people would not trust us [Labour] with government' (Robertson 1997).

Given the efforts made by the Labour Party's leadership to make themselves acceptable on matters of overseas relations, a radical move on the part of a Blair government seemed unlikely. Thus, in the last stages of the Major government, a significant study on behalf of Chatham House emphasized the prevailing conventional wisdom of the likely continuity of foreign policy under a Labour government (Martin and Garnett 1997: 82–5).[5]

Yet Labour chose to initiate an ethical dimension to foreign policy that could not other than turn into a focus that would enable critics to audit Labour's practice (Wheeler and Dunne 1998). Robin Cook launched the new approach within days of the election victory. Cook's mission statement for the Foreign and Commonwealth Office (FCO) stated that Labour 'does not accept that political values can be left behind when we check in our passports to travel on diplomatic business. Our foreign policy must have an ethical dimension and must support the demands of other peoples for the democratic rights on which we insist for ourselves.' Perhaps most significantly, he stated that the new approach 'supplies an ethical content to foreign policy and recognises that the national interest cannot be defined only by narrow realpolitik' (Cook 1997a). Cook subsequently argued that 'The right to enjoy our freedom comes with the obligation to support the human rights of others' (Cook 1997b).

These themes were taken up by Defence Secretary Robertson. He stated that

> This Government already has a clear and different foreign policy agenda. We are internationalist, not isolationist. We believe in European cooperation, not offshore scepticism. We intend Britain's foreign policy to be based on clear ethical principles and not just to be driven by sharp profit... Nor, in a world which is fast becoming a global village, can we turn our backs on human suffering and economic and social damage, even when our national interests are not directly engaged. (Robertson 1997)

New Labour's new internationalism apparently required new initiatives in the ethical realm. This was a radical departure in British foreign policy discourse in two senses. First, and most obviously, it put ethical questions at the heart of policy formation in a way that had not been seen before. Of course, this is not to suggest that ethics had been ignored previously. Lord Hurd has stressed that under his leadership, British foreign policy had also been concerned with 'ethical' questions, although without the attendant publicity. As he put it, 'What is slightly irritating ... is to pretend that a shift of two or three degrees is a shift of 180 degrees and that all his [Cook's] predecessors were immoral rogues' (Hurd 1997: 25).[6] But it is fair to say that the language of ethics strongly influenced attitudes towards foreign policy, as will be examined later.

Second, and perhaps more significantly, this was the first attempt in the history of British foreign policy to articulate a conceptual framework for policy by officials, beyond rather unfocused comments on the balance of power and the importance of national interests, whatever they may be. Holistic thinking, rather than pragmatism, seemed to be on offer. But not for long. Cook has pointedly referred to 'an ethical dimension' to foreign policy, not to an 'ethical foreign policy' (Cook 1998d). As he put it some eighteen months after the launch, 'I never said that there would be an ethical foreign policy... What we have sought to do in a practical way is to put into effect our values' (Cook 1998c: 15).

Given that the ethical dimension emerged so dramatically, and with so little prior warning, its origin is therefore a little murky. Perhaps it lay with Robin Cook and his leftist past, in which he had been a critic of the conventional wisdom governing British foreign policy in the 1970s and 1980s. 'It was one issue where he could keep some link to his left wing past, a difficult enough challenge in his new role as foreign secretary' (Norton-Taylor 1999b). Perhaps it lay in Cook's desire to play a role equal to that of his long-term political rival, Gordon

Brown, and to establish Cook's power base within the FCO. More interestingly, it may have been an attempt to give a foreign policy dimension to notions of that which subsequently became referred to as a political Third Way. Echoing New Labour's concern for the 'people' the Foreign Office developed what they called 'a people's diplomacy', to cover what previously would simply have been considered to be consular work (see for example Symons 1997). But it was not until 1998 that Cook started to make clear links between the two. In an interview in the *New Statesman* Cook suggested that the Third Way allowed the government to reject 'the polarisation of blazing rows about human rights or else leave your values behind in Britain and go out simply to seek commercial contracts. You can pursue economic co-operation without being silenced on human rights' (Cook 1998a). This was subsequently taken up by Tony Blair. On the occasion of his visit to South Africa, Blair stated that 'the Third Way is not just about what happens in our own countries. The political debate today is shaped as much by how a country sees its place in the world as by internal ideological debate.' Blair went on to locate four ethical dimension–Third Way challenges: the 'outrage that one in four people does not have enough to eat, clean water, education or basic healthcare'; guaranteeing that 'our children have the right to grow up in a greener, cleaner world'; ensuring that 'all countries must be able to benefit from globalisation'; and securing the 'right to live in peace, free from the fear of war, the horrors of ethnic cleansing and the terrifying threat of Weapons of Mass Destruction' (Blair 1999a).

Whatever its origins, the ethical dimension to foreign policy raised the question of whether ideals could be imposed on international relations. This has proved to be difficult, certainly on a unilaterial basis.

Practising the ethical dimension

The ethical dimension seemed to offer a framework for many aspects of policy, and it was deliberately sold as such. Subsequently, to ensure its application in the FCO, there were to be secondments from non-governmental organizations (NGOs) to the FCO, and secondments from the FCO to NGOs.[7] Tony Lloyd, Minister of State, told a conference organized by non-governmental organizations that

> Security, prosperity and quality of life are all very important national interests to be promoted through effective foreign policy. But so is what Robin Cook has described as the ethical dimension. Part of the UK's

national interest must be our contribution to keeping the peace of the
world and promoting human rights...The Government supports a strong
UK defence industry...We are one of the major arms exporters in the
world. But that status carries with it a responsibility, an obligation, to
ensure that the arms trade is properly regulated. (Lloyd 1997)

Despite these brave words, the ethical dimension lasted only a little
more than a year as a unifying concept in British foreign policy, before
becoming swamped by criticism. Censure focused in particular on two
issues: the continued sale of arms, especially to those states with poor
human rights records; and the breach of international law associated
with the so-called 'arms to Africa' or Sandline affair.

Labour's foreign policy has included approval of exports of armoured
vehicles to Indonesia, despite the conflict in East Timor and elsewhere on
the archipelago, machine guns to Turkey, despite the violence in Kurdish
populated areas, a range of weapons to Colombia, a country racked by
internal violence, and the continuation of a close arms sales relationship
with non-democratic Saudi Arabia (Norton-Taylor 1999b). The government invited a number of countries with poor human rights records to
the Defence Systems and Equipment International exhibition in September 1999, including Indonesia, China and Burma. Paul Flynn MP put it
rather colourfully: 'It seems that an ethical foreign policy does not
preclude collaborating with and being accessory after the fact to mass
murder by dictators' (Pallister 1999).

It was the Labour government's arms relationship with Indonesia,
however, that provoked the most outrage. The British-made Alvis (a
tracked fighting vehicle) was used in the repression of student protests,
under the post-Suharto regime of President Habibie, and were responsible for deaths when used to break up groups of protestors in November
1998. British-made Saracen and Saladin armoured vehicles were report-
edly used in the repression in East Timor. In September 1999 it was
revealed that Hawk jets had been delivered to Indonesia, on the same
day that Indonesian security forces shot and killed five protestors in the
Jakarta streets (Gittings, O'Kane and Gonclaves 1999). Hawk jets had
been reported over East Timor for some years. In addition, the EU had
imposed an arms embargo on Indonesia a week before the Hawks
departed for South East Asia, and the United States had made an announcement to the same effect two days before the British concurred,
after Cook persuaded Blair to overrule the Ministry of Defence (Black
1999). The Hawks had gone, with the Labour government protesting
that as contracts had been signed under the Conservatives, there were no
legal means of preventing the departure of the aircraft. Hence Patrick

Barkham's charge that 'Ethics haven't loomed large in Labour's arms-length relationship with Indonesia' (Barkham 1999).

Consequently, the government was subjected to constant criticism. Robin Cook found the need to defend his record at the Labour Party Conference. He told the conference that 'Your government has not sold weapons that would suppress democracy... We rejected every licence to Indonesia when the weapons might have been used for suppression. We refused them sniper rifles, we refused them silenced firearms and we refused them armoured Land-Rovers' (MacAskill 1999). Most critics found this unpersuasive. In any case, under Labour just 2.4 per cent of export applications for arms exports to Indonesia had been rejected (Barkham 1999). The Campaign Against the Arms Trade had already argued that despite the declaratory change of policy introduced by Cook towards an ethical dimension 'there is no indication that... this change of wording has made any difference to the pattern of licences accepted and refused' (Campaign Against the Arms Trade 1997: 273).

The arms-to-Indonesia criticism had come at a bad time for Labour. The winter of 1998 and the spring of 1999 had seen determined efforts to revitalize the ethical dimension, in the light of the Kosovo campaign, as will be examined below. Cook re-emphasized that 'I firmly believe that the values that inform our domestic policies must also connect with our foreign policy' (Cook 1998d). And Geoff Hoon, while still an FCO minister, argued that 'it is wrong – and unfair – to examine every deed and utterance that we make looking for absolute perfection. Because you will not find it. We live in an imperfect world' (Hoon 1999). But by seemingly seeking to impose an ethical ideal over and above interests in British foreign policy, ministers had invited critics to search for any sign of imperfection; or at least for consistency.

The restatement of policy noted above was important, not only in the context of Kosovo, but in the context of the arms-to-Africa scandal, which had run for the previous eighteen months. Labour stood accused of breaking international law in breaching a United Nations arms embargo, as well as of being unable to produce efficient management systems for the Foreign and Commonwealth office, with Robin Cook and the relevant minister, Tony Lloyd, being said to be unable to control officials. Extraordinarily, in evidence to the Commons Foreign Affairs Committee, the Permanent Under-Secretary at the FCO, Sir John Kerr, indicated that Lloyd knew of the breach of the embargo in time for the debate in the Commons on 12 March 1998, only for Kerr to modify that evidence later that same day (Foreign Affairs Committee 1999: vi).

Briefly, a coup in Sierra Leone ousted the democratically elected government of President Kabbah in 1997. Britain stated its support for

Kabbah, but said that it did not support military action; this was specifically set out by Blair in response to a personal plea by Kabbah in June 1997. However, Britain supported the work of the military arm of the Economic Community of West African states, which sought a three-level approach of negotiation, sanctions, and the threat of force. Britain led the adoption of a UN Security Council resolution in October 1997 supporting the West African approach. It supported an arms embargo on all groups in Sierra Leone: government, rebels and the West African force, as the latter was dominated by Nigeria, itself the subject of EU and Commonwealth arms embargoes. Despite this, a British 'security' company (a supplier of mercenaries to those who could pay in Africa) was selling weapons to Kabbah.[8] The British High Commissioner knew both of the agreement to sell weapons, then of their actual transfer, as did some officials in London, but according to the government's own enquiry, ministers were not informed.[9]

As the scandal broke, ministers seemed genuinely surprised. The result of the activities of the British 'security' company, Sandline, was that Kabbah was reinstated. The President's enemies in Sierra Leone had behaved in a fashion that was extraordinarily brutal to civilians, including children, who had been victims of murder and horrendous amputations among other crimes. Tony Blair seemed to think that in some ways the ends had justified the means. He explained that 'Of course it is the case that nobody should be involved deliberately in breaking a UN arms embargo... [But] Don't let us forget that what was happening was that the UN and UK were both trying to help the democratic regime from an illegal military coup... That is the background and people can see that a lot of the hoo-ha is overblown' (Blair 1998a).[10] But surely no policy with an ethical dimension that is recognizable from a Western liberal-democratic tradition could be built on a distinction between ends and means.

In one important area, ethical ends and means were united. In the Kosovo campaign, the Labour government contributed to what they saw as a just war, conducted in an ethical fashion. Was the Kosovo conflict the finest hour of Labour's ethical dimension?

Iraq and Kosovo: ethical wars?

It is often forgotten that the military campaign against Federal Yugoslav forces in Kosovo was not the first use of force by the Blair government. In December 1998, Blair authorized air attacks against Iraq, in response to a United Nations report which found Iraq in contravention of its responsibilities to cooperate with inspections regarding weapons of mass destruction (Blair 1998b, 1998d). Only the British supported the Americans militarily in this short, four-day campaign. Strangely though, in the context of Robin Cook's policy line, and in contrast to descriptions of policy that were to follow over Kosovo, the attacks on Iraq were not put in the context of the ethical dimension of foreign policy.

This omission was very strange. Clearly the government believed that it had a just position. Iraq was in contravention of United Nations demands, in clear contravention of international law. The country was run by a brutal dictator. Yet at no time was the use of force put into the context of the ethical dimension to foreign policy. (On the absence of such a context, see Blair 1998d, 1998e; Cook 1998g). Robin Cook went as far as outlining Iraq's breaches of human rights, and the FCO issued a supporting list of 'Crimes and abuses committed under Saddam's regime' (Cook 1998f; Foreign and Commonwealth Office 1999). When Robin Cook placed a chronology of over one hundred 'atrocities' in Kosovo in the Commons Library, he did so because 'I want every Member [of the Commons] to understand the evil that we are fighting ... ' (Cook 1999a). But at no time was the British action over Iraq placed in such an explicitly ethical and moralistic framework.

Clearly there was a nervousness in government about presenting the case in ethical terms. Partly this was because the action was being implemented on behalf of the international community by the Americans and British only, and that international community – especially in the Arab world, and even among NATO and EU allies – did not seem particularly supportive and grateful. That is, the action looked as much a modern version of gunboat diplomacy as it did a just intervention. In addition, the government had been on the defensive all year over public pressure to lift sanctions on Iraq, in order to prevent disease and death among the civilian population. Labour's justifiable countercase was that the importation of medical supplies and drugs was not prohibited under UN sanctions, and indeed Iraq was allowed to sell some oil to fund such purchases; but it was a case not widely heard. And beginning a military campaign in the Arab world during Ramadan did not appear very sensitive to the concerns of those from other ethical backgrounds. In short, Labour accepted that, in this context, it was not sensible to justify military action as part of the ethical dimension to foreign policy, even though it was in support of international law against a regime that brutally breached any human rights norms on a regular basis, had begun two wars, and had used weapons of mass destruction and was bent on acquiring more. What did this say about the robustness of an ethical framework for policy? Ministers actually sought to justify military action on fairly traditional grounds. For Blair, we had a stark choice. Either we could let this process (that is, Iraqi refusal to cooperate with weapons inspections) continue further.... Or, having tried every possible diplomatic avenue, and shown endless patience despite all Saddam's deception, we could decide that if UNSCOM (the UN weapons monitoring body) could not do its work, we should tackle Saddam's remaining capability through direct action of our own. In these circumstances he saw only one responsible choice to make (Blair 1998c).

And for Cook, 'No Foreign Minister can be satisfied when events compel the need for military force. The aim of diplomacy is to avert the need for such action. But diplomacy can only work if the other side is prepared to negotiate in good faith' (Cook 1998e). Such sentiments expressed by Prime Minister and Foreign Secretary would not seem out of place to Canning, Crowe, Churchill, the authors of the Maud Committee Report, or Margaret Thatcher, cited earlier.

This was in marked contrast to the Kosovo campaign. Whereas, over Iraq, Britain had apparently been compelled to act because of international responsibility based on the power of its adversary, Kosovo was about supporting ideals. As Cook put it, 'The campaign we fought in Kosovo was not fought to gain us territory or to bring us greater power. What prompted us to intervene, what motivated us to maintain the resolve of the alliance, was our values – freedom, justice, compassion – basic human decency' (Cook 1999j).

The ethical dimension of the Kosovo war had two related but distinct elements. In the first, Blair and Cook developed a clear vision of those ethics that were important enough to fight for. In the second, they developed a vision of the role values have in modern Europe, and how the past acts as a guide to the future. Both aspects will be examined in turn.

As the crisis drew close to war, the government began to raise the stakes. Whereas the Rambouillet talks, co-chaired by the French and British, had sought to project some equidistance between the British and the Serbs on the one hand and the Kosovars on the other, this effort began to collapse in the early part of 1999. Blair explained that Britain stood ready to fight with NATO not to support the balance of power, but 'primarily to avert what would otherwise be a humanitarian disaster for Kosovo' (Blair 1999c).

As the war began, Cook emphasized that 'We were left with no other way of preventing the present humanitarian crisis from becoming a catastrophe than by taking military action to limit the capacity of [Yugoslav President] Milosevic's army to repress the Kosovar Albanians' (Cook 1999b). The point was made again by Blair in a broadcast to the nation:

'To those who say the aim of military strikes is not clear, I say it is crystal clear. It is to curb Milosevic's ability to wage war on an innocent civilian population... These are our fellow human beings... We are doing what is right, for Britain, for Europe, for a world that must know that barbarity cannot be allowed to defeat justice' (Blair 1999d). And the military concurred. Chief of the Defence Staff, General Sir Charles Guthrie, told the *Evening Standard* that 'In trying to head off a humanitarian disaster unrivalled in Europe since the end of the Second World War, NATO finds itself having to use force' (Guthrie 1999).

As the war continued, the importance of values, of Western ethics, was ratcheted ever upwards. In mid-April, Blair told the *Sunday Mirror* that 'I don't use the word evil lightly. But I have no doubt that the appalling tragedy of Kosovo... is the result of real evil' (Blair 1999e). In *Newsweek* we learnt that 'We need to enter a new millennium where dictators know that they cannot get away with ethnic cleansing or repress their peoples with impunity' (Blair 1999f). By May, Blair was agreeing with Clinton that this air campaign over a small part of South Eastern Europe was a battle 'over the values of civilisation' (Blair 1999g). In June, after the conflict had ended, Blair noted that the war 'wasn't fought on behalf of NATO for one ethnic grouping against another, it was fought for the principle that all people, whatever their ethnic background, whatever their race, their religion, should be able to live together peacefully' (Blair 1999h).

Many may scoff at politicians using such language; but surely few doubt that it was meant. The ethical dimension to foreign policy seemed to be at the core. Both the Prime Minister and his Foreign Secretary reflected this in the aftermath of the conflict. Blair said that 'We began this action for a reason. We have seen it through and we will see it through. We did it for justice' (Blair 1999i). And Cook echoed this: 'we have delivered not a military victory, but a victory for our values. The real winners from Kosovo are our values of human rights, ethnic equality and humanitarian law... We fought... out of principle' (Cook 1999i). It is fair to argue that these views, so frequently repeated, were absolutely serious.

But in comparison to the values advanced by Cook in his ethical dimension to foreign policy in 1997, there was nothing particularly Labour or socialist/left-wing about them. The values espoused by the Prime Minister and his Foreign Secretary over the Kosovo conflict are those to which many from different democratic political parties could subscribe. Indeed, as the Prime Minister himself suggested, the values supported in conducting the Kosovo campaign are those of Western Europe as a whole.[11]

But not only was the government seeking to advance a particular set of (Western) ethics, they were trying to prevent a return to the past. This is true in a narrow and a broad sense. In the narrow sense, the government sought to learn the lessons of the failure of the first years of the Bosnian conflict, which were marked in the West by argument over appropriate institutional responsibility, transatlantic disagreement, and national lack of interest. Tony Blair explained that 'If we can prevent war, we should do so ... In Bosnia we underestimated what would be needed to halt the conflict, and we underestimated the consequences of failing to do so' (Blair 1999b). More significantly, though, the government believed that a failure to halt the Serbian campaign in Kosovo would lead directly to a challenge to those Western values, as had happened sixty years before.

Some years earlier, Ole Waever argued that 'Europe's "other", the enemy image, is today to no very large extent "Islamic fundamentalism", "the Russians" or anything similar – rather Europe's Other is Europe's own past which should not be allowed to become its future' (Waever 1996: 122). This important insight explains Labour's attitude to the Kosovo war. That theme was ever-present in the words of Robin Cook. In late March he told a Belgrade radio station that Milosevic's Kosovo policy 'belongs to the Middle Ages, it does not belong to Europe at the end of the twentieth century' (Cook 1999c). But medieval Europe was not Cook's main focal point; rather, that was the 1930s. In early May, Cook told the Serbs that 'The tactics that President Milosevic has employed belongs more to the dark days of the 1930s than the modern Europe of the 1990s' (Cook 1999d). Later, he said that 'We want the Serb people ... to be able to join us in that modern Europe' (Cook 1999e). At the NATO summit in Washington, he concluded that 'NATO cannot tolerate the rebirth of fascism within Europe and that is what we are witnessing at the present time. In 1945 when we looked at the Europe that we inherited, it was a Europe scarred by genocide, by mass deportation of peoples, by ethnic confrontation and ethnic aggression. The tragedy is that we witness all of those again in Kosovo today' (Cook 1999f). Later in that same visit to Washington, he argued that 'there is no place in the Europe of the end of the twentieth century for somebody pursuing the fascist policies of fifty years ago ... ' (Cook 1999g). And in an article for the *Guardian*, Cook wrote that 'There are now two Europes competing for the soul of our continent. One still follows the race ideology that blighted our continent under the fascists. The other emerged fifty years ago from behind the shadow of the Second World War. The conflict between the international community and Yugoslavia is the struggle between these two Europes. Which side prevails will determine what sort of continent we live in' (Cook 1999h).

Kosovo, for the government, saw the reintroduction of values into the language of foreign policy. But those values had become Western ones. The victory of values that Kosovo apparently represented allowed a British government and its allies to defeat the ideology of fascism; again.

Conclusion

This chapter has suggested that it is possible to argue that for the government, the Kosovo conflict was about values and an ethical foreign policy. But the meaning of 'ethical' had changed. A transformation had taken place. Originally, the ethical dimension meant the difference that a Labour government could bring. Let these be called Labour, rather than socialist values; but nevertheless, something distinctively different. But over time, these values seemed to play a greater role in rhetoric than in policy implementation, to the extent that by the time Tony Blair was ordering air-raids on Baghdad, ethics did not play a legitimizing role, even though such a case could have been made. The return of ethics and values as seen over Kosovo marked the final change in their meaning, from Labour values to Western ones.

Must this inevitably lead to a view that the ethical dimension to foreign policy (that is, the implementation of Labour values) has been a failure? There have been failures of policy, notably over Indonesia and arms-to-Africa. Important non-governmental organizations such as the Campaign Against the Arms Trade have been disappointed by the implementation of policy. Wheeler and Dunne criticized the government for a lack of intervention over Algeria (1998: 866–7). As Amnesty International put it, 'When dialogue is the UK's objective, countries such as Algeria can easily satisfy the Government by committing themselves to lengthy talks, without feeling any real need to end human rights violations' (1997: 296). And critics such as Lord Hurd have agreed, viewing the move from a Conservative to a Labour administration as having changed foreign policy by only 'two or three degrees'.

But debate over whether the ethical dimension has failed needs to be examined in greater depth. As Ken Booth argues, 'The British government does not have a choice between pursuing an "ethical" foreign policy or a "pragmatic" or a "prudent" one. The only choice it has is between different sets of ethical principles that deliver different ethical consequences' (1997: 260). That is, there has always been an ethical dimension at work; it is just an ethic with which those on the left of British politics have been traditionally uncomfortable. In 1998, Wheeler and Dunne suggested that 'the new government recognises that foreign policy should be guided by universal moral values. This represents more than a slight resetting of the compass' (1998: 870). That relatively early judgement looks generous. If, despite all the rhetoric, Labour's foreign policy ethic in practice is that of the Conservatives, then judged by their own words in 1997, ministers have not succeeded.

Perhaps much of this reflects a general disillusionment with the Labour government, perhaps inevitable given the euphoria of victory at the polls. In many areas of public policy, with the important exception of the economy, the promises of 1997 have seemed not to be fulfilled, particularly to those on the left, broadly defined. Few would have believed before 1 May 1997 that a Labour Home Secretary would allow an alleged Nazi war criminal to leave the country for Australia in full view of the cameras one week, and then find compelling 'independent' 'medical' evidence to deny the extradition of General Pinochet, an alleged mass murderer and torturer, to a fellow EU country the next. But this was exactly what Jack Straw did in December 1999 and January 2000.

But even despite such evidence, it would be wrong to suggest that Cook's ethical dimension left British foreign policy untouched. Norton-Taylor suggested, rather grudgingly, that 'The best legacy Robin Cook could leave may be to have prevented, at the risk of cabinet rows, Britain's foreign policy from being totally skewed by the arms lobby. And he should be glad to have encouraged an open debate, rather than complain about what he now considers unwelcome publicity' (Norton-Taylor 1999b).

But the issue, for the purposes of this chapter, lies deeper still. The key here is not whether there has been an ethic behind British foreign policy, for as argued above, there has. The issue is whether it has changed under Labour. And if we accept the argument that it has not, then why not? Is it the case that ideas cannot be implemented in this way in foreign policy, because they are always overwhelmed by interests? Such a simplistic conclusion is apparently supported by the history of Labour's foreign policy since 1997. But it should be resisted. There has been no coherent idea to be applied to policy. The phrase 'an ethical dimension' was never defined; left hanging, it was seen to mean many different things by different groups. Casual use of language by ministers in 1997 in particular created expectations that could not be met because they had not been defined. So the idea of an ethical foreign policy has not been weighed down by interests, because there was never a single idea in the first place. Surely the evidence of the speedy move from the 'Labour ethics' of 1997 to the 'Western ethics' of the Kosovo campaign make that clear. But ethical considerations are, as Lord Hurd among others has pointed out, ever-present in British foreign policy. Perhaps one might hold that the 1991 Gulf War was a war for oil; but British intervention over Kurdistan subsequently is hard to fit into such a framework. And British endeavours over Kosovo are about as far from the motivations and actions that lay behind the Boer War as it is possible to get in one century.

Further, it is not conceivable for the UK to have a foreign policy that does not contain ideals based on British political practice. Domestic and international politics are not separable in that way, certainly not in the context of EU-Europe. And that scandals such as the Sandline affair, or arms sales to Indonesia, are that, scandals, demonstrates the power of the idea that democratic norms should frame British foreign policy. The social understanding of foreign policy is therefore changing. Probably this was accelerated by the end of the Cold War; perhaps more precisely, by the rather slower realization that Cold War ideas needed to be replaced by new ones. Labour has allowed this debate to be framed and focused, although it has not provided answers. The debate is unlikely to disappear; notions of how to behave that develop in Britain and the EU will continue to have an impact on the way in which interests are conceived, and hence on the practice of foreign policy.

This chapter began with a quote from John Pilger. Such critics would have us believe that all is hypocrisy; that ministers of all parties have sought to deflect criticism with spin, and have pursued narrow, profit-driven and environmentally unfriendly policies. This conclusion proposes something rather different. It suggests that the argument over whether Britain should have an ethical dimension to foreign policy is over, and has been for many years, pre-dating 1997. The consensus is in the affirmative. The task now is to provide a clear definition of what that means, and of how to implement that in practice. The relationship between ideas and interests is complex, organic, and dynamic.

NOTES

Thanks to John Roper and Colin Hay for comments and to Vicky Harrison for research assistance. I would like to acknowledge ESRC support, grant L213252008, 'One Europe or Several' Programme.

1 However, Bevin's restructuring of the Foreign Office did lead to seventeen forced retirements by the end of 1947 (see Adamthwaite 1985).

2 Ministers argued that 'If it was our policy to build world peace on moral foundations rather than on the balance of power we should be prepared to apply that principle at once to the atomic bomb' (Gowing 1974: 70). At the

cabinet meeting on 8 November 1945, 'Some ministers thought it would be wiser to make an immediate offer to disclose this [atomic] information to the Soviet government.' Attlee himself was, initially, an internationalist on the nuclear issue: see Smith and Zametica 1985: 243.

3 The speech was originally given in March 1936.

4 At the 1987 Labour Party Conference, resolution Composite 30 was adopted, through which 'Conference reaffirms Labour's commitment to remain a member of NATO.'

5 Although they did emphasize the likelihood of a change in style.

6 More fully, Hurd stated that 'I think the Foreign Secretary and the Government are perfectly entitled to do what every incoming Foreign Secretary does, which is to look at the range of policies and adjust the compass by two or three points. That is what the present incumbent has done, quite understandably. What is slightly irritating... is to pretend that a shift of two or three degrees is a shift of 180 degrees and that all his predecessors were immoral rogues. It is not a matter of huge import to the country, as long as the policy itself is reasonably continuous' (Hurd 1997: 25).

7 Specifically, from Amnesty and Save the Children to the FCO; FCO staff were to be seconded to Article 19 and Minority Rights Group (see Cook 1998b).

8 This summary is based on the House of Commons Foreign Affairs Committee Report, which gives a much fuller account (see Foreign Affairs Committee 1999).

9 The government's enquiry was conducted by Sir Thomas Legg, the former Permanent Secretary at the Lord Chancellor's Department and Sir Robin Ibbs. It was published on 28 July 1998. The government refused to allow information which fell into the ambit of the Legg enquiry to be passed to the House of Commons Foreign Affairs Committee, which was conducting its own enquiry.

10 That Symons quoted Blair demonstrated that this was an accepted government view.

11 'I myself have been to Romania, Bulgaria, Macedonia, Albania, and said to them that there is a different future for the Balkans based, not on ethnic conflict, but on peace, prosperity and security, as with western Europe. But you have to adopt the values of western Europe' (Blair 1999i).

REFERENCES

Adamthwaite, Anthony (1985) 'Britain and the World 1945–9: The View from the Foreign Office', *International Affairs*, 61(2), 223–36.

Amnesty International (1997) Memorandum submitted to the House of Commons Foreign Affairs Committee, First Report, *Foreign Policy and Human Rights*, vol.3, HC 100–III. London: HMSO.

Barkham, Patrick (1999) 'Keeping Indonesia at Arms Length', *Guardian*, 8 Sept., reproduced on the Guardian website http://www.guardian.co.uk/Archive

Booth, Ken (1997) Memorandum submitted to the House of Commons Foreign Affairs Committee, First Report, *Foreign Policy and Human Rights*, vol.3, HC 100–III. London: HMSO.

Bourne, Kenneth (1970) *The Foreign Policy of Victorian England 1830–1902*. Oxford: Clarendon Press.

Black, Ian (1999) 'Cook Denies U-Turn', *Guardian*, 13 Sept., reproduced on http://www.guardian.co.uk/Archive

Blair, Tony (1998a) Cited by Baroness Symons, statement to the House of Lords, 11 May, reproduced on the Foreign and Commonwealth Office (FCO) website http://www.fco.gov.uk

—— (1998b) 'Launch of Operation Desert Fox', statement at Downing Street, 16 Dec., reproduced on http://www.fco.gov.uk

—— (1998c) Prime Minister's statement to the House of Commons, 17 Dec., reproduced on http://www.fco.gov.uk

—— (1998d) 'Cessation of Military Action against Iraq', statement at Downing Street, 19 Dec., reproduced on, http://www.fco.gov.uk

—— (1998e) 'Prime Minister's Assessment of Latest Military Action on Iraq', transcript of interview for the BBC World Service, 19 Dec., reproduced on http://www.fco.gov.uk

—— (1998f) 'Assessment of Operation Desert Fox and Forward Strategy', opening statement by the Prime Minister at press conference, 20 Dec., reproduced on http://www.fco.gov.uk

—— (1999a) 'Facing the Modern Challenge: The Third Way in Britain and South Africa', speech in Cape Town, 8 Jan., reproduced on http://www.fco.gov.uk

—— (1999b) 'Our Responsibilities Do Not End at the English Channel', *Independent on Sunday*, 14 Feb., reproduced on http://www.fco.gov.uk

—— (1999c) Prime Minister's statement on Kosovo to the House of Commons, 23 Mar. reproduced on http://www.fco.gov.uk

—— (1999d) 'Taking Action is the Only Chance for Justice in Kosovo', text of broadcast to the nation, 26 Mar., reproduced on http://www.fco.gov.uk

—— (1999e) 'There is No Compromise…We Will Win', *Sunday Mirror*, 11 Apr., reproduced on http://www.fco.gov.uk

—— (1999f) 'We are Fighting for a New Internationalism', *Newsweek*, 19 Apr., reproduced on http://www.fco.gov.uk

—— (1999g) 'PM Justifies Battle over the Values of Civilisation', interview for the *Observer*, 16 May, reproduced on http://www.fco.gov.uk

—— (1999h) Transcript of interview given by the Prime Minister in Cologne, 3 June, reproduced on http://www.fco.gov.uk

—— (1999i) Comments by the Prime Minister to the press at the European Council in Cologne, 4 June, reproduced on http://www.fco.gov.uk

—— (1999j) Interview given to GMTV, 4 June, reproduced on http://www.fco.-gov.uk

Bullock, Alan (1985) *Ernest Bevin Foreign Secretary*. Oxford: Oxford University Press.

Campaign Against the Arms Trade (1997) Memorandum, Appendix 14, House of Commons Foreign Affairs Committee, First Report, *Foreign Affairs and Human Rights*, vol.3, Appendices to the Minutes of Evidence, HC 100–III. London: HMSO.

Churchill, Winston (1961) *The Gathering Storm*. New York: Bantam Books.

Cook, Robin (1997a) 'British Foreign Policy', Mission Statement for the British Foreign and Commonwealth Office, 12 May, reproduced on the FCO website http://www.fco.gov.uk

—— (1997b) 'Human Rights into the Next Century', keynote address 17 July, reproduced on http://www.fco.gov.uk

—— (1998a) Interview in the *New Statesman*, 1 May.

—— (1998b) 'Human Rights: Making the Difference', speech to the Amnesty International Human Rights Festival, 16 Oct., reproduced on http://www.fco.gov.uk

—— (1998c) 'The NS Interview' by Steve Richards, *New Statesman*, 13 Nov.

—— (1998d) 'Beyond Good Intentions – Government, Business and the Environment', speech to the Business and the Environment Dinner, 17 Nov., reproduced on http://www.fco.gov.uk

—— (1998e) Foreign Secretary's opening statement of the emergency debate on Iraq, House of Commons, 17 Dec., reproduced on http://www.fco.gov.uk

—— (1998f) 'Standing Up to Saddam's Terror State', press conference, 19 Dec., reproduced on http://www.fco.gov.uk

—— (1998g) 'Launching a Forward Strategy of Containment for Saddam', transcript of interview for GMTV, 20 Dec., reproduced on http://www.fco.gov.uk

—— (1999a) Speech to the House of Commons, debate on Kosovo, 18 May, reproduced on http://www.fco.gov.uk

—— (1999b) Statement to the House of Commons, 25 Mar., reproduced on http://www.fco.gov.uk

—— (1999c) Interview to B92 Radio Belgrade, 29 Mar., reproduced on http://www.fco.gov.uk

—— (1999d) Message to the Serbian People, 1 Apr., reproduced on http://www.fco.gov.uk

—— (1999e) Speech to the House of Commons, Commons debate on Kosovo, 19 Apr., reproduced on http://www.fco.gov.uk

—— (1999f) Press conference with US Secretary of State Madeleine Albright, 22 Apr., reproduced on http://www.fco.gov.uk

—— (1999g) Interview with Frost, BBC television, 24 Apr., reproduced on http://www.fco.gov.uk

—— (1999h) 'It is Fascism that We are Fighting', *Guardian*, 5 May, reproduced on http://www.guardian.co.uk/archive

—— (1999i) Foreign Secretary's opening statement to the House of Commons, Commons debate on Kosovo, 17 June 1999, reproduced on http://www.fco.gov.uk

—— (1999j) Speech at the Labour Party Conference, 28 Sept., reproduced on http://www.guardian.co.uk/Archive

Dalton, Hugh (1962) *High Tide and After*. London: Frederick Muller.

Foreign Affairs Committee (1999) Second Report, *Sierra Leone*, vol. 1, HC 116–I. London: HMSO.

Foreign and Commonwealth Office (1999) *Crimes and Abuses Committed Under Saddam's Regime*, briefing paper, reproduced on http://www.fco.gov.uk

Gittings, John, O'Kane, Maggie, and Gonclaves, Eduardo (1999) 'Cook Faces New Crisis as Hawk Jets Fly In', *Guardian*, 26 Sept., reproduced on http://www.guardian.co.uk/Archive

Gooch, G. P. and Temperley, Harold (1928) *British Documents on the Origins of War 1889–1917*, vol. III. London: HMSO.

Gowing, Margaret (1964) *Britain and Atomic Energy 1939–45*. London: Macmillan.

—— (1974) *Independence and Deterrence*. London: Macmillan.

Guthrie, Sir Charles (1999) 'Why NATO Cannot Simply March In and Crush Milosevic', *Evening Standard*, 1 Apr., reproduced on the Ministry of Defence website http://www.mod.uk

Hoon, Geoffrey (1999) 'Defence and Security: A Snapshot of the Issues', speech to the Carlton Club, 25 May, reproduced on http://www.fco.gov.uk

Hurd, Douglas (1997) Minutes of evidence to the House of Commons Foreign Affairs Committee investigation into Foreign Policy and Human Rights, 16 Dec.

Labour Party (1987) *Modern Britain in a Modern World*. London: Labour Party.

—— (1997) *Because Britain Deserves Better*. London: Labour Party.

Lloyd, Tony (1997) 'Controlling the Arms Trade: A New Agenda for the 21st Century', speech to a Conference at Chatham House organized by Saferworld and the British American Security Information Council, 9 June, reproduced on http://www.fco.gov.uk

MacAskill, Ewen (1999) 'Cook Defends Record on Arms', *Guardian*, 29 Sept., reproduced on http://www.guardian.co.uk/Archive

Martin, Sir Laurence and Garnett, John (1997) *British Foreign Policy: Challenges and Choices for the 21st Century*. London: Pinter for the Royal Institute of International Affairs.

Norton-Taylor, Richard (1999a) 'Cavalier Officials Slated by MP's', *Guardian*, 10 Feb., reproduced on http://www.guardian.co.uk/Archive

—— (1999b) 'In the Swamp', *Guardian*, 2 Sept., reproduced on http://www.guardian.co.uk/Archive

Pallister, David (1999) 'Torturers on MoD Invitation List for Biggest Arms Fair', *Guardian*, 4 Sept., reproduced on http://www.guardian.co.uk/Archive

Pilger, John (1999) 'Immoral Earnings', *Guardian*, 29 June, reproduced on http://www.guardian.co.uk/Archive

Robertson, George (1997) 'Strategic Defence Review', speech at the Royal United Services Institute, London, 18 Sept., reproduced on the Ministry of Defence website http://www.mod.uk

Shlaim, Avi (1978) *Britain and the Origins of European Unity*. Reading: Graduate School of Contemporary European Studies, University of Reading.

Smith, Raymond and Zametica, John (1985) 'The Cold Warrior: Clement Attlee Reconsidered 1945–7', *International Affairs*, 61(2), 237–54.

Symons, Baroness (1997) 'New Government New Foreign Policy', speech to the Canadian Foreign Service, 10 Oct., reproduced on http://www.fco.gov.uk

Thatcher, Margaret (1988) *Hansard*, vol. 128, col. 1294, 4 Mar.

Waever, Ole (1996) 'European Security Identities', *Journal of Common Market Studies*, 34(1), 103–32.

Wheeler, Nicholas J. and Dunne, Tim (1998) 'Good International Citizenship: A Third Way for British Foreign Policy', *International Affairs*, 74(4), 847–70.

11

Towards a New Constitutional Settlement?

James Mitchell

Introduction

There is broad agreement on the radical nature of New Labour's programme of constitutional reform. The introduction to a 1999 text on the subject described it as 'wider than that of any political party taking office this century' (Blackburn and Plant 1999: 1). Indeed, fairly dramatic changes have taken place in the formal institutions of the constitution of the United Kingdom. A Scottish Parliament and Welsh assembly have been established. A new assembly in Northern Ireland and new cross-border institutions as well as institutions which might play a role in coordinating the work of these bodies are part of the new constitutional landscape. At face value, this does look like a radical restructuring of the constitution, a break with an old consensus. These are significant innovations in the constitutional development of the UK. Especially set against the perceived conservatism of so many other elements of its agenda, constitutional reform appears to provide New Labour with a radical cutting edge. However, do these changes mark a radical break with the past, a new emerging consensus or do these changes hide continuities with the past and involve less decentralization of power than appearances suggest? Or is it possible that an innate constitutional conservatism is to be found alongside this constitutional radicalism? In order to answer these questions we must first be clear about the pre-devolutionary consensus and the nature of the British constitution.[1]

Kavanagh and Morris defined consensus as 'a set of parameters which bounded the set of policy options regarded by senior politicians and civil servants as administratively practicable, economically affordable and politically acceptable' (Kavanagh and Morris 1995: 13). However, though there may be some disagreement on the existence of consensus generally (Kavanagh and Morris 1995; Pimlott 1988), there is little doubt that a broad consensus existed on territorial politics as far as Scotland and Wales were concerned. In Jim Bulpitt's terms, a 'dual polity' existed during this period, with London at the centre and the peripheries having remarkable levels of autonomy from each other (Bulpitt 1983). Occasional demands for devolution over this period amounted to little more than flurries on the fringe of politics. Neither of the two main parties gave serious thought to altering the constitutional positions of Scotland or Wales in a fundamental way. Debate on whether Wales should have a Secretary of State on a par with Scotland eventually led to the establishment of the Welsh Office in 1964, but voices calling for more radical reform were easily dismissed. A sense of grievance about the treatment of Scotland and Wales existed, but this was merely part of the game of party and electoral politics. Opposition parties accused the governing party of failing to treat Scotland and Wales with due attention and sensitivity, and in turn would face such criticisms on coming into office. These grievances, along with special procedures and institutions recognizing Scottish and Welsh distinctiveness, were significant in keeping alive the notion that these were communities which should be treated distinctively. They also may have had a ratchet-like effect, constantly forcing small but cumulative concessions. As Connor has observed, ethnonationalism 'appears to feed on adversity and denial...It also appears to feed on concessions' (Connor 1977: 21). Scottish and Welsh grievances simmered away throughout the postwar period but only really emerged as serious threats to the constitutional order from the 1960s.

Of course, it would be quite wrong to suggest that the processes leading up to the establishment of devolved government for Scotland and Wales were part of a continuous and unbroken path. There was much in Britain's postwar history which signalled a move towards greater integration of these parts within Britain and the UK. The welfare state, nationalization and the programme of government initiated by the Attlee government gave it centralizing elements which, for a period at least, became part of the consensus. However, the programme of the Attlee government was embedded in an understanding of the United Kingdom which took account of the distinctive parts of the state. The welfare state and nationalized industries, for example, had territorial aspects and were not run entirely from London, though opponents attempted, with some success at times, to suggest that centralization would result. A more enduring institutional and cultural consensus, a truly British political tradition, existed which accepted diverse institutions and practices within the centralized polity, with the 'unwritten' constitution a significant component.

The unwritten nature of the British constitution is a common starting point in discussions and debates on British politics. However, it is more accurate to view the constitution as consisting of a number of institutions, in the broadest sense of the term. Institutions, as defined by Hall, are 'the formal rules, compliance procedures, and the standard operating practices that structure the relationship between individuals in various units of the polity and economy' (Hall 1986: 19). For the purposes of a discussion of contemporary constitutional debate, it is useful to distinguish between *formal institutions*, for example legislatures, agencies in the public bureaucracy and the legal framework, and *informal institutions* such as a network of interacting organizations or a set of shared norms (Peters 1999: 18). The formal institutions of the British constitution are easily identified: Parliament at Westminster, the cabinet, Whitehall and local government are prominent 'hard' institutions. Informal institutions – the rules and *modus operandi* of the British constitution – include the 'conventions' of the constitution, described by one eminent constitutionalist as 'somewhat vague and slippery – resembling the procreation of eels' (Marshall 1984: 54–5); they include the standard operating procedures within cabinet government and Whitehall. No matter how slippery they appear to be, these are crucial elements of the British constitution. These 'rules' are the 'routines, procedures, conventions, roles, strategies, organisational forms, and technologies around which political activity is constructed... the beliefs, paradigms, codes, cultures, and knowledge that surround, support, elaborate, and contradict those roles and routines' (March and Olsen 1989: 22). Any attempt to understand the 'British' constitution means taking account of all of these.

However, the extent to which these have been accompanied by, or even necessitate, changes in the informal institutions is another matter. To what extent has there been a constitutional revolution as a result of the election of Labour in 1997 and the legislation it subsequently passed, or to what extent should devolution be seen as new formal institutions operating within old informal arrangements?

The myth of the unitary state

Textbooks on UK/British politics commonly assert that the UK/Britain is a unitary state. Rarely, however, do they seek to define or engage with the term. Even books which are sophisticated in their understanding of territorial politics and which focus on a discussion of the constituent nations of the UK use the term.[2] The fact that until fairly recently it was accepted that the state was unitary is a statement of the power of the myth of the unitary state. By myth I am not suggesting that the statement is inaccurate, though that may well be the case, but merely that its potency has lain in it being widely, perhaps unquestioningly, held. As Bogdanor expressed it in 1979, perhaps the strongest of the 'tacit understandings' underpinning the UK was the 'profoundly unitary nature of the United Kingdom, as expressed in the supremacy of Parliament' (Bogdanor 1979: 7). Albert Venn Dicey can be credited with popularizing the idea, though not with its invention, in the nineteenth century. This had far-reaching implications for debates on both the UK's domestic constitution and its relations with the rest of Europe in or 'throughout' the twentieth century. Parliamentary sovereignty was, in the opening words of chapter 1 of Dicey's *Law of the Constitution*, first published in 1885: '(from a legal point of view) the dominant characteristic of our political institutions' (Dicey 1923: 37).[3] Dicey became an inveterate opponent of (Irish) home rule. For him home rule, 'no matter in what guise it was presented by proponents, infringed the sovereignty of Parliament and portended the dissolution of the United Kingdom' (Cosgrove 1980: 114). Dicey's work offers a better understanding of the compromises, complexities and essentially pluralist territorial nature of the UK than his often strident opposition to home rule indicated, or the subsequent crude references and interpretations of his work, by devolutionists and anti-devolutionists alike, would suggest.

Leaving aside the issue of parliamentary sovereignty, Dicey was keen in his work to stress the variation which existed within the UK. In a book co-authored with a Scottish historian he had noted that the Treaty of Union,[4] establishing Britain through the creation of a British parliament, was 'the most conservative of revolutionary measures' in that it 'repealed every law or custom of England or of Scotland inconsistent with the political unity of the new State, but it did not make or attempt any change or reform which was not necessary for the creation of the new United Kingdom' (Dicey and Rait 1920: 245). In other words, there was no attempt to obliterate all signs of Scottish national identity in the process of union:

> the men who drafted the Treaty of Union carefully left every institution in England and every institution in Scotland untouched by the Act, provided that the existence of such an institution was consistent with the main objects of the Act. Hence the extraordinary success of the Act. It destroyed nothing which did not threaten the essential unity of the whole people; and

hence, lastly, the supreme glory of the Act, that while creating the political unity it kept alive the nationalism both of England and of Scotland. (Dicey and Rait 1920: 362)

Efforts were made to maintain pre-union institutions and practices. This was fully understood by Dicey. Indeed, Dicey stressed in his various works that he did not believe in uniformity across the state:

> The true watchwords which should guide English democrats in their dealings with Ireland, as in truth with every other part of the United Kingdom, are not 'equality', 'similarity', and 'simultaneity', but 'unity of government', 'equality of political rights', 'diversity of institutions'. Unless English democrats see this they will commit a double fault: they will not in reality deal with Ireland as with England, for to deal with societies in essentially different conditions in the same manner is in truth to treat them differently. (Dicey 1886: 30–1)

This is not to say that Dicey denied the existence of a UK nation. In a book formed from letters he had written to the *Spectator*, Dicey expounded on the notion of a UK nation (Dicey 1887). Dicey could not concede that the UK was a nation of nations as that would be to admit that the component nations had a right to self-determination, something he refused to accept.

The unity of government principle was provided for by parliamentary sovereignty. Accepting distinct established churches in different parts of the UK allowed for diverse institutions, while equality of political rights could be ensured through Acts of the single Parliament. Strong central government ensured the Diceyian principles of equality of political rights and unity of government, giving parliamentary sovereignty a privileged position in the constitution. To what extent, however, were Dicey's watchwords mutually compatible? He had made the point that there was an apparent contradiction in the nature of the Union of Scotland and England – it amounted to a 'conservative revolution'. Was it possible to have diverse institutions and equal political rights? This, he believed, was made possible by the limited role of distinct and separate institutions. So long as they did not interfere with the political rights then a balance might be struck. In large measure, however, it came down to an interpretation of political rights. If by that was meant access to the franchise, for example, there were indeed differences within the United Kingdom, but these appear to have been anomalies which Dicey was willing to accept. If, however, rights were extended, as happened during the twentieth century, to include social and welfare rights such as access to a public health service and an old age pension for example, then it was conceivable that rights would not be equal across the state. In Dicey's day, the state's remit was limited and it was much easier to ensure equality of rights when these were so limited, at least as compared with today. When the state's reach and remit grew, there would inevitably be problems in ensuring that every subject of the Crown had the same rights. The Scottish Board of Health, for example, set up after the First World War would not necessarily provide the same level of health and housing for people living in Scotland as was provided by the Board of Health set up at the same time but with a territorial remit limited to England and Wales. Separate institutions for pensions were set up for the constituent nations of the UK at the beginning of the century, but a centralized system was introduced after the Second World War which ensured uniformity. A pensioner in Scotland would, therefore, receive the same pension as another in England, but would have different rights when it came to health, housing and rents.

Unity of government does not sit easily with diverse political institutions, including different systems of law, especially if policies flowing from these provide different (social) rights, even if these are not political rights strictly speaking. Scots living in rented accommodation had preferential treatment compared to their southern neighbours, and access to council housing was far greater in Scotland after 1945 simply because of the differential growth of public sector housing in the constituent nations of Britain. That said, the liberal democratic welfare state was in many respects the embodiment of many of Dicey's principles. The 'national' in Bevan's National Health Service was the Diceyian nation of the UK. Any individual could expect the same basic level of healthcare regardless of which part of the state she lived in; similarly with pensions – a pensioner in Bathgate could expect the same pension as a pensioner in Bath. In other words, the mutual compatibility of Dicey's watchwords was more likely in a period of the night-watchman state than in an advanced liberal democracy. Strong central control was the most obvious means of ensuring equality of political and other rights associated with the welfare state.

While the constitution is fêted as flexible and unwritten, innovation on a number of levels has been prevented by a rigid and often grossly oversimplified interpretation of Dicey's work. Dicey himself did not help matters, particularly as his views 'gradually hardened into bitter opposition to every form of home rule' (Cosgrove 1980: 114). In essence, Dicey's doctrine of parliamentary sovereignty proved a constitutional straitjacket which prevented serious debate on aspects of constitutional development. It was a written fetter on the interpretation of an unwritten constitution. This most affected socialists and those keen on extending the scope of the state. It is one of the supreme ironies of constitutional development in the United Kingdom that Dicey, a champion of the limited state, should have so greatly influenced those who believed in exactly the opposite. British socialists accepted Diceyian principles as readily and unthinkingly as any other group in British politics. This had profound implications for the kind of state they envisaged and helped create. There is no better authority on this than Gordon Brown, Labour Chancellor of the Exchequer and sometime historian, whose doctoral thesis included an appendix on home rule and the labour movement. Here he maintained that Scottish Labour wanted to be both Scottish and British but: 'No theorist attempted in sufficient depth to reconcile the conflicting aspirations for home rule and a British socialist advance. In particular, no one was able to show how capturing power in Britain – and legislating for minimum levels of welfare, for example – could be combined with a policy of devolution for Scotland' (Brown 1981: 527). In other words, the principle of equality was incompatible with that of home rule.

The evolution of the territorial form of the state

As has frequently been pointed out, devolution in the form of an elected assembly first came to that part of the UK which had been most vehemently opposed to home rule. The Northern Ireland assembly which met from 1922 until it was prorogued in 1972 was a curious development in constitutional politics. It was a body which was established to emphasize Northern Ireland's link with the rest of the UK. It was assuredly a unionist body in every sense of the term. Dominated by the Ulster Unionist Party throughout its half-century of existence, in some respects it probably came as close to conforming with Dicey's watchwords as was possible, while utterly ignoring them in other respects.[5] The Diceyian principle of diversity of institutions was embodied in Stormont, but equality of political rights was abandoned. However, contrary to what Dicey might have expected, it was not between the devolved territory and the rest of the state that the inequality of political rights was to be found. Stormont's demise by Act of Parliament at Westminster seems to confirm that parliamentary sovereignty remained unaffected. In political terms, Terence O'Neill, the most liberal premier during Stormont's existence, remarked: 'Oddly enough, I would say that the main task of the separate government in Northern Ireland has not been to emphasise differences but to encourage conformity of standards' (O'Neill 1969: 77–8). A similar view was held by Enoch Powell, a politician who at times almost seemed to see himself as the reincarnation of Dicey in his denunciations of perceived attacks on parliamentary sovereignty and his involvement in the Irish Question. In 1955 as Conservative government minister responsible for rent restrictions at Westminster, Powell advised his counterparts in Northern Ireland against introducing a measure ahead of Westminster.[6] The denial of the Diceyian principle of equality of political rights was to be Stormont's undoing.

Other parts of the UK also had separate political institutions. Scotland, as we have seen, retained some of its pre-union rights and institutions, but some of these became less significant over time. Secularization reduced the role of the Church of Scotland while it remained as distinctly Scottish as it had been in the past. The increased reach of the state and the increased importance of Parliament in the life of the UK resulted in pressure for this central institution to take greater account of Scottish distinctiveness. The Scottish Office, established in 1885, and special parliamentary procedures in the House of Commons to deal with Scottish affairs were developed over the course of the twentieth century, embodying two of the Diceyian principles – unity of government and diversity of institutions – without infringing to a great extent on the third. The Scottish Office, like the Welsh Office which was set up in 1964, was able to carve out a role for itself and did more than simply put a kilt on public policy designed in the south. However, it was not within the powers of these territorial departments to alter the fundamental political rights of people living in Scotland and Wales. The Northern Ireland Office, set up in the wake of Stormont's demise in 1972, along with other government departments did indeed set out to alter the political rights in Northern Ireland. For most Catholics this meant giving them the same formal political rights as those enjoyed by Protestants, ending gerrymandering for example. At the same time special legislation was passed which altered the civil rights of people living in Northern Ireland.

The development of the territorial departments cannot be divorced from the development of the state more generally. As the reach of the state increased this had implications for territorial politics.[7] This was the case not least because a developed welfare state required, at the very least, local and regional agencies with which to implement policies decided at the centre. The development of such bodies provokes questions about the unitary nature of the state. The Scottish and Welsh Offices and attendant quangos and agencies fulfilled two quite different functions. They served as formal institutional embodiments of Diceyian diverse institutions, but also had more prosaic, but no less significant, public policy functions in playing a part in delivering public services. In time, these two functions became blurred. The provision of public services through distinct Scottish and Welsh institutions helped maintain the unity of the state by recognizing its diversity. In the late twentieth century, these were the manifestations of what Dicey had referred to as the 'supreme glory of union'.

Bulpitt described this as a dual polity, which he maintained existed for around forty years after 1926: 'a structure of territorial politics in which Centre and periphery had relatively little to do with each other' (Bulpitt 1983: 160). In essence, there was a consensus around the dual polity during this period. The consensus was made possible in large measure because the centre was able to govern as it saw fit and the peripheries were given sufficient and growing resources by the centre to do what they wanted, within accepted limits. Economic growth allowed for growth in public spending and made the dual polity successful. It was a consensus which followed Dicey's watchwords. Diverse institutions were able to cut out relatively distinct policies, but within a centralized polity in which Parliament remained sovereign, without (Northern Ireland apart) undermining to any significant degree uniformity of political rights. The dual polity was most evident in Northern Ireland but operated elsewhere too. This separation was, according to Bulpitt, what the centre had always desired – autonomy for itself to pursue 'high' politics, while leaving the relatively peripheral affairs of 'low' politics to local elites to manage, whether these were to be found in local government, Stormont or the Scottish Office. Between 1961 and 1969, forces emerged to challenge the dual polity. As well as problems in Northern Ireland requiring London's direct intervention, Scottish and Welsh nationalist pressures and problems around local authority spending challenged the dual polity. But the main challenge, according to Bulpitt, came from the centre itself, which was determined to pursue modernization and appease peripheral dissidents.

The challenge to the consensus

If the dual polity began to look ragged in the 1960s, it started to disintegrate in the late 1970s and to collapse in the 1990s. The downturn in the economy, frustrations with spending cuts and a general sense that all was not well undermined the territorial consensus. The rise of Scottish and Welsh nationalism in the 1960s culminated in the offer by the Labour government in the late 1970s of a measure of devolution to both Scotland and Wales. In large measure, this was a response designed to placate Scottish and Welsh public opinion rather than a measure aimed at tackling underlying problems in the British economy. Referendums were held in Scotland and Wales in 1979, resulting in a narrow majority for devolution in Scotland, though insufficient to overcome the weighted majority required by Parliament, and a massive majority against in Wales. Levels of support for devolution which had been recorded in polls some time before the referendum could not be sustained when it came to voting on a concrete set of proposals. Various explanations have been given for the outcome of the referendums, including the unpopularity of the Labour government at the time and the divisions within the Labour Party on the issue. Divisions within the Labour Party were important. Many Labour politicians could not see how devolution could operate while the party was committed to equal social rights across the state. They echoed Gordon Brown's lament on the labour movement's inability in the 1920s to find some means of reconciling devolution and minimum levels of welfare across the state.

Other Labour opponents had a much more conservative agenda, emphasizing what they saw as the challenge to the unitary nature of the state implicit in devolution. Most notable among them was Tam Dalyell, a Labour opponent of devolution. For him devolution and a unitary state were 'mutually exclusive': 'Would it not be more honest to admit that it is impossible to have an Assembly – especially any kind of subordinate Parliament – that is part, though only part of a unitary state?' (Dalyell 1977c). Dalyell's innate conservatism was even more evident when he warned that devolution was supported by women who 'tend to be more emotional about their politics than men' (Dalyell 1977a: 224). Dalyell's alliterative espousal of what became known as the 'West Lothian Question' – so named after his constituency in recognition of his persistence on the issue – became his hallmark in the devolution debates. An example was his question to Prime Minister Callaghan after a new devolution bill was introduced into the Commons in late 1977: 'Under the new Bill, shall I be able to vote on many matters in relation to West Bromwich but not West Lothian, as I was under the last Bill, and will my Right Hon. Friend be able to vote on many matters in relation to Carlisle but not Cardiff?' (Dalyell 1977b).

He was articulating a Diceyian concern. As Dicey had pointed out a century before, devolution to any one part of the state involves a 'demand for fundamental alterations in the whole Constitution of the United Kingdom' (Dicey 1886: preface). Gladstone was an earlier Prime Minister who had wrestled with the implications for Westminster of giving one part of the state (Ireland) home rule. In his speech in the Commons on his first home rule bill, Gladstone maintained that there 'cannot be a domestic legislature in Ireland dealing with Irish affairs, and

Irish Peers and Representatives sitting in Parliament at Westminster to take part in English and Scotch [sic] affairs' (Gladstone 1886).

The mixture of socialist and conservative concerns within the Labour Party provided a sizeable anti-devolution element among Labour supporters which was mobilized in the referendum. In Scotland the majority for devolution was insufficient to overcome the weighted majority demanded by Westminster: 40 per cent of the eligible electorate were required to vote Yes. In the event only 32.5 per cent of the electorate (51.6 per cent of those who voted) voted Yes and 30.4 voted No (48.4 per cent of those who voted).

Matters did not end with the defeat of devolution in 1979. Frustrations and grievances in Scotland and Wales reached new levels in the 1980s under Margaret Thatcher. Until then, the sense of grievance in Scotland and Wales had been persistent but inchoate. The Tories had ruled Britain for thirteen years after 1951 but that had been quite different from the years after 1979. Opposition politics in Scotland and Wales became more coherent, with a left-progressive agenda forming around the case for a parliament or assembly. In large measure, a perception developed in Scotland and Wales that the old territorial consensus and all that accompanied it was being undermined by the Conservatives. As in the past, the Opposition parties set out to capitalize on the governing party's difficulties but were aided by the combination of factors which had not been present together in the past. The Conservatives were a minority party in Scotland during the Thatcher years. The reduction in the number of seats they held over the years only added to the perception that they were a minority imposing their will on a reluctant majority. The very fact that they were in office so long meant that the public came to associate London rule with Conservative rule. The Conservative programme for government left no room for significant increases in public spending or giving Scotland and Wales flexibility within the system of government. Mrs Thatcher's stridency did not help and created a strong sense among Scots that she was 'anti-Scottish' (Mitchell and Bennie 1996). Suspicions that she had contempt for the territorial consensus were confirmed when she published her memoirs. Unlike any previous premier, she saw the Scottish Office as part of the problem rather than a means of managing territorial relations (Thatcher 1993: 618–24). Past Conservative premiers had celebrated the diversity of the United Kingdom, but Mrs Thatcher seemed to many people in Scotland and Wales at least to see the state as England writ large. Mrs Thatcher commented on the implications in Scotland of being seen as a 'quintessential English figure': 'I am what I am and I have no intention of wearing tartan camouflage . . . If [the Tory Party] sometimes seems English to some Scots that is because the Union is

inevitably dominated by England by reason of its greater population'
(1993: 624). She was, of course, accurate, but insensitive, her interpretation of 'union' differing markedly from that of her predecessors. In
Diceyian terms, unity of government was paramount in Mrs Thatcher's
understanding of the Union.

Under Mrs Thatcher, one feature of the Diceyian constitutional order
was emphasized but at the expense of another. Parliamentary sovereignty
and the unity of government were prioritized, while diversity of institutions was demoted. The consequence was a backlash which built on
existing distinctiveness and long-standing grievances. For many Scots,
the introduction of the poll tax, a flat rate tax to replace domestic rates,
symbolized in stark terms the Conservatives' attitude to Scotland in the
late 1980s. It was deeply unpopular, regressive in nature and provided a
focus for Scottish grievances. Support for devolution became less inchoate, more immediate and focused. In essence, devolution was perceived
as a means of blocking Conservative rule in Scotland and Wales, where
that party was in a declining minority but managed to rule by virtue of
victory in general elections across Britain.

Though the devolution proposals which emerged from this period
were not radically different in nature from those that had been put to
the peoples of Scotland and Wales in 1979, the political force behind
them was much greater. Opinion hardened inside the Labour Party.
Devolution was no longer simply a means of responding to electoral
pressure from Scottish and Welsh nationalism. Labour members and
supporters saw devolution as a way of having power in Scotland and
keeping the Tories out. Though it failed to achieve the levels of support it
had won in the 1970s, the Scottish National Party (SNP) was in many
respects more of a threat than it had been in the 1970s. Increasing
numbers of Labour voters saw it as a realistic alternative and viewed it
as their second choice, with support for independence becoming increasingly attractive (Bennie, Brand and Mitchell 1997). Labour prevented its
support haemorrhaging to the SNP by firming up its support for a
Scottish Parliament and adopting neo-nationalist rhetoric. Similiar developments in Wales altered opinion there, though Scotland made the
running.

Between the general elections of 1979 and 1997 the most significant
development as far as devolution was concerned was the growth in the
depth of support (levels of conviction) – if not in its breadth (extent of
support) – for constitutional change. In Scotland, support for a parliament continued to run at around 75 per cent but, crucially, that component which supported independence grew within this total. Most
significant was the hardening of support within the Labour Party. In

opposition, Labour in Scotland and Wales refined its policy over that period, culminating after 1989 in Scottish Labour's involvement in the Constitutional Convention, a cross-party grouping with the support of trade unions, local authorities, churches and others which advocated home rule. Supporters referred to it as representative of 'Scottish civil society', though it looked and sounded more like Scottish bourgeois society. The convention made few changes to Labour's devolution policy. The party had already decided that the remit of the Scottish Parliament should be wider than that proposed in the 1970s and that it should have tax-varying powers. However, the issue of representation was altered, with the convention and Labour agreeing that a future Scottish Parliament should be elected using some more proportional form of representation and that efforts should be made to increase women's representation.

The rhetoric surrounding the constitutional Convention, especially in its early days, was nationalistic. A grandiosely entitled 'Claim of Right for Scotland' was signed by participants, including all Scottish Labour MPs except Tam Dalyell, which proclaimed that sovereignty lay with the people of Scotland not Parliament at Westminster. At face value, it was a direct challenge to Diceyian constitutionalism. In reality, the rhetoric was radical but the proposals were reformist. The Scottish devolution White Paper stated that the 'UK Parliament is, and will remain sovereign in all matters' and 'Westminster will be choosing to exercise that sovereignty by devolving legislative responsibilities to a Scottish Parliament without in any way diminishing its own powers' (Scottish Office 1997: para. 4.2). The Scotland Act 1998 establishing the Scottish Parliament reiterated this point in a section on Acts of the Scottish Parliament: 'This section does not affect the power of the Parliament of the United Kingdom to make laws for Scotland' (Scotland Act, clause 27(7)). Unity of government is protected. As Tony Blair made clear after he became leader of the Labour Party, parliamentary sovereignty would not be undermined by the establishment of a Scottish Parliament.[8]

The 'settled will'?

The new Labour government's devolution proposals appeared in White Papers in July 1997 (HMSO 1997a, 1997b) and were put to referendums in September. Two questions were put to the people of Scotland: whether they wanted a Scottish Parliament and whether they wanted it to have tax-varying powers. Scots voted overwhelmingly for a parliament and tax-varying powers. In Wales, the narrowest majority voted for a Welsh assembly (table 11.1). The result in Scotland was a foregone conclusion with little change of opinion during the actual campaign. An effective campaign was waged by pro-devolution forces, especially as compared with the referendum in 1979. In voting for a parliament, Scots were quite clear what they expected as a consequence. Seven out ten expected taxes to rise, but, more significantly, 86 per cent expected the economy to improve as a consequence of having a Scottish Parliament and 89 per cent expected the quality of education to improve (table 11.2) (Denver et al. 2000). In voting for a tax-varying parliament, Scots expected that it would 'improve the quality of welfare in Scotland' (Surridge and McCrone 1999: 47).

However, in the event, many matters relating to welfare are retained at Westminster. The overall size of the Scottish Parliament's budget and redistributive policies such as pensions, welfare payments and the tax system are beyond its scope. The capacity of the Scottish Parliament to deliver improved welfare is, therefore, far from certain (Mitchell 1998). Expectations triumphed over judgement among the electorate, though many supporters of devolution may have felt reluctant to admit that the new institution would be unable to make a difference. It is, however, notable that expectations with regard to improvements in the economy, standards of the health service and quality of education exceed the proportion of those who voted for the Parliament. There is a 'capability–expectations gap' in Scottish politics, with the Scottish Parliament unable, given its limited powers, to meet the expectations the electorate have of it.[9] This will create a dynamic for further change unless either these expectations are lowered or London delivers.

Much had been made in debates on devolution of the description by the then Labour leader John Smith of devolution as the 'settled will of the Scottish people'. In reality, there was only a settled will against the status quo ante. No settled will exists regarding the future constitutional status of Scotland, as polls since the referendum indicating continued high levels of support for independence show. It is conceivable that high levels of support for independence, even majority support for that option, will not be translated into support for the SNP, as Labour now has a substantial element of its vote which supports independence but which, presumably, views other, non-constitutional issues of greater importance. So long as Labour is perceived to deliver on welfare then it may be safe from a nationalist assault on its support. However, if the expectations previously projected on to devolution are not delivered, it is possible that these expectations will be re-projected on to independence. In Wales the change from the 1979 referendum was greater than it had been in Scotland. Devolution was endorsed by a tiny majority but great expectations surrounded the creation of the Welsh Assembly, though to a

Table 11.1 Results of devolution referendums in Scotland and Wales (percentages)

	Yes	No	Turnout
1979			
Scotland	51.6	48.4	62.9
Wales	20.2	79.8	58.3
1997			
Scottish Parliament	74.3	25.7	60.4
Tax-varying powers	63.5	36.5	
Wales	50.3	49.7	50.1

Table 11.2 Expectations of a Scottish parliament

	A lot (%)	A little (%)	Total (%)
A Scottish parliament would:			
Increase unemployment ·	2	9	11
Increase taxes	2	68	70
Improve the economy	26	60	86
Improve the standard of the NHS	36	46	82
Improve the quality of education	39	50	89
Improve the standard of social welfare	19	52	71

Source: D. Denver et al., *Scotland Decides* (London: Frank Cass, 2000), p. 200.

lesser degree than in Scotland. Almost 50 per cent thought that it would lead to an improvement in the standard of the National Health Service and improvement in the economy (Jones and Trystan 1999: 81–2). Legislation establishing the new Scottish and Welsh institutions was then passed through Parliament. The new Scottish Parliament and Welsh Assembly were elected in May 1999, resulting in Labour becoming the largest party but without an overall majority in either.

The likelihood of further change after devolution is indicated by a number of factors. As with the 'expectations–capability gap', little thought had gone into the implications for Westminster and Whitehall of the devolution 'settlement'. In Scotland, the Constitutional Convention had little to say on this and had concentrated on making a nationalist 'claim' for a parliament. As far as its impact on the centre is concerned, devolution has simply been allowed to evolve piecemeal. Late one night, as the Scottish legislation was passing through the Lords, the government minister in charge announced the intention to establish 'standing arrangements for the devolved administrations to be

involved by the UK Government at ministerial level when they consider
reserved matters which impinge on devolved responsibilities' (Ramsay
1998). It took a number of months and many revisions before a 'Memorandum of Understanding and supplementary agreements' between the
UK government and the devolved administrations was issued (Scottish
Executive 1999). It proved less significant than had been initially suggested. The issue of relations between London and Edinburgh/Cardiff
remained and remains contentious.

The 'West Lothian Question' remains unresolved. It was less significant in the debates in the 1990s for three main reasons. First, there was
much more concern about what were perceived as existing anomalies
allowing a minority Conservative government to impose its policies on
Scotland and Wales than about possible new anomalies as a consequence
of devolution. Second, the referendum was held before a devolution
measure was debated in Parliament. MPs would be more likely to be
concerned with the West Lothian Question than voters in Scotland. In the
1970s the devolution legislation had preceded the referendum, allowing
Parliament to set the terms of the debate. Third, the myth of the unitary
state which had given such force to the West Lothian Question was being
questioned. There was greater acceptance that the unreformed UK constitution was already full of anomalies as far as territorial politics was
concerned. What almost amounted to a paradigm shift had taken place in
Labour Party thinking on this matter, at least in Scotland.

However, it was perhaps inevitable that following the establishment of
the Scottish Parliament and the Welsh Assembly, an English backlash
would begin to emerge and that old Diceyian objections to devolution
would resurface. The issue of territorial representation at Westminster
and the future of the territorial departments after devolution were raised,
especially by devolution's opponents. In a debate on the consequences of
devolution for Parliament at Westminster, the Conservative opposition
spokesman warned that the country as a whole had not 'fully woken up
to all the changes that devolution will bring about' and that for England
the present scheme is 'neither stable nor defensible' (Young 1999). The
prospect of further change was confirmed when the Leader of the Opposition announced his intention if elected of abolishing the posts of
Secretaries of State for Scotland and Wales (*Herald*, 26 Oct. 1999).

Conclusions

There are a number of reasons for concluding that the legislation creating
the Scottish Parliament and the Welsh Assembly are only a stage in the

process of constitutional change. Ron Davies, the former Welsh Secretary, has argued that devolution is a 'process not an event' (Davies 1999),
indicating its path-dependent qualities. The reasons for the rise in the
demand for devolution may not have gone away. National pride played
its part in the votes for the new institutions but the spur which brought
about their creation was more prosaic and, ironically, was concerned
with protecting much that had in the recent past been associated with
Britishness. The interventionist welfare (British) state was perceived to be
under attack. New Labour shows little sign that it will remove all the
fears which were exhibited in Scotland and Wales in the 1980s and
1990s. On the other hand, the election successes of Labour mean that
the largest party in Scotland and Wales is now in government. But past
experience has shown that whichever party is in government faces the
accusation that it is not sensitive to Scottish and Welsh needs and aspirations. Though this is less likely to be as immediate a problem for Labour
as it was for the Conservatives, Labour now faces the Scottish National
Party and Plaid Cymru as the main opposition parties in Scotland and
Wales. The existence of a Scottish Parliament and a Welsh Assembly can
be expected to augment, not diminish, the need for parties to demonstrate their Scottish and Welsh credentials. In a sense, there has been
another turn of the nationalist ratchet.

In addition, the capability–expectations gap creates a dynamic the
consequence of which is difficult to predict. There may be a tendency
in London to assume that devolution removes the problem, that it
involves the devolution of penury. Difficult decisions will have to be
taken and there is an advantage for the centre in forcing the devolved
institutions to confront them and face the consequences than having to
take these decisions itself. Unfortunately for the centre, it still controls
much that is important for potentially closing the capability–expectations gap. Redistributive powers are retained at Westminster and considerable power over spending matters will still be held in London. More
important may prove to be culpability for problems and conflicts that are
bound to arise. Who will people in Scotland and Wales blame when
things go wrong and when expectations are not met? Will they turn on
the new institutions or on London? Any settlement, in the sense of the
establishment of new consensus, does not yet seem in sight. A new
consensus will require a diminishing of the political differences between
Scotland/Wales and England, but devolution seems set to increase these.
In addition, though the Conservatives have accepted the outcome of the
referendums in Scotland and Wales and the establishment of the new
institutions, they do not accept that that the current arrangements are
either stable or defensible.

One factor may prove to be the informal institutions of the constitution. Though devolutionary institutions have been established, it is not clear whether a less unitary culture now exists at the centre. It is conceivable that a belief will develop that the Scottish Parliament and the Welsh Assembly are enough, and indeed that the centre need no longer be so sensitive. The temptation to see devolution as requiring the reduction of Scottish and Welsh rights at the centre might provoke a backlash there or at least be used by nationalists and others to mobilize support for further change. Conversely, the failure to do so might provoke a backlash in England or encourage some politicians to 'play the English card' just as the 'Scottish card' has been played in the past. As perceptions of the centre's insensitivities proved crucial in the mobilization of support for devolution in the past, and with so much remaining under the control of the centre, it cannot be assumed that the devolved institutions will necessarily be enough. The arrangements for dealing with Scotland and Wales at the centre are crucial but have not for the most part been written into the legislation. It is the informal institutions which in the past were perceived to have caused the problems and may do so again. How these operate in the future will play a large part in determining the future constitutional development of the United Kingdom.

The Diceyian principles may need to be reconsidered in light of the new institutions. Devolution involves greater emphasis on the diversity of institutions but at the expense, potentially at least, of unity of government and even possibly of equality of political rights. If equality of rights, though not necessarily political rights, is maintained across the state this may prove unpopular in those places where expectations of devolution making a difference has developed. As far as territorial politics is concerned, Dicey's most significant contribution was his understanding of what can best be described as the harmonious contradictions in the constitution, the 'conservative revolution' which union between Scotland and England entailed. Devolution's ultimate success and the best hopes for the emergence of a new consensus around devolution may require greater uniformity of expectations across the state, whether this involves accepting more or less state intervention.

The old constitutional settlement has been shaken as a result of devolution. That has been obvious in the formal institutions. Less obvious has been any parallel shake-up in the informal institutions. The interaction of the new formal institutions with old ones is still evolving and as yet unsettled. At the same time, there is as yet no obvious set of new shared values, though this may not be necessary if the informal arrangements prove less radical than conventional wisdom suggests. Much of this depends on what happens at the centre. It seems certain that devolved parliaments – providing for Dicey's 'diversity of institutions' – will have some impact on Dicey's other 'watchwords', 'unity of government' and 'equality of political rights'. John Smith, former leader of the Labour Party, is frequently quoted as referring to devolution as 'unfinished business'. Even after the election of the new institutions in Belfast, Cardiff and Edinburgh, there remains much unfinished business. The old settlement may have been shaken, but the United Kingdom has yet to find a new one.

NOTES

1   The term 'British' is commonly used, though of course it is not entirely accurate. The discussion which follows will say little about Northern Ireland, which is dealt with in chapter 12.
2   A good example of the changing thinking on this is found in the work of Vernon Bogdanor, one of the foremost scholars on territorial politics in the UK. Though offering a sophisticated understanding of the national components of the state in his 1979 book on devolution, he nonetheless referred to Britain as a unitary state (Bogdanor 1979: 7). In later works (1997, 1999), he has adopted the term 'union state', reflecting changes in the terms of the debate. Another example, nearer to home, is a textbook on Scottish politics in which it was asserted that 'the United Kingdom remains a unitary state, in which ultimate sovereignty resides in parliament' (Midwinter, Keating and Mitchell 1991:2)
3   All references from this work are taken from the eighth edition published in 1923. This edition includes an introduction in which the author considers some of the changes since the first edition was published. Dicey died in 1922. Two books on Dicey which shed light particularly on his views on territorial politics are Cosgrove 1980 and Ford 1985. The former makes the point that the Irish Question 'came to dominate his life' (p. 114).
4   The term 'Treaty' rather than 'Act' of Union is used here to denote the existence of two independent states reaching agreement. This distinction is more than a matter of pedantry but is seen, especially but by no means exclusively, by supporters of Scottish devolution as important as it signifies that the creation of Britain involved more than simply England writ larger.
5   Dicey had maintained in correspondence with a friend that he would continue his support for Ulster Unionism in its campaign against home rule only so long as the protest did not degenerate into attacks on Catholics (Cosgrove 1980: 242).
6   Though in this instance this meant for England and Wales (not Britain), as Scotland had separate legislation dealing with rent restrictions.

7 Territorial politics can be defined as 'that arena of political activity concerned with the relations between the central political institutions in the capital city and those interests, communities, political organisations and governmental bodies outside the central institutional complex, but within the accepted boundaries of the state, which possess, or are commonly perceived to possess, a significant geographical or local/regional character' (Bulpitt 1983: 1).

8 In an interview during the 1997 election campaign, Blair explained how he would explain devolution to his English constituents: 'I will say to them we have devolved these matters to the Scottish Parliament but as far as we are concerned sovereignty rests with me as an English MP and that's the way it will stay' (4 April 1997).

9 This phrase is drawn from Hill (1993) in his discussion of the European Community's capabilities and its international role.

REFERENCES

Bennie, Lynn, Brand, Jack and Mitchell, James (1997) *How Scotland Votes*. Manchester: Manchester University Press.

Blackburn, Robert and Plant, Raymond (eds) (1999) *Constitutional Reform: The Labour Government's Constitutional Reform Agenda*. London: Longman.

Bogdanor, Vernon (1979) *Devolution*. Oxford: Oxford University Press.

—— (1997) *Power and the People*. London: Gollancz.

—— (1997) *Devolution in the United Kingdom*. Oxford: Oxford University Press.

Brown, Gordon (1981) 'The Labour Party and Political Change in Scotland, 1918–1929: The Politics of Five Elections', Ph.D. thesis, Edinburgh University.

Bulpitt, Jim (1983) *Territory and Power in the United Kingdom*. Manchester: Manchester University Press.

Connor, Walker (1997) 'The Politics of Ethnonationalism', *Journal of International Affairs*, 27, 1–21.

Cosgrove, Richard (1980) *The Rule of Law: Albert Venn Dicey, Victorian Jurist*. London: Basingstoke.

Dalyell, Tam (1977a) *Devolution: The End of Britain?* London: Cape.

—— (1977b) Question from Tam Dalyell, House of Commons, *Hansard*, vol. 938, 3 Nov., col. 31.

—— (1977c) Question from Tam Dalyell, House of Commons, *Hansard*, vol. 939, 14 Nov., cols 78–9.

Davies, Ron (1999) *Devolution: A Process Not an Event*. Cardiff: Institute of Welsh Affairs.

Denver, David, Mitchell, James, Pattie, Charles and Bochel, Hugh (2000) *Scotland Decides: The Devolution Issue and the 1997 Referendum*. London: Frank Cass.

Dicey, Albert Venn (1886) *England's Case against Home Rule*. London: John Murray.

—— (1887) *Letters on Unionist Delusions*. London: Macmillan.

—— (1893) *A Leap in the Dark: A Criticism of the Principles of Home Rule as Illustrated by the Bill of 1893*. London: John Murray.

—— (1913) *A Fool's Paradise: Being a Constitutionalist's Criticism on the Home Rule Bill of 1912*. London: John Murray.

—— (1923) *Law of the Constitution*, 8th ed. London: Macmillan.

Dicey, A. V. and Rait, Robert (1920) *Thoughts on the Union Between England and Scotland*. London: Macmillan.

Ford, Trowbridge (1985) *Albert Venn Dicey: The Man and his Times*. Chichester: Barry Rose.

Gladstone, W. E: (1886) Speech by W. E. Gladstone, House of Commons, *Hansard*, vol. 304, 8 Apr., col. 1055.

Hall, Peter (1986) *Governing the Economy: The Politics of State Intervention in Britain and France*. Oxford: Oxford University Press.

Hill, Christopher (1993) 'The Capability–Expectations Gap, or Conceptualizing Europe's International Role', *Journal of Common Market Studies*, 31, 305–28.

Procedure Committee (1999) *The Procedural Consequences of Devolution*, HC 185. London: House of Commons.

HMSO (1997a) *Scotland's Parliament* Cm. 3658. Edinburgh: HMSO.

HMSO (1997b) *A Voice for Wales*, Cm. 3718. London: HMSO.

Jones, Richard Wyn and Trystan, Dafydd (1999) 'The 1997 Welsh Referendum Vote', in B. Taylor and K. Thomson (eds), *Scotland and Wales: Nations Again?* Cardiff: University of Wales Press.

Kavanagh, Dennis and Morris, Peter (1995) *Consensus Politics: From Attlee to Major*, 2 edn. Oxford: Blackwell.

March, James G. and Olsen, Johan P. (1989) *Rediscovering Institutions: The Organizational Basis of Politics*. New York: Free Press.

Marshall, Geoffrey (1984) *Constitutional Conventions*. Oxford: Clarendon Press.

Midwinter, A., Keating M. and Mitchell, J. (1981) *Politics and Public Policy in Scotland*. Houndmills: Macmillan.

Mitchell, James (1988) 'What Could a Scottish Parliament Do?', *Regional and Federal Studies*, 8, 68–85.

Mitchell, James and Bennie, Lynn (1996) 'Thatcherism and the Scottish Question', *British Elections and Parties Yearbook, 1995*. London: Frank Cass.

O'Neill, Terence (1969) *Ulster at the Crossroads*. London: Faber.

Peters, B. Guy (1999) *Institutional Theory in Political Science: The 'New Institutionalism'*. London: Pinter.

Pimlott, Ben (1988) 'The Myth of Consensus', in L. M. Smith (ed.), *The Making of Britain: Echoes of Greatness*. London: Macmillan.

Ramsay, Baroness of Cartvale (1998) Statement in House of Lords, 28 July, col. 1487.

Scottish Executive (1999) *Memorandum of Understanding and Supplementary Agreements*, SE/99/36. Edinburgh: Scottish Executive.

Scottish Office (1997) *Scotland's Parliament*. Edinburgh: HMSO.

Surridge, Paula and McCrone, David (1999) 'The 1997 Referendum Vote', in Bridget Taylor and Katarina Thomson (eds), *Scotland and Wales: Nations Again?* Cardiff: University of Wales Press.

Thatcher, Margaret (1993) *The Downing Street Years*. London: HarperCollins.

Young, George (1999) Speech by Sir George Young, House of Commons, *Hansard*, 21 Oct. col. 610.

12

The Belfast Agreement: The Making, Management and Mismanagement of a Complex Consociation

Brendan O'Leary

The Belfast Agreement of 10 April 1998, reached within a year of its general election victory, was the most surprising co-achievement of the new Labour government. The new government should not be praised too much, however. Credit was largely owed to others: the two men awarded the Nobel Peace Prize, John Hume and David Trimble, and their party colleagues and advisers; the representatives of republicans and loyalists, notably Gerry Adams, Martin McGuinness, David Ervine and Gary McMichael; two Irish governments, the Fianna Fáil–Labour coalition of 1992–4, and the Fianna Fáil–Progressive Democrat coalition of 1997 – including their officials in Ireland's Department of Foreign Affairs (DFA); and an array of others, including significant Americans. Tony Blair and his colleagues contributed no fresh ideas to the Agreement, despite courtier Charles Leadbetter's claim that it exemplified 'the Third Way'. Most of the ideas were articulated or prefigured before Blair took office. The Labour government's role was that of an enthusiastic first-time midwife.

Before history's hand

The bulk of the design of the political architecture agreed in Belfast on 10 April 1998 originated with Irish nationalists of all hues, within and without the Social Democratic and Labour Party (SDLP), Sinn Féin, and the Irish government. Their demands were sculpted into a coherent negotiating package by the Irish DFA, acting under the skilful leadership of diplomat Sean O Huiginn, now the Irish ambassador in Washington, and embedded in the Irish contributions to the Joint Framework Documents (JFDs), agreed by the Irish and British governments in February 1995 (O'Leary 1995). The JFDs arose from an established 'three-standard' negotiating process in which matters internal to Northern Ireland, North–South issues, and East–West (British–Irish) issues, were respectively addressed.[1] The JFDs anticipated a power-sharing assembly and executive in Northern Ireland, extensive consultative, harmonizing and executive functions for an all-Ireland North–South body, and an innovative model of 'double protection' of rights. They also anticipated referendums in both parts of Ireland, the brainchild of Hume, to give expression to Irish national self-determination. The Belfast Agreement was the baby of the JFDs, though its conception and birth were long and painful, and even though it was mildly genetically modified by the negotiators of the Ulster Unionist Party (UUP) who diminished the powers and autonomy of the proposed North–South Ministerial Council, and added the British–Irish Council.

The outgoing Conservative government deserved little credit for innovative ideas. Fortunately, and partly because of President Clinton's pressure, it avoided its instincts and refused to kill outright the political opportunity created by the antecedents and the materialization of the IRA ceasefire of 31 August 1994. Whitehall's civil servants, but not the local Northern Ireland Office, contributed positively to the agenda for the multiparty negotiations. Quentin Thomas, best known for leading the initial exploratory talks with Sinn Féin's Chief Negotiator Martin McGuinness, was crucial. In drafting the British contribution to the JFDs, he split the differences between the UUP's and the SDLP's preferences for the internal government of Northern Ireland from the previous interparty negotiations of 1991–2 (O'Leary and McGarry 1996: 327–69).

Labour's first Prime Minister for eighteen years had no profound agenda on Ireland, North or South – even though much was made of the fact that he had an Irish mother and a Catholic wife. 'New' Labour's role in Opposition had apparently been simple. It had supported the peace process, and offered bipartisan support for the Major government in its death throes. Behind the scenes the story was less perfumed. Blair's priority was to win the next general election, and Northern Ireland policy, like all others, was utterly subordinated to that objective. In 1994–5 his closest advisers believed some of Labour's existing policies, viz. support for Irish unification by consent and opposition to the draconian powers in the UK's antiterrorism legislation, were electorally counterproductive – not in themselves, but because they thought they were gifts to the right-wing press, identifying Labour with being soft on terrorism, and with political extremism. In fact, polls showed that weakening British sovereignty over Northern Ireland, and indeed troop withdrawal, enjoyed consistent majority support in Great Britain (O'Leary 1992). But Blair's coterie was driven by the fear that the party might appear soft on crime and terrorism. Blair had established himself with the mantra that he would be tough on crime and tough on the causes of crime. In the summer of 1994, he unilaterally ditched Labour's policy of seeking Irish unity by consent – without the formal approval of the Labour Party Conference – and modified the party's stance on the Prevention of Terrorism Act (PTA). Then he supported whatever the Major government did, whatever contradictions it created (for a mildly jaundiced if accurate view of this see O'Leary 1997).

There was a *prima facie* case for Labour's policy shift. Dropping the policy of encouraging unity by consent appeared to move Labour to a neutral stance on the future of Northern Ireland, at odds with the Sinn Féin demand that a British government become a persuader for Irish unity. Thereby it made unionists more likely to enter into negotiations with republicans and others. This *prima facie* case was not, however, the determining factor in the policy shift, though it would be used retrospectively by the leader's spin-doctors. The case was also doubtful because the Conservatives were persuaders for the Union, and New Labour's shift meant that both the UK's 'parties of government' favoured maintaining the Union, albeit in different formats and with different intensities, and thereby destabilized one of the premises of the republican initiative.

In October 1994 Blair replaced Kevin McNamara in the Northern Ireland portfolio with Dr Marjorie (Mo) Mowlam – an elected member of the shadow cabinet. McNamara concluded that Blair deemed him too old Labour, and too 'fat and bald and green' (Langdon 2000: 269). His able number two, Jim Marshall, was dismissed. Roger Stott MP, another junior spokesman, who had unintentionally embarrassed Blair when he was Shadow Home Secretary by opposing the PTA, also suffered loss of office, and went into a downward spiral that led to his premature death. Clive Soley MP, a former spokesman on Northern Ireland, soon to be a sycophantic chairman of the Parliamentary Labour Party, rationalized Blair's policy shifts as designed to support Major against right-wing Conservatives opposed to the peace process.[2] That appeared plausible, but it was misleading. The Labour leadership's focus was entirely electoral. Northern Ireland policy was wholly constrained by the objective of minimizing enemies in the right-wing press – which supported the right-wing Conservatives opposed to the peace process. Blair would take no risks for peace while in Opposition. Notes of meetings with Dr Mowlam record her prosaic and characteristically honest appraisal in 1995: 'They [Blair and Mandelson] think we should be so far up Major's **** that he can never accuse us of not being behind him' (personal notes).

Removing McNamara, on the pretext that he did not win a place in the shadow cabinet elections, eased the Labour leadership's parliamentary relations with the UUP, whom they hoped might one day support them in bringing down the Major government in a parliamentary 'no confidence' motion, or at least remain neutral. Mowlam, in contrast to McNamara, was a reluctant appointee who would have preferred the education portfolio. But she embraced the post with characteristic energy, mental sharpness and superb networking skills. She had been appointed a junior Northern Ireland front-bench spokesperson by Neil Kinnock in 1988–9, at McNamara's suggestion, and knew the terrain. She was, in contrast to Blair, not a unionist as far as the Union of Great Britain and Northern Ireland was concerned. She believed that Irish unification by consent was fine in principle but not feasible within this generation. In 1988 with McNamara and others she deliberated over how best to achieve either a negotiated settlement, or, failing that, a system of shared British and Irish sovereignty which would involve a devolved component – work that was later developed and encouraged by Neil Kinnock, and later by John Smith (see, *inter alia*, O'Leary et al. 1993). She had no time for Labour's electoral integrationists – who claimed that bringing Labour's organization and message to the region would salve working-class divisions and transcend sectarianism and nationalism.[3] In private her sympathies lay with the SDLP, though she found its leader, John Hume, remote and unapproachable.[4] Though many of the UUP's MPs called for McNamara's dismissal, Mowlam was not exactly what they wanted; though some unionists harboured illusions about her. On becoming Shadow Secretary of State she supported the agenda of the emerging JFDs, and endorsed them on their publication. She was fun and pragmatic, but had settled principles on the peace process: the priority was an inclusive agreement with which peaceful republicans, nationalists and moderate unionists would be content. Schooled in political science and political anthropology, she was knowledgeable about consociational and federal principles, and had written a Ph.D. dissertation on referendums. She was unusually skilled at making warm connections with people, irrespective of nationality, class or sex, and mastered her new brief. She did not go down well with the UUP's older males, for whom the flirtatious Redcar MP was the embodiment of secular, profane and liberated woman.

Blair's support for whatever Major did had one negative consequence. After the IRA ceasefire of 31 August 1994, and its reciprocation by loyalists six weeks later, there was a long hiatus of eighteen months, and no rush to start the inclusive negotiations for parties with democratic mandates that had been promised by Major and Albert Reynolds's joint declaration of December 1993. Instead Sinn Féin was put in quarantine in the UK. The blockage to negotiations was simple: Unionists and some Conservative MPs strongly opposed negotiations commencing without prior decommissioning of its weapons by the IRA and without a declaration that its ceasefire was permanent. The blockage strengthened as Major's majority diminished. Blair did not offer, and Major apparently did not seek, his support to bypass these obstacles to negotiations, even though there would have been a cross-party majority in the Commons for such an initiative. The blockage eventually won a name, viz. 'Washington 3', after a clause in a speech made by Secretary of State Sir Patrick Mayhew in March 1995, which demanded some prior decommissioning before inclusive negotiations.

The Irish government, under Taoiseach Reynolds (1992–4), and most Irish nationalists, north and south, took the view that the IRA ceasefire was permanent, and that decommissioning should be left until negotiations were completed. The two governments, steered by Irish officials and with American good offices, agreed to establish an international body, composed of former US Senator Majority Leader George Mitchell, Canadian General Jean de Chastelain and former Finnish premier Harri Holkeri, to propose ways out of the impasse. On 23 January 1996 they did the obvious, but in lucid and effective language. They proposed six peaceful and democratic principles to which parties to the negotiations would be obliged to commit themselves. They also proposed that 'parallel decommissioning' begin *during* the negotiations rather than *before* (the British suggestion) or *after* (the Irish suggestion) (Mitchell, de Chastelain and Holkeri 1996).[5] Major responded by appearing both to accept and reject the report. If prior decommissioning was not to happen, a certainty, then he would call for elections to a Peace Forum, playing fast and loose with a clause in the report,[6] so that parties would have mandates for negotiations, and then decommissioning could be handled as Mitchell had proposed. This was playing with fire. It required Sinn Féin, which already had a mandate, to legitimate a new forum, and thereby the status of Northern Ireland, in advance of negotiations, and to agree to elections that postponed negotiation.[7]

Blair supported Major's manoeuvre. Their myopic consensus had predictable consequences: the IRA went back to war, bombing Canary Wharf on 9 February 1996, killing two British citizens. It was a restart of bombing to force negotiations to begin, rather than a complete republican exit from their new strategy. But the breakdown of the IRA ceasefire deeply damaged the peace process, both in the short and longer run. It heightened distrust all around, and confirmed unionist presumptions that the ceasefire was purely tactical. The same events confirmed republican suspicions that the British political class would behave as perfidiously and as slowly as it could, despite the good offices of international mediators. Fortunately, however, the IRA's bombing campaign in 1996–7 was limited, both in the sense of being largely confined to small-scale operations in Great Britain, and in its impact on the public (with several IRA personnel proving incompetent).[8] Elections to the Forum took place

Table 12.1 Parties' shares of the vote and of seats in the 30 May 1996 elections to the Northern Ireland Forum

	Votes %	Seats No.	Seats %
Unionists			
Ulster Unionist Party (UUP)	24.2	30	27.3
Democratic Unionist Party (DUP)	18.8	24	21.8
United Kingdom Unionist Party (UKUP)	3.7	3	2.7
Progressive Unionist Party (PUP)	3.5	2	1.8
Ulster Democratic Party (UDP)	2.2	2	1.8
Others			
Alliance Party of Northern Ireland (APNI)	6.6	7	6.4
Northern Ireland Women's Coalition (NIWC)	1.0	2	1.8
(Northern Ireland) Labour	0.8	2	1.8
Nationalists			
Social Democratic and Labour Party of Northern Ireland (SDLP)	21.4	21	19.1
Sinn Féin	15.5	17	15.5

Election system: PR-list system (using the Droop quota, followed by d'Hondt, equivalent to pure d'Hondt) with two seats guaranteed to the top ten parties (four parties achieved representation solely through this mechanism). Deviation from proportionality was quite high ($d = (1/2) \Sigma [s_i - v_i] = 7.85$) and led to the DUP winning more seats than the SDLP on a lower share of the vote.
Source: B. O'Leary and G. Evans, 'Northern Ireland: La Fin de Siècle, the Twilight of the Second Protestant Ascendancy and Sinn Féin's Second Coming', *Parliamentary Affairs*, 50, (1997), 672–80.

Table 12.2 Parties' shares of the vote and of seats in Westminster elections, 1997

	Votes %	Seats No.	Seats %
Unionists			
Ulster Unionist Party (UUP)	32.7	10	55.6
Democratic Unionist Party (DUP)	13.6	2	11.1
United Kingdom Unionist Party (UKUP)	1.6	1	5.6
Progressive Unionist Party (PUP)	–	–	–
Ulster Democratic Party (UDP)	–	–	–
Others			
Alliance Party of Northern Ireland (APNI)	8.0	–	–
Northern Ireland Women's Coalition (NIWC)	–	–	–
(Northern Ireland) Labour	–	–	–
Nationalists			
Social Democratic and Labour Party of Northern Ireland (SDLP)	24.1	3	16.7
Sinn Féin	16.7	2	11.1

Election system: Plurality rule in eighteen single member districts.
Source: B. O'Leary and G. Evans, 'Northern Ireland', *Parliamentary Affairs*, 50 (1997), 672–80.

in May. Sinn Féin increased its vote share significantly – see table 12.1 – while the unionist vote fragmented, a significant pointer for the future.[9] Negotiations, in principle open to the top ten parties with democratic mandates, began in June 1996, with Sinn Féin excluded. Negotiating teams were separated from the Forum, and nationalists boycotted the Forum. The negotiations remained procedural until the Westminster elections were called in May 1997. In Northern Ireland – see table 12.2 – they led to a further rise in Sinn Féin's vote share, and confirmation of the thesis that the vote for overtly unionist parties was in secular decline (O'Leary and Evans 1997).

The functional, but not entirely intended, consequence of Blair's constant following of Major was mildly to relax the UUP's fear of a new Labour government. Its London supporters started to have fond memories of the Callaghan premiership, and of Callaghan's royalist, unionist and brutish Secretary of State, Roy Mason. This worried Labour's Irish nationalist sympathizers, but they were relaxed because Mowlam had the key portfolio, and was patently the best prepared prospective office-holder since the post was invented in 1972. Blair privately promised Irish officials that once elected he would deliver; he did not disappoint.

Taking the cards dealt by history

In the summer of 1997 the new government, with Blair and Mowlam at the helm, orchestrated the renewal of the IRA's ceasefire as the first significant non-economic initiative of the new regime. They correctly judged that the IRA's campaign had been intended to persuade the UK government to change its stance, and to force Sinn Féin's entry into negotiations, rather than to dictate the outcome of the negotiations. The government's judgement would make Sinn Féin's entry into negotiations possible, and was preceded by a speech made by the new Premier in Belfast to assure unionists of Blair's commitment to maintaining the Union as long as a local majority so wished. He declared that 'A political settlement is not a slippery slope to a united Ireland' (speech, Belfast, 16 May 1997), and that he did not expect the latter within his lifetime. The message was intended to keep the UUP at the negotiating tables while bringing Sinn Féin to join them. It would succeed. 'The settlement train is leaving' Blair told republicans, 'I want you on that train . . . So end the violence now' (ibid.).

The Labour government facilitated the eight parties which would make the Agreement – the UUP, the loyalist PUP and UDP, the SDLP, Sinn Féin, the Alliance, the Women's Coalition and (Northern Ireland) Labour. It was not distressed by the decision of Paisley's DUP and McCartney's United Kingdom Unionist Party (UKUP) to withdraw from the negotiating process after Sinn Féin was admitted – that eased the making of the Agreement. The government's unsung hero would prove to be Minister of State Paul Murphy, the future Secretary of State for Wales, who chaired long months of negotiations about negotiations between the summer of 1997 and the spring of 1998. The crucial performance of the new government, especially of its Premier, was to exhort, cajole and persuade the UUP, and its leader David Trimble, to negotiate and make the Agreement. Trimble had succeeded James Molyneaux after the latter's resignation – the production of the JFDs had been a green bridge too far for his party colleagues. Trimble had been elected because he was seen as a hardliner, the 'hero of Drumcree' and the brightest of the UUP's Westminster MPs.[10] He was also sensitive, underconfident, prickly, and terrified, sensibly, that he might face the fate of previous UUP leaders who had decided to accommodate Irish nationalism, such as Terence O'Neill, Brian Faulkner and Bill Craig. The government's delicate task, with its Irish counterpart, was to encourage Trimble to negotiate on the basis of the JFDs while enabling him to maintain that he had repudiated them. Blair's charm mattered. Trimble had sworn he would not fall for the same trap as Molyneaux, that is, seduction through bilaterals with Number 10. Instead he resolved always to be accompanied by party colleagues when he met the PM. This was a resolution that Blair would wear away, partly because Mowlam's relations with Trimble deteriorated radically.

Blair's government got off to a good start with the Irish government and its officials, and neither Blair nor Mowlam displayed the same sensitivities to America's benign interventions as their Conservative predecessors.[11] This ensured that there were three governments strongly mission-committed to the success of the negotiations. The replacement of the rainbow coalition in Dublin (1994–7) with a new Fianna Fáil-led coalition invigorated the Irish commitment because the new Taoiseach, Bertie Ahern, enjoyed the confidence of Northern nationalists, unlike his predecessor, Fine Gael's John Bruton.[12] The British and Irish governments' decisions to act through Senator Mitchell, the chair of the negotiations, when they concurred, and their decision to set a deadline for completing the negotiations,[13] were important components in delivering a successful outcome.

When the IRA renewed its ceasefire in July 1997 Mowlam took responsibility for monitoring it with the understanding that Sinn Féin would join the negotiations in September if the IRA's conduct withstood scrutiny. At Mitchell's initiative in August the two governments established an Independent International Commission on Decommissioning (IICD), chaired by de Chastelain. This was intended to facilitate the UUP's acceptance of Sinn Féin's presence at the negotiations, and, tacitly, to enable decommissioning to be parked while other substantive issues were addressed. In September Sinn Féin signed up to the Mitchell principles. Despite the provocation occasioned by an IRA statement that it did not accept the Mitchell principles and was not a party to the talks (*An Phoblacht*, 11 September 1997), and a bomb planted by the dissident republican faction, the Continuity-IRA, the UUP, flanked by the loyalist parties, agreed to participate in negotiations with Sinn Féin.

A tacit division of labour developed. The Prime Minister was seen as more empathetic to unionists, the Secretary of State to nationalists – a correct perception. This would mean that in the final negotiations of April 1998 Blair's role was visibly more important, since nationalists bargained on behalf of themselves with the back-up of the Irish government, whereas the unionists looked to Blair for sympathy. Before and during the negotiations Blair and Mowlam overrode the timidity of some of their ministerial colleagues, accepting that the full-scale release of all paramilitaries on ceasefire must form an essential component of the peace process. Mowlam in particular displayed political courage and nous in visiting the Maze prison to calm loyalist paramilitaries in January 1998, earning the sobriquet 'Mighty Mo'. In the new year the two governments produced 'Heads of Agreement', prefiguring the eventual settlement, while Mowlam and Mitchell successfully managed temporary suspensions of the UDP and Sinn Féin from the negotiations because of violations of their ceasefires by the UDA and the IRA respectively.

The final negotiations were held in late March and April 1998, with a deadline of Thursday 9 April. Strand One, the internal government of Northern Ireland, was negotiated head-to-head by the SDLP and the UUP, with the SDLP making the proposals, and the UUP choosing to reject or accept them. In Strand Two Blair and Ahern agreed to dilute the powers and scope of the proposed North–South Ministerial Council previously agreed by their officials to meet Trimble's and the UUP's requirements. They resisted an explicit linkage between inclusive executive formation in the North and prior decommissioning by the IRA. In Strand Three the governments negotiated constitutional and other peace and confidence-building measures, sometimes with loyalists and republicans. The Agreement was finally produced on 10 April, Good Friday, but not without difficulties. Jeffrey Donaldson MP of the UUP walked out because he was not satisfied that the Agreement required decommissioning before executive formation, and two independent commissions had to be established on policing and the administration of criminal justice because all the parties could agree on was their terms of reference. Nevertheless the Agreement was made, and justified Blair's comment that he had felt the hand of history upon his shoulder. Now what was required was to have it endorsed in referendums and implemented, without fear or favour.

Building institutions or a house of cards?

The Agreement was endorsed in both parts of Ireland, with a 95 and a 71 per cent 'Yes' vote in the South and North respectively. Blair, posing as a fully fledged unionist, was successful in persuading at least some unionists to vote 'Yes' – though he also gave hostages to fortune inconsistent with the text of the Agreement. He had almost done the same on the day of the Agreement in an ambiguous letter to Trimble, which suggested that the Prime Minister agreed that decommissioning of its weapons by the IRA 'should' commence before the new executive could be formed with Sinn Féin's participation. The 'should' was subjunctive: the text of the Agreement, by contrast, did not warrant Trimble's position, or that of Blair in some of his later statements, and, in any case, the words of a UK premier are not law, outside the ranks of New Labour. After the Agreement was made and ratified in the two referendums Mowlam helped override obstruction from some of her Northern Ireland Office's officials and ensured that the Agreement was mostly faithfully reflected in the Northern Ireland 1998 Act.[14] But in general the Blair government would prove much better at managing the making of the Agreement than in managing its successful implementation.

In part, of course, this was because implementation was more difficult. The government could not be faulted, initially, on the hours it put in. Blair was astonished at the time he had to devote to Irish matters, and so were his advisers. At one stage, Jonathan Powell, to his chagrin, ended up trying to micro-manage the Drumcree dispute, occasioned by the Orange Order's demand that its members should be able to parade down the Garvaghy Road without the prior consent of local (mostly nationalist) residents. The government's difficulties in implementation were not, of course, entirely of its own making. The deep polarization that the Agreement occasioned within the unionist bloc as a whole, and more particularly the polarization within the UUP, were obviously not Labour's responsibility. In the elections to the new Assembly in June 1998 – see table 12.3 – the SDLP outpolled the UUP, the 'No Unionists' performed slightly better than they had in the referendum, and Trimble's Westminster parliamentary colleagues mostly opposed the Agreement. Trimble's responses to these intra-unionist crises were to be a key source of tension in the Agreement's implementation. Republican (and loyalist) dilatoriness on the matter of decommissioning would be another.

The proportionality of the election results was evident, both with respect to blocs and with respect to parties. But the deviations in seats won compared to the first preference vote benefited the pro-Agreement parties. The UUP was the principal beneficiary of the transfer of lower order preferences, taking its seat share (25.9 per cent) significantly above its first-preference vote-share (21.3 per cent) – though these lower order preferences came from voters who voted 'No' as well as those who voted 'Yes' to the Agreement. The net transfers by voters to the pro-Agreement candidates, though not as significant as had been hoped, converted a bare 'Anti-Agreement' majority of the first preference vote (25.5 per cent) within the unionist bloc of voters into a bare 'pro-Agreement' majority (27.8 per cent) among seats won by unionists, a result that was essential for the Agreement's (partial) stabilization. The Labour government could not be faulted for the palpably evident intra-unionist divisions, but it would significantly contribute to the difficulties in implementing the Agreement, not least in managing its own responsibilities, and the new institutions. This would become especially manifest in a series of

Table 12.3   The June 1998 elections to the Northern Ireland Assembly

	First preference vote %	Seats	
		No.	%
Social Democratic and Labour Party of Northern Ireland (SDLP)	22.0	24	22.2
Sinn Féin (SF)	17.7	18	16.7
Other nationalists	0.1	–	–
All Nationalists	**39.8**	**42**	**38.9**
Alliance Party of Northern Ireland (APNI)	6.4	6	5.5
Women's Coalition	1.7	2	1.8
Other 'Others'	1.3	–	–
All Others	**9.4**	**8**	**7.3**
Ulster Unionist Party (UUP)	21.0	28	25.9
Progressive Unionist Party (PUP)	2.5	2	1.8
Ulster Democratic Party (UDP)	1.2	–	–
Other Yes Unionists	0.3	–	–
All Yes Unionists	**25.0**	**30**	**27.7**
Democratic Unionist Party (DUP)	18.0	20	18.5
United Kingdom Unionist Party (UKUP)	4.5	5	4.6
Independent No Unionists	3.0	3	2.8
All No Unionists	**25.5**	**28**	**25.9**

Per cent figures for votes and seat shares rounded to one decimal place.
Source: B. O'Leary, 'The Nature of the Agreement', *Fordham Journal of International Law*, 22 (1999).

unilateral and ill-judged actions, inactions and public lies on the part of Peter Mandelson, who replaced Dr Mowlam as Secretary of State in October 1999.

Mandelson was Blair's best known and least liked confidante, his Prince of Darkness. In 1999 Blair wanted to rehabilitate him after his sins committed in the Notting Hill housing market with the pockets of Geoffrey Robinson. He hoped Mandelson's appointment would spare him endless unionist deputations – largely occasioned by their refusal to engage Mowlam, who had been suffering from treatment of a benign brain tumour, and had, partly in consequence, become immensely popular, more popular than the PM, but whom some UUP MPs nevertheless treated with a mixture of political and sexist disdain. Mowlam had wanted to be promoted to the Foreign Office, which Blair would not entertain, and at one stage contemplated requesting that she have Mandelson as her deputy. Mandelson saw Northern Ireland as the route to his rehabilitation – given that other ministers would be happy with his 'relegation'. He also thought of it as a route to the ministry he most coveted, the Foreign Office. He had once been friendly with Mowlam – they had holidayed together in Spain – but now was said to regard her as 'terminally undisciplined' (*Sunday Telegraph*, 27 July 1997, cited in Langdon 2000: 8). He, by contrast, tended to be terminally disloyal to past friends, commitments, and the truth. In the spring and summer of 1999 he and his associates, including Labour's unionists, started to damage Mowlam's reputation in the press in much the same manner as they had once defamed David Clark, when Mandelson had coveted his cabinet position.

Mandelson came to Northern Ireland with no obvious preparation in Opposition, unlike Mowlam, though his more credible supporters spun the line that he had made programmes on the region for *Weekend World* in his days as a TV producer. That at least was accurate. Some in the UUP, including Trimble, called for Mandelson's appointment – much as some had once called for Mowlam to replace McNamara. The DUP, by contrast, were not pleased: 'we do not want a sodomite' as one of its typically homophobic members put it.[15] Blair calculated that it was more important to calm Trimble and his party than to continue with the balanced ticket of a soft unionist PM and a soft nationalist Secretary of State. Indeed 'saving Trimble to save the Agreement' would become the government's priority in 1999–2000. The world was told that Mandelson possessed remarkable negotiating skills and diplomatic finesse. This was not evident in his opening parliamentary statement when he described himself as Secretary of State for Ireland – rather than Northern Ireland. He would also quickly demonstrate that he lacked one important element of the normal job description of a normal Foreign Secretary, the capacity to get on with and be appreciated by foreigners. If Blair deserves credit for making the Agreement with Mowlam, as he does, then he must also share with Mandelson the blame for mismanaging its implementation.

The nature of the agreement(s)

The Belfast Agreement, incorporated in the British–Irish Agreement (1999), an international treaty, was an exemplary constitutional design. Internally it was 'consociational' (O'Leary 1999a, 1999b). Externally it established confederal relationships, and prefigured imaginative federalist relationships and a novel model of double protection. If the Agreement fails, debate will arise over whether flaws in its design or in its implementation were the principal factors. The rest of this chapter anticipates that debate. By contrast, if the Agreement is fully successful, albeit outside its scheduled timetable and its own agreed procedures, I hope it will become an export model for conflict regulators. What follows appraises the Agreement's novelties, possible design flaws, and the contributions of Labour's decision-makers to its implementation. Three evaluative arguments are advanced:

1   The Labour government correctly grasped that the conflict required external as well as internal resolution, and realized that the sovereignty and self-determination disputes needed to be resolved. But it failed to follow through on its treaty commitments, and broke international law when it unilaterally suspended some of the Agreement's institutions between February and May 2000, and thereby destabilized the Agreement by making all its provisions and commissions negotiable.
2   The novel dual premiership, designed by the major moderate parties, the SDLP and the UUP, in the heat of the negotiations, has proved its major institutional weakness, suggesting, paradoxically, that moderates are not always the best designers or caretakers of power-sharing systems.
3   The Labour government's, especially Mandelson's, mismanagement of policing reform severely threatened the stabilization of the Agreement, and the reversal of Mandelson's stances was necessary for the resolution of November 2001.

These propositions require a prior analysis of the Agreement as a 'constitution'.

A consociational federacy

The Agreement met all four standard consociational criteria (Lijphart 1977).

A. Cross-community executive power-sharing   This was manifest in:

1   the creation of a quasi-presidential dual premiership, elected by a concurrent majority of unionists and nationalists in the Assembly, and expected to preside over:

2 the inclusive grand coalition ten-member executive cabinet of ministers, whose portfolios are allocated according to the d'Hondt voting procedure.

B. *Proportionality norms*   These were evident in:

1 the d'Hondt procedure used to determine the composition of the cabinet – which resulted in five unionists (three UUP, two DUP) and five nationalists (three SDLP and two Sinn Féin) holding ministries between November 1999 and February 2000, and again from May 2000;
2 the electoral system (the Single Transferable Vote in eighteen six-member districts) used to elect the Assembly;
3 the d'Hondt procedure used to allocate Assembly members to committees with powers of oversight and legislative initiative; and
4 existing and additional legislative provisions to ensure fair and representative employment, especially throughout the public sector, and the promise of a representative police service.

C. *Community autonomy and equality*   These commitments were evident in:

1 the official recognition of unionists', nationalists' and others' political ethos and identities, notably in the Assembly's procedures, and in a declaration of 'parity of esteem' between the communities and a promise of 'rigorous impartiality' in administration from the current and possibly future sovereign states;
2 the decision to leave alone the existing separate but recently equally funded forms of Catholic, Protestant and integrated schooling;
3 the renewed outlawing of discrimination on grounds of political or religious belief;
4 the replacement of an oath of loyalty to the Crown with a pledge of office for ministers;
5 the establishment of a Human Rights Commission tasked with protecting individual equality and liberty, and identity rights;
6 the entrenchment of vigorous equality provisions, eventually incorporated in section 75 of the Northern Ireland Act (1998);
7 the promise of better legislative and institutional treatment of the Irish language and Ulster Scots – both of which became languages of record in the Assembly; and
8 the promise of a civic forum, and 'participatory norms of governance', to facilitate the representation of voices that might not be

heard purely through electoral or party mechanisms (McCrudden 1999).

D. Veto rights for minorities and mutual veto rights   These were evident in:

1   the legislative procedures in the Assembly which require 'key decisions' to be passed either with a *concurrent majority* (under the 'parallel consent' procedure) of registered nationalists and unionists, or with a *weighted majority* (60 per cent majority including the support of at least 40 per cent of registered nationalists and registered unionists);
2   the mutual interdependency of office acquisition and maintenance by the First Minister and Deputy First Minister; and of the running of the Northern Ireland Assembly and the North–South Ministerial Council; and
3   the legal incorporation of the European Convention on Human Rights and Freedoms in UK public law and (the promise of) other legal enactments to give Northern Ireland a tailor-made Bill of Rights.

The Agreement led to a devolved government,[16] with full executive and legislative competence for economic development, education, health and social services, agriculture, environment and finance (including the local civil service), though plainly it is constrained by both UK and EU budgetary and other policies in these domains. Non-devolved powers remain with Westminster and the Secretary of State, who continues to be appointed by the UK premier. The form of devolved government originally envisaged few limits on Northern Ireland's capacity to expand its autonomy. Through 'cross-community agreement' the Assembly is entitled to agree to expand its competencies; and, again through such agreement, and the consent of the Secretary of State and Westminster, the Assembly is empowered to legislate for non-devolved functions. Security functions, policing and the courts were not devolved, but could be if sought by 'cross-community' consent. Maximum feasible autonomy was therefore within the scope of the local decision-makers. A convention may have arisen in which the Secretary of State and Westminster 'rubber stamped' the legislative measures of the Assembly. Indeed public policy in Ireland, North and South, might eventually have been made without direct British ministerial involvement.

For these reasons and others, had the Agreement been fully implemented and developed Northern Ireland would have become a specimen of what Elazar terms a 'federacy' (1987). A federal relationship exists where there are at least two tiers of government over the same territory, and when neither can unilaterally alter the constitutional capacities of the other. Such a relationship is a necessary element of a federal system, but whether it is sufficient is controversial. Normally a federation has subcentral units that are co-sovereign with the centre throughout most of the territory and population of the state. Plainly it is premature to call new Labour's reconstructed UK a federation. But any system of constitutionally entrenched autonomy for one region makes the relationship between that region and the centre functionally equivalent to a federal relationship, and following Elazar, I call such a region – and its relationships with the centre – a federacy. The term 'federacy' captures how Irish nationalists understood the Agreement's institutions, and their entrenchment in the treaty.

Through standard legislative majority rules, the Assembly is empowered to pass 'normal laws', though there is provision for a minority, of 30 of the 108 members, to trigger procedures that require special majorities. Controversial legislation, 'key decisions', including the Budget, require these special procedures demonstrating 'cross-community' support. Two rules, parallel consent and weighted majority, were designed for this purpose (see D1 above). There is also one supermajority rule, which was not explicitly concurrent, cross-community or consociational. The Assembly is entitled by a two-thirds resolution of its membership to call an extraordinary general election before its four-year term expires. This was agreed by the parties, after the Agreement, in preference to a proposal that the Secretary of State should have the power to dissolve the Assembly.

This distinctive consociation, or consociational federacy, challenges the conventional wisdom of the post-1945 political science of ethnonational questions. For a long time 'external' self-determination, in law and political science, as well as political practice, was accepted solely as a once only right of colonial territories. The Agreement was, in part, a striking rejection of this wisdom. It contained agreed procedures on how a border might be changed, or rather abolished. The Agreement accepted the legitimacy of an irredentist aspiration: the desire of the Irish nation in both parts of Ireland to unify in one state, though its realization was made conditional on the consent of majorities in both current jurisdictions, and the recognition of the aspiration was accompanied by the removal of an irredentist territorial claim-of-right in the 1937 Irish constitution. The Agreement, like the negotiations that preceded it, contained recognition by the UK of the right of the people of Ireland, North and South, to exercise their self-determination to create a united

Ireland. The UK has never officially recognized Northern Ireland as a colonial territory, but its employment of the language of self-determination in the making of the Agreement was an interesting departure. In addition, the Agreement established elaborate cross-border arrangements explicitly seen by nationalist parties as mechanisms to facilitate national reunification. Lastly, the Agreement contained features of an externally protected minority rights regime, a tacit 'double protection model' – laced with elements of co-sovereignty, and designed to withstand major demographic and electoral change. The UK and Irish governments promised to develop functionally equivalent legal protections of rights, collective and individual, on both sides of the present border, promising protection to Northern Irish nationalists now on the same terms that would be given to Ulster unionists if they ever became a minority in a unified Ireland. National communities were to be protected whether they were majorities or minorities, irrespective of the sovereign stateholder – whence the expression 'double protection'. The two governments affirmed that 'whatever choice is freely exercised by a majority of the people of Northern Ireland, the power of the sovereign government with jurisdiction there shall be exercised with *rigorous impartiality* on behalf of all the people in the diversity of their identities and traditions and shall be founded on the principles of full respect for, and equality of, civil, political, social and cultural rights, of freedom from discrimination for all citizens, and of *parity of esteem and of just and equal treatment* for the identity, ethos and aspirations of both communities' (author's emphases).

If conventional postwar political science was correct, then all these linkages, between an internal consociational settlement and measures that envisaged the possibility of a transformation in borders and of sovereignty regimes, should be the key sources of instability in the Agreement, raising expectations among the nationalist minority and arousing deep fears among the local unionist majority. Indeed for nearly ten years after the collapse of the 1973–4 Sunningdale settlement it was an axiom of faith among UK policy-makers that an internal consociational agreement – power-sharing – should be reached without an external agreement – an Irish dimension. Alternatively, it was held that an internal agreement should precede an external agreement. This thinking was reversed in the making of the Anglo-Irish Agreement. Recognizing that the absence of an Irish dimension facilitated republican militancy, the two governments established an intergovernmental conference, giving the Irish government unlimited rights of consultation over UK public policy on Northern Ireland, while encouraging the local parties to agree internal power-sharing. This combination of external and internal arrangements and incentives, 'coercive consociation', was unacceptable to unionists, in the short term. But since they could not destroy the Anglo-Irish Agreement, through strikes, paramilitarism, civil disobedience or conventional parliamentary tactics, unionists eventually negotiated the Belfast Agreement in return for the modification of what they regarded as deeply unsatisfactory external arrangements.

Northern nationalists certainly had their expectations raised, and unionists certainly had, and still have, anxieties about the Agreement's external dimensions, but both the making of the 1998 Agreement and its stalling in 2000 suggest that the postwar wisdom of political science needs revision. Consociational arrangements can be effectively combined with cross-border regimes, which enable a change in sovereignty, without engendering massive instability. The 'No Unionists' who rejected the Agreement did not like its external features, but they focused their rhetorical fire on the prospects of gunmen getting into (the internal) government, terrorists being released early from jail, the failure to secure the decommissioning of (republican) paramilitaries' weapons, and on those parts of the Agreement, including proposed policing arrangements, which implied the full equality of nationalists with unionists within Northern Ireland. By contrast, the 'Yes Unionists' trumpeted some of the external aspects of the Agreement, pointing out that the Agreement had led to changes in the Irish Republic's constitution, which now requires the active consent of majorities in both parts of Ireland before Irish unification, and claiming that they had 'negotiated away' the Anglo-Irish Agreement of 1985. 'Yes Unionists' defended the cross-border institutions as minimal rational functional cooperation between neighbouring states, and observed, correctly, that they had succeeded in trimming down the more ambitious cross-border institutions advocated by the Irish government, the SDLP and by Sinn Féin. In short, the primary unionist concerns with the Agreement cannot reasonably be said to have lain with its external dimensions.

Con/federalizing arrangements

Confederations exist when political units delegate powers and functions to bodies that can exercise power across their jurisdictions, while retaining veto and opt-out rights. Two confederal relationships were established under the Agreement: the North–South Ministerial Council and the British–Irish Council.

The North–South Ministerial Council (NSMC) brings together those with executive responsibilities in Northern Ireland and in the Republic.

Nationalists were concerned that if the Assembly could outlast the NSMC, it would provide incentives for unionists to undermine the latter. Unionists, by contrast, worried that if the NSMC could survive the destruction of the Assembly, nationalists would seek to bring this about. The Agreement was a tightly written contract. Internal consociation and all-Ireland external confederalism went together: the Assembly and the NSMC were made 'mutually interdependent'; one could not function without the other. Unionists were unable to destroy the NSMC while retaining the Assembly, and nationalists were not able to destroy the Assembly while keeping the NSMC. The NSMC satisfactorily linked northern nationalists to their preferred nation-state. The Irish government successfully recommended a change in its constitution to ensure that the NSMC, and its delegated implementation bodies, would be able to exercise island-wide jurisdiction in those functional activities where unionists were willing to cooperate. The NSMC functions much like the Council of Ministers in the European Union, with ministers having considerable discretion to reach decisions, but ultimately being accountable to their respective legislatures. The NSMC meets in plenary format twice a year, and in smaller groups to discuss specific sectors on a 'regular and frequent basis'. Provision was made for the Council to discuss matters that cut across sectors, and to resolve disagreements. In addition, the Agreement provided for 'implementation' bodies. The scope of these institutions was somewhat open-ended. The Agreement, however, required a meaningful Council. It stated that the Council '*will*' (not 'may') identify at least six matters, where 'existing bodies' will be the appropriate mechanisms for cooperation within each separate jurisdiction, and at least six matters where cooperation will take place through implementation bodies. The latter were subsequently agreed to be inland waterways, food safety, trade and business development, special EU programmes, the Irish and Ulster Scots languages, and aquaculture and marine matters. The parties further agreed on six functional areas of cooperation – including some aspects of transport, agriculture, education, health, the environment and tourism, where a joint North–South public company was established.

The NSMC differed from the Council of Ireland of 1974. The name change was significant: a concession to unionist sensibilities. There was no provision for a joint parliamentary forum but the Northern Assembly and the Irish Oireachtas (Ireland's houses of parliament) were asked 'to consider' one. Nationalists wanted the NSMC established by legislation from Westminister and the Oireachtas – to emphasize its autonomy from the Northern Assembly. Unionists wanted it established by the Northern Assembly and its counterpart in Dublin. The Agreement split these differences. The NSMC and the implementation bodies were brought into existence by British and Irish legislation, but during the transitional period it was for the Northern executive and the Republic's government to decide how cooperation should take place, and in what areas the North–South institutions should cooperate. Once agreed, the Assembly was unable to change these agreements – except by cross-community consent. The signatories to the Agreement promised to work 'in good faith' to bring the NSMC into being. There was not, however, sufficient good faith to prevent the first material break in the timetable scheduled in the Agreement occurring over the NSMC – but this was patently a by-product of the crisis over executive formation and decommissioning. The signatories were required to use 'best endeavours' to reach agreement and to make 'determined efforts' to overcome disagreements over functions where there was a 'mutual cross-border and all-island benefit'.

A second weaker confederal relationship was established, affecting all the islands of Britain and Ireland.[17] Under the new British–Irish Council (BIC) the two governments of the sovereign states, and all the devolved governments and neighbouring insular dependent territories of the UK, can meet, agree to delegate functions, and may agree common policies. This proposal met unionists' concerns for reciprocity in linkages – and provides a mechanism through which they might in future be linked to the UK even if Northern Ireland becomes part of the Republic. Unionists originally wanted the NSMC subordinated to a British–Irish, or East–West, Council. This did not happen. There is no hierarchical relationship between the two councils. Two textual warrants suggest that the NSMC is more far-reaching than the BIC. The Agreement required the establishment of North–South implementation bodies, leaving the formation of East–West bodies a voluntary matter, and stated explicitly that the Assembly and the NSMC were interdependent, making no equivalent provision for the BIC.

The Agreement opened other linkages for Northern Ireland, one within the UK, and another as a possibility with the Republic, which held federalist as opposed to confederalist promise. The Agreement, unlike Scottish and Welsh devolution, was embedded in a treaty between two states, based on the UK's recognition of Irish national self-determination. The UK officially acknowledged that Northern Ireland has the right to join the Republic, on the basis of a local referendum, and it recognized, in a treaty, the authority of Irish national self-determination throughout the island of Ireland. The Agreement's institutions were brought into being by the will of the people of Ireland, North and South, and not just by the people of Northern Ireland – recall the referendums and the interdependence of the NSMC and the Assembly. In consequence, under the Agreement, the UK's relationship to Northern Ireland, at least in international law, in my view, has an explicitly federal character: Northern Ireland had become a federacy. The Westminster Parliament and executive could not, except through breaking its treaty obligations, and except through denying Irish national self-determination, exercise power in any manner that affected Northern Ireland's autonomy inconsistent with the Agreement. This was believed to be the case immediately after the Agreement was made. Plainly the suspension of the Agreement by Mandelson in February 2000 showed that the UK's authorities did not feel constrained by that reasoning.

The Agreement also opened federalist avenues in the Republic – one of the most centralized states in Europe. The Irish government and its people did not abandon Irish unification. Instead it became 'the firm will of the Irish nation, in harmony and friendship, to unite all the people who share the territory of the island of Ireland, in all the diversity of their identities and traditions, recognising that a united Ireland shall be brought about only by peaceful means with the consent of a majority of the people expressed, in both jurisdictions in the island' (from the new Article 3). Irish unification cannot be precluded because of present demographic and electoral trends – which have led to a steady rise in the nationalist share of the vote across different electoral systems. The unification envisaged in the redrafted Irish constitution is, however, now different. It no longer resembles a programme of assimilation. The Republic is bound to structure its laws to prepare for the possibility of a con/federal as well as a unitary Ireland. Northern Ireland is a recognized legal entity within the Irish constitution, and its elimination as a political unit is no longer a programmatic feature of Bunreacht na hÉireann (Constitution of Ireland).

Externally protecting the Agreement

The two states signed a treaty and created two intergovernmental devices to protect their respective national communities. The most important was the successor to that of the Anglo-Irish Agreement, viz. the new British–Irish intergovernmental conference (BIGC) that guarantees the Republic's government access to policy formulation on all matters not (yet) devolved to the Northern Assembly or the NSMC. The Irish government retains rights of consultation in those Northern Irish matters that have not been devolved to the Assembly, as was the case under Article 4 of the Anglo-Irish Agreement, and as with that agreement, there continues to be an intergovernmental conference, chaired by the Minister for Foreign Affairs and the Northern Ireland Secretary of State, to deal with non-devolved matters, and it continues to be serviced by a standing secretariat. The new Agreement, moreover, promised to 'intensify cooperation' between the two governments on all-island or cross-border aspects of rights, justice, prison and policing (unless and until these matters are devolved). There is provision for representatives of the Assembly to be involved in the intergovernmental conference – a welcome parliamentarization – but they will not have the same status as the representatives of the governments of the sovereign states. The Anglo-Irish Agreement fully anticipated these arrangements, so it is as accurate to claim that it has been fulfilled as to say it has been deleted.

Formal joint sovereignty over Northern Ireland was not established, but the governments guaranteed the Agreement, and embedded it in an international treaty. Irish officials had been wary since the early 1990s of trading constitutional changes that were likely to be irreversible for institutions that might share the same fate as the Sunningdale settlement. That is why they argued that the Agreement should be incorporated in a treaty. The official Irish belief, and the Irish nationalist belief, was that the Agreement, like Northern Ireland's constitutional choice between membership of the UK and the Republic, now rested on the consent of the Irish people, through the joint act of self-determination of the North and South. The UK government would not, on this view, have the authority to do anything that was not legitimate under the Agreement's procedures. The UK government, under Mowlam, shared this understanding. Under Mandelson it did not. In February 2000 Mandelson obtained from the UK Parliament emergency statutory powers to suspend the Assembly and Executive. In doing so he acted in classic Diceyian fashion, using the doctrine of parliamentary sovereignty to arrogate to himself the power of suspension – which had not been granted in the making of the Agreement, or in its (UK) legislative enactment. The UK government's officials knew that suspension would breach the formal Agreement – because in the summer of 1999, when both governments contemplated a suspension mechanism, Mowlam's officials proposed that the treaty that was about to be signed by the two governments, which incorporated the Belfast Agreement, should be amended, to make it compatible with suspension. No such amendment was made.

Mandelson's justification of suspension in February 2000 was that it was necessary to save the First Minister, David Trimble. His threat to resign because the IRA had not delivered on decommissioning, in advance of the deadline mandated by the Agreement, would have become operative in an environment in which 'Yes Unionists' no longer commanded an absolute majority of the registered unionists in the Assembly.[18] Therefore, it was feared, Trimble could not have been resurrected as First Minister if he did resign. This reasoning was false: the Assembly, by weighted majority, was entitled to pass any measure to amend its current rules for electing the dual premiers, and to send this measure to Westminster for statutory ratification. So there was a mechanism, within the Agreement, under which Trimble could have regained the position of First Minister. But even if Mandelson's justification had been true, the suspension was an unconstitutional and a partisan act. It was unconstitutional in Irish eyes because the suspensory power had not been endorsed with cross-community consent through the negotiation of the Agreement, or in the referendums, or in the UK's legislative enactment of the Agreement. It was partisan because neither the Agreement, nor the Mitchell Review of the Agreement that took place in late 1999, required Sinn Féin to deliver decommissioning by the IRA because of a new deadline set by the leader of the UUP. The then formally agreed deadline for decommissioning required all political parties to use their best endeavours to achieve full decommissioning by 22 May 2000.

One passage of the Agreement referred to procedures for review if difficulties arose across the range of institutions established on the entering into force of the international treaty: 'If difficulties arise which require remedial action across the range of institutions, or otherwise require amendment of the British–Irish Agreement or relevant legislation, *the process of review will fall to the two Governments in consultation with the parties in the Assembly. Each Government will be responsible for action in its own jurisdiction*' (emphasis added). The italicized passages, read in conjunction with the whole Agreement, suggest that the UK government was obligated formally to consult the parties in the Assembly and the Irish government over obtaining any power of suspension, and that any remedial action required the joint support of the two governments, especially as regards their treaty. That each government would be 'responsible for action in its own jurisdiction' was not taken by the Irish side to mean that the Westminster Parliament had unilateral discretion to alter, amend, suspend or abolish the institutions of the Agreement. It merely meant that for agreed remedial action there would not be joint sovereignty but rather parallel legislative procedures.

The central purpose of the UK's agreement to delete section 75 of the Government of Ireland Act of 1920, and of the Irish state's agreement to modify Articles 2 and 3 of the Irish constitution, had been to show that both states were engaged in 'balanced' constitutional change, confirming that Northern Ireland's status as part of the UK or the Republic rested with its people alone. The UK's Diceyians, including Ulster Unionists, have obviously interpreted the UK's deletion of section 75 of the Government of Ireland Act as meaningless because in their eyes Parliament's sovereignty remains intact in a given domain even when it removes a statutory statement which says it remains intact! Irish negotiators obviously should have been more careful: the UK's 'constitution' is Ireland's British problem. Had the Agreement fully bedded down, perhaps Northern Ireland status as a federacy would have developed the status of a constitutional convention – the UK's mysterious functional poor cousin of constitutionality.

The suspension had four messages. First, it made plain that every aspect of the Agreement is vulnerable to Westminster's sovereignty. Everything in the Agreement – its institutions, its confidence-building measures, its commissions, the promise that Irish unification will take place if there is majority consent for it in both parts of Ireland – is revisable by the current Parliament, and any future Parliament, and that Parliament's Secretaries of State, irrespective of international law, or the solemn promises made by UK negotiators in the making of the Agreement. No UK parliamentarian can look an Irish nationalist or republican in the eye and say that Northern Ireland's status and its institutional arrangements rest on the consent of its people. By its actions the Westminster Parliament has affirmed that it regards its sovereignty as unconstrained by the Agreement. Had it sought and obtained the assent of the Northern Assembly – by cross-community consent – to its possession of the power of the suspension, that would have been a different matter. It did not. Even if the Secretary of State's motives were entirely benign – and that has been questioned – his decision to obtain the power of suspension destroyed the assumptions of nearly a decade of negotiation.

Secondly, the suspension spells out to official Irish negotiators, and Northern nationalists, the necessity, in any new round of major negotiations, of entrenching Northern Ireland's status as a 'federacy', perhaps in the same manner as the UK's courts are instructed to make European law supreme over law(s) made by the Westminster Parliament, through full domestic incorporation and entrenchment of the relevant treaty. Without such protection the Agreement cannot be constitutionalized consistently with Irish national self-determination, North and South. This will require Ireland's negotiators to require Westminster to repeal the suspension Act and to declare that its sovereignty is circumscribed by the Agreement.

Thirdly, unionists must, eventually, consider the constitutional consequences of suspension. The 'Yes Unionists', in embracing the doctrine of parliamentary sovereignty, forget that they may one day suffer from the consequences of the sword they urged Westminster to deploy. What Westminster did on behalf of unionists may be used at their expense tomorrow – including taking from them membership of the Union. Mandelson's action means that the Union does not rest on the consent of its component parts, but rather on Westminster's say so: Westminster is free to modify the Union in any way it likes, for example, through full-scale joint sovereignty over Northern Ireland with the Republic, or through expelling Northern Ireland from its jurisdiction.

Lastly, the suspension spells a blunt warning to the Scottish Parliament and the Welsh Assembly – bodies created with smaller proportions of popular support and lower electoral turnouts than their Northern Irish counterpart. Sovereignty remains indivisibly in Westminster's possession: even under 'modernizing' New Labour.

The dual premiership

Among its institutional novelties the Agreement established two quasi-presidential figures, a dyarchy, to preside over an executive formed through the d'Hondt allocation process.[19] An executive presidency is an executive that cannot be destroyed by an assembly except through impeachment; the dual premiership has presidential characteristics because it is almost impossible to depose the two office-holders, provided they remain united as a team, until the next general election. The First and Deputy First Minister are elected together by the *parallel consent procedure*, an idea that flowed out of the making of the Agreement which required propositions to have the support of a majority of parties, including parties representing a majority of nationalists and of unionists. The carry-over of this concurrent rule of negotiation into the election of the two premiers gave very strong incentives to unionists and nationalists to nominate a candidate for one of these positions who was acceptable to a majority of the other bloc's members. It also meant that the respective unionist and nationalist moderates were guaranteeing their control of these positions. In the first elections for these posts in *designate* or *shadow* form pro-Agreement unionists in the UUP and the Progressive Unionist Party, who between them then had a majority of registered unionists (30 out of 58), voted solidly for the combination of David Trimble of the UUP and Seamus Mallon of the SDLP. Naturally so did the SDLP, which enjoyed a majority among registered nationalists (24 out of 42). (The 'No Unionists' voted against this combination, while Sinn Féin abstained.)

The Agreement and its UK legislative enactment, the Northern Ireland Act (1998), made clear that both posts had identical symbolic and external representation functions. Indeed both have identical powers, the sole difference being in their titles: both preside over the 'Executive Committee' of ministers, and have a role in coordinating its work. Their implicit and explicit coordinating functions, as approved by the Shadow Assembly, were elaborated in February 1999. A Department of the First and Deputy First Ministers was created. It was to have an Economic Policy Unit, and an Equality Unit, and was tasked with liaising with the NSMC, the BIC and the Secretary of State on reserved and excepted UK powers, EU/international matters, and cross-departmental coordination.

The prime ministerial dyarchy is quasi-presidential, because neither the First nor the Deputy First Minister formally appoint the other ministers to the Executive – save where one of them is a party leader entitled to nominate the ministries to which his or her party is entitled. Posts in the Executive are allocated to parties in proportion to their strength in the Assembly, according to a mechanical rule, the d'Hondt rule. The rule's consequences were simple: any party that won a significant share of seats and was willing to abide by the new rules established by the Agreement had a reasonable chance of access to the executive. It creates a voluntary grand coalition government because parties are free to exclude themselves from the Executive Committee, and because no programme of government has to be negotiated in advance. The design created strong incentives for parties to take their entitlement to ministries because if they did not, the seats would go either to their ethnonational rivals or to competitors in their own bloc.

This dual premiership critically depends on the personal cooperation of the two holders of these posts, and on the cooperation of their respective majorities (or pluralities – under the weighted majority rule). The Northern Ireland Act (1998) reinforced their interdependence by requiring that 'if either the First Minister or the deputy First Minister ceases to hold office, whether by resignation or otherwise, the other shall also cease to hold office' (Article 14 (6)). This power of resignation has been strategically deployed by both elected office-holders.

In the summer of 1999 the SDLP's Mallon resigned as Deputy First Minister (designate), complaining that the UUP was 'dishonouring' the Agreement and 'insulting its principles' by insisting on decommissioning before executive formation. He did so to speed an intergovernmental review of the implementation of the Agreement. The question immediately arose: did Mallon's resignation automatically trigger Trimble's departure from office, and require fresh elections to these positions within six weeks? The Initial Presiding Officer's answer to this question was that it did not, because the Assembly was not yet functioning under the Northern Ireland Act. This answer was accepted, and in November 1999 Mallon's resignation was subsequently rescinded with the assent of the Assembly with no requirement that the two men would have to re-stand for office.

Shortly afterwards, however, when the Assembly and Executive came fully 'on line' in November 1999, and ceased to be in designate form, David Trimble was to use the threat of resignation, helping thereby to precipitate the suspension of February 2000. He wrote a postdated letter of resignation to the chairman of his party, who was authorized to deliver it to the Secretary of State if Sinn Féin failed to achieve IRA movement on the decommissioning of its weapons – in the form of 'product' – within a specified period after the Ulster Unionist Party had agreed to full-scale executive formation. As we have seen, the fear that this resignation would become operative was the proximate cause of the Secretary of State's decision to suspend the Assembly.

How should we appraise the executive design in the Agreement? The skill of the designers/negotiators was to create strong incentives for executive power-sharing and power division, but without requiring parties to have any prior formal coalition agreement – other than the institutional agreement – and without requiring any party to renounce its long-run aspirations. The dual premiership, by contrast, was designed to tie moderate representatives of each bloc together, and to give some drive towards overall policy coherence. It was intended to strengthen moderates and to give them significant steering powers over the rest of the executive. The d'Hondt mechanism, by contrast, ensured inclusivity and was carefully explained to the public as achieving precisely that. Distinctive coalitions could form around different issues within the Executive, permitting flexibility, but inhibiting chaos (given the requirement that the budget be agreed by cross-community consent).

In these respects and others the Agreement differed positively from the Sunningdale experiment of 1973. Yet the Executive, and the dual premiership in particular, have proven unstable – and for reasons that go beyond the holders' personalities. Two causes have mattered: the precariousness of the 'Yes Unionist' bloc, and the potency of the resignation weapon available to each premier. Arguably the inter-moderate party deal was a weak spot in institutional design. Had the first and deputy first premierships been allocated according to the d'Hondt procedure, and had parties which threatened not to take up their Executive seats simply lost access to executive power, then there would have been very strong incentives for the Executive to be sustained, especially if the

Secretary of State had decided to take a hands-off approach to any threats of non-participation in the executive.

Using the d'Hondt rule to allocate the dual premierships, with the same Mitchell-inspired ministerial pledge of office, perhaps modified by a rule that one premiership had to go to the unionist party with the highest number of seats and the other to the nationalist party with the highest number of seats, would, however, have had the consequence of making more likely the future success of harder-line party leaders, such as Paisley or Adams. That, of course, was one motivation behind the construction of the dual premiership. However, the prospect feared by the moderates may not have spelled disaster: the prospect of the highest offices might have further moderated the stances of the respective hardline parties. It is a heretical thought.

What was not foreseen was that failure to timetable the formation of the rest of the Executive immediately after the election of the premiers would precipitate a protracted crisis of Executive formation. Trimble availed himself of this loophole to prevent Executive formation until November 1999. If the Agreement survives, amendments to the Northern Ireland Act (1998) could be adopted by the UK Parliament, or by the Assembly, to prevent any recurrence of this type of crisis. In future, candidates for First and Deputy First Minister could be obliged to state the number of Executive portfolios that will be available, and the formation of the Executive should be required immediately after their election. That would plug this particular constitutional hole. It may, however, be unnecessary. It is unlikely that future candidates for First and Deputy First Minister will agree to be nominated without a firm agreement on the number of portfolios and the date of cabinet formation.

The crisis of Executive formation, which dogged the implementation of the Agreement between June 1998 and November 1999, arose for political and constitutional reasons. Trimble insisted that Sinn Féin deliver some IRA decommissioning before its members would take their seats in the Executive: 'no government before guns'. Under the text of the Agreement, Trimble had no warrant to exercise this veto:

1 no party can veto another party's membership of the Executive, though the Assembly as a whole, through cross-community consent, may deem a party unfit for office (it has not done so);

2 the Agreement did not specify a starting date for decommissioning, though it did require parties to use their best endeavours to achieve the completion of decommissioning within two years, that is, by 22 May 2000;

3   any natural reading of the Agreement mandated Executive formation
    as the first step in bringing all the Agreement's institutions 'on line'.

Trimble's concern was to appease critics of the Agreement within his own
party, and he was initially facilitated in exercising this tacit veto by the
UK and Irish governments who were sympathetic to his exposed position. One flexible provision in the Agreement gave Trimble time to stall.
The Agreement stated that there must be at least six 'other ministers', but
that there can be 'up to' ten. The number of ministries was to be decided
by cross-community consent and that gave an opportunity to delay
Executive formation. It would be December 1998 before the parties
reached agreement on ten ministries.

   In mid-November 1999 it looked as if the crisis over Executive formation would finally be resolved. The UUP accepted that the running of the
d'Hondt procedure to fill the cabinet could occur after the *process* of
decommissioning began – with the IRA appointing an interlocutor to
negotiate with the IICD – while actual decommissioning, consistent with
the text of the Agreement, would not be required until after Executive
formation. Senator Mitchell in concluding his Review of the Agreement,
and with the consent of the pro-Agreement parties, stated that 'Devolution should take effect, then the executive should meet, and then the
paramilitary groups should appoint their authorised representatives, all
on the same day, in that order.' This was an honourable resolution to
what looked like becoming a fundamental impasse – though the Ulster
Unionist Council rendered it problematic. To get their support Trimble
offered the previously cited postdated resignation letter to become operative within a specified period not negotiated under the Mitchell
Review. The IRA did not deliver, at least not in the way that Mandelson
believed was required; suspensory powers were obtained and used. Had
the Agreement been followed to the letter, the parties in the Assembly
could have determined by cross-community consent that Sinn Féin and
the PUP were not fit for office because they had not used their best
endeavours to achieve comprehensive decommissioning. That avenue
was not deployed.

   Suspension did not completely save Trimble from the wrath of his
party: 43 per cent of them voted for a stalking horse to replace him,
the Reverend Martin Smyth MP. Trimble remained leader but bound by a
mandate for reformation of the Executive that neither the UK government or republicans seemed likely to deliver. The 'Yes Unionists' had
failed decisively to rout the 'No Unionists', partly through misjudgement
and mismanagement, and partly through the over-representation of 'No'
and 'soft Yes' unionists among the UUP's activists as opposed to its

voters. Their failure was, of course, rendered more likely by the republican position on decommissioning. The Republicans were locked in a ghetto of insecurity – determined that, at best, the decommissioning of their weapons would be the last or joint last act of implementation.

In May 2000, however, republicans promised to deliver a 'confidence-building measure', viz. inspections of some of the IRA's arms dumps, by two international observers, Cyril Rhamaposa, the former African National Congress negotiator, and Marti Ahtisaari, the former general and premier of Finland. It also seemed clear that they would re-engage with the IICD. In return Trimble promised to lift his resignation threat and Mandelson took the Executive and Assembly out of suspended animation. It was agreed that completing decommissioning be delayed for one year. Republicans appeared to be engaging in the decommissioning process in return for the restoration of the Executive, side-payments for their prisoners and those still facing extradition, and for assurances on demilitarization and police reform: Mandelson appeared vindicated in the eyes of his supporters. Blair gave assurances that the UK government would implement the Patten Commission's proposals on policing, which Trimble was known to oppose. Trimble warned republicans to engage with the IICD; republicans warned Mandelson to deliver on his obligations under the Agreement, which takes us to the crisis over Executive maintenance and policing reform.[20]

Policing reform and spinning out of control

The institution building of the Belfast Agreement was flanked by confidence-building processes involving ceasefires by paramilitaries, the release of their incarcerated prisoners, and commitments to protect human rights, entrench equality, demilitarize the region, assist in decommissioning, and to the reform of the administration of justice and policing. As of 2000, just four of these items awaited full or effective beginnings in implementation: decommissioning by paramilitaries; the reform of the system of criminal justice; demilitarization; and policing reform. These items were interlinked.

The Labour government initially welcomed the Patten Report issued by the Independent Commission on Policing for charting 'the way forward in the interests of all'. Blair, Mandelson, and the 'Explanatory Notes' issued by the Northern Ireland Office accompanying the Police Bill put before the UK Parliament in the spring of 2000, flatly declared their intention to give effect to Patten's 175 recommendations. That was not true. The UK government also implied, usually in off-the-record briefings, that it could not implement the Patten Report in full because of the 'security situation'. This position, in dissembling contradiction with its official one, would have had credibility if the necessary preparatory steps to implement Patten in full when the security situation was satisfactory had been taken. They were not.[21]

Policing was so controversial that the parties to the Agreement could not concur on future arrangements (see McGarry and O'Leary 1999).[22] They did agree the terms of reference of a commission, eventually chaired by Christopher Patten, a former minister in the region and now a European Commissioner. To have effective police rooted in, and legitimate with, both major communities was vital to the settlement. Eight criteria for policing arrangements were mandated in the commission's terms of reference. They were to be impartial; representative; free from partisan political control; efficient and effective; infused with a human rights culture; decentralized; democratically accountable 'at all levels'; and consistent with the letter and the spirit of the Agreement. The Patten Commission engaged in extensive research and interaction with the affected parties, interest groups and citizens, and published its report in September 1999. It did not, and could not, meet the hopes, or match the fears, of all, but the commissioners undoubtedly met their terms of reference (see Patten et al. 1999; O'Leary 1999c).

The Patten Report was a thorough, careful and imaginative compromise between unionists who maintained that the existing Royal Ulster Constabulary already met the terms of reference of the Agreement and those nationalists, especially republicans, who maintained that the RUC's record mandated its disbanding. However the Police Bill presented to Parliament in the spring of 2000 was an evisceration of Patten, and condemned as such by the SDLP, Sinn Féin, the Women's Coalition, the Catholic Church, and non-governmental and human rights organizations, such as the Committee on the Administration of Justice. It was also criticized by the Irish government, the US House of Representatives (H. Res. 447, 106th Congress) and Irish Americans, including President Clinton.[23] The veracity of the critics' complaints can be demonstrated by comparing some of Patten's recommendations with the initial bill presented to Parliament:

1   Patten recommended a neutral name, the Northern Ireland Police Service. The Royal Ulster Constabulary was not a neutral title so it was recommended to go. Patten also recommended that the display of the Union flag and the portrait of the Queen at police stations should go. Symbols should be 'free from association with the British or Irish states'. These recommendations were a consequence of

Patten's terms of reference, the Agreement's explicit commitment to establishing 'parity of esteem' between the national traditions, and the UK's solemn commitment to 'rigorous impartiality' in its administration. The original bill, by contrast, proposed that the Secretary of State have the power to decide on the issues of names and emblems.

2   Patten recommended affirmative action to change rapidly the proportion of cultural Catholics in the police. Even critics of affirmative action recognized the need to correct the existing imbalance – in which over 90 per cent of the police are local cultural Protestants. The original bill reduced the period in which the police would be recruited on a 50:50 ratio of cultural Catholics and cultural Protestants from ten to three years, requiring the Secretary of State to make any extension, and was silent on 'aggregation', the proposed policy for shortfalls in the recruitment of suitably qualified cultural Catholics.

3   Patten proposed a Policing Board consisting of ten representatives from political parties, in proportion to their shares of seats on the Executive, and nine members nominated by the First and Deputy First Ministers. These recommendations guaranteed a politically representative board in which neither unionists nor nationalists would have partisan control. The original bill introduced a requirement that the board should operate according to a weighted majority when recommending an inquiry, tantamount to giving unionist and unionist-nominated members a veto over inquiries, that is, partisan political control, and a direct violation of Patten's terms of reference.

4   Patten avoided false economies when recommending a downsizing of the service, advocated a strong board empowered to set performance targets, and proposed enabling local District Policing Partnership Boards to engage in the market-testing of police effectiveness. The original bill empowered the Secretary of State, not the Policing Board, to set performance targets, made no statutory provision for disbanding the police reserve, and deflated the proposed District Policing Partnership Boards, because of assertions that they would lead to paramilitaries being subsidized by taxpayers.

5   Patten proposed that new and serving officers should have knowledge of human rights built into their training, and retraining, and their codes of practice. In addition to the European Convention, due to become part of UK domestic law, the Commission held out international norms as benchmarks (Patten et al. 1999: para. 5.17). Patten's proposals for normalizing the police – through merging the special branch into criminal investigations – and demilitarizing the police

met the Agreement's human rights objectives. The original bill was a parody. The new oath was to be confined to new officers. No standards of rights higher than those in the European Convention were to be incorporated into police training and practice. Responsibility for a code of ethics was left with the Chief Constable. Patten's proposed requirement that the oath of service 'respect the traditions and beliefs of people' was excluded. Normalization and demilitarization were left unclear in the bill and the implementation plan.

6 Patten envisaged enabling local governments to influence the Policing Board through their own District Policing Partnership Boards, and giving the latter powers 'to purchase additional services from the police or statutory agencies, or from the private sector', and matching police internal management units to local government districts. The original bill, by contrast, maintained or strengthened centralization: the Secretary of State obtained powers that Patten proposed for the First and Deputy First Ministers and the Policing Board, and powers to issue instructions to District Policing Partnership Boards; and neither the bill nor the implementation plan implemented Patten's proposed experiment in community policing.

7 Patten envisaged that the Policing Board would be strong, independent and powerful to hold the police to account, and to replace the discredited Police Authority (Patten et al. 1999: para. 6.23). The police would have 'operational responsibility' but be held to account by the board, and required to interact with the Human Rights Commission, the Ombudsman and the Equality Commission. The bill watered down Patten's proposals, empowering the Secretary of State to oversee and veto the board's powers, empowering the Chief Constable to refuse to respond to reasonable requests from the board, and preventing the board from making inquiries into past misconduct.

8 Patten was consistent with the terms of reference and spirit of the Belfast Agreement. The original bill was not, being incompatible with the 'parity of esteem' and 'rigorous impartiality' in administration. Manifestly it would not encourage 'widespread community support' since it fell far short of the compromise that moderate nationalists had accepted and that Patten had proposed to mark a 'new beginning'.

What explains the radical discrepancy between the Patten Report and the original police bill? The short answer is that the Northern Ireland Office's officials under Mandelson's supervision drafted the bill. They appeared to 'forget' that the terms of reference came from the Belfast Agreement. They treated the Patten Report as a nationalist report, which they had to modify as benign mediators. Although Patten warned against 'cherry-picking', the Secretary of State and his officials believed that they had the right to implement what they found acceptable, and to leave aside what they found unacceptable, premature, or likely to cause difficulties for pro-Agreement unionists or the RUC. The Police Bill suggested that the UK government was determined to avoid the police being subject to rigorous democratic accountability; deeply distrustful of the capacity of the local parties to manage policing at any level; and concerned to minimize the difficulties that the partial implementation of Patten would occasion for Trimble, by minimizing radical change to become mere reforms of the RUC.

Under pressure Mandelson beat a partial retreat, whether to a position prepared in advance only others can know. Some speculated that he designed an obviously defective bill so that nationalists would then be mollified by subsequent improvements. That is to make the characteristic error of endowing him with greater political intelligence than his record suggests: all that the defective bill achieved, according to Seamus Mallon, was to 'shatter already fragile faith in the Government's commitment to police reform'.

Accusing his critics of 'hype', 'rhetoric' and 'hyperbole', Mandelson promised to 'listen' and to modify the bill. He declared that he might have been too cautious in the powers granted to the Policing Board. Indeed the government was subsequently to accept over sixty SDLP-driven amendments to bring the bill more into line with Patten. The bill was improved in the Commons and Lords. The quota for the recruitment of cultural Catholics is now better protected. The Policing Board has been given power over the setting of short-run objectives, and final responsibility for the police's code of ethics. Consultation procedures involving the Ombudsman and the Equality Commission have been strengthened, and the First and Deputy First Ministers will now be consulted over the appointment of non-party members to the board. The weighted majority provisions for an inquiry by the board have gone. Yet any honest appraisal of the Act had to conclude that it was still not the whole Patten; it rectifies some of the original bill's more overt deviations, but on the crucial issues of symbolic neutrality and police accountability, vital for a 'new beginning', it was at odds with Patten's explicit recommendations.[24]

Symbolic neutrality

Patten wanted a police rooted in both communities, not just one. That is why he recommended that the name of the service be *entirely* new: The

Northern Ireland Police Service. The Act, because of a government decision to accept an amendment tabled by the UUP, styles the service 'The
Police Service of Northern Ireland (incorporating the Royal Ulster Constabulary)'. The Secretary of State promised an amendment to define it
'for operational purposes', to ensure that the full title would rarely be
used and that the parenthetic past generally be excluded. He broke this
commitment at the report stage of the bill's passage through parliament.
Mandelson was mendaciously misleading in declaring that he was merely
following Patten's wishes that the new service be connected to the old,
avoiding suggestions of disbanding. Patten proposed an entirely new and
fresh name, and proposed linkages between the old and new services
through police memorials, and *not* the renaming adopted by the government.

Patten unambiguously recommended that the police's new badge and
emblems be free of association with the British or Irish states, and that the
Union flag should not fly from police buildings. The Act postpones these
matters. Avoiding responsibility, the government passed the parcel to the
local parties to reach agreement, while providing reassuring but vague
words for the parliamentary record. Since Mandelson had already ruled
that only the Union Jack, albeit just on specified days, should fly over the
buildings of the devolved administration, some nationalists lacked faith
that the UK would deliver on cultural neutrality and impartiality.

Why do these symbolic issues matter? Simply because the best way to
win widespread acceptance for police reform was to confirm Patten's
promised new beginning by following his proposed strategy of symbolic
neutrality.[25] Full renaming and symbolic neutrality would spell a double
message: that the new police are to be everyone's, and the new police are
no longer to be primarily the unionists' police. This symbolic shift would
mightily assist in obtaining representative cultural Catholic recruitment
and in winning consent for the new order among nationalists as well as
unionists.

Oversight and accountability

Patten recommended an Oversight Commissioner to 'supervise the implementation of our recommendations'. The Labour government – under
pressure – put the commissioner's office on a statutory basis, which it did
not intend to do originally, but confined the commissioner's role to
overseeing changes 'decided by the government'. Had Mandelson and
his colleagues been committed to Patten they would have charged the
commissioner with recommending, now or in the future, any legislative

and management changes necessary for the full and effective implementation of the Patten Report. Patten recommended a Policing Board to hold the police to account, and to initiate inquiries into police conduct and practices. Mandelson in effect prevented the board from inquiring into any act or omission arising before the eventual Act applies. This was tantamount to an undeclared amnesty for past police misconduct, not proposed by Patten. The Secretary of State will additionally have the authority to approve or veto the person appointed to conduct any present or future inquiry (Police Act 2000, clause 58 (9)). Patten also recommended that the Ombudsman should have significant powers (Patten et al. 1999: para. 6.42) and should 'exercise the right to investigate and comment on police policies and practices', whereas in the Act the Ombudsman may make reports, but not investigate (so it is not a crime to obstruct her work). The Ombudsman is additionally restricted in her retrospective powers (Police Act 2000, clause 62), again circumscribing the police's accountability for past misconduct.

Mandelson suggested his critics were petty, arguing that they were ungrateful, pointing out just how much he had done to implement Patten, and how radical Patten is by comparison with elsewhere. This 'spin' was utterly unconvincing. The proposed arrangements effectively seal off past, present and future avenues through which the police might be held to account for misconduct, for instance in colluding with loyalist paramilitaries or covering up assassinations; and are recipes for leaving the police outside the effective ambit of the law. And be it noted: Patten is not radical, especially by the standards of Canada and the USA that have long made their police democratically accountable and socially representative. Patten is only radical by the past standards of Northern Ireland.

There was a small ray of hope, noted by the SDLP, viz. if the implementation plan on policing brought the UK government much closer into line with Patten then there might be a basis for a new beginning. Over 300 police had been killed in the conflict, the number emphasized by unionists, but nationalists remembered that seven of the first eight deaths in 1969 were partly caused by an illegitimate unreformed police. In the mind-set of the Provisional IRA their formation was the result of the police standing by, or assisting in, the burning of nationalists' homes in the summer of 1969. So, Mandelson's dilution of the Patten report threatened to decouple republicans from the Agreement.[26]

Generously disposed analysts believe Mandelson's conduct was motivated to help Trimble and the UUP who were in a precarious position – aggravated by the absence of a start to decommissioning by the IRA. Perhaps, but that does not account for his efforts to block an accountable service in the future – here the Secretary of State appeared to succumb to lobbying to prevent the unearthing of past and present policing scandals. And, it neglects the fact that his conduct continued a practice he had established by obtaining the power of suspension, of unilaterally rewriting the rules of the game – perhaps appropriate in normal politics, but entirely inappropriate in bedding down a new constitutional settlement.

Avoiding a meltdown?

In January 2001 it was difficult to avoid pessimism about the prospects for the Agreement. The passage of the Police (Northern Ireland) Act in November 2000 had left the SDLP, Sinn Féin and the Irish government strongly dissatisfied. Even though the final Act was better than the original bill it was still 'Patten lite'. The IRA had not formally re-engaged with the IICD, partly, it seemed, to put pressure on Mandelson to deliver on Patten and demilitarization – though it did facilitate a second inspection of its arms dumps. The UK government was refusing to move fast on demilitarization because of its security concerns, especially about dissident republicans, who were strongest in areas which have historically been vigorously republican – and where there is the greatest demand for demilitarization. The discipline of loyalist paramilitaries was breaking down: there was internal feuding, and sections of the UDA were targeting vulnerable Catholics with pipe-bomb attacks in predominantly unionist towns.

On top of all this Trimble decided to play Executive hardball. At the end of 2000, besieged by internal party critics demanding a fast exist from the Executive because of the IRA's obstinate stance on decommissioning, he decided to take what was called proportionate action. Acting on poor legal advice, he availed himself of a technical clause in the Northern Ireland (1998) Act and refused to nominate the two Sinn Féin ministers to carry out their obligations under meetings of the North–South Ministerial Council. Sinn Féin's two ministers, Bairbre de Bruin and Martin McGuiness, and the Deputy First Minister, Seamus Mallon, announced they would test the legality of Trimble's decision in the courts. Trimble's lawyer justified his action as intended to put pressure on Sinn Féin to get the IRA to deliver on its obligations. Judge Kerr ruled Trimble's action unlawful on 30 January 2001, partly because Trimble could not inhibit or frustrate one part of the Agreement, cross-border cooperation, to ensure progress on another, viz. decommissioning. He also ruled that Trimble had acted beyond his powers. Trimble immediately decided to appeal.

The political stalemate and legal showdown threatened an acrimonious and messy meltdown. However, on 24 January 2001 something unexpected happened. Peter Mandelson was forced to resign as Secretary of State because of events that had nothing to do with Northern Ireland. He was replaced by Dr John Reid, the former Secretary of State for Scotland.

Mandelson's exit left nationalists, republicans and the Irish government almost as happy as Labour's backbenchers. In the course of the next ten months Dr Reid would establish much better relations with the SDLP and Sinn Fein, while generally retaining the confidence of the UUP.

The remarkable formal political institutions of the Agreement, which merit the description of a complex consociation, had all been established in 1998–9, albeit with delays in their scheduled timetables. But key implementation difficulties were evident in 2000–1:

1   The UK government obtained and used the unilateral power of suspension – immensely disliked by nationalists, but sought by unionists, especially as a bargaining chip to compel IRA decommissioning.
2   The dual premiership was vulnerable to resignation threats from both the First and Deputy First Ministers – creating reasons for either intra-Agreement Reviews, or extra-Agreement suspensions.
3   Unionists who rejected, and unionists who supported, the Agreement tried to create difficulties within the Executive, by refusing to attend plenary sessions of the NSMC and rotating their ministerial nominees in the case of the DUP; by initially refusing in the case of both the UUP and the DUP to nominate their MLAs to their ministerial entitlements, and later obliging their withdrawal from those entitlements; and by refusing to establish or maintain the Executive in the absence of IRA decommissioning.
4   The First Minister acted unlawfully in refusing to nominate Sinn Féin ministers to carry out their duties on the NSMC.

The institution-building of the Agreement had, however, led to an ironic historic reversal. Whereas nationalists and republicans had once boycotted devolved arrangements in Stormont (O'Leary and McGarry 1996: ch. 3), it was now unionists who threatened to do so. The difficulties in institutional maintenance, magnified by Mandelson's mismanagement, flowed directly from two sources:

1   Unionist dissatisfaction with the failure of the confidence-building measures attached to the Agreement, especially decommissioning, and their dissatisfaction with the inevitable repercussions of

appropriate implementation of the confidence-building measures, especially with regard to police reform, and prisoner releases.

2   Internal unionist political competition, within the UUP, and between the UUP and the DUP, rendered it extremely difficult for the UUP to be a confident coalition partner with the nationalists and the republicans who made the Agreement.

The confidence-building measures embedded in the making of the Agreement have been of two kinds: the responsibilities of the two sovereign governments, and the responsibility of agents within Northern Ireland. The Irish government fulfilled its immediate obligations, including the organization of the change of its constitution through a referendum – though it has been slow in building the human rights institutions and measures that would demonstrate its full commitment to the double protection model embedded in the Agreement. The UK government had a much more mixed track record, though it had the most to do. It was the most vulnerable to lobbying, and there has been erratic conduct partly because of three different Secretaries of State. The UK fulfilled its obligations with regard to prisoner releases, organized better arrangements for the victims of violence, made promising starts with respect to better human rights protections and laws on equality – though some of its reforms in this area and the administration of justice are yet to be specified. It has initiated some demilitarization, but, reasonably, has awaited decommissioning before completion. On police reform it zigzagged dramatically. It radically diluted the Patten Commission's proposals, then moved to satisfy the SDLP's complaints that it had done so, but lost Sinn Féin's confidence that it wanted it be part of new policing arrangements. Its conduct, especially over suspensions, was partial to the interests and threats of the divided moderate unionists. It made it less likely that the IRA would deliver on decommissioning because, especially on police reform, it patently dishonoured its commitments.

The confidence-building measures that lie outside the two governments' control rested with paramilitaries who did not directly negotiate the Agreement. They have, albeit to varying degrees, broadly maintained their ceasefires, and the worst atrocities, on a generally lower scale than before, have been carried out by smaller dissident organizations. The IRA played tit-for-tat with the UK on police reform and decommissioning, and tit-for-tat with the UK and the UUP on the institutions of the Agreement and decommissioning. Nothing in the Agreement warranted its lateness in starting, let alone completing, decommissioning. What inhibited it was the failure of the UK and the UUP fully to honour their obligations, and the fear – among the IRA and its constituents – that they should not be left defenceless against unreformed police and active loyalists.

Loyalists have failed to prosper politically (Bruce 2001), which partly explains their disorganization, disarray and greater descent into criminality. By contrast Sinn Féin has been the prime electoral beneficiary of the peace process (Mitchell, O'Leary and Evans 2001), because it is seen by cultural Catholics as their (increasingly constitutional) nationalist champion, and because it is the beneficiary of demographic transformations (O'Leary and Evans 1997). And it would be the interplay of electoral calculations and deft manoeuvring by all parties that would produce a remarkable political game in the summer and autumn of 2001 that terminated with the apparent stabilization of the Agreement in November 2001.

Just before the Westminster general elections of June 2001 Trimble decided to gamble, resigning as First Minister, both to position his party for competition with the anti-Agreement DUP in the forthcoming election, and to put pressure on Sinn Féin to deliver the IRA on decommissioning in accordance with the now postponed deadline. His resignation required the UK Secretary of State either to suspend the institutions – thereby provoking nationalists – or to call fresh Assembly elections – widely seen as likely to benefit the 'No Unionists'. In the Westminster general elections Sinn Fein did remarkably well, edging ahead of the SDLP for the first time, both in share of the vote, and in seats won (for full details see Mitchell, O'Leary and Evans 2001). Shortly afterwards the SDLP leader John Hume announced his resignation as party leader, and Seamus Mallon indicated that he would not stand for the next Assembly elections. The DUP also did very well, winning its highest ever share of the vote and of seats in a Westminster election. The conventional wisdom was that all this boded very badly for the Agreement, even though both Sinn Féin and the DUP had done well on much more moderate platforms – Sinn Féin supporting the Agreement, the DUP calling for its renegotiation.

Shortly after the Westminster elections a review of the Agreement was convened by the two governments at Weston Park, Shropshire. The UK government indicated its willingness to deliver further administrative and legislative changes to come very close to the full implementation of the Patten Report – in effect, conceding that Mandelson's critics had been correct. It also promised a series of inquiries on controversial cases involving police collusion in the killing of nationalists and lawyers identified as nationalists – and the Irish government balanced that by permitting the possibility of inquiries into alleged Garda collusion with the IRA. The UK government promised that specific demilitarization moves would accompany moves by the IRA on decommissioning. The UK's shifts were sufficient to prompt the SDLP soon afterwards to accept its positions on the new police board – which Sinn Féin decided to boycott. The IRA did not, however, move on decommissioning, though it had organized another inspection of its arms dumps during the course of the election campaign. It looked as if republicans were determined to extract further concessions on policing, or that they were internally divided over beginning decommissioning, especially given loyalist activities in North Belfast.

Dr Reid and his advisers found a (unanticipated) loophole in the suspension legislation, and twice opted for one-day unilateral suspensions of the Agreement's institutions – which each time enabled the Assembly to function for a further six weeks without an elected First Minister. The prospects for institutional collapse worsened in mid-summer, partly because of loyalist breaches of their ceasefires in Northern Ireland, and because a team of IRA and Sinn Féin cadres were arrested in Colombia, accused of being engaged in international terrorist advisory counsel. Then came the suicide missions by Islamist militants in New York and Washington on September 11 – which shook US and European public opinion on the capacity of terrorism in general. Trimble and his ministerial colleagues in the UUP threatened to withdraw from the Executive completely – which would force the Secretary of State to choose between a long suspension and fresh elections. These events provided the catalysts for the leadership of Sinn Féin to persuade hardliners in the IRA that it was time to begin decommissioning, to consolidate Sinn Féin's electoral progress, North and South, and to save the institutions of the Agreement. They would likely have done so anyway – September 11 made rapid movement more urgent, and in some respects easier.

When the IRA started to decommission, the UK reciprocated with the promised demilitarization actions it had made at Weston Park, but a new institutional crisis emerged. Trimble and his colleagues were prepared to accept the authenticity of the IRA's actions, as verified by the International Commission, but hardline unionists were not. When the Assembly would vote to try to restore Trimble to office, together with the new prospective leader of the SDLP, Mark Durkan, two of Trimble's party looked likely to desert him. There was not a sufficient – majority – level of support within the unionist bloc for the election of a First Minister and Deputy First Minister, though there was a very large majority in the Assembly overall. Time seemed to have run out. The Secretary of State could not, it seemed, avoid calling for fresh Assembly elections – he had ruled out another suspension, which would have been tantamount to throwing dust in the faces of the IRA. Pressure was accordingly exerted on the 'Others' to redesignate themselves as unionists to save the Agreement. The Women's Coalition divided in two, designating one of its members as a nationalist and the other as a unionist. It was not sufficient: Trimble and Durkan were not elected, falling one vote short of the required concurrent majority. The Alliance Party demanded a Review of the Agreement, seeking to change its rules, and seeking to end the practice of obligatory designation – even though it was an entrenched part of the Agreement. Over a fateful weekend, and under intense political and media criticism, it reversed its position, and some of its members agreed to be unionists. The Assembly would twice change its standing orders, on a Friday and a Monday, by weighted majority, on how designation might be changed – first to accommodate the Women's Coalition's shift, and then to accommodate the Alliance Party's shift. It would prove enough to put Trimble and Durkan into office. The DUP challenged the legality of the Secretary of State's decision to permit the Assembly to elect new First and Deputy First Ministers, arguing that the UK's legislation required him to call fresh Assembly elections. But because the Secretary of State acknowledged he did indeed have to call such elections – but was not yet required to specify the date – a judge threw out the DUP's legal action, though it was given subsequent leave to appeal.

The complex consociation had therefore obtained a vital new lease of life. The apparently unattainable had occurred. The IRA had started to decommission; the RUC had passed into history. Sinn Féin and the IRA had acted to save the Agreement and Sinn Féin had voted for Trimble and Durkan – whereas in the case of Trimble and Mallon it had simply abstained. Eighteen months of relative stability looked likely before the next Assembly elections. While no one can discount the prospect of fresh crises – over the completion of decommissioning in the case of the IRA, in starting decommissioning in the cases of loyalists, the worst moments seem to be over. The Agreement will not be fully tested on its robustness until Sinn Féin and the DUP emerge as the respective majority parties in their blocs, but for the moment that lies in the future. There will be a Review of the rules on designation and on voting procedures in general. The UK and Irish governments and the makers of the Agreement deserve credit for the making of the Agreement, and more for its implementation – though some of them, as I have argued, had seemed likely to ruin its progress. In the course of the peace process, poet Seamus Heaney coined the phrase that he wanted to see if hope and history could rhyme. The words can certainly now go together, even though both assonance and dissonance will accompany them.

NOTES

1 The origin of most of the ideas for the internal government of Northern Ireland, in Strand One, also stemmed from Irish nationalists, led by the SDLP, and advised by Irish officials and others.

2 According to Langdon, Soley was 'acting as a secret and unacknowledged emissary between the Conservative British Government and the leaders of Sinn Féin' (2000: 271ff.). In fact he was one of numerous channels through which Sinn Féin attempted to persuade the UK's parties of government that they were serious about negotiations.

3 McNamara's salvo against Labour's electoral integrationists led the party's unionists to argue that he was unfit for office (see McNamara et al. 1992). Electoral integrationists were especially salient among Scottish MPs (convinced that the Scottish sectarian question was the same as the Irish national question), members with communist pasts, those influenced by Ireland's Workers' Party, and those who are Northern Irish cultural Protestants. They campaigned against McNamara, much as they would later campaign against Mowlam, by the politics of 'malicious gossip', a trait they shared with New Labour's principal apparatchiks – for a sharp statement see Ken Follett, *Observer*, 2 July 2000.

4 Evidence of her empathy with Irish nationalists was manifest in her willingness to use Ken Livingstone to inform her of Sinn Fén's positions, and her (rejected) proposal to Blair that Livingstone become part of her ministerial team at the Northern Ireland Office (Langdon 2000: 4).

5 For the Senator's account of matters see Mitchell 2000, esp. ch. 3.

6 The International Body's text had suggested elections if they were widely agreed, viz. 'If it were broadly acceptable, with an appropriate mandate, and within the three-strand structure, an elective process could contribute to the building of confidence.' An elective process was not 'broadly acceptable' to the SDLP and Sinn Féin.

7 Mitchell puts matters with characteristic tact: Major's response 'wasn't support, but it wasn't exactly a dumping. It was a temporary sidestep to get to negotiations by a different route' (2000: 39).

8 At a meeting with Adams and McGuinness in 1997–8 Blair is said to have told them that he would do everything he could to find an agreement, 'But if you ever do a Canary Wharf on me, I will never talk to you again' (Rawnsley 2000: 123). The irony would not have been lost on them. Canary Wharf prompted the two premiers, Major and Bruton, to specify the date on which negotiations would begin, and the modalities through which negotiations would take place. A year and half's relative inaction by the UK government after the IRA's ceasefire ended three weeks after the bomb. None other than Tony Blair supported the two governments' rapid volte-face.

9 For the details, and the state of public opinion at that time, see Evans and O'Leary 1996.

10   For a hasty biography of the UUP leader see MacDonald 2000, and for a critical notice see O'Leary in *Sunday Business Post*, 13 April 2000.

11   For a treatment of the Clinton administration on Ireland see O'Clery 1996; he does not miss the significance of the Morrison delegation, Clinton's undeclared 'envoy'. See also Mitchell 2000, *passim*.

12   Irish Labour leader, Dick Spring, Tánaiste (deputy prime minister) 1992–7, was an essential figure in shaping the Agreement's focus on the protection of rights in both parts of Ireland.

13   The legislation establishing the Forum envisaged its termination in May 1998. Though it did not require the negotiations to be concluded by that date, the government argued that since the negotiators' mandates stemmed from their elections to the Forum it was the authorized deadline.

14   Some officials of the Northern Ireland office sought to dilute or block the potentially far-reaching equality clauses, mandated by the Belfast Agreement, and now embedded as §75 of the 1998 Northern Ireland Act. Mowlam was critical in blocking these efforts. Her conduct was in striking contrast to that of her successor who allowed his officials to dilute the proposals of the Patten Commission.

15   Ian Paisley had once run a campaign to 'Save Ulster from Sodomy'; his party is notoriously homophobic.

16   Northern Ireland's devolution arrangements may be contrasted with those of Scotland and Wales, described in James Mitchell's chapter above. In Northern Ireland interparty power sharing and proportionality are required and UK Labour has no party interest at stake. The Northern Ireland Assembly is larger and more powerful than the Welsh National Assembly and may, by the agreement of its blocs, expand its autonomy to the same degree as the Scottish Parliament, and indeed beyond. Northern Ireland's autonomy is both more open-ended, and more constrained. It is tied to the all Ireland North–South Ministerial Council. It has a specified right of secession, to join a unified Ireland (see also Hazell and O'Leary 1999).

17   The NSMC also linked Ireland, North and South, to another confederation, the European Union. It required the Council to consider the implementation of EU policies and programmes as well as proposals under way at the EU, and made provisions for the Council's views to be 'taken into account' at relevant EU meetings.

18   The resignation of one UUP member from the party whip meant that twenty-nine 'Yes Unionists' exactly matched twenty-nine 'No Unionists' in the Assembly.

19   For a fuller discussion of the d'Hondt allocation process see O'Leary 1999a.

20   The following section draws on evidence presented in 'Why Failing to Implement the Patten Report Matters', Testimony for the Hearing of the Commission on Security and Co-operation in Europe (the Helsinki Commission), entitled 'Protecting Human Rights and Securing Peace in Northern Ireland: The Vital Role of Police Reform', Friday 22 Sept. 2000, International Relations Committee Room, Raeburn Building, Washington DC.

21 Despite the Omagh atrocity of 1998, the key indicators of political violence demonstrate that the security situation has been much better in the period since 1995 than it was in the period running up to 1994, and significantly so by comparison with the entire period of fully active conflict which preceded the first IRA ceasefire (i.e. 1969–93). The death toll during 1995–9 more than halved by comparison with 1990–4.

22 A former Irish prime minister, Dr Garret FitzGerald, has described policing in Northern Ireland as having the status of Jerusalem in the Israeli-Palestinian peace process (*Irish Times*, 12 Aug. 2000).

23 I described it as betraying Patten's 'substantive intentions in most of its thinly disguised legislative window-dressing' (O'Leary 2000).

24 For the defects in the police Bill and the accompanying implementation plan with regard to community policing see Paddy Hillyard's comments (*Irish Times*, 2 Aug. 2000).

25 An alternative path, legitimate under the Agreement, would have been to pursue a fully binational symbolic strategy (McGarry and O'Leary 1999). However, even if the police were to have both an English and Irish title in each case, the name should be neutral: Northern Ireland Police Service or Coras Siochana Thuaisceart Eireann.

26 The careful and detailed denunciation of Mandelson by Mitchel McLaughlin, Sinn Féin's leading moderate, suggests the depth of the crisis ('The Mandelson Factor', *Belfast Telegraph*, 1 Dec. 2000). It specifically accuses Mandelson of failing to deliver on explicit commitments and obligations.

REFERENCES

Bruce, S. (2001) 'Terrorists and Politics: The Case of Northern Ireland's Loyalist Paramilitaries', *Terrorism and Political Violence*, 13(2), 27–48.

Elazar, D. (1987) *Exploring Federalism*. Tuscaloosa: University of Alabama Press.

Evans, G. and O'Leary, B. (1997) 'Frameworked Futures: Intransigence and Flexibility in the Northern Ireland Elections of May 30 1996', *Irish Political Studies*, 12, 23–47.

—— (2000) 'Northern Irish Voters and the British-Irish Agreement: Foundations of a Stable Consociational Settlement?', *Political Quarterly*, 71, 78–101.

Hazell, R. and O'Leary, B. (1999) 'A Rolling Programme of Devolution: Slippery Slope or Safeguard of the Union?', in R. Hazell (ed.), *Constitutional Futures: A History of the Next Ten Years*. Oxford: Oxford University Press.

Langdon, J. (2000) *Mo Mowlam: The Biography*. London: Little, Brown.

Lijphart, A. (1977) *Democracy in Plural Societies: A Comparative Exploration*. London: Yale University Press.

McCrudden, C. (1999) 'Mainstreaming Equality in the Governance of Northern Ireland', *Fordham International Law Journal*, 22, 1696–1775.

MacDonald, H. (2000) *Trimble*. London: Bloomsbury.

McGarry, J. and O'Leary, B. (1999) *Policing Northern Ireland: Proposals for a New Start*. Belfast: Blackstaff.

McNamara, K. et al. (1992) 'Oranges or Lemons? Should Labour Organise in Northern Ireland?' House of Commons, London.

Mitchell, G. J. (2000) *Making Peace*, 2nd edn. Berkeley: University of California Press.

Mitchell, G. J., de Chastelain, J. and Holkeri, H. (1996) *Report of the International Body on Arms Decommissioning* (The Mitchell Report). Dublin and London.

Mitchell, P., O'Leary, B. and Evans, G. (2001) 'Northern Ireland: Flanking Extremists Bite the Moderates and Emerge in Their Clothes', *Parliamentary Affairs*, special issue 'Britain Votes 2001'.

O'Clery, C. (1996). *The Greening of the White House*. Dublin: Gill and Macmillan.

O'Leary, B. (1992) 'Public Opinion and Northern Irish Futures', *Political Quarterly*, 63(2), 143–70.

——(1995) 'Afterword: What is Framed in the Framework Documents?', *Ethnic and Racial Studies*, 18(4), 862–72.

——(1997) 'The Conservative Stewardship of Northern Ireland 1979–97: Sound-Bottomed Contradictions or Slow Learning?', *Political Studies*, 45(4), 663–76.

——(1999a) 'The Nature of the Agreement', *Fordham Journal of International Law*, 22, 1628–67.

——(1999b) 'The Nature of the British–Irish Agreement', *New Left Review*, 233, 66–96.

——(1999c) 'A Bright Future and Less Orange (Review of the Independent Commission on Policing for Northern Ireland)', *Times Higher Education Supplement*, 19 Nov.

——(2000) 'What a Travesty: Police Bill is Just a Parody of Patten', *Sunday Business Post* (Dublin), 30 Apr.

O'Leary, B. and Evans, G. (1997) 'Northern Ireland: La Fin de Siècle, the Twilight of the Second Protestant Ascendancy and Sinn Féin's Second Coming', *Parliamentary Affairs*, 50, 672–80.

O'Leary, B. and McGarry, J. (1996) *The Politics of Antagonism: Understanding Northern Ireland*. London and Atlantic Heights: Athlone.

O'Leary, B., Lyne, T., Marshall, J. and Rowthorn, B. (1993) *Northern Ireland: Sharing Authority*. London: Institute of Public Policy Research.

Patten, C. et al. (1999) *A New Beginning: The Report of the Independent Commission on Policing for Northern Ireland*. Belfast and London: HMSO.

Rawnsley, A. (2000) *Servants of the People: The Inside Story of New Labour*. London: Hamish Hamilton.

Index

Richardson, J. 191, 196
Robertson, G. 219, 220
Robins, L. 122
Robson, W. 101
Roper, J. 231
Rorty, R. 111
Rosamond, B. 3, 7, 190, 191, 201, 206
Rose, N. 131, 132, 138, 139
Royal Ulster Constabulary 290, 293, 294

Sanders, D. 7, 8, 12, 28, 73, 79, 82, 83, 202
Sandline affair 222
Sargent, Sir O. 210
Schröder, G. 135–6
Schuman Plan 188
Scottish Constitutional Convention 48,
    249, 251
Scottish Nationalist Party 48, 90, 92, 93,
    98–9, 248, 250, 253
Scottish Parliament 39, 41, 48, 61, 79, 85,
    89, 237, 249, 250, 252, 253, 254, 256,
    284
Seawright, D. 191, 194
Seldon, A. 2, 5, 65, 67
Short, C. 39, 41, 45
Sinn Féin 259, 260, 261, 263, 265, 267,
    268, 273, 277, 282, 284, 286, 287,
    290, 296, 297, 298, 299, 300, 301,
    302, 304
Smith, J. 45, 63, 71, 255, 262
Smith, M. J. 15, 19, 29, 32, 34
Smyth, M. 288
social class 81, 164–5, 167
social class, and voting 81–2
Social Democratic and Labour Party 259,
    260, 268, 269, 272, 273, 277, 284, 285,
    290, 293, 295, 296, 297, 298, 299, 300,
    302
Social Democratic Party 62, 190
social mobility 28
Socialist International Women 44
Soley, C. 261, 302
Spring, D. 303
stability 3–5
Stanyer, J. 64, 65, 74
statecraft 61, 202–3
Stewart, M. 28, 83
Stormont 243, 244, 245
Stott, R. 261
Straw, J. 230
Symons, Baroness 221, 232

Tant, T 29, 31
Thatcher, M. 27, 67, 70, 106, 129, 178,
    190, 191, 218
Thatcher, government 176–7, 198, 204
Thatcherism 5, 31, 127, 177–8, 190, 205,
    226, 247–8
third way 115, 122, 127, 131–2, 135–6,
    139, 143, 176, 177, 221, 259
Thompson, G. 5, 25
Thompson, H. 193, 202
Thrasher, M. 44, 56
Timmins, N. 145, 146
trade unions 45, 64–5
Tribune 44
Trimble, D. 259, 266, 267, 268, 269, 271,
    281–2, 284, 285, 287, 289, 296, 299,
    300, 301
Truman, D. 15, 16
two-party system 61, 79–81

UK Independence Party 194
Ulster Democratic Party 267, 268
Ulster Unionist Party 243, 260, 262, 263,
    265, 266, 267, 268, 269, 272, 273, 284,
    285, 288, 294, 297, 298, 303
unitary state 7, 108, 239–43
United Nations 224, 225, 226
US, as policy model 63
US political science 17–18

Walker, A. 133, 140, 149
Wallace, H. 204, 206
Watson, M. 25, 33
welfare reform 9
welfare state 8, 9, 238; see also new welfare
    state
Wells, J. 161, 169, 170
Welsh Assembly 39, 41, 48, 61, 79, 85, 89,
    90, 237, 249, 250, 251, 252, 253, 254,
    284
Westminster 39–40, 47, 56, 80
Wheeler, N. 219, 229–30
Wilkes, G. 189, 198
Wilks, S. 198, 199
Wilson, H. 176, 190
Wilson, Sir R. 109
women, representation of 8, 40–9
World Trade Organization 195

Young, H. 135, 187, 192
Young, J. W. 187, 188